Contes de mr Phle Le Feuvre surveillant

Le 19me Mars 1711 il me Cousta vingt six sous neuf ~~~~~~~~ ₶ ₷ ₫
deniers avecq les Causeur lors quil vindrent visiter
Le travail de Leglise ~~~~~~~~~~~~~~~~~~~~~~~~~~~~~~~~~~~~ 01=06=0

Le 20me Juillet 1712 Payé a Thomas Tailleur quarante
Six Livres huit sous pour achevement de poiment ~~~~~~~~~~~ 46=08=0
pour le travail de Leglise ~~~~~~~~~~~~~~~

Le mesme jour & an Payé a George le Fou
Livres Dix sous por Service a Leglis ~~~~~~~~~~~~~~~~~~~~~~ =10=0

Le 25me Juillet 1712 payé a Jean
trente Deux Livres huit sous pour ~~~~~~~~~~~~~~ nent ~~~~~ 32=08=0
de poiment pour le travail de Leglise

Jy le 29e septemb 1712 payé a mr Abraham Bertram
& a Phle Gorey por des Chariage quil ont fait pour ~~~~~~~ 07=10=00
du gravier por Leglise sept livres Dix sous ~~~~~~~~~~~~~~ 97=02=09

            Recepte dudr surveillant
                                                        ₶ ₷ ₫

Receu en plussieurs fois de Tho: Lempriere gents &
Conestables nonante sept livres deux sous neuf dens ~~~~~~ 97=02=9

Ce 29me Septemb 1712 mr Phle le Feuvre L'un des surveillant de cette
paroise a rendu les Contes suscrits les poyments monte a la
fome de nonante sept Livres Deux sous neuf deniers & les
recepte a la mesme some de sorte qt est quite de ce jour

Dumaresq   Fr: Le Couseur Rt

                    Tho: Lempriere fonest

                    Pierre Machon Centenir

                    Phle Collas Centenir

                    Francois Lempriere surveillan

To Elizabeth.

Just a small gift to wish you a happy retirement and to remind you of St Martin.

Helen Blampied

Maggie Dodd

Betty Herivel

5th October 1999.

ST MARTIN
JERSEY

The Story of an Island Parish

J. B. Germain .

ST MARTIN
JERSEY

The Story of an Island Parish

edited by

Chris Blackstone and Katie Le Quesne

with contributions by the editors and
Monica Amy, Christopher Aubin, Helen Baker, Helen Blampied, Betty Brooke,
Graham Crosby, Jackie De Gruchy, Hugh Fauvel, Peter Germain, Mary Gibb,
Percy Gicquel, Michael Ginns, Trevor Green, Bob Hill, Sarah Johnson,
Gerald Le Cocq, Nigel Le Gresley, Beatrice Le Huquet, Maurice Lees, Louise Magris,
Hamish Marett-Crosby, Anthony Paines, Jenny Pallot, Amelia Perchard,
Anne Perchard, Pauline Perchard, Stan Perchard, John Renouf, Kath Richardson,
Paul Richardson, Christopher Scholefield, Nicol Spence, Mike Stentiford, Peter Tabb,
Nancy Thelland, Lawrence Turner and Eunice Whiteside

PHILLIMORE

1999

Published by
PHILLIMORE & CO. LTD.
Shopwyke Manor Barn, Chichester, West Sussex
for the
Parish of St Martin

ISBN 1 86077 104 1

Dedicated to the memory of
all those Parishioners of
St Martin,
who gave their lives in two
World Wars
(1914-1918)
(1939-1945)

Note: While every attempt has been made to ensure the accuracy of all the material contained in this book, the editors, individual contributors and members of St Martin's Parish History Committee accept no responsibility or liability for any inaccuracies or mis-statements which may appear in the text.

Printed and bound in Great Britain by
BUTLER AND TANNER LTD.
London and Frome

CONTENTS

LIST OF ILLUSTRATIONS

Front endpaper (left): Minutes of a Parish Assembly held on 25 January 1785. The sale of the goods of Philip Bertram jnr was ordered for non-payment of rates. The top signature in the right-hand column is that of Reverend François Le Couteur, who played a prominent part in the Battle of Jersey, three years earlier.
Front endpaper (right): Receipted and certified account of Philippe Le Feuvre, surveillant (churchwarden) for the period 19 March 1711-29 September 1712.

Back endpaper (left): Minutes of two Parish Assemblies, 3 August 1709 and 12 April 1710. In both cases, the business at hand was the reservation of pews in the Parish Church.
Back endpaper (right): Minutes of a Parish Assembly of 5 April 1796, setting the rate.

LIST OF COLOUR PLATES

ACKNOWLEDGEMENTS

Our first thanks must be to the Parishioners of St Martin who voted from the parish rate the funds which made this publication possible.

The idea of a book of parish history was conceived in March 1998 by members of the St Martin's Parish Millennium Committee, which had been appointed to select one or more suitable projects by which the Parish might celebrate the advent of the 21st century.

Subsequently, the St Martin's Parish History Committee was created to pursue the idea of a book and, once this had been approved by the Parish, to bring it to fruition. This Committee, consisting of Helen Baker, Mary Gibb, Gerald Le Cocq, Anthony Paines, Anne Perchard and Jenny Pallot, has made individual contributions to the text and, over a period of 15 months attended to all the administrative work involved. The Committee would like particularly to record its appreciation of the support and assistance of Connétable John Germain and the staff of St Martin's Public Hall: Helen Blampied, Betty Herivel and Maggie Poole.

The Société Jersiaise has played a vital rôle in making all its archives available for research. Unstinting assistance has been given by Mary Billot and Sally Knight of the Lord Coutanche Library, by Julia Coutanche of the photographic archive and by Roger and Margaret Long who have read the copy with diligence and attention to detail.

A special mention is due to Jan Hedley of the *Jersey Evening Post*, who has sought out many photographs from its archives.

This book has been a combined effort by many people, both St Martinais and others. The contributors of sections of text are acknowledged in the chapter notes and illustrations are also accredited. In addition we would like to thank the following for all their help, in many cases including the loan of treasured photographs and other historic material: Donald Ahier, Gerald Amy, Stan Barnard, Kathleen Binet, Betty Bois, John Brewster, Faye Buesnel, Paul Cobden, Gordon and Muriel Cobden, Dave Crawford, Beryl Crimp, Harold and Jackie De Gruchy, Stanley and Christine De La Haye, Anne de Wolff, Ailsa Dorey, Laurence Dorey, Mike Dryden, Frank Falle, Jack Falle, Hugh Fauvel, Janet Ferbrache, Derrick Frigot, Cyril Gaudin, Paul and Megan Gaudin, John Gavey, John D. Germain, Michael Ginns, Alex Glendinning, Pat Gruchy, Rhona Lady Guthrie, Deputy Bob Hill, John Jean, Philip Jeune, Jayn Johnson, Margaret Le Cornu, Beatrice Le Huquet, Reverend David Le Seelleur, John Le Seelleur, Brigadier Raoul and Mrs. Sheelagh Lemprière-Robin, Violet Lort-Phillips, Alec McFadyen, Marjorie Marett, Richard Miles, Paul Mimmack, Alan Mollet, Irene Morley, Tony Newcombe, Madeleine Noël, David Pallot, Garnet Perchard, Alec Podger, Glenn Rankine, William Renouf, Andalusia Richardson, Gerald Richardson, Marjorie Robins, Peter and Sonya Scott Graham, Richard Stent, Frank Tadier, Reverend Lawrence Turner, Michael and Nancy Vautier, Anne Walton, Tony Watton, Eunice Whiteside, Christine Wilson, Steve Woods, Jack Worrall.

It is through the help and support of all these people that St Martin, *Jersey – The Story of an Island Parish* has been completed. Without it, it would have been quite impossible to produce such a comprehensive publication.

Chris Blackstone
Katie Le Quesne
St Martin, Jersey
March 1999

PREFACE

by Brigadier R.C. Lemprière-Robin, O.B.E., Seigneur de Rosel.

This excellent book is a history of both the land and the community of St Martin. It is a mainly rural Parish where my ancestors and I have been fortunate enough to live for many generations, and in the process have reaped the benefits of that association. It is a Parish of singular beauty, with its wonderful coastline, harbours and beaches, and of great history, as we can see by studying the churches, the castle, the neolithic monuments and the breakwater. But above all it is the community spirit which holds it all together, and this is portrayed in this book.

The many Parishioners who have given so freely of their time and knowledge to put this book together have not only shown themselves to be true St Martinais, but have done something which should help to kindle a pride and interest in this Parish community throughout future generations.

Courtesy of Sheelagh Lemprière-Robin

Raoul Lemprière-Robin
Rosel Manor
January 1999

THE PARISH OF ST MARTIN

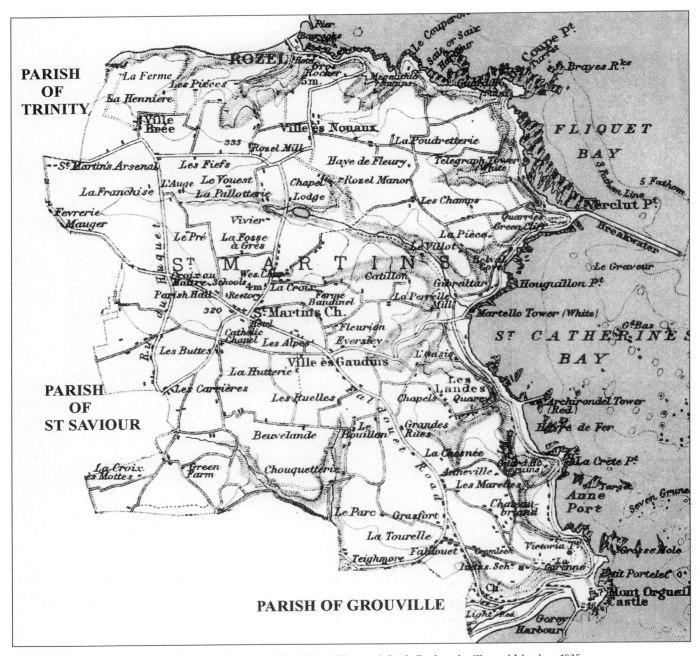

This map has been adapted from Ward Lock & Co.'s Illustrated Guide Book to the Channel Islands, c.*1935.*

Ancient Times

THE GEOLOGY AND TOPOGRAPHY OF ST MARTIN

The granite rocks of Les Écréhous – along with their westward extensions in the reefs of the Diroûilles and Paternosters – have been in existence for something like six hundred million years. These rocks were separated from the rocks of Jersey by an important fault line along Le Ruau which, even now, has potential for movement. This fault must loom large in any history of the rocks of St Martin since it has had a significant effect on past and present relationships between the Island and the reefs. In effect, it is a fault of great age and importance.

To discover how St Martin's rocks developed, we must look back between 500 and 600 million years, to examine a time of mountain-building and its later consequences.

The granitic rocks of the reefs began as a molten magma deep in the heart of a truly ancient range of mountains which are known as the Cadomian Range, a range in fact not very different in nature from the present day Andes. This range dominated the northern coasts of an equally ancient land mass known as Gondwanaland. But time passed and that minute speck of Gondwanaland which was to become Jersey found itself in a situation more akin to the island chain of Sumatra-Java, where volcanoes grew out of the sea at that time just as those of the East Indies have in the recent past, and are continuing to do today.

These dramatic events are recorded in the Parish in a major outcrop of volcanic rocks extending from the Tête des Hougues in Trinity to the Gorey area. They form a very varied series of rocks recording many different types of volcanic activity and are superbly exposed from Archirondel along to Petit Portelet, below Mont Orgueil Castle. There is even a remnant of the marine deposits from the sea out of which the volcanoes grew, though the main deposits of this sea, the strata of the Jersey shale formation, composed mainly of shaly and silty rocks, are to be found in the central and western parishes. The most exciting of the volcanic outcrops exists immediately to the south of Anne Port on the upper foreshore, where hexagonal prisms are strikingly exposed, turned on their side, just like a smaller version of the Giant's Causeway, though in a different rock type (Fig. 2).

The upheavals associated with the formation of the Cadomian mountain-building episode thus created first the deep molten magmas now forming the Écréhous reef, then the volcanoes growing out of the seas of the time.

During these events and following them the whole area was folded and faulted and uplifted to make the Cadomian mountain chain. One of the most important faults formed was that of Le Ruau. It was a profound fault extending deep into the earth's crust and activity on it was considerable during the uplift of the Cadomian mountains. In fact it was so active that the northern side was uplifted more than the south and, on the north side, steep high cliffs were formed from which

1 This photograph, taken in the Salt Range of the Punjab shows very clearly what the landscape of St Martin might have looked like at the time of deposition of the conglomerate nearly 500 million years ago. (Photo: Dercyk Laming)

rivers rushed out of *gulches* and *wadis* onto a plain comparable to that of valley floors such as Death Valley in Nevada today. These rivers in flood (Fig. 1) carried huge amounts of debris of all sizes, from silt to boulders two metres or more across, and deposited them all on the valley floors as layers of sediment varying in thickness from a few centimetres to several metres. The coarsest deposits to be seen today are in Trinity near the Tour de Rozel but one huge boulder, known modestly as The Pebble, is on show at the beginning of St Catherine's Breakwater.

The finest-grained sediments are well displayed in the bank opposite La Solitude Farm. These are of varied colour, either a pale green or purple mauve, and are the result of deposition in a temporary *playa* lake of the time. The choice of words used in this and the preceding paragraph – *gulch, wadi, playa* – is deliberate for they evoke the language and scenery of the desert areas of the world. This was what St Martin looked like at this late stage of the Cadomian mountain-building episode, with bare landscapes, rocky walled gorges, extensive walls of cliff fronting the valley plains, *playa* lakes and from time to time raging flash floods. The rocks and boulders caught up in the floods were roughly rounded and this gives the deposit in St Martin the choice of two names – Rozel Conglomerate or Rozel Pudding Stone (Plates 3 and 4). Every bit of coast from Rozel Bay itself to St Catherine has its conglomerate cliffs.

At some much later time the deposit was folded and fractured, producing tilted strata dipping up to a maximum of 36 degrees and also causing major joint planes. These last are what create those strange flat surfaces seen to best advantage in the vertical faces of the old Verclut quarries at the Breakwater but visible in all outcrops. It is also remarkable that original rounded pebbles are cut across indiscriminately by these joint planes. The gullies cut back into the conglomerate around the coast are distinctive and quite different from those in the volcanics, granites or shales elsewhere in the Island; they are characterised by near-vertical sides and flat bottoms, with tumbled boulders of great size forming occasional pseudo-caves.

With the close of the Cadomian mountain-building episode 500 million years ago, almost all the hard rocks of Jersey were in existence including the principal Island granites which are not represented in St Martin. Of these rocks, the Rozel Conglomerate is the youngest. However, much was to happen before the present geography of the Channel Islands and adjacent areas of Brittany, the Channel and south-west England would appear in any form that we would recognise today.

From 500 million years ago to a mere 1.8 million years before this new millennium, huge changes took place. The Cadomian mountains were worn down flat; they were submerged beneath the sea, and sandstones, shales and limestones were deposited over the areas which included the Channel Islands-to-be.

These sediments were caught up in a new episode of mountain formation some 300 million years ago, the Variscan. The basic forms of Brittany/Lower Normandy (known as Armorica), south-west England and the Channel were to emerge from this new convulsive episode of mountain building. As the plate tectonic-generated opening of the Atlantic Ocean began some 250 million years ago it caused major uplifting of south-west England and Armorica on the northern and southern sides of a relatively downfaulted Channel and Western Approaches.

The down-faulting of the Channel resulted in thick layers of sands, muds and limestones accumulating over its central parts, between the Channel Islands and south-west England, during the next 190 million years. This brings the story to within some 60 to 70 million years of the present – and incidentally to that well-known event, the extinction of the dinosaurs.

Accumulation of sediments over the Channel Islands area was limited, since the whole area was a very shallow shelf sea, a mere embayment of the shores of Armorica, which was only flooded by the sea every now and then. However, the flooding did lead to important deposits in the embayment. In particular, about 60 million years ago, a tongue of the sea at that time caused limestones to form on the shelf. It is likely, though not finally proven, that these limestones, known to lie beneath the waters of Le Ruau between Jersey and Les Écréhous where scuba divers have sampled them, are proof that the Channel Islands existed in a form similar to how we know them today.

But of even greater interest is the fact that the deep water separating Jersey from Les Écréhous, Diroûilles and Paternosters occupies a valley lying on the line of that ancient Le Ruau fault which is still wielding its influence after some 500 million years. And so another rock entirely is added to the count in St Martin, that of the Eocene nummulitic limestones of the Le Ruau Channel.

There are interesting implications arising from the likely existence of the Channel Islands in a recognisable form at this period. If the waters of the Channel Islands' shelf were to be removed – as they have been in practice during the many ice ages of the last two million years – there would be revealed not a true seabed but an ancient drowned landscape. The origin in time of this landscape is uncertain, but from the form and distribution of the nummulitic limestones and allied

2   The rhyolite columns of Anne Port are similar in form and origin to the columns of the Giant's Causeway. Note the square to hexagonal ends of the columns, which lie at an angle of 20-30 degrees to the horizontal. They can be seen by looking down onto the rocks from the picnic area at La Crête Point. (Photo: John Renouf)

rocks of comparable age it is very possible that it was formed on land considerably earlier, even before the Channel began to subside some 250 million years ago.

Not only do we have these extensive flat areas around the Channel Islands forming the shelf, but there are many dissected flat areas or plateaux at a variety of levels in surrounding Armorica. Some of the lower ones, of about 100 metres and lower, are also found in Jersey. The significant crest running from near Tête des Hougues to Rozel Mill forms the northern edge, somewhat degraded, of this 100-metre plateau in the Parish. The crest also marks the junction between the Rozel Conglomerate and the harder-weathering volcanic rocks. The Rozel Conglomerate has been more easily eroded and forms a gently-shelving slope to the coast, which is something unique on Jersey's northern coastline.

Plateaux which are more or less at the present sea level form extensive flats around the edge of the Island and include St Catherine's Bay. Beyond the Island itself, Les Écréhous were also probably shaped at their present tidal levels, as were the Minquiers and other tidal reefs between the Channel Islands and France. All these plateaux, low and high, were certainly more or less as they are now by the time that the most recent geological period, the Pleistocene, started soon after two million years ago.

The Pleistocene was the period when what is now St Martin saw glacials, interglacials and exotic animals, and welcomed for the first time people onto the scene.

The Pleistocene was marked by a succession of extremes of climate with alternating cold glacials and warmer interglacials. It contrasts sharply with the 60 million years which had gone before, when the climate was much milder, even subtropical, as shown, for instance, by the nummulitic limestones.

The Channel Islands shelf is so shallow that relatively minor changes in sea level cause large tracts of seabed to be revealed. St Martin would become one with Les Écréhous if the sea level were to drop by 20–30 metres though there would be a significant river to be crossed, occupying the drowned valley of the Le Ruau channel. This river could be traced westward, out towards the larger drowned river valleys of the central Channel and eastward back to its headwaters, the present River Ay near Lessay in the Cotentin. During the last third of the Pleistocene, from about 600 thousand years ago, the glacials were usually long and very cold and the wild animals associated with these times were those adapted to the climate: the woolly mammoth, the woolly rhinoceros, large deer, arctic fox, wild horse and others. On the journey from Rozel out to Les Écréhous across the emergent plain and the River Ay, these are all animals which might have been encountered.

But who would have encountered them? From the cave deposits in La Cotte de St Brelade have come the remains of the Neanderthalers, that early race of humankind that was the dominant form to live in Europe for several hundred thousand years down to about 35,000 years ago. At this time of writing there is still heated debate about the fate of the Neanderthalers, who were supplanted about 30,000 years ago by modern man. Across the plain to Les Écréhous the Neanderthalers roamed during the less extreme climates of the glacials and hunted their prey – a scene which appears so exotic in our imagination today (Plate 2).

The end of the Neanderthalers was followed in the Channel Islands area by the onset of the extreme cold of the latest of the known glacials – the Devensian. As close to St Martin as Green Island there is evidence of permafrost 28 thousand years ago. There would have been very little which would have survived this climate and human beings would have rarely visited. The unrelenting cold continued more or less unabated for another 10 thousand years. During this time, and for several thousand years after, the cold climate caused the formation of two very typical deposits seen around all the coastlands of northern Armorica and the Channel Islands: *head* and *loess*.

Along valley sides and cliffs the harsh weather caused the shattering of the rocks by frost, and their subsequent collapse downslope, taking with them any finer material to form the typical orange-brown cliffs of *head* so conspicuous behind bays such as Bonne Nuit. *Head* is also present to a lesser extent in St Martin but the conglomerate cliffs were too low to allow any great thicknesses to accumulate.

During drier spells, strong long-lasting winds blew along the plains stretching from the Western Approaches to Poland and beyond. These winds picked up the rock flour ground beneath the vast northern ice sheets and spread it as an all-carpeting layer on most surfaces. Some got blown into the *head* deposits but most formed sheets of *loess* varying greatly in thickness from place to place. Near the River Seine, thicknesses up to tens of metres are known while in Jersey the maximum over the plateau is just over a metre. The plateau from near Tête des Hougues in the north to Faldouet in the south is covered by this *loess* carpet and forms the basis of the fertile farm soils of the area.

Along the coastal cliffs there are thin deposits of *loess* up to a few tens of centimetres to be found locally between St Catherine's Tower and the Breakwater. These *loesses* have one particular feature of interest: in one or two places there was enough calcium carbonate to lead to the formation of hard lumps or concretions of carbonate a few centimetres across, which have the picturesque German name of Loëssmännchen – little *loess* dolls.

With the final ending of the Devensian glacial some 10,000 years ago, the climate warmed up all over the northern hemisphere and the world entered the present interglacial. The sea level rose as the water which had been locked up in the great ice sheets and glaciers melted, and was returned to the oceans. By the opening of Neolithic times in the Channel Islands area, the high tide was more or less the same as the present low of our spring tides. From this point on, i.e. from sometime after 5000 BC, the sea continued rising and began the active erosion of the deposits of the last glacial, the *loesses* and *heads*. This was most effective around the coasts and eventually led to the laying bare of the cliffs as we see them today.

The story of the rocks of St Martin does not end with the sea at its present level. With the coming of the first farmers, the Neolithic people, to the Island soon after 5000 BC, serious use began to be made of the different rocks and soils left behind by the various geological episodes of the remote past. First the Neolithic people sought out the flatter fertile areas of the Island on the coastal plains and the plateau. From Faldouet to La Ville Brée the plateau is unbroken by deep valleys. The Neolithic people cleared the forests and from then on, in an unbroken tradition down to the present day, this area has been well farmed.

During the Neolithic period and the beginning of more or less continuous habitation of the Channel Islands and adjacent parts of Armorica, the purely natural evolution of the whole area came to an end. But that is not to say that geological processes did not continue. The continuing changes were important. The sea level continued to rise until probably the late third millennium BC, since when it has fluctuated within a metre or so of where it is today.

The sea has continued to encroach on the land right up to our own times – with perhaps an acceleration in sight if some forecasts of sea level rise are correct. One vexed question concerns the issue of vanished land and even buildings, for instance Le Manoir de La Brecquette in St Ouen, the Forest of Scissy between us and the Cotentin, and the story of the Bishop of Coutances and the plank. This has also been of considerable interest to the history of Les Écréhous.

From a purely geological point of view, there is no difficulty in supposing, for example, that the sands of St Catherine's Bay and the whole of the low tide area at Les Écréhous were once dry land. The known low sea level of the glacials which exposed the whole of the Channel Islands shelf is not in question and the sea level rise after the last glacial brought sea levels to about that of our present spring low tides near 5000 BC. The presence of Neolithic peats at intertidal levels on many island beaches proves land existed over areas where the tides now wash. However, in the absence of a datable sequence of deposits above the peats, it is not now possible to say when the inundation of the land represented by the peats took place. The most that can be stated geologically is that the encroachment of the sea occurred at some unknown time after the peat formed. The problem is that once soft sediment has been removed by the sea and the hard rocks exposed, there is no geological evidence to show when it was removed or even that it was ever there. This is the situation, geologically speaking, for Les Écréhous and the Forest of Scissy and any supposed bishop's plank.

But of course geology is not the only source of information about the extent of land on Les Écréhous, or between the islands and France. Human records have something to contribute too. The best evidence would have been unambiguous maps, but these do not exist for the period in question – the mid-first millennium AD to late medieval times. We do have legend, but the interpretation of it is fraught with uncertainties at all levels.

Unquestionably there is a body of indirect historical evidence, very well summarised in the article by C. P. Le Cornu (1883) suggesting strongly that there was a considerable extent of low land at both L'Étacq and off Le Hocq up to about the 12th or 13th centuries. Similar lines of argument can be used to suggest that there were some forested lands extending off the coast of the Cotentin and further south to Mont St Michel which may or may not correlate with the Forest of Scissy. However, there is no strong evidence to indicate that there was anything remotely resembling a causeway in historical times linking either La Rocque or Les Écréhous to the Cotentin with the only hurdle to be crossed a stream or river. The archaeological and historical investigations carried out at Les Écréhous recently (Rodwell, 1996) demand a greater land area there than exists at present, but at its maximum this would never have extended beyond the present low-tide limits. When such of this land as existed was destroyed by the sea is likely to remain imponderable for ever.

Stone has always had its uses. The Neolithic people were the first to make organised use of stone, not in the construction of their homes, but in their special burial monuments. Faldouet dolmen, or passage grave, as it should really be known, is notable for its huge 25-ton capstone of autobrecciated rhyolite (Plate 5). Since the rhyolite is the bedrock on the plateau here, we shall never know whether the great block was found in place on the heights or whether it was found on the seashore below and brought up the steep coastal slopes to its present position, though the seashore source is much the more likely. The other surviving uprights of the tomb are mostly granite which must have been brought up from the south east somewhere, but their relatively small size must have made the task comparatively easy for these skilled people.

At a later stage in the Neolithic, a different tomb type, the *allée couverte*, was constructed. Le Couperon de Rozel, in St Martin, is one of the Island's two most important survivors. The stone in this area is the Rozel Conglomerate and this tomb is made exclusively of this rock. For normal building purposes the Rozel Conglomerate is poor, since it cannot be split in a controlled manner, and it is water permeable along the multiplicity of small cracks that open up between its constituent pebbles. However, for the sort of tomb structure at Le Couperon this did not present a problem, and the builders chose the local stone with the minimum of transport required.

Tomb construction by the Neolithic peoples represented a major communal effort taking up a significant proportion of the total workforce over a considerable time. No comparable task devoted to religious observances occurred again in north-west France and the Channel Islands until the building of Christian churches began some three millennia later. Other prehistoric peoples, notably those of the Iron Age, created imposing structures but these were for purposes of fortification. In St Martin the mound on which Mont Orgueil Castle is built was fortified throughout most of its prehistoric existence with a succession of ramparts but these structures used only local rubble. However, Mont Orgueil Castle itself at the end of the 12th century AD became the first major construction in the Parish after the Neolithic.

Building techniques by this time were such that the Island granites could be fashioned into quoins and ashlars to enable the masons to make strong corners and openings with the rougher stone used to infill between. This technique, once perfected, has remained in use ever since, in both vernacular and public building. The stone used for Mont Orgueil Castle was granite from outside the Parish, while infill came both from the neighbourhood and even from England, particularly limestones from Dorset, which were used for special purposes.

Most vernacular houses in the Island right up to the 18th century were built principally of wood. The iron tools of quarrymen in medieval and earlier times were expensive, and the work of shaping stone involved much labour, which was also expensive then – even though cheap by modern standards. A further influence was lack of wealth; though not poor by contemporary standards, the farmers in the Island were not wealthy enough until the 18th century to create stone-built homes. In St Martin most of the stone-built farmhouses, as others in the Island, date from the 18th century even if they have been extensively changed since. The only stone in the Island really suitable for house walls is granite, because the other rocks are all seamed through with planes and lines of weakness and cannot be squared to shape. For this reason the local volcanics and conglomerates are only rarely found in houses and even then used almost exclusively as infill between shaped granite blocks.

Sometimes outbuildings contain more local rock as for these, appearance was deemed to be less important. There is however, one other local stone that was important for a few houses in the north of the Parish: that is Les Écréhous granite.

Until the modern transport revolution of this century all the granite used in the Parish had to be brought by horse and cart from the quarry, mostly from Mont Mado. The stone from Les Écréhous had not only to be quarried or selected from beach material on the island but had to be transported by boat to Jersey before being transferred to carts. The extra cost of this seems to make little sense unless it is assumed that the stone itself was quarried or selected by those who had rights of some sort to it. This is a possible explanation for much of the stone being concentrated in local family clusters or *Villes*, of which the most typical is La Palloterie.

Any mention of the use of stone in the Parish of St Martin must also include the 18th- and 19th-century fortifications by the British military in their attempt to create defences against the French, and a major harbour to compete with that of Cherbourg. Much conglomerate was used for the two defensive towers, Archirondel and St Catherine, but the *pièce de résistance* must be the Breakwater. Granite has been used to form major corners and edges, but the bulk of the giant structure is made out of the conglomerate quarried nearby, which has created a major alteration to the landscape of this area. Because it was cut into blocks of the size required for this huge breakwater, the many joints did not prove a hindrance, and because of the job required of it, water permeability of the stone was not particularly relevant.

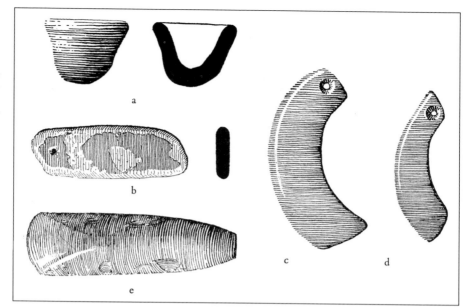

*3 A pot, pendants and flint axe
excavated at La Pouquelaye de
Faldouet by Mr. Fauvel.
(Courtesy of Société Jersiaise
Photographic Archive, Jersey)*

ST MARTIN IN PRE-HISTORY: THE FIRST FARMERS OF THE NEOLITHIC

There is no direct evidence of the presence of man in St Martin during the Old Stone Age but the important archaeological finds in La Cotte de St Brelade show that Neanderthal people were living and hunting in Jersey before 30,000 BC. At that time Jersey was part of the continent of Europe, although the glaciers to the north were beginning to retreat, producing a milder climate and a slow rise in sea levels. The landscape too was beginning to change, from an icy inhospitable tundra to park-like woodland. Here, as on what is now the continent, woolly mammoths, wild pigs and deer flourished, all of which were hunted by the wandering bands of Palaeolithic men and women.

While the sea level was rising and the climate improving, sometime after 10,000 BC, new people arrived in the area. These were the Mesolithic hunters, fishers and gatherers who lived along the extensive shorelines of the period; Jersey was still joined to France, but not the islands to the north. These early wanderers have left all too little evidence of their passing, since much of the coastal zones they inhabited was later submerged by the rising sea. They are only known from their flint-chipping areas found on most exposed headlands, heathlands and dunes in the island.

Even after Jersey became a true island the fertile coastal plains remained extensive for a millennium or more. It was on these plains and the flatter plateaux that the first pioneer Neolithic farmers settled around 5000 BC.

The sea crossing at this time was short and easy for boats of the coracle type, and the sea itself provided a rich harvest of fish and shellfish to supplement a diet of hunted birds and animals, gathered nuts and berries, as well as the first grain harvests and the products of the first domesticated animals. It is thought that these farmers came from Normandy, having travelled there from further east.

The high tide level of 5000 BC was probably more or less the same as the lowest tide mark of today, so for at least a thousand years, when the Atlantic civilisations of the Neolithic reached their peak, there would have been much good land to farm on coastal plains around the islands and the coast of Brittany.

It has proved impossible as yet to find the settlement sites or villages of these early people, but this must in part be because the sea has washed them away gradually as it rose, taking the Neolithic farmlands together with their dwellings. There have, however, been many random finds of stone tools, particularly arrowheads and axes, which attest to a Neolithic presence in St Martin.

These early farmers were joined by others who had a strong tradition of megalithic building, especially of passage graves. We cannot now know or even imagine the thinking behind this religion. We can only wonder at the achievements of these primitive farmers who built the monuments known by the name of 'Dolmens'. St Martin has two outstanding examples in La Pouquelaye de Faldouet, a chambered tomb of the peak of Neolithic civilisation in Jersey, and the Dolmen du Couperon, a late gallery grave or *allée couverte*. It is clear that, at the time Faldouet Dolmen was built, there must have been a population of at least two thousand in Jersey to provide the labour needed for this and other such constructions. It is true to say that these people left a more indelible mark on the landscape of the time than all their successors down to the time of the Normans.

From 5000 BC to 3000 BC the population of Jersey increased in number and in efficiency at farming, hunting and food gathering. They learned to grow wheat, barley and beans on land which was probably cleared by cutting and burning. Flax was grown for making cloth. Domesticated animals provided many materials such as skin, leather, horn and bone as well as food. The making of pottery became important and skilful; not made on a wheel, but decorated and burnished and increasingly well fired. Stone tools, especially axes and adzes, were manufactured to ever higher standards.

Basketry, mat-making, spinning and weaving all flourished. It is known that trade was carried on with people from the mainland, because so many of the fine stone tools found in Jersey are made of stone which does not exist in the island, notably flint and jadeite. The ability to trade meant, of course, the Jersey Neolithic communities were able to produce goods and food in excess of their needs for day-to-day living. Above all, the population was sufficient to provide a workforce which could spare the time from food production to build the Dolmens.

No doubt St Martin followed the fortunes of the Island as a whole during the later Neolithic after 3500 BC, when it is likely that the higher land was increasingly cleared and farmed as the inexorable rise of the sea drowned the fertile lowlands. By the end of the third millennium BC, the St Martin coastline probably took on a form much as at present. In addition, there were problems with the weather. It is now thought that the climate deteriorated, bringing storms and summer rains which damaged land and crops. In Jersey, as in the other islands and the coastal areas of the mainland, the population began to decline and Neolithic civilisation stagnated or regressed.

However, sometime after 2000 BC there seems to have been an improvement in conditions in Jersey. Perhaps the climate was better, so that farming was more successful. At all events, a new kind of pottery appeared, called Beaker ware, bell-shaped and decorated with care and elegance. This seems to have been an indication of cultural improvement and a renewed ability to trade with the mainland.

Around 1500 BC the technology of making bronze had been perfected. Before this, some copper axes had appeared in Jersey, but it is thought that these were more of a status symbol than

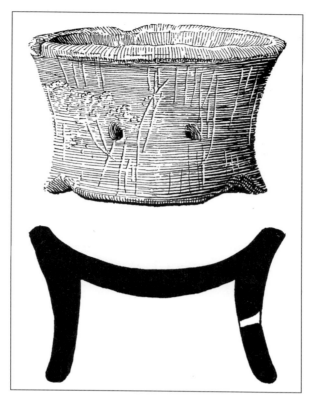

4 A vase support from La Pouquelaye de Faldouet. (Courtesy of Société Jersiaise Photographic Archive, Jersey)

a useful tool. Bronze is a much harder metal, which led to the introduction of the plough and other more efficient methods of farming. Ploughing was a more feasible proposition, but the loss of the lower lands meant that Jersey could not sustain as large a population as it had during the thousand or more years of the 'high' Neolithic era. The Bronze and early Iron Age also ushered in a long period of unsettled times, when it is clear that the Island population needed places of refuge from marauding invaders. Fortifications were built round easily defended sites, one of the largest of these being the Câtel de Rozel. From the excavations in the Middle Ward of Gorey Castle we know that this place was defended in the Iron Age. Before that, there is some evidence that it was also a safe settlement site for Neolithic farmers.

Secure farmlands must have been in short supply and no doubt the population was reduced by war and want. By 500 BC an important new chapter was beginning in Island history with the burgeoning of Iron-Age societies in north-west Europe. It was this Iron-Age society in Gaul and the Channel Islands that the Romans were to encounter and conquer in the middle of the first century BC.

THE DOLMENS OF ST MARTIN

There may be no evidence to show where and how the Neolithic farmers of St Martin lived, but the Parish is fortunate to have two important megalithic monuments within its boundaries. Fortunate, because so many other relics of the powerful religion which guided the farmers' lives have been destroyed in past times. There were people who took stones for other buildings; farmers who needed to plough land which was encumbered with ancient monuments, and those who

5 *An excavation party at Le Couperon. This could well be the 1868 excavation by the Reverend F. Porter. (Courtesy of Société Jersiaise Photographic Archive, Jersey)*

thought that treasure was there for the taking. Last, and possibly most dangerous, were the antiquarians, whose motives were a mixture of treasure-seeking and the desire to excavate with little experience or knowledge.

Both the dolmen of Le Couperon (a long-cist or *allée couverte*) and La Pouquelaye de Faldouet (a passage grave) have suffered in these ways. Le Couperon was first mentioned in 1734, Faldouet as early as 1682. It is clear from these early descriptions that both were originally buried beneath mounds of earth and rubble in the same manner as La Hougue Bie. However, the various writers from the past have left us with conflicting and confusing descriptions of the arrangement of the stones.

In 1868 the Reverend F. Porter (who was the chaplain of the Naval School above Gorey and a keen antiquarian) found Le Couperon in a sad state of ruin. He set out to excavate and replace the stones where he thought they should be. Unfortunately his ideas were not always archaeologically sound; one stone in particular which has a kind of circular hole in it was certainly not put back where it was originally. If only Porter had made plans of his excavations, modern archaeologists would have blessed him instead of reviling his efforts. The only thing we can say with certainty is that the general plan of Le Couperon dolmen is that of a type well known in France, where it is called an *allée couverte*. The probable date of such a monument is around 2500 BC, considerably later than the probable date of Faldouet dolmen. The stone used for Le Couperon is the local Rozel Conglomerate. There is no knowing what happened to finds made by Porter, since he only mentions broken pieces of urns and flints, with no record of what he did with them.

Faldouet dolmen also suffered from the attentions of Porter in 1868. The tenant of the site (leased from the Crown) was a Mr. Fauvel. He had been excavating beneath the capstone and in the side chambers since 1839, and allowed Porter to help him finish the job. Fauvel had been searching for treasure, and had charged visitors an entrance fee, but had not removed most of the mound. Plans of what he had found were made by the Lukis brothers from Guernsey, showing side chambers on the northern side, one with a capstone in place, and a note that human bones

6 *La Pouquelaye de Faldouet, viewed from the east. The capstone weighs about 23 tons and was probably dragged from the foreshore at Anne Port. (Courtesy of Société Jersiaise Photographic Archive, Jersey)*

were found there. There was no side chamber on the southern side in this plan, nor did it show the entrance passageway which, presumably, had not then been uncovered.

A year after Porter had finished excavating and reconstructing the dolmen, he was severely criticised by a Lieutenant S. P. Oliver, who was writing a book called *The Megalithic Structures of the Channel Islands.* Lieutenant Oliver accused the excavators of 'throwing down a small capstone and displacing other blocks', while Porter had allegedly 'altered the dry-walling at the exit to the passageway and falsely reconstructed a side-kist'.

There is no record of there having been capstones found over the passageway or the central chamber but there is no doubt that capstones were commonly removed for building material – perhaps some had found their way to Gorey Castle walls – and Ahier reports in 1852 that one capstone was used as a hearthstone in a nearby cottage. Lieutenant Oliver reported the height of the passageway stones as three feet six inches, which is some six inches lower than the passageway at La Hougue Bie.

The last reconstruction of Faldouet dolmen was undertaken in 1910 by the Société Jersiaise, largely because the upright stones were falling, owing to the lack of drainage in the interior. The fallen uprights were put back into position and the floor of the dolmen was raised, using the earth which had been heaped round the stones, and an open drainage gutter was built.

Finally an effort was made to excavate so as to find the outer walls of the mound, which had been reported by Oliver. These walls were not found, but numbers of large stones were found mixed with the rubble of the mound, which seemed to show that the walls had been destroyed. However, across the eastern entrance to the passageway and about three feet from the first stones were discovered the foundations of the encircling wall right across the entrance. This seemed to confirm Oliver's statement that Porter had rearranged the entrance walls.

Jean Fauvel kept the finds he made, with the exception of the human bones, and these were bought by the Société Jersiaise from his heirs in 1932. Porter gave some of his finds to a friend and these eventually found their way to the British Museum. Fauvel's finds included bowls and vase supports, polished axes and pendants, which are now in the care of the Jersey Museums Service.

7   *The gallery grave or* allée couverte *at La Couperon, built around 2500 BC. (Courtesy of Société Jersiaise Photographic Archive, Jersey)*

It is of interest to note that most of the upright stones are of the dark red granite from the Mont Orgueil area. These stones must have been carried about a quarter of a mile and raised at least 130 feet. The nearest outcrop of the special rhyolite of the great capstone (which has been estimated to weigh 23 to 24 tons) is a quarter of a mile away, but at the same height as the dolmen; but a more likely source are the outcrops of the same rock at shore level near Anne Port, where large blocks are more common. There is no proper evidence for dating the Faldouet dolmen. All that can be said is that it is of a type which was being built between 4000 and 3500 BC.

In modern times we have been fortunate to find a less damaged passage grave in La Hougue Bie, so that we can appreciate better the mysterious religious nature of these megalithic monuments. It is clear that they could not have been merely graves, since a population capable of building them would have filled them up in no time. Perhaps they should be thought of as something more akin to a parish church, where seasonal festivals of worship were held to encourage mother earth to bless the farmers and their crops each year.

The megalithic religion had considerable knowledge of astronomy and the direction of the entrances to the passage graves seems to have been important. Both Faldouet and La Hougue Bie are built to the same orientation, which is some 19 degrees south of east. Those who care to climb on the great capstone of Faldouet dolmen on the evening of the September full moon will find that the moon rises from the sea on the line of the passageway of the dolmen. It would be fascinating to know whether this was the intention of the original builders – a time to celebrate the harvest festival perhaps – or whether the September full moon had some other special spiritual significance for them.

We nowadays can only wonder at this amazing architecture and remember that the religion of the passage graves lasted for at least 4,000 years. Our millennium is celebrating a mere 2,000 years from the birth of Jesus Christ.

Two
Medieval History

MONT ORGUEIL CASTLE

Mont Orgueil Castle's towering silhouette has almost come to symbolise Jersey. Some would say it is the Island's finest building.

It is a magnificent example of military architecture, spanning the ages and being constantly remodelled and extended so that it could respond to advances in siegecraft over the passing centuries. It has been a useful fortification from (or even before) the Iron Age, through until the end of the German Occupation in 1945. The ancient site has remained unchanged, but the building and the style of warfare, with which it was expected to cope, have altered dramatically.

Every advance in weaponry and military thinking had to be met with new methods of defence. And so for several hundred years new towers, new bastions, new battlements and new defensive weapons were constantly being added. The massive structure we see today is the result of a long process of military and defensive evolution.

The name by which the castle is known has also changed over the years. In the 13th and 14th centuries it was usually called the Castle in Jersey or the King's Castle in Jersey, though it was also sometimes called the Castle of Gurry or Gores. In the 15th century, during the French Occupation (1461-1468), the name Mont Orgueil was coined and it has generally been known as Mont Orgueil or Gorey Castle ever since, though it has been called the Old Castle (Le Vieux Chateau) to differentiate it from the 'new' castle built in the 16th century in St Aubin's Bay.

The promontory on which Mont Orgueil stands was occupied in the Neolithic era (probably from the third and early second millennium BC). Pottery dating from this period has been discovered, but no proof of structures has been found. Some of this pottery was collected from a thick black layer of deposit in the earth, dating from the Iron Age, but very little is known of the Iron-Age occupation of this headland, although some wheel-made pottery has been found. Archaeological excavations in the 1970s in the Middle Ward of the castle exposed a row of large boulders, 'grounders' or foundation stones, for the construction of a dry stone wall fronting an earth and turf rampart.

The site then fades from historical and archaeological records until the turbulent reign of King John. Richard the Lionheart died in France in 1199. He was succeeded by his younger brother, John, who was crowned as Duke of Normandy and King of England. While England and Normandy were united, there was no threat to the Island of Jersey –

8   From Richard Popinjay's 'Platte of Jersey', 1563.

9   '*An attempted reconstruction of Gorey castle in 1400' by Major N.V.L. Rybot in 1931. Major Rybot was a respected archaeologist and president of La Société Jersiaise.*

it lay safely tucked away in the King's dominions. But when John lost Normandy in 1204, it found itself in the front line in sight of the enemy shore, but loyal to its Duke, King John. Obviously, Jersey had to be fortified.

The position was precarious. The castle was mentioned in 1212, when King John appointed Philippe d'Aubigny, the Crusader buried outside the Church of the Holy Sepulchre in Jerusalem, Keeper of the Islands. On his appointment in November 1212 he received 'the custody of Jersey with our Castle'. This is the first reference. Since at least 1209, however, there is evidence for munitions being sent to the Island, but it is not known who owned the site before the construction of the castle.

Once work began in earnest on building the castle, it became the spotlight for industry in the Island. Timber and lead were sent to Jersey in 1225-6 and money was spent on repairs and improvements between May 1226 and May 1227. A further period of building lasted from 1241 to 1244. Other 13th-century records of expenditure have not survived, except for a small fragment from 1294-7. The Island had again been attacked by the French in 1294 and extensive repairs were carried out after 1328. A report on the condition was ordered in 1252, but this has not survived either.

The Pipe Rolls of Edward III include the accounts of Sir John des Roches, Keeper of the Isles for the years 1328-1330. During his third year in office des Roches spent *74 sous 6 deniers* on bows, arrows, quarrels, crossbow winches, *sulphur vivum*, and other essential military supplies for the archers and other men. *Sulphur vivum* is probably an early reference to gunpowder.

The Island was attacked again in 1338 and in 1339 but on neither occasion was the castle taken, though Jean de Barentin was killed leading a sortie against the French in 1338. The French frequently overran the Island during the Hundred Years War, but Mont Orgueil appeared impregnable. In 1338 Admiral Béhuchet failed to take the castle after laying siege to it for six months. A few months later Sir Robert Bertrand, Marshal of France, summoned it to surrender. The report

10 *The arms of Du Guesclin.*

sent later to the King said, 'We made no answer. Not while ten men are alive in it.' There were many other smaller, but devastating, raids on the Island. A further Commission into the state of the castle was sent in 1342.

In late July 1373, Bertrand du Guesclin, who was regarded as the most formidable military commander of this time, landed in the Island and went to the castle with a force said to number 2,000 soldiers. The defences had been neglected and William de Asthorp, commanding the castle, faced a carefully-planned attack. Du Guesclin did not try to force his way in: instead his sappers set to work undermining the foundations of the outer wall. What happened afterwards is a matter for conjecture, but in September the English fleet arrived and the castle was saved.

On 7 October 1406 a force under Hector de Pontbriand and Pero Nino attacked the Island. After extracting a ransom and deciding not to attack the castle, they left on the 9th.

During the reigns of Henry V and Henry VI much work was carried out at the castle largely in connection with the new use of cannon.

11 *Sir Thomas Overay's belfry on the Grand Rampart (1499).*

The Island was embroiled in the Wars of the Roses, not so much because it was partisan, but because Margaret of Anjou, wife of Henry VI, tried to stoke up the flagging Lancastrian cause by dealing directly with her cousin, Pierre de Brezé, Comte de Maulevrier and Grand Senechal of Normandy, for military assistance from the King of France. Precise details of what transpired are unknown but, during the summer of 1461, Jean de Carbonnel, on behalf of de Brezé, captured the castle with the assistance of the local de St Martin family and possibly also with that of the Governor, John Nanfan.

The castle and the Island remained under French rule, with a French Lord of the Isles for seven years. With the change in fortunes so common in history, the castle was besieged by Sir Richard Harliston for the Yorkist cause, in the spring of 1468. Renaud Lemprière, Seigneur of Rosel, 'reckless in personal courage', lost his life during a sortie from the castle. Early in October, de Carbonnel was compelled to surrender and retired with his garrison to France. Fortunes changed again, with the arrival of Henry VII on the throne: Harliston, a staunch Yorkist,

12   *The Middle Ward and Grand Battery. The concrete roofs added by German forces during the Occupation are visible on the turrets.*

found himself besieged at the castle. Harliston eventually retired to Flanders in the service of Edward IV's sister. He is remembered at the castle by the first gateway, the Harliston Tower, built during his governorship.

After this period, the castle was allowed to fall into disrepair. A Royal Commission visited in 1531 to inspect it. The garrison, on paper, numbered 54 but in reality was only 18 with four watchmen. Of the impressive list of stores and supplies held there the Commissioners eventually learnt that the majority had been 'purchased' before their arrival with an agreement to sell back to the original owners upon the Commission's departure! Only the Bousgros Tower had a night watch but it was necessary for a watch to be kept in both the Harliston and Rochefort Towers as of old. The Governor was replaced. A further enquiry was held in 1540.

During the 1540s Henry Cornish commenced work on the extension of the keep known as the Somerset Tower (named after the Governor, Sir Edward Seymour, who became Duke of Somerset) as a platform for heavy cannon. After the French attack of 1549, the first of the Poulets was sent to the Island to enquire again into the state of the castle. Cornish resigned in 1549 and was replaced by Sir Hugh Poulet, followed by yet another Commission in 1551. In 1558 the castle was still too weakly manned and lacked powder and munitions; the following year the French were again reported as having designs on the castle. A further Commission reported on the state of the castle in 1562-3. In both 1567 and 1573 the Poulets asked for money from the Treasury to finish Somerset Tower.

By 1593 the position of the old castle was insecure. It appeared to have outlived its usefulness, partly because the newer types of cannon could bombard it from the opposite hill. It was said, 'We have been credibly informed that the castle is very ill-seated, and lieth subject to a mighty hill but 400 feet distant, and so overtopt by it, that no man can show his face in defence on this side'. The advice was to press on with the building of Elizabeth Castle in St Aubin's Bay, which was being built, and the Crown decided not to spend any further sums on restoring Mont Orgueil.

It is often said that we owe the preservation of Mont Orgueil Castle to Sir Walter Raleigh who, at this time, was Governor of Jersey. The usual practice of the time when a castle was of no further use was to slight it – to throw down the walls and put it out of action. But, in a letter to Sir Robert Cecil, Secretary of State, in 1600, Raleigh said 'it is stately fort of great capacatye … it were a pitty to cast it down'. Queen Elizabeth did not insist.

Reference is made in the early 17th century to 20 houses in the lower ward maintained by the inhabitants of the Island for their safety in time of war; these also were in poor repair. The Commission of 1617 resulted in ordinances for the running of the castle being made in 1618 and repairs carried out, but in 1623 another Commission again asked for funds for repairs. Repairs

13   *A fascinating drawing, dated 1 May 1846, from* Harwood's Illustrations. *Prominence is given to the oyster boats, whose trade was then at its height. The cliff line at the left is difficult to relate to the topography today.*

were eventually carried out in 1634-7 shortly before the arrival of the celebrated Puritan, William Prynne, as a prisoner at the castle, where he remained for two and a half years. He arrived with twice-cropped ears and S.L. (seditious libeller) branded on each cheek. £10 was spent on iron for his windows. His relations with the de Carteret family, which were very good – he was almost treated as a family guest – may have helped the Island remain on the Royalist side in the Civil War. His stay there drew attention to the fact that Mont Orgueil was also used as a prison for political offenders.

In the late 1660s various repair works were carried out to the castle. In 1680 the whole Island was surveyed by Lieutenant-Colonel George Legge and Thomas Phillips (the military engineer) with maps and plans of bays and defences drawn up, and the old castle was included. Sir Bernard de Gomme, Engineer-General, and Captain Richard Leake, Master Gunner of England, also reported on the castle, but once again very little appears to have been done as a result. In 1693 the ancient role the castle had played as a prison was also discontinued with the building of a prison in St Helier.

In the 18th century the English garrison in the Island was greatly increased. The castles were both insufficient and too neglected to hold them and the troops were billeted on the inhabitants; this inevitably led to many disputes and troubles. Some repairs and re-arming were carried out in the 1730s and in 1770 it is recorded that rooms were available for officers and men at the castle with an additional facility made in St Mary's chapel for 60 men in 1778.

Captain Philippe d'Auvergne was in command of the Jersey Naval Station from 1793 to 1812. He later became Vice-Admiral and was also titular Duke of Bouillon (having been adopted as his heir by the last Duke) and as such had a vested interest in preserving the French monarchy. From Mont Orgueil, d'Auvergne played a significant role in the French Royalist cause, the castle itself acting as an *entrepôt* and meeting point for the *emigrés*, as well as a base for secret negotiations and for rallying the cause. Unfortunately for the French Royalist cause, it came to nothing with the defeat at Quiberon.

By 1835 the castle was no longer used for garrisoning troops as Fort Regent had been built.

Responsibility for Mont Orgueil was transferred to the States of Jersey on 6 April 1907 but the Crown retained the right to maintain a signal station and to repossess the castle in time of war. A grand ceremony marked the handing over of the keys on 28 June. War was not far away, though thankfully it did not touch the Island. Many Islanders saw active service and some, including the son-in-law of the Seigneur of Rosel, did not return. Mont Orgueil itself was used as an observation post manned by detachments of the Coast Guards and the Royal Militia of Jersey.

Peace returned to British shores and the castle became a tourist attraction. King George V and Queen Mary visited in 1921. The museum opened in 1929 and many archaeological excavations were carried out to investigate its long and varied history.

Unfortunately war loomed again, and this time the Island was occupied for five years by the Germans. They made Mont Orgueil into a self-contained strongpoint with fire-control and observation towers, dug-outs, trenches, and small arms positions. Even a flame thrower was placed covering the steps leading to the keep. The north-east outworks were converted to form a concrete-encased battle headquarters. Luckily there was no need to besiege the castle! After the Occupation, the castle was re-opened to the public in 1946.

During the Royal Visit by Elizabeth II in 1989 Mont Orgueil provided a splendid backdrop for the ceremony of homage by local Seigneurs to the visiting Crown. The Seigneur of Trinity presented Her Majesty with two mallards, as is his due; and the Seigneurs des Augrès and de Rosel acted as butlers.

In 1998, the ownership of the castle was transferred from the Crown to the States of Jersey. It remains one of the most important historical sites in the Channel Islands and recent archaeological work shows how little we really know of it. There is much yet to be learned from a detailed study of the standing structures, and local archaeologists and historians believe that it is imperative that these should be properly understood before any future structural works are carried out.

ROSEL AND THE LEMPRIÈRE-ROBINS

The Lemprières of Rosel Manor can trace their ancestry back to 1367, when the estate was in the hands of Raoul Lemprière – the first member of this family to live in Jersey. He, as a native of Brittany, had to have a special licence from Richard II before he was allowed to take up permanent residence in the Island.

Plate 1. John Baudains Germain
Connétable of St Martin
Prévôt 1958-68, Constable's Officer 1971-81, Centenier 1981-94.
Direct descendant in the 13th generation of Julien Noël of St Martin (c.1480).
(Photo: Stuart McAlister)

Plate 2. An Ice-Age Hunting Scene in St Martin
The scene in the foreground shows men of the Neanderthal race butchering a deer, while further off roam a woolly rhinoceros and a family of woolly mammoth. The foreground may be recognised by the little hill at La Coupe, while the horizon shows a faint and distant prospect of Les Écréhous. (Original watercolour by Alan Copp)

GEOLOGICAL SPECIMENTS

Plate 3. The finer grained and uncommon type of Rozel Conglomerate, found near La Solitude. Deposited originally in a playa-type lake. Layers seen become younger from the bottom up. (Photo: John Renouf)

Plate 4. Typical Rozel Conglomerate, with a range of pebble sizes and colours. The larger the included pebbles, the rounder they are. (Photo: John Renouf)

Plate 5. Rhyolitic lava. This particular type of broken-up and contorted lava referred to as auto- or self- brecciated is common between Archirondel and Anne Port. One of its more spectacular occurrences is the Faldouet dolmen capstone suggesting the derivation of this massive block from the shore below. (Photo: John Renouf)

ALAN COPP '98

Plate 6. The fascinating altar in Rosel Manor chapel is unlikely to be the original: the chapel was closed at the Reformation and was used as a potato store, until resanctified in the 19th century. The front panel of the altar dates from about 1600. (Photo: Chris Blackstone)

Plate 7. At spring sunrise, the 12th-century chapel at Rosel Manor is reflected in the waters of the upper pond. (Photo: Chris Blackstone)

Rosel Manor was always one of the five chief manor houses, together with St Ouen, Samarès, Trinity and Mélesches. They were known as *fiefs haubert*, and their importance and seniority is properly understood when contrasted with the 116 subordinate fiefs which existed in Jersey in feudal times.

Today the Lemprières and the other Jersey Seigneurs have been stripped of almost all their feudal powers. But the ancient titles remain and, with them, some of the old traditions which have never died.

When the Queen came to Jersey in 1989, Brigadier Raoul Lemprière-Robin waited upon her at table with a glass of wine – one of the ancient duties of the Seigneurs of Rosel was to act as Butler to the Monarch whenever he or she visited the Island. This task had probably never been performed or required for many hundreds of years, but Jersey's Bailiff of the time, Sir Peter Crill, and the Brigadier thought that it might be amusing to revive it.

The first recorded Seigneur of Rosel was Ingram de Fourneaux, whose reign was relatively brief. Before the fiefdom of Rosel passed into the hands of the Lemprières it was held for 120 years by the de Barentins. On 18 November 1247, Henry III gave to Drouet de Barentin 10 *livres* of land at Rosel. He and his heirs were to hold this land until England and Normandy were reunited. Drouet, who was also known as Drogo or Dreux, also received from Henry III another 60 *livres* of land in Trinity, which was probably the Fief de Diélament. Rosel was his home, however, and the de Barentin family became the dominant family in Jersey for the following century.

By 1299 Drouet I's grandson, Drouet II, held power and there are reports that he abused his position. He was accused of withholding payments, taking other people's land and produce, and of tearing up third party's deeds when he wanted more land. His brother Jean was also accused of carrying off women and committing outrages and assaults on them. Jean and Drouet II had dispossessed their brother of his inheritance. To make matters worse, Drouet II's prévôt had been accused of stealing cattle and his warrener had been accused of extortion and assault. The Justices were called in and, even though several of the accusations were in the end withdrawn, Drogo II was fined 300 *livres* for his transgressions.

He was also in trouble with the Crown. His right to have gallows, prison, varech, éperquerie, warren and pleas of the Crown were all challenged. Drouet denied holding pleas of the Crown or prison, which he admitted were rights which rested with the Crown, but the rest he claimed for himself, saying they were privileges which had gone with the fief since time immemorial.

Despite challenges to his title to Rosel, the de Barentin family held the estate until the mid-14th century. Tragedy forced the last of the Seigneurial de Barentins to leave the Island. An old manuscript relates the sad tale:

> One day the wife of Philippe de Barentin said to her sons, 'Jehannet de St Martin has called me an adulteress. Avenge this insult on your mother.' So the sons set an ambush, and put a boy to whistle when de St Martin drew near. When he came, they seized him, stabbed him to death and tore out his tongue. They presented the tongue to their mother.

This happened where the cross of Jehannet now stands on the road from St Martin to Trinity (Croix au Maître). After seeking sanctuary in St Martin's Church the sons fled to Normandy,

14 *The arms of Lemprière. The last time the Seigneurial coat of arms was seen proudly flying from the top of the Manor's tower was in November 1997, when Brigadier and Mrs. Lemprière-Robin's grandson was born.*

using the perquage or sanctuary path. One was arrested and hanged. The other made his home near Rouen.

De Barentin, maybe not surprisingly after such a scandal, sold up in Jersey and went to live in England. In 1362 he appointed Raoul Lemprière and Guillaume Payn, who were Jurats of the Royal Court, as his attorneys in Jersey. In 1367 he sold his lands in Jersey to Lemprière and Payn. These included not just Rosel, but also the fiefs of Samarès, Diélament and St Jean la Hougue Böete.

In 1382 Payn and Lemprière divided the estates by *partage*. Lemprière took the fiefs of Rosel, Longueville and la Hougue Böete, and the family then held Rosel for four generations.

The Rosel Manor that we know today was built in 1770 by the Seigneur of the time, Charles Lemprière, a distinguished Jerseyman who was solicitor general, a jurat and, later, Lieutenant-Bailiff. All that remains of the original house is an old granite archway in a corner of the farm outbuildings, close to which the original Manor once stood. He had found the house he inherited impossible to live in and, as he was also Seigneur of Diélament, had chosen to live there instead.

Maybe he did not find Diélament entirely suitable either for, after living there for 35 years, he decided to build a new Rosel Manor on a piece of land that was known as Mont Ste Marguerite.

Fifty years later, his grandson believed he could further improve the new Georgian granite house by adding gothic-style turrets and encasing the whole thing in cement: something that was the height of fashion in those days. The design was greatly criticised in a book published in 1950, *The Charm of the Channel Islands* by R.M. Lockley, who lived in St Martin. He said:

> Ansted describes Rozel Manor, the residence of the Lemprières … as 'rebuilt in recent years in an exquisite Gothic style.' But nowhere else is there to be noted a favourable remark upon this pretentious modern mansion. One can only hope that the present hideous imitation block walls of Rozel Manor will be quickly covered with a creeper or ivy, or colour-washed, or else the concrete surface removed to show the granite, if it exists, beneath.

Strong criticism indeed.

While the archway is all that remains of the original Manor, the old chapel and colombier, dating from medieval times, still stand in the lovely gardens. In the chapel there is a beautiful glass window designed by Millais, who was often a visitor to Rosel.

Rosel is the old French version of the word *roseau*, a reed. The reeds after which Rosel Manor is named did not grow in Jersey, but in France. In Normandy, almost directly across the Bay of St Michel, stands the Castle of Rosel, whose Seigneurs carried three reeds in their coat of arms.

The best known of the early ancestors of the present Seigneur was Renaud, who lived at Rosel during the mid-15th century. Even then, Rosel Manor was know for its beautiful gardens, and Renaud Lemprière took great pride in them. He was obviously a most welcoming host, and kept open house: even the most unwelcome guest was pressed to stay for dinner, and everyone was expected to admire the gardens. For his younger guests he kept a tennis court in the barn and

15 The Manor on Mont Ste Marguerite was built as a Georgian granite house by Charles Lemprière in 1770. Fifty years later, his grandson, keeping abreast with fashion, added crenellated turrets and encased the building in cement. (Gerald Amy Collection)

in the evening he played chess. Every day began with Mass in the chapel and twice a week he rode into St Helier to perform his duties as a jurat.

These details of life at a Jersey Manor House in the 15th century came to light from evidence in a trial against Renaud Lemprière. In 1463, during the French Occupation, he was accused of bribery and colluding to leave a gate unbarred at Gorey Castle so that the French forces might be surprised and driven out. This amounted to treason and it was only thanks to the gallant testimony of his 22-year-old wife, who was half his age, and who stood up to one and a half days' gruelling cross-examination, that his name was cleared and he was acquitted. Four years later he was killed in the final assault on the castle which drove out the French.

The fifth Lemprière Seigneur died childless, and the title and lands passed to another branch of the family, the Perrins of Guernsey. In 1625 Rosel was sold to the de Carterets of St Ouen's Manor and it was held by them with their other estates for over one hundred years, until it came back by marriage to the Lemprière family, who have held it ever since.

In 1931, Jurat Reginald Raoul Lemprière died without a male heir, and the property passed to his eldest daughter, who became La Dame de Rosel. In 1913 she had married Charles Harold Robin of Steephill, St Saviour, who was killed fighting in France in 1917. They had one son, Raoul Charles, who in turn became Seigneur of Rosel. The heir to the Rosel Manor estates is now Brigadier and Mrs. Lemprière-Robin's daughter Emma.

Brigadier Lemprière-Robin and his wife, Sheelagh, came back to live in Jersey in the 1960s, following the death of La Dame de Rosel, who drowned in a boating accident at Les Écréhous. The garden, since their return, has been given much love and attention and is known as one of the finest in the Island.

Emma and her husband have a son, William Stewart Lemprière-Johnston, born in November 1997. He is the latest in a long family line which has given great service to the Island: so far, one Governor, one Lieutenant-Governor, five Bailiffs, three Lieutenant-Bailiffs, two Attorneys General, two Viscounts, four Solicitors General, 26 Jurats and one States Deputy.

16   A fine Norman doorway graces the west front of 12th-century Rosel Manor Chapel. (Courtesy of Sheelagh Lemprière-Robin)

The Seigneurs are one of the last vestiges of the feudal system imposed upon the Island by the Normans, and which has not yet been – maybe never will be – shaken off.

William Longsword, the conquering Duke who captured the Islands, divided his new territory into Fiefs. Some of these he kept for himself, and these later formed the basis of the Crown Estates. The rest he distributed among some of his chosen followers, but some had greater powers than others. It has been reported that great fiefs like St Ouen's, Trinity, Rosel and Samarès received powers of *haute, moyenne, et basse justice*. This meant that the Seigneur held his feudal court and had the power to hang, imprison, and flog his tenants. However, historian Christopher Aubin states that this is untrue and that no Jersey fief ever held these rights. But Rosel did have feudal gallows, and these stood on Mont Daubignie. Smaller fiefs had much more restricted powers.

The Seigneur's tenants would be responsible for working separate parcels of the seigneurial estates, and would have to pay *rentes* in the form of produce – very often wheat, eggs or capons, each Michaelmas Day. Seigneurs also had the rights to seize flotsam and jetsam washed up on their shores, and the right to claim the vraic for fertilising and conditioning their arable land.

It was not until 1966 that a law was introduced in Jersey abolishing most of these ancient feudal rights – including the one which enabled Seigneurs to seize property, when an owner had died intestate, and to keep it for a year and a day, before handing it on to the heir.

However, the Seigneurs still enjoy some of their more colourful rights and privileges. Once a year, they must appear at an Assize d'Héritage in the Royal Court and swear an oath of allegiance

17 *The colombier. In medieval times the right to keep pigeons was a seigneurial privilege. (Courtesy of Sheelagh Lemprière-Robin)*

to the Crown. If they default in this three times, they will lose their fief. Some of the greater fiefdoms – and this includes Rosel – also carry the right and obligation to make homage to the monarch on arrival in Jersey.

Sadly for the historian, little of the original manor houses remain, as prosperous Seigneurs have, over the centuries, drastically modernised their feudal homes. But Rosel still has its pre-Reformation manorial chapel, and its colombier, in which hundreds of pigeons would have guaranteed the Seigneur and his family a plentiful supply of food. Permission to build a colombier was a highly-prized privilege. The number of pigeons had to be limited, as they devoured surrounding crops, and it was a privilege which the Seigneurs tended to keep for themselves. The Lemprière responsible for building this one apparently overlooked the fact that he should have asked the King's permission first. When his omission was discovered, he was banned from the Royal presence for 20 years.

LE SAUT GEOFFROI

Convicted of a heinous crime,
One Geoffrey was by statute old
Condemned to death,
A cruel death –
Compelled was he
To leap from rocky headland bold
Into the angry, surging sea.

From rugged rock exceeding high
Standing 'twixt pleasant bays –
And to St Martin's nigh
The prisoner, guarded by two halbardiers
By masked executioner was flung
Into the raging sea, where by
Deft swimming and emboldened strategy
He soon regained the land.

18 *Geoffrey's Leap, with Anne Port Bay in the background. From a colour postcard c.1920. (John Le Seelleur Collection)*

The crowd divided in opinion cried
'Let sentence just be truly carried out.'
Others who praised bold Geoffrey thus did shout
'The sentence has been truly carried out.'
But Geoffrey – bold in his success –
In exultation cried
'The Leap again, I will repeat'
And from the rock leapt down
This time to meet a dread defeat,
For falling, he his head struck on a rock
And in the swirling torrents – died.

This poem, published in the *Jersey Evening Post* in the early 1940s and credited to local resident F.W. Killer, tells the story of Geoffrey's Leap, or Le Saut Geoffroi. Very little is known about who Geoffrey actually was, and indeed, no-one seems entirely sure how to spell his name. Sometimes it is spelled Geoffrey, or Jeffrey, or Geoffroi, or Jeoffrey. Equally, it could be Geoffroy, or Geff Ray, or Jeffroi.

But what does seem to be generally agreed is that, in medieval times, this small pinnacle of rock at the southern end of Anne Port Bay was used as a site for executions. They were carried out simply by pushing the victims off the rock onto the crags below. The prisoners were first marched from their cell at Mont Orgueil Castle with an escort of halberdiers, before being handed over to a masked executioner who took hold of the prisoner and threw him down into the sea.

Geoffrey had been convicted of a capital crime, and many Islanders came to see justice done. They watched him being pushed off, but were amazed to see that – despite the huge drop – he had survived the fall and was swimming back to shore.

It is reported that some of the ladies present shouted that the 'execution' should be repeated. The masked executioner had obviously failed to do his job properly. Others, no doubt suspecting that Geoffrey's survival might well be a sign that there had been a miscarriage of justice in the first place, shouted that justice had been done and he should be allowed to walk free.

In all this mayhem, it was Geoffrey himself who settled the argument. Believing that he had the skill to survive a second descent, he volunteered to throw himself off the cliff to show

19 *This photograph, taken in or before 1922, shows the degree of erosion that has occurred near Geoffrey's Leap. Then there was a cultivated field between the road and the cliff edge; today virtually none of this remains. (John Le Seelleur Collection)*

how easily it could be done. Sadly, despite his bravado, he struck his head on a rock and was killed.

The story has enough sufficiently enticing ingredients to have stood the test of time. The site still features as a tourist attraction and in 1997, when St Martin Deputy Bob Hill pointed out that the picturesque headland was in danger of falling into the sea because of coastal erosion, the States of Jersey voted by 48 votes to two to make money available to enable stabilisation work to be carried out.

Anne Port Bay had been subjected to severe coastal erosion for several years. The beach levels had decreased and the sea had undermined the sea walls. However, while a great deal of work had been done to stabilise the northern and eastern headlands, Geoffrey's Leap, which was privately owned, continued to be vulnerable. Deputy Hill pointed out that if it was not preserved, it could well tumble down into the sea taking the road and Geoffrey's Leap Café with it, and bring an end to one of Jersey's best-loved pieces of folklore.

LES CHEFS TENANTS DU FIEF DE LA REINE

The Parish's links with ancient feudal times are in part kept alive by the immensely grand-sounding title 'Chef Tenant de la Commune du Fief de la Reine en Saint-Martin' which is the privilege of the owners of certain properties in the Parish.

Sadly, there are no records telling how it came to exist, but this old title is one of the few remaining relics of the feudal system. The Commune is that area of the Fief de la Reine (the name is perpetuated in the Vingtaine de la Reine) which is now generally known as St Catherine's Woods or Rozel Woods. Seven Jersey parishes (originally ten) contained land which formed part of the Ancient Demesne of the Dukes of Normandy: these were lands possessed and held by the Duke or, later, the King, since 'time immemorial'. The Duke or the King granted tenures in respect of these lands, from which he derived the income and services that were needed for the defence and administration of his possessions and of his subjects. The Jersey lands of the Demesne were treated as a separate entity from the lands of the Ancient Demesne in Normandy, and for the purposes of the collection of rents and the organisation of other services due to the Crown they were divided into units (fiefs), one for each parish in which land of the Demesne was situated. One such parish was St Martin.

Each of the King's tenants in these fiefs held an area of land known as a *bouvée*, equivalent to about 24 vergées. The holdings comprised only arable land but the tenants also had rights in, or a share of, the waste, meadows and woodlands. In the Fief de la Reine (or Fief du Roi when the reigning monarch is a King), La Commune is the mainly woodland area over which the tenants of the fief enjoyed such rights in common. The *bouvée* system originally formed the basis for the election of the Prévôt (whose functions are described below) but by the 16th century it had been superseded by a system under which the head of a group of property owners on a fief was called Chef de Charette, or Chef Tenant or Chef de Prévôté. (In recent years, the term Chef Tenant has been used. The spelling of the plural can be found as Chefs Tenants, Chef Tenants and Cheftenants. Chefs Tenants is used here in accordance with 19th-century records.)

Under the new system, an 'Appériement' was prepared about every thirty years. This was a formal list of the tenants of a fief who owed the obligation of 'prévôté' (also described below) and of their holdings on that fief. The tenants were divided into Chefs de Charette and Aides (the Aides were tenants inferior to the Chefs), and were grouped so that each Chef and his Aides held approximately the same land area. When a new Appériement was drawn up, the Aides were reapportioned among the Chefs to counterbalance any changes in the land holdings of the Chefs which had occurred since the previous Appériement. The Chefs became responsible in turn for serving as, or providing, the Prévôt and the Aides contributed financially to the cost. The oldest record in the possession of the Chefs Tenants du Fief de la Reine is a beautiful manuscript Appériement of 1701.

That document records that at the *Requête* of the Connétable and the procureurs du bien publique it was ordered

> qu'il sera publié par le Prévôt du Roi en la dite Parroisse, par trois dimanches consécutifs, Issue du Service Divin, & une quatrième fois pour toutes, que tous les Tenants du Fief du Roi, en la dite Paroisse, ayent à apporter une vrai mesure de leurs terres en forme d'Aveu, entre les mains dudit Prévôt, pour procéder à un Appériement des Prévôtés à peine qu'en cas de défaut, leurs terres soient saisies …

The autorisés who undertook the Appériement were appointed by the Cour d'Héritage and their subsequent Record was enrolled in the Actes of that Court.

As already indicated, the Chefs Tenants had obligations as well as rights, as was the basic feature of the feudal system. The obligation of 'Prévôté' was to appoint a Prévôt, whose functions were to provide the Crown with services which included collecting the *ferme* (the rent payable by the tenants themselves and which remained at about the same level from the 16th to the 20th centuries), and the serving of summonses.

An interesting document dated 1806 is a *Lettre* passed between Philippe Raoul Lemprière, Seigneur of Rosel, and his 15 Chefs Tenants and Francs Tenants. The Chefs Tenants, 13 in number, had to fulfil the following duties; to give a day (*corvée*) before Christmas and another after, for spreading manure; to clear the stables of manure; to give a day before Christmas and another

20 *The introduction to the Appériement of 1701. This has been bound in book form as '… appartient aux Chefs de Charette du Fief du Roi en la Paroisse de St Martin'. (Anthony Paines Collection)*

L'An Mille sept cents un le vingt quatrième jour d'Avril, à la Requête du Connétable & Procureurs du bien public, de la Paroisse de St. Martin. Il est ordonné qu'il sera publié par le Prévôt de Roi en la dite Paroisse par trois dimanches consécutifs, Issue du Service Divin, & une quatrième fois pour toutes, que tous les Tenans du Fief du Roi, en la dite Paroisse, ayent à apporter une vraie mesure de leurs terres en forme d'Aveu, entre les mains dudit Prévôt pour procéder à un Appériement des Prévôtés à peine qu'en cas de défaut, leurs terres soient saisies, & sont Monsr. Charles Dumaresq Justicier, & George Bandinel gent: autorisés par la cour pour faire le dit Appériement où le Procureur du Roi sera requis d'être présent. _____

after for ploughing (*aerer*) one vergée of land; to cart wine and logs within the Fief; to clean (*nestier*) the stackyard and stack the champart corn; to bring meat from the market; to work at the water mill (La Perrelle); to provide help for (*servir*) the masons and thatchers; to cart the grinding stones for the said mill; to clean the leat, except an arm's length on each side of the conduit (*goulet*); to keep the ferrets earthed for three days if they cannot be found, working with one of the Seigneur's men; to gather fern at La Lande and stack it on the Fief, as is laid down in the Extente of the said Fief, renewed and confirmed in 1758.

The Francs Tenants, Edouard Noel, Philippe Nicolle and Clement Richardson sr, did not have to fulfil all these services. The Seigneur then released all the Tenants of these dues, the Chefs Tenants paying £666 13s. 4d. per tenement, and the Francs Tenants paying £200 each, in Order Money. However, they still had to perform the duty of Prévôt, each one in turn, and they still had to cart the champart corn and bring wheat and other seigneurial dues which they owed, as in olden times and pay *la ferme* and do any duty not expressly excluded by the affranchisement.

The Prévôt's duties extended over the whole of his fief. He attended the Cour d'Héritage where he made a declaration under oath as to whatever had occurred within his district which might add to the revenues of the Crown. The Oath was:

> Vous jurez et promettez par la foi et serment que vous devez à Dieu, que bien et fidèlement vous exercerez la Charge de Prévôt du Roi en la Paroisse de …; que vous ferez tous bons et loyaux Ajournements et Records, que vous verez que le droit de Sa Majesté soit gardé et maintenu en toutes choses; et ferez les déclarations ordinaires et requises; vous leverez les Fermes et Extraites, pour en tenir compte, et ferez généralement tous autres devoirs qui dépendent ladite charge.

21 TRANSFER OF MONT ORGUEIL CASTLE TO THE STATES OF JERSEY
Ceremony of handing over of the keys – 28 June 1907.'At noon prompt, the guns on the greensward below boomed forth, and as the seventh gun was fired, the troops on the outer edge of the castle battlements fired a "Feu de joie", which starting from the summit, gradually reached the base of the old pile. The band played the National Anthem, and after the third salute, His Excellency called for three cheers for the King, which were lustily given, the cheering echoing from all parts of the well-garrisoned castle. The Jersey ensign was then hoisted to the top of the flagstaff, this being the signal for loud applause from the spectators below, and on the neighbouring hillside.' (Jersey Post)

The halberdiers: Philippe Le Huquet (Chef Sergent), Thomas Renouf De Gruchy, Charles William Journeaux, William Whitel jnr., Philip Bertram Le Huquet, Nicolas Dumaresq Noël, John Thomas Blampied, George R. Blampied, Walter Falle, Walter Du Feu, Edmund Le Boutillier. Among the other dignitaries present were: The Very Reverend Samuel Falle (Dean of Jersey), Adolphus H. Turner (Attorney-General), Reginald Raoul Lemprière (Viscount – with the mace – and Seigneur of Rosel), Charles E. Malet de Carteret (H.M.'s Receiver-General), Charles Perchard (Connétable of St Martin), George Journeaux (Deputy of St Martin), G.P. Balleine (Rector of St Martin). Front centre, behind the keys: Lieutenant-Governor Major-General H.S. Gough, C.B., C.M.G., Bailiff Sir William Henry Venables Vernon.

(Beatrice Le Huquet Collection)

The office of Prévôt was abolished by the Royal Court Rules, 1968. The last Prévôt in St Martin was the present Connétable, John Germain, who succeeded his father in that office in the 1960s. By the time of his period of office the duties of the Prévôt had dwindled. He no longer collected any revenues for the Crown and his only duty was the serving of summonses in court proceedings. Summonses were received by him on Fridays from the lawyers who had issued them and his task was to serve the summonses, making sure that they were served upon the correct person, and to return the signed acknowledgements of service to the lawyers on the following Monday. He received a fee of one shilling for each summons and in addition was paid an annual fee of £7 10s. 0d. by the tenants. Although the Prévôts continued to attend the Cour d'Héritage, reports concerning Crown revenues were no longer given.

Another duty of the tenants was 'Chariage', the obligation to harvest and carry the King's hay and wood – a duty which will later be shown to have become an onerous one.

The Chefs Tenants were also amongst the Halberdiers (there are various spellings of this title) who had the obligation to render a kind of military service in the form of the provision, together with some from Grouville and St Saviour, of 150 men armed with halberds to provide a guard of honour for the Governor on certain occasions and to guard prisoners being taken to and from trial.

An article about the restoration of La Côte au Palier, one of the properties whose owner is a Chef Tenant, describes the latter duty as collecting prisoners from Mont Orgueil Castle and marching them to the Royal Square, where they were placed in an iron cage pending their turn in Court. The cage was removed in 1697 when a new prison was built and thereafter prisoners were no longer detained at the castle, '… so that the Halbardiers had not so far to march. But as in those harsh times flogging was the usual penalty for felonies, it was the pikemen's grim task to march alongside the convicts, guarding them as they were flogged from the Court House to prison …' There is a record of Halberdiers providing an escort for King George V on his visit to Jersey in 1921.

Whilst the Chefs Tenants of the Jersey fiefs were of very minor importance in the overall context of the feudal system, they nevertheless exemplify, in a small way, the purposes for which the feudal system had evolved. Nowadays, the term 'feudal' is often used in a pejorative sense, implying that a system or regime is archaic, undemocratic and oppressive. Certainly the feudal system may now be called archaic; and it was not, and could not have been in the social circumstances of that time, in any way democratic. It was not, however, oppressive. De Gruchy points out that the destruction of civilised life, including law, learning, administration and communications following the barbarian invasions and the break-up of the Roman Empire, left the northwestern regions of Europe in a state of chaos. The one essential need was to cultivate the fertile land to provide food for the people, both the conquerors and the conquered, who would otherwise face starvation. So a system evolved during the Dark Ages and into the Middle Ages in which the cultivators were grouped under the protection of a lord. Gradually, order was brought out of chaos, neglected lands were restored to cultivation and the population increased. Tenants were granted lands to till, as here in this parish, and in return for their lands and protection they provided services and other resources to their lord. De Gruchy writes,

> I think that any great system which has for a time dominated the history of an important part of mankind is fairly entitled to be judged by its fruits; if so, then the feudal system

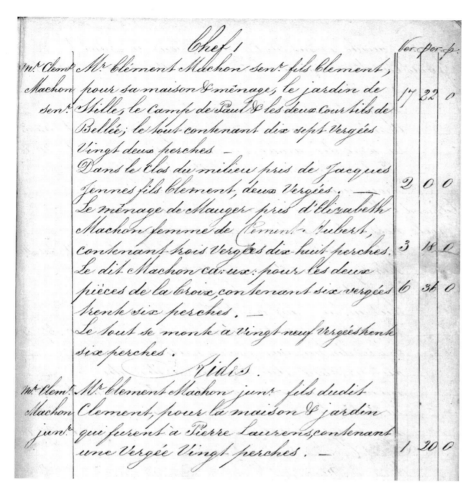

22 Extract from the Appériement of 1701, detailing the property of Clement Machon and of his son. (Anthony Paines Collection)

which dominated the history of north-western Europe in the Middle Ages can put in a strong claim to success. Under it there grew up an intelligent system of finance, law and administration, which strengthened the central governments enormously until they were able to kick away the feudal ladder by which they had climbed.

Wealth, raw materials and technical skills increased, so that surplus funds became available enabling the construction of such architectural masterpieces, never surpassed, as the great cathedrals and churches of France and England.

Few relics of the system now remain. In Jersey, seigneurial rights were abolished by the Seigneurial Rights (Abolition) (Jersey) Law, 1966, and the vestigial powers of the Seigneurs of the great fiefs are now reduced to ceremonial duties at the Cour d'Héritage and on royal visits to the Island. Those powers were once very great. The Seigneur de Rosel was one of the few who possessed the right of gallows, that is to say to hang criminals sentenced to death by the Royal Court so that they died on his fief.

To revert to the Fief de la Reine in St Martin, it is unfortunate that the history over the last hundred years has major gaps. The records in the possession of the Chefs Tenants commence in 1871 but contain no minutes of meetings of the tenants between 1897 and 1928, except for one held in 1909. Curiously, the minutes of that 1909 meeting were subsequently signed on 7 February 1920, although there is no other record of a meeting on that date. The lack of minutes is difficult to understand, since the 19th-century minute book has many blank pages after the minutes and contains, towards the end of the book, accounts of the Chefs Tenants for the years up to 1928 for which there are no minutes. The manuscript minutes are in the French language, meticulous in their detail and written in a legalistic style. There are no minutes of meetings during the Occupation years, nor between 1975 and 1993.

It is evident that by 1871, when the existing records begin, the tenants were finding their ancient duties irksome or even burdensome. In May of that year they appointed a committee to approach H.M. Attorney General and the Receiver General on behalf of all the Tenants and their Aides to propose that the Tenants should yield all their rights to Her Majesty and that in return the Tenants should 'obtain from Her Majesty a quittance to the said Tenants of the Prévôté ,"Ferme", making and carting of the hay from the Queen's Meadow and other duties and obligations which the said Tenants and their Aides might owe to Her Majesty'. If that proposal was not acceptable, the Commune should be let and the rent applied to pay the costs of the Prévôté and any other charges to which the Tenants were subject. The office of Prévôt was auctioned to the lowest bidder (*bannie au rabais*). The office was offered 'par trois fois et une quatrième pour toutes selon l'usage' before being awarded. A survey of the boundaries of the Commune was carried out in 1879 by Thomas Messervy, arpenteur, and the distances between the 74 boundary stones were measured and recorded. Letting of the Commune continued over subsequent years but with a provision for termination if an arrangement could be come to with Her Majesty.

After the minutes of a meeting of the tenants held on 9 September 1892 there is set out, in the same handwriting and on the same page but without explanation, the text of a petition dated March 1896 (three and a half years after the previous meeting) to the Treasury of the United Kingdom Government as follows:

St Martin's
Jersey
March 1896

To the Right Honourable the Lords Commissioners of Her Majesty's Treasury,
Your Lordships,
We the undersigned have the honour to respectfully represent:

That the landowners 'Chefs tenants' and 'Chefs de Prévôté' on the Queen's Fief in this Parish are subject to certain services and dues on account of our respective holdings such as performance of the duties of 'Prévôt' (Summoning Officer), harvesting the hay on Her Majesty's meadow and carting the same, collecting the 'Ferme', and to serve as halbardiers (guard of honour) at executions of criminals condemned to death etc etc. That we have a right to, and enjoy the 'Utile' (pasturage and underwood) as users of the Queen's Commons which Her Majesty possesses 'en directe' (by Tenure in Capite). That considering the time has come when it is desirable and expedient that those old feudal services and rights should be abolished we would humbly ask that Her Majesty's pleasure may be obtained to the effect that we should cede or surrender all our rights and privileges as Commoners to the said 'Utile' and in compensation or exchange that we should be liberated of all the above services and dues we now owe. That by this arrangement Her Majesty being in possession not only of the 'directe' would also have all the rights to the 'Utile' and so be enabled to dispose of the said Commons advantageously inasmuch as the proceeds

23 *Visit of King George V in 1921. St Martin halberdier, Vivian Richardson, guards the entrance to the Royal Court. (Courtesy of the Richardson family)*

of the sale would, we beg to submit, realize considerably more than necessary to pay such person or persons as might be employed to perform the said services which could be effected by imposing on the purchaser a certain rent charge sufficient to acquit the same as in part payment of the purchase money.

The Petition was signed by all the tenants. It appears to have been presented to the Treasury, since the minutes of the last meeting before the records temporarily cease refers to a lease of La Grande Commune to R.R. Lemprière for five years on terms that, if the cession to Her Majesty should occur, the lessor should give up possession. However the outcome of the Petition is not recorded in any document available to the author of this chapter, and neither the Receiver-General, nor the Lieutenant-Governor's office, through which such a petition would normally be passed, has any record of it. An enquiry of H.M. Treasury has elicited no response. However, since the tenants continue to receive a rental from the land, it is evident that their rights were not surrendered. The duties of harvesting the hay and providing halberdiers no longer exist. Whether they were formally released or simply fell into disuse is not now known. The accounts show no payments to the Receiver-General subsequent to the abolition of the office of Prévôt. Nevertheless, the ancient title of Chef Tenant remains as a relic of an earlier social, economic and political system. In recent years, there has been a resurgence of interest in the heritage of the Chefs Tenants and they now meet socially once or twice a year.

Properties in St Martin whose Owners are Chefs Tenants

Devon Villa	Roselea	Le Huquet	Les Fontaines
Le Côtil	Le Taillis	La Mâitrerie	La Vignette
Spring Farm	St Martin's House	La Préférence	La Rué
Beauchamp	Fieldend (formerly White House)		La Caruée (formerly Lynfield)
La Fresnaie	La Côte au Palier	Le Pavillon	Le Câtillon
La Chasse	Meanskirk (formerly Les Charrières)		Brantwood
Little Manor (formerly Les Alpes Cottages)			

Three

17th to 19th Centuries

THE DON ROADS

The erratic network of lanes which existed in St Martin until the late 18th century would have been well described by G.K. Chesterton's *Rolling English Road*. This was thought to have been inspired by the meandering of a rolling English drunkard but, in fact, described rather well the meanderings of the Parish lanes and byways.

> They were nothing but narrow lanes, too narrow for carts to pass, which wound to and fro in bewildering fashion to avoid encroaching on this or that farmer's field.
>
> These apologies for roads were divided in all into three classes: Le chemin de roi, with foot walks 16 feet wide between hedge banks; Le chemin de huit pieds, or cross roads, 8 feet wide, and Le chemin de quatre pieds, or extremely narrow bridle-ways.

This was the topography of the Parish, charming, leafy, but utterly without system which General Don discovered when he arrived in Jersey on his appointment as Lieutenant-Governor in 1806. Within the space of 10 years Don had transformed St Martin from its essentially medieval structure to the Parish which we know today.

Don is credited quite correctly with the overall improvement of the Island's main road system and certainly it was his determination and diplomatic skill which carried through the overall enterprise; but it is one of the Parish heroes, the Reverend François Le Couteur, who should be given the credit for much of the work in St Martin. In 1790 he had founded and become President of the Jersey Agricultural Society whose first stated object was: 'improvements in road-making'. He had, therefore, been working for an improved road system for some years prior to Don's arrival and was no doubt enthusiastic in his support for the initiative of the new Lieutenant-Governor.

We are lucky to possess two key pieces of evidence which graphically highlight the differences between the St Martin of 1795 and that of 1849. The Richmond map of 1795 was the first systematic and scientific survey of the Island, effectively its first Ordnance Survey map: It shows an Island of byways, narrow lanes and a mass of cider orchards but few

24   General Don, Lieutenant-Governor of Jersey from 1806 until 1814.

effective lines of communication. The Godfray map of 1849, drawn to an almost identical scale and equally complete, reveals a very different picture: the Island is now dissected by a network of main roads, the Grandes Routes which Don had created.

His motives were, of course, largely those of a military governor determined to ensure the rapid movement of men and arms but his plans were not universally approved. Many argued that a system of narrow lanes and high hedges provided an excellent defensive system and that Don's plans were both dangerous and an unwelcome interference in parish affairs.

Building on the groundwork of the Reverend Le Couteur, Don recognised that, for St Martin, three lines of communication, all radiating from the parish church, were essential for the effective movement of artillery: a road from the church to Five Oaks (and so on to St Helier); a road from the church direct to Gorey Harbour; and a road from the church to Rozel Bay. In 1795 no such direct routes existed.

The route from the church to Five Oaks, today's Grande Route de St Martin, was, in 1795, anything but grand and certainly not direct. Travellers setting out from St Martin would have journeyed, as we do, towards La Préférence and on for some two hundred yards towards Maufant; and there the journey would have ended, for at the point where Poplar Stores stands today they would have met open fields. A quarter of a mile beyond, at today's Three Mile Garage, another track might have been glimpsed but a large cider orchard lay between. Don's answer was to cut straight through and to create the Grande Route de Saint Martin, the first direct link between the Parish and St Helier.

25   *The arms of General Don.*

The route from the church to Gorey Harbour, the present Grande Route de Faldouet, can already be seen on the Richmond map following much the same path as it does today, that is until it reached the top of Gorey Hill. For the most part, Don's task was simply to widen the existing *chemin de roi* and to reinforce it with the lines of stone walls, here the local diorite rather than granite, which today border the road for much of its length. The descent to Gorey, however, posed a difficult problem. The Richmond map shows a pattern of narrow and no doubt rutted pathways running down the hillside towards the village. Daisy Hill is evident but Gorey Hill, as we know it, is not. Don's solution was typically direct. He linked an existing *chemin*, which ran down the top part of the hill, to the zig-zag of roads which lay below it. The clearest sign of the link is the sweeping bend which today drops below the high buttress wall of Gouray Church.

Creating the present Grande Route de Rozel was clearly Don's most challenging task. Even today, the route from the church to Rozel is tortuous and, in places, seemingly arbitrary. A glance at the Richmond map shows a confusion of lanes and byways which must have faced the traveller in 1795. From the church, the descent to Wrentham Hall and the road to the bridge and the Lodge are clearly evident; but there the journey would have ended. What is today the slope up to the T-junction with La Rue des Alleurs would have been open fields. Don, like the Romans before him, cut straight through. His problems, however, were just beginning. The pathway he met did indeed run past the Manor and on towards the Rozel headland, but from there nothing more than open fields and rough trackways existed. He had, in effect, to create a new road, the present, winding Grande Route de Rozel.

Within a space of ten years, Don, with Le Couteur's help, had changed not just the physical structure of the Parish but also its social and economic relationship with the rest of the Island. It was now part of a larger network of communications which were to have a profound impact on its development in the 19th century.

THE JERSEY EASTERN RAILWAY

Gorey is five miles by road from St Helier, but in the 18th century it was much more, as the traveller was forced to follow a route through many meandering lanes. The advent of the 19th century brought the east physically closer to town, when the first direct road was built by General Don. But it was the advent of the Jersey Eastern Railway which provided a comparatively fast and easily-accessible public link between St Helier and the outlying eastern villages.

It was the success of Jersey's first railway, from St Helier to St Aubin in 1870, which provided the inspiration for another line heading east to Gorey. Work started in May 1872 and, despite at least one workmen's strike, was completed as far as Grouville in July 1873. This was just in time to provide free transport for three militia regiments and two batteries of artillery who were beginning manoeuvres on Grouville Common. The extension to Gorey was completed the following month.

The States of Jersey had passed an appropriate enabling Bill two years previously. Some of its clauses give illuminating information about life in Jersey at the time:

Article 45. Authorised the railway to run from Snow Hill to Gorey and from there to St Catherine's Bay.

Article 47. Provided for access to shipyards along the route.

Article 54. Stipulated that the *Clameur de Haro* could not be raised in the event of disagreement over any property situated within the limits indicated on the plans.

Article 55. Fixed a maximum fare between St Helier and Gorey of 1½d per mile, or fraction of a mile. 1d for second class.

Article 59. Provided a minimum of four services each day, in each direction.

Article 61. Fixed that the St Helier – Gorey section must be completed within three years, and the remainder in ten.

In fact, the extension to St Catherine was never built, and indeed, it would have been a very major undertaking. From Gorey Pier, the line was to have entered a tunnel next to the site of the *Dolphin Hotel*, which would have run under Castle Green to Anne Port. The contours of the coastline from this point are varied and often precipitous, and a huge amount of costly levelling would have been required to run the track on to St Catherine. As the construction of the harbour

26   *Calvados stands ready to pull out from Gorey Harbour station. (Michael Ginns Collection)*

there had been abandoned and the Breakwater itself transferred to the States, there was little likelihood of there ever being sufficient traffic to justify such work.

The traffic on the line to Gorey was initially good and in 1876 the June horse races on Gorey Common meant that 28 trains were needed each day to carry passengers from St Helier. On the day in 1907 when Mont Orgueil Castle was handed over to the States by the British Government, 32 return journeys were made, carrying a total of 6,200 passengers.

In 1881, the Carteret-Carentan Railway was opened and the *Compagnie Rouenaise de Navigation* offered a steamship service from Gorey to Carteret. Using this connection it was possible, a few years later, to book a direct ticket from St Helier to Paris via Gorey. Encouraged by the possibilities opened up by this new service, the States decided in 1891 that the railway line should be extended to a new Gorey Pier Station. The line ran between the sea wall and the new coast road. In those days the journey time from St Helier to Gorey Pier was 24 minutes. This compares very favourably with the bus timetable 100 years later!

The 11.30 a.m. departure from Snow Hill was the mail train, and flew a blue pennant on its journey to Gorey Pier to signal its importance. The early morning train on Saturdays was equipped with an extra van upon which to load fish at La Rocque, destined for St Helier market. It was known as the 'fish train'. There was also a limited traffic in cattle, imported from France and taken to the abattoir in St Helier for slaughter.

27   A train leaving Gorey Harbour en route for St Helier. (Michael Ginns Collection)

The first two engines were the *Caesarea* and *Calvados*, which were built in Leeds, costing £1,800 each. The *North Western* was purchased from the Jersey Railway in 1878, but this was not a successful engine. It lacked steam brakes, and had difficulty in stopping when required to do so. The *Mont Orgueil* was acquired in 1886, and two years later the troublesome *North Western* was replaced by a new locomotive, the *Carteret*. These five engines and two steam-powered rail cars supplied all the power on the route for the 56 years of the Eastern Railway's existence. The engines usually stopped at Gorey Village Station, where they obtained free water from the brook. The station itself survives as a private house, but sadly there are no remnants of the railway in St Martin.

Little is known about the Eastern Railway Company's fortunes in the early years of the 20th century. The challenge of motor buses emerged in 1926, and the Railway could not compete. It was forced to close on 21 June 1929. The locomotives, and much of the other metal, were shipped to Poland as scrap.

A railway of sorts did run again in St Martin in the Occupation years. After Hitler's instruction that the Channel Islands should be made impregnable, the major fortifications which were constructed around the Island needed building materials. It was reported that 'Funny little railways were constructed for these operations, particularly at Gorey and La Pulente'. The Gorey line was built initially to carry sand from Grouville Bay to Gorey Village Station. Later, it was extended along the roadbed to Gorey Pier, so that the sand could be barged to St Helier and other parts of the Island.

It seems now that the Jersey Eastern Railway was little more than a short-lived and expensive anachronism. However, it provided a glorious 60 years of reasonably-priced and efficient everyday transport for those who lived along its route, and it helped to open up and popularise travel to the east of the Island.

THE MILLS OF ROZEL

The mills of St Martin were once a vital part of parish life. Today, with a plentiful supply of convenience foods, easy transport and first-class roads leading to the numerous shops vying to supply them, it is hard to imagine the former importance and prestige of the parish mills.

In 1309 a watermill was built at Rosel Manor, because it had its own stream. However, it was inadequate, and it led Drogo de Barentin to erect a windmill on a high point roughly half a mile away in an excellent situation for wind to drive the sails. It was the only windmill in the Parish and in medieval times was the property of the Seigneur. The tenants of the fief owed *suite de moulin* to their Seigneur, which meant that they were obliged to grind their corn at his mill and also to render service in the form of labour, cartage and materials for the upkeep of the mill buildings. To the tenants the mill was essential as the only means of grinding corn for their

28   Rozel Mill at the turn of the century.

bread. To the Seigneur it was important as a source of revenue.

Rozel Mill or Le Moulin à St Martin is first mentioned in 1618 and it was sold by Jean Perrin (the then Lord of Rosel) to Jean le Hardy. The occupant in 1698, 1701 and 1707 was François Messervy. It is likely that, after the corn-grinding season, it was used for fulling. It was a seigneurial mill until 1702 when it was bought by Philippe le Maistre. It has been rebuilt several times during its history. In 1849 it was sold by D. Anley to Philip Vardon and was then passed down to his son and grandson. In 1909 the wooden dome was removed and in 1916 the mill machinery dismantled. The States bought it in 1920 and conserved and whitened it as a navigating landmark, particularly for fishermen returning from Les Écréhous, allowing them to steer clear of the Dirouîlles and the Paternosters.

During the Occupation by the Germans the tower was used as an observation platform and gun emplacement, which provided them with an ideal position for keeping watch towards the coast of France. It is now in private ownership.

THE DEFENSIVE TOWERS OF ST MARTIN

When General Henry Seymour Conway took office as Governor of Jersey in 1772, the American War of Independence had begun and the colonists had found an ally in the French. Conway rightly worried that France would dearly love to conquer the Channel Islands, if only to spite the

29 *St Catherine's Tower with its prominent machicoulis, now painted white on the seaward side as a navigational aid. (Photo: Chris Blackstone)*

British Government. In 1778 Conway paid his first visit to Jersey, where he was horrified to find that the Island was virtually defenceless against a sea-borne invasion, if it took place out of range of Gorey or Elizabeth Castles. Conway, who had studied the art of fortification, particularly in a book written by Marshal Maurice, the Comte de Saxe, realised the advantages of towers in a defensive strategy. Economical in manpower as well as materials, they could be armed with several small cannon to repulse an enemy landing.

General Conway quickly convinced the British Government and the King that 30 towers should be built in Jersey to cover possible landing places and that similar towers should also be built in Guernsey. Building began almost immediately, supervised by Captain Frederick Basset, who was then the resident engineer officer. The original estimate given to the British Board of Ordnance was £4,680 – £156 for each tower.

The design of the towers is interesting because it is peculiar to Jersey. Each tower was equipped with machicoulis at the top, as a defence against enemy mining operations at the base. No drawing has been found to show who designed the towers, but it seems logical to suppose that General Conway had a hand in the design, possibly helped by Captain Frederick Basset. However, when Captain Basset was sent to Guernsey later, the towers he built there were not built to the Jersey design, in spite of the fact that the States of Guernsey had been instructed to build to the same design as that of the larger island.

In St Martin there are four defensive towers, three of which are 'Conway' towers of the Jersey design, although none is exactly the same. The fourth, Victoria Tower above Gorey Castle, is a Martello tower, built some years after the others.

The tower at St Catherine's Bay was built well before Archirondel Tower, as was Fliquet Tower. The stretch of beach between St Catherine's Tower and Archirondel was covered by a small battery halfway between them. Both St Catherine's and Fliquet Towers appear on the famous Richmond map, which implies that they were built before 1787.

St Catherine's Tower (also known as La Mare Tower) is of Conway's original design with four machicoulis. It is fortunate that a sea wall was built here, as it has saved the tower from coastal erosion. Fliquet Tower has been altered, its machicoulis having been removed for unknown reasons at an unknown date. It is also known as 'Telegraph Tower', because it was here that the telegraph and telephone cable from France was brought ashore, many years later.

30 In contrast to the other defensive towers, Victoria Tower, built in 1837, follows the Martello pattern. Squat and solid, a heavy gun could be mounted on its summit. The range of fire extended from St Catherine to The Royal Bay of Grouville. (Photo: Chris Blackstone)

Archirondel Tower was the last one to be built while General Conway was still alive, and it was his idea to construct a masonry gun platform round its base. Unfortunately, by 1793, when Archirondel Tower was begun, the cost of building had risen from £156 to £1,000 per tower. The British Board of Ordnance objected to the extra cost of putting a gun platform there and suggested that the proposed Anne Port Tower be dispensed with to save money. Conway did not like this, but had to content himself with altering the design of Archirondel Tower to the extent that its machicoulis were double the size of the other towers, but there are only three of them instead of four. Archirondel Tower was completed in 1794, and became the prototype for La Rocco Tower in St Ouen's Bay, although the battery at Archirondel was built for four 13-pounder guns while that at La Rocco for five 32-pounder guns.

The last tower which belongs in St Martin is Victoria Tower, built on Mont St Nicolas, opposite the keep of Mont Orgueil Castle, and overlooking Anne Port Bay. There were two reasons for building here: firstly to prevent an enemy occupying the headland which commanded the keep of Mont Orgueil Castle; secondly to make an enemy landing on Anne Port beach difficult. The tower was built in 1837 and was named after the new young Queen, who had just been crowned.

Victoria Tower is basically a Martello tower. The name 'Martello' is taken to be an English corruption of Mortella Bay in Corsica, where a round tower had held the British fleet at bay in 1794, the date when Archirondel Tower was completed. The idea of Martello towers was to make them strong enough to support larger guns at the top. They were therefore shorter and wider than the Conway towers, but because they had no machicoulis were presumably cheaper to build. However, the danger of mining seems to have been recognised in the case of Victoria Tower, in that its base is set below ground and a defensive moat surrounds it with a traditional drawbridge to protect the entrance.

It must be said that Victoria Tower is an unsophisticated version of the Martello towers which were built in England, being completely circular and of a smaller size, so that only one gun could be mounted on top. Kempt Tower in St Ouen's is much nearer to the English design. Victoria Tower has the distinction of being the last defensive round tower to be built in Jersey.

31 Fliquet Tower, c.1910. Built as a 'Conway' tower, by the time of the photograph, it has been shortened. It was also known as 'Telegraph Tower', as the first communication lines from France came ashore here. (John Le Seelleur Collection)

The purpose of all the towers was to defend any possible landing places from an invading French army. Baron de Rullecourt had shown the authorities in charge of the defence of the Island in 1781 that a surprise landing was not only possible, but likely to be effective in subduing Jersey. Thereafter, the coastal defences and communications between them were enhanced wherever possible, culminating in the building of Fort Regent and the military roads of Lieutenant-Governor General Don.

In this connection it is sad to note that the No. 1 Tower of Grouville built on La Rocque Point north of La Rocque harbour, had been completed before Baron de Rullecourt's landing, but the guard there did not notice his arrival at Platte Rocque. Platte Rocque itself had a Guard House and a gun emplacement on it, where the Militia Guard, under a Sergeant Falle, also failed to see de Rullecourt's troops landing; nor did the guard at Seymour Tower (not the present one but an earlier building) realise that a French fleet was sailing up the Violet Channel. The inevitable conclusion is that a tower or any other defensive position is only as good as its garrison when it comes to preventing an enemy landing.

ROZEL, OR LE COUPERON, BARRACKS

In 1810 the barracks at Rozel were built by the British Board of Ordnance and were named 'Le Couperon Barracks' after the name of the southern point of Rozel harbour. General Don, then Lieutenant-Governor of Jersey, had been working to improve the defences of the Island since his

Plate 8. La Côte au Palier. The house, which dates from the middle of the 16th century, is one of the properties of the Chefs Tenants du Fief de la Reine (see Chapter 2). In the 19th century, it was acquired by the Whitley family and later by inheritance, by the Renoufs. After lying derelict for a period, it was completely restored and extended in the 1960s. (Anthony Paines Collection)

Plate 9. The 19th-century batons of St Martin Honorary Police are exhibited at the Public Hall. (Photo: Chris Blackstone)

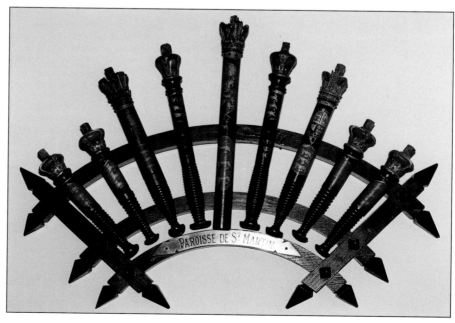
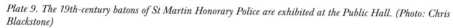

Plate 10. La Tourelle at Faldouet is an outstanding example of the classic 17th-century Jersey farmhouse. The voussoir arch is particularly fine. (Photo: Jenny Pallot)

Plate 11. La Chaumière, one of the very few houses in the Island to have retained a thatched roof, nestles into the hillside at La Ville Brée. (Anthony Paines Collection)

Plate 12. *The Old School House, Rozel. Edmund Blampied attended school here. (Photo: Chris Blackstone)*

Plate 13. *Les Alpes, on La Grande Route de Faldouet, built in 1900, an example of high Victorian style. It housed Touzel's School and later St Martin's Collegiate School. (Photo: Chris Blackstone)*

DATE STONES

Plate 14. Edouard Noël 1694 on one of the oldest buildings at Ville ès Nouaux. The design on the right appears to be a fleur-de-lis, indicating the family's origin in France. (Photo: Chris Blackstone)

Plate 15. George Noël and Anne Aubin 1842 at Rozel Hamlet. The house has been extended since and this stone is now over an internal doorway. (Photo: Chris Blackstone)

Plate 16. Thomas Le Seelleur and Susanne Le Seelleur 1820 at Haye Hogard. Thomas and Susanne were third cousins. (Photo: Chris Blackstone)

Plate 17. Nicholas Ralph Richardson 1839 at La Ferme. The design on the left refers to Philippe Richardson and the monogramme is that of his mother, Abigail Dumaresq. It is possible that this, together with the 1663 date, refers to an earlier house on the site. (Photo: Chris Blackstone)

arrival in 1806. Napoleon and the French were formidable enemies, who had already shown in 1781 that an invasion of Jersey was possible. General Don's strategy was to build defences which could contain an enemy invasion long enough for troops and artillery to arrive as reinforcements at all likely landing places.

Rozel harbour had no defences; moreover, there were no regular troops stationed in the north-east of Jersey, so it was decided to build the barracks at Rozel to be both a strong defensive fortress and a station for regular army troops. The British government negotiated a 99-year lease, for the sum of £4 10s. 0d. per annum, on land owned by Mr. Lemprière of Rosel Manor, on which to build.

It was not a sound construction, for four years after the building was completed it was found that the whole wall along the sea side was likely to collapse, because it had been built on loose gravel and the sea was washing away such foundations as the wall had. The sea side of the barracks had then to be underpinned with masonry foundations at a cost of £800, but this operation was done well, so that the walls on the sea side are as sound today as they ever were.

The barracks were built to quarter 68 men (three of these were officers) together with stabling for the officers' horses. The walls were holed for musketry on the sea side, and there were embrasures for 9lb or 12lb guns, four at least, with a 6ft parapet, also holed for musketry. The sea wall had a small parapet to protect the men lying down there firing their muskets. It would certainly not have been easy for an enemy to make a successful landing at Rozel against this firepower.

In 1816 a French ship called *La Balane*, which was on its way to Canada filled with emigrating families, was wrecked on Les Diroûilles rocks. Seventy people were rescued with the help of boats from Jersey and many were landed at Rozel, where the soldiers of the 8th Royal Veteran Battalion were quartered. This garrison showed great kindness to the survivors, many of whom were lodged at the barracks for a time.

Sometime after 1821, Rozel's barracks became the residence of the Lieutenant-Governor of Jersey. Sir John Halkett, who was Lieutenant-Governor from 1821 to 1830, decided to live there while Government House on St Saviour's Hill was being made ready for him. Interestingly, it is known that a well was provided for the barracks in 1838. Where His Excellency and the soldiers had got water from before this is a mystery.

A guide book for Jersey written in 1850 states that the barracks were untenanted at that time, but we are told by a Colonel W.D. Mills that a Frenchman, the Prince de Vienne, was in residence there in 1860. Ten years later the Franco-Prussian war began, and it was thought necessary to bring extra troops to Jersey. It was at this time that a cook-house, ablution house and a washhouse were added to the barracks, to help accommodate the extra troops. One must suppose that the troops who garrisoned the barracks when it was first built managed without any of these amenities.

One local man recounts a most interesting legal case which went on appeal to the Privy Council, whose legal Lords delivered their judgment in 1954. The case concerned the ownership of the road which the War Department had made to the north and west of Le Couperon Barracks, originally to replace a road which had been built over within the barracks area.

32   *Le Couperon Barracks at Rozel, c.1905. Built in 1810, they have been in private ownership since 1924 and are now an hotel. (John Le Seelleur Collection)*

The case was brought by Arthur Villeneuve Nicolle, who had bought the barracks from a Mrs. Rose in 1932, Mrs. Rose having bought the property from the War Department in 1924. Mr. Nicolle claimed that this road was his property and that the respondent in the case had no right to build windows in his house only three feet from the road, nor to put sewage disposal pipes under it. Mr. Wigram, the respondent, claimed that the road belonged to the Parish of St Martin, whose permission he had obtained to do both the things complained of. This meant that Henry Ahier, who was then Constable of St Martin, also became a respondent, because the rights of the Parish were involved.

The case turned on whether a road could be transferred to the ownership of the Parish by an Acte of the Comité des Chemins of the Parish of St Martin, without the necessity of registering the transfer of ownership in the Royal Court. The Parish had passed two such Actes, one in 1911 when Major Brooker had offered the road to the Parish on behalf of the War Department, and the second in 1925 when Mrs. Rose's solicitors queried whether the Parish had confirmed acceptance of the road from the War Department in 1911. The Lords of the Privy Council found in favour of Mr. Wigram and the Parish of St Martin, which then continued to look after the road as they had done for many years before.

Four years after this case was settled, Mr. and Mrs. Charles Sharp arrived from Yorkshire, bought the Barracks from Mr. Nicolle, and set about turning the building into an hotel. An upper storey faced with cedarwood was built to provide bedrooms, while a swimming pool and garden replaced much of the barrack square. The hotel is still flourishing under new ownership, providing an example of how to adapt historic buildings to modern use.

ST MARTIN'S ARSENAL

In 1806, when General Don arrived in Jersey as Lieutenant-Governor, there was considerable anxiety both in England and in Jersey about the threat of an invasion from France. Napoleon was still a formidable enemy with naval forces available to him all along the French channel coasts.

There were already a number of defensive towers built and ready for action round Jersey's shores, but these strong points had to be manned by the Jersey Militia. There were not enough regular Army troops available and General Don was not impressed by the Militia's equipment, arms, or even its ability to use them. The Militia artillery pieces were kept in the parish churches; other equipment and uniforms were kept by each man in his home and were not always well looked after. The militia regiments had no buildings in which to train and no properly-organised rallying points. Lastly, the roads which would be so necessary to enable either militia or regular army units to move quickly to possible invasion points were lacking or inadequate.

General Don applied himself to the task, with the help of General Sir John Le Couteur, of solving these problems and turning the Militia into a good fighting force. New roads were constructed by the regular Army engineers. Drill sheds were built in each parish near the churches. In 1783 the States of Jersey had organised a lottery to raise the money needed for building these drill sheds and the newly-proposed arsenals. However, the arsenals, although they had been started, were not completed until 1835, by which time they were more necessary than ever to accommodate the larger guns which had been brought to the Island for the use of the militia's artillery regiment.

Five arsenals were built to the same plan, one of which was St Martin's, while the sixth in St Helier was an altogether larger building. It is not known who the architect was, but it is tempting to suppose that Colonel Humfrey, the Royal Engineer who designed and built Fort Regent, had a hand in the design. At any rate, St Martin's Arsenal is a handsome well-constructed granite building of three two-storey blocks, joined by triple-arched links on the ground floor. Here were kept the field pieces with their limbers, ready to be taken to the point of action. Here also were the men's uniforms and weapons, together with the necessary ammunition.

In the event of a general stand-to the Arsenal was the rallying point for the Militia of the north and east regiments, and for the artillery men with their horses. Its position was chosen as a convenient central point, but also so that it would not be more than two miles from any likely point of attack. This was thought to be the longest distance a fully-equipped infantryman could travel with any speed and still be fit to fight at the end of his journey. There were paths which the Militia used from the arsenal as well as the roads, which provided short cuts to strong points. One such led to Les Pièces, where there was a gun.

A law governing the arsenals had been passed in 1844. General Sir John Le Couteur wanted to make it compulsory for all principals of the parishes to supply the horses for hauling the guns, or if they could not do so they had to pay an annual fee for exemption. It is said that Sir John encouraged racing on Grouville Common in order to improve the breeding of horses for his military purposes; but whether a good racehorse would also make a good horse for pulling guns does seem a little doubtful.

33 St Martin's Arsenal dates from 1835. It is now part of a States Housing project. (Photo: Chris Blackstone)

In the Second World War the Arsenal was again used as a collecting point, but this time by the occupying German forces. The farmers of Trinity and St Martin were ordered to bring all their horses to the arsenal for inspection. The Germans then chose the best horses which were requisitioned for the use of the German army.

On 20 June 1940 the Jersey Militia sailed for England to fight with the Hampshire Regiment. The arsenal was no longer needed for militia purposes and two families, the Fennels and the Parkers, made their homes there for the duration of the war.

After the war, in 1946, the Jersey Militia was disbanded and all the arsenals were redundant. It was not until 1948 that the States of Jersey Housing Department took over St Martin's Arsenal. A second pebble-dashed storey was added to the arched linking structures; the arches were filled in and given doors and windows so that the whole arsenal could be turned into housing. This is now surrounded by other States houses built at that time, but it remains a handsome granite building, still serving a useful purpose, unlike some of the other parish arsenals which have unfortunately been destroyed.

HAUT DE LA GARENNE

Life was very much tougher 150 years ago than it is today. Few places illustrate this better than the Jersey Industrial School – now Haut de la Garenne – in St Martin.

Those who set up this establishment 'for young people of the lower classes of society and for children neglected and in a state of destitution' were regarded as benevolent philanthropists. And so they were. A report in 1871 read:

> It is a source of real pleasure to the friends of youth to see steps taken … for the protection and education of the outcast and parentless portion of the rising generation … The boy who has been bereft of his natural protectors and guardians finds himself alone and the perhaps not unwilling prey of the vicious and unprincipled; easily led into temptation he requires that someone should take him by the hand and shew him the beacon of light which warns him of the shoals and quicksands upon which he may make shipwreck. And this the Industrial School at Gorey professes to do and actually accomplishes.

34 *The Jersey Home for Boys, 1953. Although the regime was strict, it provided a secure refuge for boys who were homeless. (Stanley Barnard Collection)*

Philanthropic, yes, but the living conditions for these boys, who were not convicted of crimes and had merely fallen on hard times, were very far from the 'politically correct' standards which would be acceptable today.

The same writer eulogised the regime:

> The boys numbering in all 99, are clean though ordinarily clad, and have their hair, through necessity rather than choice we should suppose, cropped close. At their meals they are assembled in a spacious and airy apartment where they are ranged in four rows, each boy with his bowl of cocoa – or tea – and a good junk of bread and treacle beside him. At a given signal they all rise and, with their eyes closed and hands reverentially joined, they sing grace. Few more touching sights than this it is impossible to witness.

The States of Jersey found earlier in the 19th century that there was a 'lamentable amount of juvenile crime'. At that time offending boys found themselves confined to a corner of the General Hospital where they led a Dickensian existence, a few of them learning shoemaking, but most doing scrubbing and washing, some learning to read and write, but emerging with a profound ignorance of the world outside. The Lieutenant-Governor of the time, Major-General Sir James Love, laid before the States several works and publications on the establishment of Industrial Schools. The plight of the boys confined to that corner of the General Hospital aroused sympathy – their situation probably mirrored the conditions in England at the time which had prompted Charles Dickens to write about social evils – and it was recommended that they should be transferred to a 70-vergée farm at Anne Port. The report quoted above, which was published in 1871, made it clear that 'No boy, as a rule, is admitted into the establishment who has been convicted before a Magistrate, although we believe, in some exceptional cases, this rule has not been strictly enforced.' It is not clear what happened to most boys who had been convicted of petty crimes, and who would previously have found themselves confined in the General Hospital.

35 *The interior courtyard, c.1950. The Home was closed in 1986. (Stanley Barnard Collection)*

In June 1867 the gaunt building, which is now a local landmark, was opened for them and they were transferred there. Its day-to-day running, although in the hands of an experienced headmaster, was overseen by a States Committee which included many prominent Jerseymen, such as Dean Le Breton (Lillie Langtry's father), Clement Hemery, C.W. Robin and Colonel J. Le Couteur, who gave a silver watch and chain as an annual prize to the boy who gained highest proficiency in Christian knowledge. It was seen as a place to 'provide a home for the moral, intellectual and industrial training of boys, who, through parental neglect or any other cause, are deprived of the means of education and are in danger of contracting idle and disorderly habits'.

If they behaved well there were treats, such as an outing to play cricket on Grouville Common, or a good tea which included cakes. But for those who fell short of expected standards of behaviour life was not so good. Minor punishments included being deprived of treacle or butter for four days, or sent on the arduous task of pumping water. But consistent offenders really had it tough – what an outcry there would be if the same conditions prevailed today! One stripe each, drilled for 15 minutes was the usual for some misdemeanours, but up to six stripes could be received or even a flogging. For those deemed to be 'very wicked' there was solitary confinement for 24 hours in the cells.

The general timetable can only be described as formidable:

6.00am	seniors rise, dress, air beds, say prayers, open windows, wash, clean boots
6.15am	the same procedure for the juniors
7.00am	first and second companies make beds, third pumps water, fourth cleans boots
7.15am	prepare breakfast
7.30am	breakfast for staff, servants and boys
8.00am	playground
8.45am	parade for inspection of clothes, etc.
9.00am	prayers and report on conduct
9.15am	work boys sent to their respective employments, the remainder to school
12.25pm	workshops and farming ceased (schoolboys dismissed at noon)
12.30pm	prepare for dinner

12.45pm	dinner
1.10pm	playground
1.45pm	parade and drill
2.00pm	work and school again
4.30pm	assemble for bathing in fine weather or remain in school until 4.45
5.30pm	prepare for tea
5.45pm	tea
6.15pm	playground, night-school in winter
7.45pm	assemble for prayers
8.40pm	boys sent to bed
10.00pm	all assistants and servants to be in and doors closed
10.00pm	all lights in the staff and servants' quarters to be extinguished

There was not much time off, but the boys did get an extra 45 minutes in bed on Sunday mornings before being twice marched to Gouray Church, where some of them were in the choir.

In 1900, the Industrial School was renamed the Jersey Home for Boys, and a former resident, the late Frank Lewis, recalled the hard regime in a retirement interview which he gave to the *Jersey Evening Post* 79 years later:

> We were made to bath 25 at a time in a huge stone bath filled with water and Jeyes fluid. Any boy who failed to remove every trace of dirt was ordered, naked and trembling, from the water to be flogged or kicked by the master in attendance.
>
> Towards the end of my time there, I was head boy and had to sit next to a new headmaster – a Mr. Badham. On the first day he came in with a cane and a bible, and told the boys that he didn't rule with the former but with the latter. Within a week he'd flogged me till I bled in front of the whole school and had cut off a boy's finger with a sharp cane. I heard later, after I had left the home, that he had been sacked for ill-treatment. Life was very very tough but the love and attention from the ladies on the staff made up for all the cruelty.

In the early days of this institution Gorey abounded with shipbuilding yards; there was a Royal Naval Training School next door to Haut de la Garenne from 1860 to 1875, so it must have seemed strange to the boys that the Admiralty would not allow them to join the Navy except 'by special permission after strict inquiry into their antecedents'. However, this appears to have been due to confusion of the name of the school with the similarly named English Industrial Schools for young offenders. When the status of the Jersey school was explained and the name eventually changed to the Jersey Home for Boys, the boys could join the Navy in the usual way.

The boys were encouraged to compete with the Island elementary schools and won their fair share of prizes, particularly in swimming. The school band had a great reputation and was in constant demand at Island functions. A fife and drum band was started in 1869 which in turn was superseded by a brass band in 1894, made possible by the generosity of subscribers. The first conductor was Band-Sergeant Hall of the Gloucester Regiment, followed by two of the well-known McKee family under whose tuition there was rapid progress. Also from about this time we have a glowing report from a visitor to the Jersey Industrial School: he found it well run by the headmaster, Michael Garry, and his wife (who fulfilled the role of Matron), together with the Committee.

36   August 1946. A group from the Jersey Home for Boys visits Jersey Airport. The aircraft is a Wayfarer of Channel Islands Airways. The tour was organised by the Rotary Club and hosted by Deputy Wilfred Krichefski, who is standing under the engine. (Photo: Jersey Evening Post)

In April 1996 there was an invitation to the public from Haut de la Garenne's custodian, Ian Robinson, to tour the property and to talk to former staff and residents.

One of them, Reg Norman, who spent nine years there from 1936-45, showed the visitors the study of Mr. Watkins, their headmaster. 'It used to be beautifully furnished, and the walls were lined with shelves full of books. When I see this place now it makes my heart bleed.' In the corridor he recalled the creaking staircase and remembered how the brown lino on the floors was cleaned by the boys with carbolic soap, and all the stair railings were polished regularly, every boy responsible for doing his own bit. In the dining room meals were taken silently, he said. If you were late, there would be nothing left for you. Breakfast was a bowl of porridge or bread and dripping. Each boy tried to get the largest portion.

Mr. Norman remembered that, during the Occupation the hungry boys climbed out of the dormitory windows at night on knotted sheets, while others kept watch. At the approach of danger the watch had only to whisper the alarm, 'digseye', and the prefect would find every boy asleep in his bunk. Jack Mourant, who was at Haut de la Garenne for five years from 1915 to

1920, particularly remembered Sergeant-Major McClintock, the Boer War veteran Drill Sergeant, who took the boys for parade twice a day, teaching children discipline by the tried and tested means of scaring them rigid. All this was in the interests of preparing the boys for a life either at sea or on the farm.

Stanley Barnard was a resident at the home from 9 July 1940, when his mother died, and he has many memories of life there during the Occupation. The boys did their best to undermine the German soldiers at every opportunity. On one occasion he remembers the boys adding horse manure to the German soldiers' lunchtime soup, and standing to watch them eat it. Another time, he and his friends drew the British flag on one of the German swastika banners, erected for a special parade for Hitler's birthday. Mr. Barnard, who was known as a child as Stanley Coussens, recalls:

> The Germans used to signal to France from the bell tower with a very powerful light. They ran an electric cable to it along the corridor from a power point in our dormitory. One boy used to get out of bed and pull out the plug in the middle of the signalling. This happened a couple of times before the Germans posted a guard near the power point. On one occasion a boy pretended to sleepwalk. He proceeded along the corridor while the Germans were signalling and began ringing the bell and, in doing so, knocked a German soldier's helmet off. Another bit of mischief happened when the Germans tethered their horses on the field by the home. Some boys let them loose and they galloped down the lane with soldiers chasing after them while we all had a good laugh.

The Home was renamed Haut de la Garenne. Garenne means rabbit-warren, and the name harks back to the time when this was the site of the warren for Mont Orgueil. Medieval warrens were the jealously-guarded right of the Crown and the Seigneurs, and the rabbits were preserved there for hunting by the feudal lord.

The Home was taken over and run by the Education Department until it finally closed in 1986, superseded by more modern establishments and practices. Since then it has remained something of a white elephant: a solid piece of Victorian architecture, situated high above Gorey, a building which is, in its own way, magnificent, but which does not now have an obvious use. It has not been completely ignored, however, and has been used recently as a youth club, a camping site, a hostel for visiting groups and even as a film studio. Its grounds include the only sports field in that part of the Island and some sports fixtures are still held there.

SASH WINDOWS, ROUND ARCHES AND SHUTTERS
Some of the architecturally interesting houses of the Parish of St Martin

To the crisply logical bureaucrats of the Jersey Post Office, a St Martin address means just one thing: the postcode JE36. To the inhabitants of these 5,732 vergées, however, an infinite variety of accommodation is on offer, providing tangible evidence of the history of St Martin. The range of housing in the Parish reflects not only the passage of time but also St Martin's half-share in two of the Island's four principal harbours.

Compared with a similar area in England or France, St Martin is almost without really old houses. Half-timber-framed houses, so evident in nearby Dinan, are completely absent (unless

37 A fine example of the Jersey round arch on La Rue du Bouillon. No longer associated with an historic house, this wall surrounds a modern property. (Photo: Chris Blackstone)

you count the cheerfully bogus Geoffrey's Leap Tea Room). It is doubtful if more than one or two houses now standing in the whole of Jersey can claim an earlier date than 1500. There is a good reason for this state of affairs. Although well-wooded by Jersey standards, even St Martin could not supply sufficient timber for the needs of its inhabitants and so houses were built of stone, of which there is an abundance.

However, the Island has no lime. Instead the stones were not very satisfactorily glued together with a mixture of clay, chopped straw, cow dung, cow hair and sea sand which never dried completely and so did not crack. This only worked so long as rainwater was excluded. If ever the thatched roof was allowed to decay the walls generally followed not long after, providing a useful source of stone for use on a new building.

The typical St Martin farmhouse of that period was a solid, rectangular, gabled building with a blank gable against the road, preferably in a sheltered location and facing south. It would be hopeless to seek an inland residence of that period that was not also a farmhouse, there being no other reason to live in the Parish but to earn a living by farming. A fine example of this sort of house is La Bachauderie in La Rue St Julien, hard against the St Saviour boundary. The appeal of this particular site is reinforced by a never-failing spring that rises just across the road.

Special mention must be made at this stage of the Jersey round arch, thought to have arrived from France before 1550 and very sensibly adopted by the Jersey Museums Service as its emblem. The arch is comprised of two outer stones with shoulders, which project sideways into the surrounding masonry, and a central keystone. These three stones, known as voussoirs, are usually supported on each side by three base stones. The arch is slightly flatter than a perfect semi-circle and generally spans between 36 and 40 inches.

St Martin can boast numerous fine examples of this archetypal Jersey feature. Les Carrières on the Grande Route de St Martin and Devon Villa on the Grande Route de Faldouet show it in use on roadside gateways. As a front door, it can be seen at Houguemont on La Rue d'Aval, Oxford House in Faldouet Lane, La Haie Fleurie in La Rue de la Haie Fleurie and Bandinel in La Chasse ès Demoiselles Bandinel (all 17th-century properties, or earlier in the case of Houguemont).

Particularly fine examples of the round arch, both as a gateway and as a doorway, are to be found at La Tourelle in La Rue d'Aval, but then everything about La Tourelle is fine. It is the best 17th-century house and farm complex in the Parish and rightly renowned for its 30-step tourelle staircase, illustrated in 1841 with a thatched roof, secured at its apex to a striking central pinnacle.

38   La Tourelle in an 1841 drawing by George Bandinel. At that date, all the buildings were thatched, including the tourelle, which had a dramatic needle point. (Jersey Museums Service Collection)

The main façade of La Tourelle, with its carefully enlarged windows set into a wall of squared and dressed granite of just the right colour, sums up entirely the appeal of the Jersey farmhouse. A St Martinais in exile anywhere in the world would, upon seeing a picture of La Tourelle, be instantly reminded of home.

The round arch fell out of fashion after 1700 and doorways were built square or were squared off. A round arch in exile is to be found in the garden wall of a new house known as The Gables at the northern end of La Rue du Bouillon. It has a twin, but with a less well-fitting keystone in the garden wall of Faldouet Lodge on the other side of the road.

The 18th century was the golden age of the Jersey granite farmhouse. Beauchamp in La Rue des Fontaines was built almost exactly in the middle of the century and would be a particularly pleasing example were it not for its plastic windows. Of the 94 houses featured in the Parish Treasury, 84 have sash windows and, of these, all but two are painted white or, occasionally, cream. Parts of St Martin are closer to France than they are to St Ouen and yet the sash window is unheard of in France. It arrived from England in the 18th century and its impact on the houses of the Parish could scarcely be overstated. The French in particular, who describe it as the fenêtre guillotine, are at a loss to understand its appeal. Unlike the casement, or French window, it allows only half the window to be opened at most. It involves a complicated boxed-in mechanism of cords, weights and pulleys and is inherently draughty because, far from butting tight together, the two halves of the window have to be free to slide past each other. In older buildings, window openings were

39 Single-frame Victorian sash window at La Cour Normande. (Photo: Christopher Scholefield)

frequently enlarged to accommodate the new 12-pane sashes. Yet, by some happy accident, the visual character of the finest houses in the Parish depends, above all else, on the relationship thereby created between the solid walls and the window apertures, and thereafter the subdivision of these windows into ever larger panes of glass as technology permitted. The Victorians were always alive to new areas of decorative potential. Although able to use single pane sashes, as at La Cour Normande in La Rue du Bouillon, they also used slim quarter lights for ornament's sake, as at Le Fleurion in La Rue de la Forge. Political affiliations were also declared with red-painted windows for the Rose Party and green for the Conservative Laurels, the latter strikingly handsome and until very recently still to be seen at Le Pont in La Rue des Cabarettes.

Some of these granite houses have achieved distinction for reasons other than their windows. Next door to Le Pont is La Chasse. This house is approached from the public road by a miniature avenue announced by a pair of round two-tier dressed granite flanking walls with decorative gateposts, dated 1823. Such grandeur is unexpected in the heart of rural St Martin, where precious land is generally put to more practical uses. Another impressive entrance and carriage-drive is to be found serving the grandly-named Chateaubriand from La Rue des Marettes. In fact, the house itself belonged not to the famous French man of letters, Viscomte François René de Châteaubriand, who lived for a year in Parade Place, but to his cousin Armand.

Three otherwise typical granite houses whose roof treatments command attention are, in order of antiquity, La Chaumière in La Rue de la Ville Brée (re-thatched in 1989 after an unhappy 60-year interlude under asbestos tiles), Le Fleurion (hipped and sporting a classically-inspired central pediment) and Faldouet Lodge, La Rue du Bouillon (hipped and covered with sea-green glazed tiles in 1938, following fire damage).

Outside the confines of the Parish the Napoleonic Wars and their conclusion had trans-formed life in St Helier and brought with them changes in architectural taste that were soon felt in St Martin itself. The change that was to have a permanent effect was not the arrival, after the French Revolution, of a colony of 4,000 aristocratic exiles, but of a more permanent colony of half-pay military men who retired from England once the war was won. For them local speculators were quick to build Regency and early Victorian crescents, villas and terraces. Crucially these new developments were never finished in local granite or brick but in smooth, creamy stucco, which needed painting, or Roman cement which did not.

40 The imposing entrance to La Chasse (1823) seems strangely incompatible with its rural environment. (Photo: Christopher Scholefield)

41 Wrentham Hall in La Grande Route de Faldouet was built in 1822 by the Rector's widow, to house herself and her 12 children. (Photo: Chris Blackstone)

There is a most urbane pair of such houses known as Two Trees and Les Murailles, complete with an 'in and out' carriage drive, opposite the parish cemetery in La Grande Route de Rozel. A short distance away to the north stands Wrentham Hall, built by the widow of the Rector of St Martin for herself and her 12 children in 1822. The contrast between the shape of, and materials used in, these houses, as compared with every other building so far considered, could not be more marked. To their contemporaries they must have seemed revolutionary.

However novel they may have been, such buildings are disciplined and work well in groups. Above all, they have inspired the character and appearance of St Martin's most urban area, Gorey. This divides into two distinct parts: Le Mont de Gouray, heading up the hill from the pier to Gouray Church, and the pier proper. The road is too wide and the houses too varied in quality for Le Mont de Gouray to have the appeal of St Aubin's High Street. The houses on the pier are marginally more consistent in appearance and were among the first structures in Jersey to enjoy the distinction of statutory designation in 1974. This has not protected them from a rash of ill-considered and unsightly dormer windows, whose appearance the famously massive bulk of the castle, rising sheer behind them, just manages to keep under control.

Away from Gorey, the vicinity of the Parish Church and Rozel Harbour, the conventional Jersey pattern of settlement scattered in hamlets rather than clustered in villages is evident. These hamlets can be very diverse in nature. The row of workers' cottages on the lower reaches of Le Mont des Landes and the grander houses further up that hill provide an intriguing insight into the sort of development that might have spread all along the coast, had the naval base at St Catherine been completed.

Altogether more rural in feel are La Ville Brée and La Ville ès Nouaux. They are lost among the fields, principally granite-built, and with varying types and sizes of building clustered together informally.

Yet a third type of hamlet are the strings of formal gentlemen's stucco residences, standing side by side, seemingly in the middle of nowhere. The fine houses lining La Rue de Fliquet, La Grande Route de Faldouet just west of Carrefour Messervy, and near Rozel Mill are cases in

42 The Old Cadet House at Mont Mallet once served as part of the Royal Naval Training School.

point. In all three, stucco houses which have, or used to have, shutters predominated. In all three there is clear evidence of shops (at Mont Alto at Fliquet, Kenilworth at Faldouet and Highlands near Rozel Mill), now converted to other uses. Happily, all three hamlets still have their post boxes.

The larger free-standing properties of the 19th century reveal a rewarding diversity of appearance in line with the evolution in architectural taste. As befits its military origins, the more severe is the just restored Old Cadet House at Le Mont Mallet. Pictures exist of this property in the days when it had a full-rigged ship's mast in its grounds for the cadets to practise on. Next door, Seymour Farm betrays its earlier purpose as the naval officers' married quarters. No other Jersey farm has a full-length, covered, wooden balcony at first-floor level.

43 Valmont (1840) in La Rue St Julien displays the Victorian passion for elaborate decoration. (Photo: Chris Blackstone)

Clearly built to enjoy its panoramic views across Grouville, Beaulieu on Le Mont de Gouray is of a more complicated design and yet still rigidly symmetrical. There is a centre section with a hipped roof and a pavilion at each end. On the other hand, Cedar Valley off La Rue de Fliquet is boldly asymmetrical. This is a house whose proportions, bay windows and gables proclaim it to be Victorian in the generally accepted sense of the word. Exuberantly Victorian detail is evident at Valmont in La Rue St Julien which boasts decorated chimneys, ornamental ridge slates on the roof, decorated dormers, three sash windows, bay windows, a three-floor design with steps to a half-glazed front door and, for good measure, a farm bell under a pitched roof bracket on the eastern gable. The house is dated 1840. Le Côtil, next door, preceded it by a mere 20 years and yet has infinitely more in common with La Bachauderie than with Valmont.

However, for most parishioners the house that represents the ultimate high-Victorian period-piece is Les Alpes on La Grande Route de

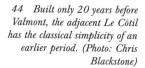

44 Built only 20 years before Valmont, the adjacent Le Côtil has the classical simplicity of an earlier period. (Photo: Chris Blackstone)

Faldouet. Built in 1900 this boasts most of the decorative features of Valmont and more besides, all set off in a brilliant wedding-cake white. Les Alpes has an unusual (for Jersey) formal driveway and its central roof pediment peeps over the hedgerows towards Les Ruettes some distance away to the south. At night this feature is illuminated; for a building so consumed by its mission to impress, nothing less would be appropriate.

The range of styles and techniques available to the Victorians led inevitably to a breakdown in the tacit consensus as to what a home should look like. A direct contemporary of Valmont is La Rive in Rozel Valley. Tantalisingly difficult to see, owing to its setting on the valley's richly-wooded, south-facing slopes, La Rive has beyond doubt the most original and the smartest paint scheme in the Parish: bone-coloured walls, ink-black woodwork (including the windows) and soft-green shutters.

The divergence of style illustrated by the contrast between Valmont and La Rive is most easily seen if you compare the prettily gothic Old School House in Rue des Alleurs (the Rozel one, not the Faldouet one) with the more classical La Campagne, next door. Some houses have a foot in both camps. Der-a-Rose atop the Mont des Landes has shutters and sash windows surmounted by a jaunty little gable with decorative barge-boarding. Springside on La Grande Route de Faldouet is all classical rigour outside, but boasts no less than four massive pairs of gothic arch doors within.

With the arrival of the 20th century, the uniformity which had begun to lose ground in the Victorian period collapsed altogether – swept away by changing fashions and financial pragmatism. Scores of new buildings sprang up of a diversity in appearance that has changed the character of the Parish for good. The generous and ornate comfort of the Edwardian gentleman's residence is best illustrated by the *Château La Chaire Hotel* in La Vallée de Rozel. The reaction to this was the international style of plain white walls, large windows and crisp, almost nautical detailing, just about evident beneath the more recent alterations made to Moonrakers at Anne Port. This break with earlier conventions led ultimately to the many bungalows and seaside houses that follow no particular style or design except a desire to make the most of a good view whilst combining low

45 Classical-modern, Longpré, above the Gorey côtils, was built very recently, although its style harks back to Regency times. (Photo: Chris Blackstone)

maintenance with the need to keep costs under control. All too rarely a building emerges whose simplicity and integrity of design have nothing to do with the churlish pragmatism of so much post-war building. Hidden away up a tributary of La Vallée de Rozel, Moulin Bleu, built in 1962, is such a house. In its front garden stands a very pretty fisherman's cottage of ornate Flemish bond bricks with white spacers. Although 300 metres from the sea, it was thoughtfully located next to the brook-side reed beds which provided the raw material for its owner's lobster pots.

Inevitably the tide of fashion turned yet again, so that the largest of the new houses built in the Parish since the Occupation aim to recapture the spirit of a more august age. There is the massive and austerely classical Longpré squeezed into the southern end of its plot on Le Mont de la Guérande. Anne Port Farm, on the other hand, is all but hidden from the gaze of passers-by. It is faced in granite and yet built to a design which, in its time, would inevitably have been finished in stucco. But the greatest paradox of all must be Fliquet Castle, wedged into the last bend before the sea of La Rue de la Perruque. This has been many years in the making and not so much built as assembled. The owner began his work decades ago and anticipated by many years the current craze for architectural salvage. The result is a triumphant folly far too romantic to be identified by anything so mundane as a postcode.

DATE STONES

One of the features of Jersey's fine stock of old houses is the carved granite date stones which contribute to their very individual and charismatic style. The earliest inscribed upon a building in St Martin are those at Mont Orgueil Castle – recording the years 1547, 1551 and 1593; but on private houses they came later – starting at the beginning of the 17th century.

46 At Mont Orgueil, this is possibly the earliest dated stone in St Martin and displays the arms of Henry Cornish.

These date stones have frequently been taken as the date when the house was built, but to assume this is a mistake. Joan Stevens, in her much-respected book *Old Jersey Houses*, warned:

47 *The earliest known date stone at a private property in the Parish, Le Taillis, Rue de la Croix. It probably relates to Collas Baudains, whose first wife died that year. (After Joan Stevens)*

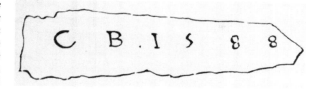

48 *Philippe Fauvel and Elizabeth Bandinel, 1715, at Holly Bank, La Ville Brée. This incorporates an early version of the heart motif. (After Joan Stevens)*

The carved date stones which abound can be most misleading, and they must be interpreted with care, and never accepted at face value. One can quote a typical 17th century window lintel on which the date 1831 has been incised, or, conversely, an earlier date added to a later feature. So one tends to be sceptical, but one should neither trust nor distrust date stones without supporting evidence.

A good example of how date stones should never be taken at face value is a small granite building at La Chasse crossroads in St Martin. It has the date 1626 carved above the door, but was in fact built in around 1900 by the eccentric Constable Messervy who, it is claimed in Balleine's book, *The Bailiwick of Jersey*, spent large sums of money on creating bogus antiquities.

The local custom of a marriage stone placed above the front door can also be misleading. These stones usually depict two inter-twined hearts, with the husband's initials on the left and the bride's on the right. But the date need have no bearing on the date of the construction of the house: it may record the date of an extension, or the date in which the newly-married couple moved into an existing house. Joan Stevens pointed out that the practice of carving interlocking hearts on marriage stones was not a very old Jersey custom '… actually it only started in the middle of the 18th century, and is not found on the early stones, and in no case on a round arch'.

An illustration of the risks of relying upon marriage stones for accuracy occurs at Cloverly at Faldouet. The date stone in the main house reads D.L.S.L – E.S.B.N. 1895. In fact, David Le Seelleur and Sophie Binet, who lived there, were married on 6 June 1888 and the date recorded is probably that when the house was completed. At the end of the 20th century, Cloverly is occupied by Peter David Le Seelleur and Lynne Le Seelleur. A date stone has been placed above the front door reading P.D.L.S. 1997 L.L.S. This marriage stone does not incorporate a maiden name, which, in Mrs. Le Seelleur's case was Hayden. At La Préférence Cottage, the date stone reads IC.RB 1688: Jean Collas married Rachel Baudayne in 1678.

The earliest recorded date stone in a private house in the Parish is at Le Taillis, with the initial CB (Collas Baudains) and the date 1588. Another early one is at Bandinel. This is featured in Joan Stevens' much-respected book, and is inscribed with the date 1619 and the initials ILM and a small heart. These are the initials of Jean Le Manquais, who married Anne La Cloche in 1612.

Dates are inscribed either in incised or embossed numerals. Sometimes both methods are used on one stone. The choice was probably governed by cost as the embossed type would be more time-consuming and therefore more expensive to produce.

The custom of carving names, dates and heraldic symbols was not confined to conventional buildings: the Island has a fine stock of roadside monuments which often carry dates and names or initials of those responsible for creating them. Photographs of a representative selection of these engraved plaques, lavoirs, parish boundary stones and many others were assembled by Roger Long in 1997 for a mobile display, sponsored by Planning and Environment Committee's Historic Buildings Section. Several of the subjects depicted may be seen in St Martin, for example, the fine road sign at the foot of Le Mont des Landes, and the interesting douet à laver in La Rue des Vaux de l'Église.

The practice of erecting date stones in new buildings is undergoing something of a renaissance, both in private houses and public schemes. A recent example, recording the names of all who were involved with the St Martin's Village development, is the handsome stone placed at the entrance to the new estate.

49   The douet à laver in La Rue des Vaux de l'Église. The inscribed initials are of those families entitled to use the lavoir. (Photo: Roger Long)

Four
The Great War 1914-1918

The Great War of 1914-1918 shook the whole world with its ferocity and its appalling level of killing. As Wilfred Owen recorded: 'War broke: and now the winter of the world with perishing darkness closed in.' In the Parish of St Martin, the shock and horror was great. As in most other parts of the British Isles, young men thought war was an adventure, a form of crusade and were quick to offer to fight. Their sacrifice is remembered each year in a touching service at the Parish War Memorial. 'At the going down of the sun and in the morning, we will remember them'.

Britain declared war on Germany on 4 August 1914, and ordered the mobilisation of its small professional army, which was heavily outnumbered by the German force. The conflict involved 6,292 young men from the Island of Jersey, of whom 862 lost their lives.

The part played by the Parish of St Martin should never be forgotten. A significant part of a generation was wiped out, and for those who did survive, life had changed with an evil vengeance. The experience of trench warfare was one that was impossible to forget. The Parish War Memorial lists 50 of its sons who perished, but the list is incomplete, and there are others who were also closely associated with the Parish who died in the dreadful battles of the Great War. For example, many of the boys living at the Boys' Home – now Haut de la Garenne – went to fight. The names of those who died are listed on the northern gable of St Martin's Church, Gouray, but are not listed on the War Memorial, even though they had been living in the Parish: their own war memorial has been removed to Highlands, but there are now plans to return it to its rightful place at Faldouet. Three of the boys were killed on the same day, serving on HMS *Black Prince*, an armoured cruiser of 13,550 tons, which sank at the Battle of Jutland on 31 May 1916.

Thirteen other men have also been omitted from the Parish Roll of Honour. The full list of those who were either killed in action, or who later died of wounds, and who had a genuine connection with the Parish of St Martin is shown below. The Parish War Memorial does show the names of French nationals who died in the War who had been residing in the Parish. They were not slow in returning to defend their country against the German attacks. Indeed one of them, Paul Gibout, may well have been the first representative of the Parish to lay down his life. He was killed on 19 October 1914.

It was not until nearly two years after the end of the war, in August 1920, that a Parish meeting was held to consider building a permanent memorial. A large and influential committee was set up to organise it: Connétable John Pallot (president), the Reverend R. Le Sueur, Mr. J.S. Le Gresley, Mr. P.J. Noël, Jurat R.R. Lemprière, Colonel W.A. Stocker, Lieutenant J.E. Dorey, Mr. P.N. Richardson, Mr. C.W. Binet, Mr. J.E. Le Huquet, Mr. P. Lamy and Mr. A.F. Mortimer. Charles de Gruchy, Professor of Architecture at the Royal Academy of Arts, agreed to advise on the scheme. Another large group of collectors was appointed to canvass for voluntary contributions from parishioners to fund the building work.

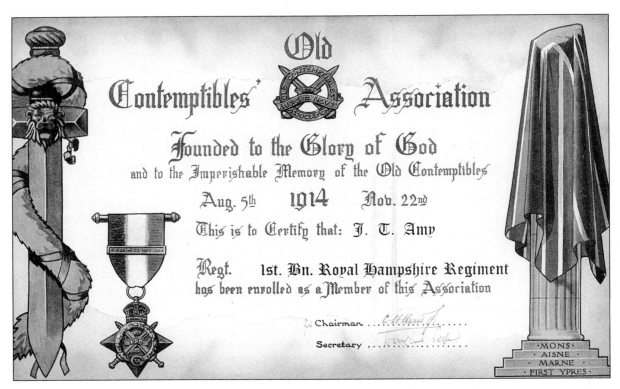

50 *The British Expeditionary Force of 1914 was described by the Germans as 'that contemptible little army'. This certificate was awarded to John Thomas Amy, who was captured at the battle of Mons and spent the remainder of the war in a prison camp. (Gerald Amy Collection)*

51 *The peace celebrations of 1919. The St Martin's Brass Band leads the procession past the Parish Church, on its way to Rosel Manor. (John Le Seelleur Collection)*

52   The peace celebrations, 1919. Part of the tableau in the grounds of Rosel Manor. (John D. Germain Collection)

The Parish War Memorial was officially unveiled and dedicated on 24 February 1924, in a service involving the Bailiff and the Lieutenant-Governor. Ex-servicemen, *anciens combattants* of the French army and local schoolchildren were requested to meet and process to the new monument, led by the St Martin's Brass Band. The War Memorial had been built into the old wall of the churchyard at a point where it closed the end of the vista from the main approach road from St Helier. To accommodate it, a small gateway and the *tronc des pauvres* were removed. It was built entirely from local granite, designed as a simple cross bearing upon its face a crusader's sword in bronze, and rising above the top of the wall from a pedestal in the centre of a curved hemicycle. The dedicatory inscription reads: A SES ENFANTS MORTS POUR LA PATRIE, LA PAROISSE DE SAINT MARTIN RECONNAISSANTE. Below, the names of the fallen are recorded in parallel columns. It is simple, un-fussy and dignified. Indeed, the official Order of Service for the dedication explained: 'A simple and severe treatment has been adopted as being more in accord with the purpose of the memorial and with the nature of the material used, and also more in harmony with the simple surroundings than any elaboration of detail.'

After the end of the war, and before the memorial was finished, the Parish organised a great celebration of peace. It had been a war which had lasted longer than almost everyone had believed possible. It was supposed to have been the war to end all wars. How quickly the world's hopes were dashed. But the immediate aftermath brought joy and relief because the killing had at last come to an end. St Martin's Peace Celebrations were held at Rosel Manor on 31 July 1919. The programme described it as a children's fête and sports. The children of the Parish, with as many parishioners as possible, were asked to meet at the Public Hall at 1 p.m. to form a procession under the leadership of the chief marshal, Major C.E. Lloyd, to march to Rosel Manor with the band and banners.

Three huge committees were set up to plan the events – the Seigneur, Jurat R.R. Lemprière, was the patron and also sat on the general committee and the sports committee. There was also a

53 *The peace celebrations: the programme. (John Le Seelleur Collection)*

decoration committee, a sports executive committee, and a tea committee, which alone had 36 members. It was a huge parochial effort and reflected the impact that the years of fighting had had upon the Parish.

Tea was served from 4.30 p.m. and at 8 p.m. the procession reformed to march to the south façade of the Manor, where prizes and commemorative medals were handed out by Madame de Rosel. After that, the children sang *La Marseillaise*, and the British national anthem, and gave three cheers for King and Empire. The colours of the allies were saluted and the procession, led by the band, finally dispersed after marching back along the drive to the Manor gates. Truly a day for the Parish to remember.

54 *Thomas Chandler Stent, teacher to Edmund Blampied at Rozel School, with his family in 1917. His two elder sons, Everard and Ernest, were both in the Royal Artillery. Everard was killed in the penultimate week of the war. (Courtesy of Richard Stent)*

1914-1918
A ses enfants morts pour la Patrie
La Paroisse de St Martin Reconnaissante

The Parish War Memorial

Amy, Philip Thomas	Private, Canadian Forces	28. 9.1918
Aubin, John Richard		
Bastard, Alfred Alexandre	Corporal, Canadian Forces	10. 4.1917
Baudains, Fred Adolphus	Private, Hampshire Regiment	4.10.1917
Bihet, Jean Austin		
Carrel, Charles Philip	Corporal, Royal Engineers	23. 5.1917
Ching, Wilfred Arthur	Private, Hampshire Regiment	4.10.1917
Courtman, Walter Herbert		
De La Haye, Josué Blampied	Corporal, Hampshire Regiment	6. 8.1915
Falle, John Cantell	Private, Hampshire Regiment	4.10.1917
Ferret, Amand		
Gallichan, Elias	Private, Canadian Forces	3.1917
Gaslonde, Pierre	French national resident in St Martin	6. 9.1915
Gautier, Louis	French national resident in St Martin	24. 9.1916
Godfray, Edwin de Vismes		
Guégan, Jean		
Gibout, Paul	French national resident in St Martin	9.10.1914
Holland, Edward William Herbert	Artificer's Mate, Royal Navy	21. 1.1918
Holland, Harold Edward	CQMS, East Surrey Regiment	1. 9.1918
Houel, Henri	French national resident in St Martin	9.10.1914
Johnson, George Mitchell		
Le Cocq, George	Private, Duke of Cornwall's Light Infantry	6.11.1918
Le Huquet, John Stanley		
Le Méhauté, Jean	French national resident in St Martin	4.1916
Le Seelleur, Hedley	Private, Medical Corps, Canadian Forces	1. 3.1918
Mackay, Arthur Jack	Private, London Scottish Regiment	20.10.1916
Mackay, Edgar Leslie		
Mackay, Walter Henry	Canadian Forces	2.10.1918
Mourant, Thomas George	Private, Duke of Cornwall's Light Infantry	30. 6.1918
Noël, Philip John		
Perchard, Edwin William	Private, Hampshire Regiment	4.10.1917
Perchard, Sydney John	Private, Duke of Cornwall's Light Infantry	6.11.1917
Renouf, Stanley John	Private, Australian Imperial Force	16. 1.1917
Renouf, Wilford Vautier	Private, Hampshire Regiment	14. 5.1917
Richards, Albert		
Richomme, Alfred George	Private, Dorset Regiment	29. 9.1918
Robert, Francis Philip		
Robert, Frederick Charles	Private, Yorkshire & Lancashire Regiment	2.10.1918
Robert, Henry George		
Robin, Charles Harold	Captain, Yorkshire & Lancashire Regiment	11. 5.1917
Ruaux, Ernest William		
Stent, Everard Chandler	Bombardier, Royal Artillery	27.10.1918

Stevens, Neville Claude	Gunner, Royal Artillery	10. 4.1918
Tachon, John	Sapper, Australian Imperial Force	22.10.1918
Tachon, Philip	Stoker, Royal Navy	15.10.1918
Tirel, Paul	French national resident in St Martin	4. 9.1916
Walden, Harold Eugene Montague		
Whitley, George Stanley	Private, New Zealand Forces	11.10.1918
Whitley, Philip Harold	Private, East Surrey Regiment	31.10.1918

1919 Roll of Honour
(Additional to names appearing on the War Memorial)

Amy, Rauline Anthoine	Corporal, Canadian Forces	28. 6.1918
Bihet, James	Gunner, Royal Artillery	26. 5.1917
De Quetteville, Alfred P.	Sergeant, Canadian Forces	8. 8.1918
Gibaut, Frederick A.	2nd Lieutenant, Canadian Forces	3.1917
Le Quesne, George Reve	Private, Royal Garrison Artillery	19. 8.1917
Lewis, Arthur Charles	Drummer, Canadian Forces	9.10.1918
Mackay, Arthur Jack	Canadian Forces	4. 9.1917
Mallett, Charles Edwin Ralph	Rifleman, Royal Irish Rifles	9. 9.1918
Martin, Thomas Leonard Franklin	Sergeant, Canadian Forces	30. 9.1918
Quaux, Ernest William	HM Submarines, E18	4. 4.1916
Smith, George Harry	Private, London Regiment	22. 8.1918
Vigot, Cyril Clifford	Private, Canadian Forces	29.11.1915

Jersey Home for Boys
(Names appearing on memorial in Gorey Church)

Abbott, Herbert John	Private, Royal Army Medical Corps	19. 5.1918
Barker, Henry John	Able Seaman, HM Submarines, E 15	15. 5.1916
Bechemin, E.	Private, Duke of Cornwall's Light Infantry	16.10.1918
Brunker, William	Private, Devon Regiment	25. 9.1915
Carreau, Jean		
Collins, John	Private, Devon Regiment	18.12.1914
De Ste Croix, Henry A.	Corporal, Hampshire Regiment	21. 5.1918
Dumont, Alphonse		
Dumont, George	HMS *Burka*	
Drube, Otto	1st Petty Officer, HMS *Black Prince*	31. 5.1916
Gold, Alfred	Corporal, Royal Irish Rifles	
Gregory, Francis	Petty Officer, HMS *Black Prince*	31. 5.1916
Hamon, Alfred	Private, Middlesex Regiment	
Hodge, Frederick Charles	Lance Corporal, Dorset Regiment	11. 8.1918
Igo, Frederick Cyril	Private, Middlesex Regiment	1. 7.1916
Laverty, John William	Gunner, Royal Field Artillery	6. 9.1918
Le Feuvre, William Edward	Lance Corporal, Royal Irish Rifles	23. 5.1917
Le Gros, Alfred Reginald	Royal Navy	2. 8.1918
Le Lievre, Clarence Charles	Able Seaman, HMS *Briton*	21. 8.1917
Lillicrap, John George	Private, Middlesex Regiment	
Marie, Philip John	Lance Corporal, Hampshire Regiment	28. 3.1915
Marshall, H		
Michel, John	Private, Devon Regiment	14. 3.1918

Ozard, George	Rifleman, Devon Regiment	14. 7.1916
Redden, Edward John	Sapper, Canadian Forces	10.1915
Rowe, Walter	Private, Munster Fusiliers	29. 3.1918
Rumsey, Frederick	Able Seaman, Royal Navy	
Sollett, Cyril	Private, Dorset Regiment	22. 7.1917
Stanbury, Arthur Alfred	Private, Duke of Cornwall's Light Infantry	6.11.1917
Tisson, Alfred Peter	Able Seaman, HMS *Black Prince*	31. 5.1916
Wooston, Albert	Corporal, Royal Irish Rifles	16. 8.1917
Wooston, William	Private, Dorset Regiment	15. 6.1918

55 Private Sydney Perchard, Duke of Cornwall's Light Infantry (seated). He was killed in action, aged 24, on 6 November 1917. (Courtesy of Irene Morley)

Five

Microcosm No More - the forces for change

ST MARTIN AND THE MOTOR CAR

In St Martin, as in the rest of western Europe, the turn of the century saw muscle, sweat and wind-power giving way to heat and hydrocarbons.

56   Quieter days. A pony and trap on La Grande Route de Rozel. (John Le Seelleur Collection)

There will always be many arguments as to which concept has had the most effect on human life in the 20th century, but it would be a stern and pernickety historian who would deny that 'internal combustion' was, literally, the engine of the developments that made the century now ending the most dynamic in the history of the world.

As the 19th century turned into the 20th, St Martinais would not have seen too many differences from conditions observed by their ancestors, one hundred years before. True, the train had come to Gorey; steam-driven tank engines reversing out of town at the head of rakes of clattering carriages that promised, at the St Helier terminal at Snow Hill, to convey the traveller to the horse races (held on what is now the Royal Jersey golf links), to Paris or even to Moscow! There were

even steam-driven vessels sitting on the mud of Gorey harbour waiting for the tide (presumably to provide the second phase in that journey from St Helier, via Carteret, to imperial Russia), but inland, road vehicles and the plough still relied almost entirely on equine and human muscle.

The first motor car powered by a fuming internal combustion engine to turn a tyre on Jersey's roads did so in 1899. It is reported to have been a Benz imported by a solicitor who lived in St John; very soon others followed. Of what makes these were is a matter of surmise since many motor carriages of those days were bought as a kit of parts and assembled by blacksmiths or even shipbuilders. Petrol (where it was available) was sold over the counter at pharmacies. What these motor cars certainly did was raise a lot of dust, since metalled roads were unknown. As the century turned, the number of motor vehicles could still be counted in dozens, rather than hundreds, but by the outbreak of global war in 1914, there were some five hundred motor vehicles on Jersey's roads and the car was already starting to exert the fascination and appeal it has yet to lose.

As a primarily agrarian community with few main highways, the motor car came rather more genteelly to St Martin than to the more populous communities that surround it. But nevertheless it came. Parishioners could hardly have welcomed a device that so clearly would frighten horses, cause cattle to miscarry and generally disturb the peaceful countryside. That the motor vehicle could one day replace the horse as the driving engine of the farming community would have caused many a sardonic chuckle in the public bar of the *Royal Hotel.*

Drink-driving (and licensing) laws were unknown at the turn of the century and a motorist who might have indulged in a pot of porter too many was just another hazard along the St Martin's byways, along with runaway horses and straying cows. Furthermore, since a terrifying din always preceded him, the merry motorist gave ample warning of his approach.

In 1908 the Jersey Motor Association was founded along similar lines to the Automobile Association (AA) which had been founded in Britain three years before. The JMA published its own highway code including such helpful suggestions as keeping to the left and overtaking on the right!

58 *A Spyker Landaulette c.1906 at Rosel Manor. Its owner, Seigneur R.R. Lemprière, was one of the first to pay a parking fine in St Helier. (John Le Seelleur Collection)*

A prominent St Martinais, HM Viscount R.R. Lemprière, Seigneur of Rosel, was fined in 1912 for leaving his car unattended for the better part of a day in the now defunct Royal Court Road. He maintained that the road was private and refused to pay the fine. The Connétable of St Helier, Mr. J.E. Pinel, agreed to reduce his fine to a third, the princely sum of five shillings; under the *Loi d'Encombrement des Routes,* the road actually being owned by the States (hence not private) and under the terms of the *Loi*, it was forbidden for anyone to allow 'a charette which he drives to stand in the streets of St Helier'. The Seigneur further argued that his car was not a 'charette' since that was a two-wheeled horse-drawn vehicle! The Connétable retorted that as far as he was concerned the term 'charette' applied to any vehicle. The Viscount, having – typically for a St Martinais – put up a good fight against parting with his money, duly paid his five shillings.

Like the aeroplane, the motor vehicle came of age during the First World War. This conflict was hardly visible in St Martin, the few Germans who were incarcerated in Jersey being behind wire erected on Les Blanches Banques on the other side of the Island and, while the occasional Zeppelin was noted, its presence high in the skies owed much more to its being blown mightily off course than any evil intent towards the Islanders.

After the war, the popularity of the car increased dramatically. As today, prices of both cars and petrol were cheaper than in the United Kingdom, and by the onset of the Second World War there were 11,000 motor vehicles in the Island. Despite this upsurge in popularity, St Martin managed to keep motoring with just one petrol forecourt, at St Martin's Garage in La Grande Route de Faldouet, as indeed it does to this very day.

Jersey's first motor bus appeared in 1910 and plied between St Helier and St Aubin. The Jersey Motor Transport Company began operations in 1923 and within six years had seen off the Jersey Eastern Railway, severing the Parish's iron road link with the Island's capital.

Until the 1920s and before the widespread use of tarmacadam, the Parish's roads were surfaced with broken stone and gravel flattened by a steam roller, the labour actually being provided by the Parish's ratepayers!

With the widespread use of the car came also the lorry and the farm tractor. However, farmers and growers tended to accept commercial vehicles rather more slowly than they did the car and, right up until the Second World War, the horse was still widely used for ploughing and taking the produce to St Helier. That the horse needed little guidance in front of the plough and knew the way home from the *Terminus Hotel* at the Weighbridge might have had something to do with it!

Things, of course, were turned upside down when, on 1 July 1940, German forces landed in the Channel Islands; the enemy was not only at the door, he had opened it and come inside. Within months of the Occupation, public transport was largely suspended and private cars had either been commandeered or were laid up for lack of spares and, very soon, lack of petrol. The Germans, indefatigable builders, 'recreated' the Jersey Eastern Railway with a 60cm narrow gauge line that followed most of the original JER route to Gorey, although they actually extended the track along the bulwarks to the top of the pier. Branch lines near the Parish boundary darted off into Les Maltières quarry and on to the Royal Jersey's hallowed golf links from where the *Organisation Todt* extracted most of the sand they used in the concrete to build their bunkers all around the Island.

Although there were relatively few vehicles on the roads, driving immediately became hazardous as the Germans soon insisted on everyone driving on the right, introduced their own alien road signs, and were themselves, by all accounts, not the best of drivers.

Compared with some of the parishes St Martin was relatively lightly fortified and, for once, the occupying forces, not noted elsewhere for their sensitivity towards ancient monuments, treated the venerable pile of Mont Orgueil with a modicum of consideration, creating only two observation towers at its summit which, today, are as familiar as old friends. And, of course, they happened to leave behind the powerful searchlights that first enabled the castle to be floodlit.

The Occupation also witnessed the unwelcome introduction of armoured vehicles rumbling around the Island's roads, although most were little Renault tanks dating back to the early 1930s and looked rather more fearsome than they actually were. However, they did batter the road surfaces and hedgerows and generally leave a trail of debris in their wake.

Jersey's love affair with the motor car really began immediately after the Liberation, as soon as the manufacturers were able to gear themselves up for peaceful production. In 1946 7,682 cars, trucks and motorcycles were taxed in the Island. Just two years later this number had grown to 12,202, including 75 buses, 100 coaches and 101 tractors! This number had doubled by 1961, doubled again by 1971 and doubled again by 1998. Today, if you count all motor vehicles including fork lifts and other such oddities, they actually outnumber the population by several hundred!

There was no formal speed limit in Jersey until the early 1960s when the now ubiquitous 40 m.p.h. was introduced. Today speed limits of 40, 30, 20 and 15 m.p.h. abound, depending on 'how green is your roadway'. St Martin has its fair share of Green Lanes where the pedestrian and the cyclist have the right of way.

Driving tests were introduced in the mid-'30s; until then licences were granted on application although some parishes insisted on the applicant driving a parish official 'around the block' to prove that he or she at least knew where the steering wheel and brakes were!

The first road traffic law seems to have been *La Loi sur la Circulation d'Automobiles* promulgated in 1935. This has subsequently led to a plethora of legislation covering every aspect of motoring, from how big the digits on a number plate must be to how and when you can or cannot use a mobile 'phone. Incidentally the law which dictates what makes a vehicle roadworthy or otherwise – the 1956 *Construction and Use Order,* and which was still in being in 1999 – banned the use of flushing toilets in motor cars but did allow colour television!

With some of the Island's most attractive countryside, St Martin inevitably attracts much visitor traffic, particularly around the narrow lanes above St Catherine and Rozel. With, at peak season, up to 4,000 hire cars on the road, the Parish could be forgiven for regarding the motor vehicle with awe and even trepidation. The reality is a little different. St Martin copes with the motor car very well and even featured on two of the six commemorative Jersey stamps devoted to the motor car (remembering that the artist had all 12 parishes to choose from) which were released in 1992. The 28p stamp showed a 1924 Chenard et Walcker T5 near St Catherine and the 33p stamp a 1932 Packard 900 Series Light Eight on the Parish's north-east coast.

59 *1992 stamp issue. In the background is Archirondel Cottage and St Catherine's Breakwater. (Courtesy of Jersey Post Office)*

Like it or loathe it, the motor car is likely to be a feature of the Parish for some time to come. Whether today's internal combustion engine, which relies on a diminishing resource, will be ousted by the electric motor remains to be seen. It appears that the number of electrically driven vehicles in Jersey at the millennium will in reality be few more than at the time of writing. Electric power will probably be confined to milk floats and a very few experimental vehicles, since the cost of batteries is unlikely to have come down sufficiently for the electric car to be a viable alternative. The perceived wisdom is that it could well be at least one hundred years before battery technology will be advanced sufficiently for the cost and efficiency of the electric fuel cell to approach that of the internal combustion engine. Indeed, the State of California, which had once decreed 'zero emissions by the year 2000', with the implication that only electric vehicles would be permitted in the state from the millennium onwards, have modified that dictum to 10 per cent of the vehicles in the state being electrically driven by the year 2010.

There is a growing school of thought that the future lies not with electric power – which had already been abandoned in the early 1900s when an electric propelled vehicle actually held the World Land Speed Record – but with the refinement of the internal combustion engine to burn liquid petroleum gas (rather than other petroleum derivatives like petrol and diesel oil) or wood-alcohol. This would then be used to drive a dynamo which in turn would drive an electric motor to be used in urban conditions, where speed and range are not major requirements, but reverting to direct drive from the internal combustion unit on the 'open road'.

60   Le Mont de Gouray, 1896
and 1999. Many Islanders now
feel that Jersey's roads are over-
burdened with traffic signs. (top:
Courtesy of Société Jersiaise
Photographic Archive, Jersey;
bottom: Chris Blackstone)

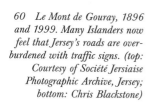

The advantages of this hybrid system are that it does not rely on battery technology, offers the prospect of low emissions (negligible in towns) and relatively low unit and running costs while maintaining the range and performance that the modern motorist demands, even if he, as in Jersey, never gets to use it. Perhaps the greatest advantage of all is that the concept is being developed by the multinational fuel companies who will, whatever we might like to think, actually determine, even in St Martin, what the future holds for the motor car.

Anyone interested in the history of the car in Jersey is recommended to read *The Motor Car in Jersey* by David Scott Warren (Seaflower Books) which chronicles not only the growth in popularity of the car, but describes the work of the Motor Traffic Office and the local motor trade in considerable detail. However, it does not often mention St Martin!

THE BUS FAMILY SLADE

The history of the Slade family between the mid-19th and mid-20th centuries epitomises the kind of industry which has given St Martin its special character: that special mix of vigorous enterprise and staunch individualism which has been such a feature of this Parish over hundreds of years.

Three places were special to the Slades: El Hassa, the family home, and the two Methodist chapels in the parish, St Martin's Wesleyan and the small chapel on Les Landes Hill, now a private house. Against this background of ardent Methodism lies the interesting story of a very special scarifier, and a successful fleet of buses.

Edward Slade was born in Somerset in 1834 and in 1860 married a young St Martin girl named Mary Ann Richardson, whose family had moved to Southampton in the 1850s. Edward

61 Edward Slade and the patented scarifier which he designed and built at El Hassa. (Courtesy of Jayn Johnson)

62   The first of Slade's buses. It has an ingenious home-built body on a Ford Model-T chassis. (Courtesy of Jayn Johnson)

and his new wife maintained contact with the Island and in 1875 their son, also named Edward, came to St Martin as a young boy of 14 to live with some Jersey relations, Jean Ferey and his family, who worked as blacksmiths at La Forge.

Clearly young Edward was a man of enterprise and independence, for in 1886 he bought the house now known as El Hassa and pursued his trade as a blacksmith in the forge at the back of the house. In 1889, he married a St Martin girl named Mary Elizabeth Noël. Edward's skills as a blacksmith were soon to develop beyond that of routine trade into the world of engineering and invention, and in the early years of the new century he produced a scarifier patented to his own design.

Before we can pursue the history of the scarifier we must turn to what must have been the real centre of the young couple's life, which was their involvement with the religious and social life of the Methodist community in St Martin.

By the latter half of the 19th century, much of the hostility which had surrounded noncon-formism in its early years had disappeared and many of our finest Methodist chapels were built at this time, St Martin's Wesleyan in 1850 and the first Les Landes Chapel in 1883. When the new chapel was opened in 1908 it soon became a much-loved centre for the religious and social life of many Parish Methodists. A charming letter to the *J.E.P.* written in 1980 by Linda L. Noël, a Slade cousin, reveals the pleasure gained from being a part of this evidently close-knit religious community.

> My mother, a true Christian, attended this place of worship for practically her whole life, being at one time a relief organist and also a trustee. She sent us to Sunday school regu-larly in the afternoons for 2 o'clock and this was followed by a service in the chapel at 3 o'clock till 4. We also went to service with her in the evenings and we enjoyed it all as we did not go far in those days.
>
> How we loved going to the practices for the anniversary services which were so well attended! For a time, Philip Le Gresley was the organist and after day-school we would gather at St Agatha, where he lived with his parents, and kind-hearted Mrs. Le Gresley would regale us with a lovely tea before we practised our 'action' songs.
>
> At a later time, Edward and George Slade [Edward Slade's two sons] came to help in practising the hymns with a willing band of helpers from St Martin's Wesleyenne.

For Edward Slade senior, however, and for many others of the Methodist community, this evident warmth and comradeship was not without an underlying sense of injustice at the fact that

63 A Slade bus at St Catherine in 1938. The Slade timetable advertised 'All our drivers are total abstainers'. (Stanley Barnard Collection)

parish rates were (and still are) used in part for the direct upkeep of the Established Church. A matter of principle was involved and a principled stand was their response. In 1907, with the full support of the Reverend G.T. Allpress, Edward Slade decided to withhold payment of his parish rates.

As might have been expected, his action proved unsuccessful, and in March 1907, Edward was ordered by the Petty Debts Court to pay the full amount of rates plus costs; and here our story might have ended had it not been for a most revealing account of the aftermath, recorded with an appropriate touch of drama, in the *Evening Post* of 5 April 1907.

As Edward Slade was a parish centenier, it must have been a curious scene indeed when the Constable, Mr. C. Perchard, along with an officer of the court, arrived at El Hassa to auction goods to the amount of the parish rate. A number of articles had been placed under arrest, among them a pony, a small pony chaise and, of course, Edward Slade's newly patented scarifier.

In the event, the auction appears to have become little more that a formality; one of Edward's Methodist colleagues, Mr. J. Renouf, made a bid corresponding exactly to the amount due for rates and costs. The auctioneer immediately closed the bidding on that amount being reached.

Whether Mr. Renouf returned the scarifier to Edward Slade is not recorded, but they were clearly in sympathy. Mr. Renouf, had made his position on the matter clear to all: 'When I go cycling on a Sunday, I do not expect the church folk to pay for the repairs to my tyres and consequently I do not think that I ought to be called upon to pay for the expense of their services.' Edward Slade and his friends had made their point and, in the words of the *Evening Post* chronicler: 'The proceedings, which had lasted but a few minutes, terminated at 11.15, and the forge at El Hassa quickly resumed its normal appearance.'

In 1890, Edward's son – another Edward – had been born, and it was natural with a family background of innovation and engineering skills that the younger Edward should engage himself in the rapidly developing world of motor transport. It is for the formation of his bus company that Edward Slade junior will be remembered.

His first move was to turn the blacksmith's forge at El Hassa into a garage. He then acquired a Model-T Ford chassis on which were constructed two open rows of seats covered, rather

64 *The Slade bus garage on La Grande Route de Faldouet, decorated for the coronation of King George VI in 1937. (Stanley Barnard Collection)*

appealingly, by a canvas roof with side curtains. Other vehicles soon followed, including Morris Commercials, and, by the end of 1934, two massive Dennis Lancet 36-seaters and a number of newer Morris Commercials.

His first route, which began operation in 1923, was from St Helier (Minden Place) to Greencliffe via St Martin's Church. By 1934 Edward Slade was operating three routes: to Faldouet via La Hougue Bie, to Archirondel via St Martin's Church and to Rozel via Greencliffe. In addition, a cross-country service operated during the summer months from Gorey Village to Plémont via the north coast, these coaches being named Waverley Tours.

The family's Methodist principles had not been forgotten: intending passengers were able to take courage from a notice which appeared in the Slade's Bus timetable reading: 'All our drivers are total abstainers.'

The splendid 1937 photograph shows the Slade Bus Depot decorated for the coronation, with five buses proudly on display. This depot, which can still be glimpsed from the road, was built on the field immediately opposite El Hassa, the same field in which Edward's father had shown off his patented scarifier.

The German Occupation brought about some minor changes, with the rule of the road altered from left to right and passengers picked up and set down in the middle of the road, but otherwise Edward Slade was able to operate his bus company much as before.

As petrol supplies became an increasing problem, some buses were converted to run on a French system using charcoal for fuel. The effectiveness of the system was often severely tested; parishioners have fond memories of getting off the bus to ensure its successful ascent of St Saviour's Hill, and on one occasion a Slade Dennis Lancet hit the headlines when it caught fire while ascending this same hill on Route 3.

With the end of the Occupation came the end of the Slade Bus Service and the end of our story. In 1946 it was announced that Slade's Blue and White Bus Service was to be taken over by the Jersey Motor Transport Company, an event which took place on 1 May 1946. Gone but not forgotten, Slade's individualistic bus services are still remembered with affection by the older members of St Martin's Parish.

65 *Successor to Slade's. A double-decker of Jersey Motor Transport at Gorey Pier in the 1960s. (Stanley Barnard Collection)*

TOURISM AND ST MARTIN

St Martin still boasts an unrivalled coastline, an extensive network of beautiful green lanes (the whole of the vingtaine of Quéruée being so designated) and, in Gorey, the Island's definitive tourist image. The Parish has remained largely unspoiled by the development of tourism in the 19th and 20th centuries, and this must be a matter of pride to all St Martinais.

In part, it has been the result of comparative isolation, a quiet seclusion even more apparent to 19th-century tourists who were inclined to describe the north-east coast of St Martin with an almost Wordsworthian rapture. One such, a gentleman with the superb name of Octavius Rooke, has left us with a vivid picture of the Parish as it must have appeared to an English visitor in 1856.

By then, steamships had revolutionised sea travel to and from the Island and it is from this period that the importance of Jersey's tourism industry developed. Steam packets carrying mail travelled from Southampton to Jersey and Guernsey every Monday, Wednesday and Friday; there was a weekly steamer from Plymouth and, in 1856, the first of the steam packets from Weymouth.

Having arrived by steamer from Plymouth and settled into his St Helier lodging, Rooke and his companion set about exploring the Island, making their way on foot along the coast to Gorey. First impressions were not favourable; the 'tidy looking inns' along the harbour did not match up to their expectations, offering them 'the most indigestible and scanty fare'; however, the Castle delighted Rooke, and he notes an early tourist concession at the castle gate: 'Here you may purchase books of sea-weed and other little things made by the hands of charity and sold for the support of schools.'

It was the coast to the north of the castle which was to provide Rooke and his companion with their greatest pleasure: 'Few people coming to the Island see this part, there being no carriage road; and generally our modern tourists seem only to arrive, glance at and depart.'

The little road which ran north from the castle past Petit Portelet eventually brought Rooke to Geoffrey's Leap and Anne Port and a view which remains virtually unchanged:

> Standing upon this rock, we look around and see a happy combination of natural charms:
> a clear blue sky, a clear blue sea, grey rocks gold-tinted with over-creeping lichens, cliffs

66 Cantell's British Hotel *and* Mont Orgueil Hotel *in 1895. At around this time, Gorey Pier also boasted the* Elphine Hotel, *the* Taunton Inn, *Marshall's Cadena Tea Rooms, Stevens' Eastern Railway Tearooms and the* Temperance Hotel. *(Courtesy of Société Jersiaise Photographic Archive, Jersey)*

covered with greensward, and tangled briers on which the ripe and luscious blackberries cling; here, reared against the sky, are leafy clumps of picturesquely stemmed trees; and there, beneath, is Saint Catherine's Bay, with smooth shiny pebbles glistening through the transparent waves. Beyond, stretching out its strong protecting arm, there is a Pier of massive stone, which gives shelter to the ships that here may harbour.

Rooke followed the narrow road down to Anne Port Bay, where it petered out to little more than a footpath leading up to La Crête Point, and it was with difficulty that he and his companion made their way through the orchards and open fields above La Crête down to the new road above Archirondel which had been constructed as an approach to the breakwater:

After a brief rest the shady lanes again give us their shelter, till at last they guide us to the north-eastern promontory of the island, called La Coupe. 'To the left hand, Monsieur, et vous trouverez les ruines that the Druides make,' a countryman informs us. And on a cliff called La Couperon, a few yards off, we find some stones that were, according to our friend, made ruins by the Druids.

Eventually, after scrambling through a tangled mass of shrubs, they reached Rozel, 'nestling with its pretty bay beneath its fort; some half-dozen boats are lying there at anchor, the very picture of repose. Here ends our walk; for the carriage road is gained (La Grande Route de Rozel) and your vehicle can meet you.'

Rooke's account is typical of many tourist guides produced around this time written by English tourists for English readers; all stress the quiet and charm of the Parish, even if facilities for travellers were occasionally less than civilised. A description of the horse-drawn omnibus service which enabled visitors to tour the country parishes on 'the great round' is provided in *Stanford's Guide* for 1868 and reminds us that unruly behaviour is not the sole preserve of the 20th century: 'The conductor of the vehicle was the chief instigator of mischief on each occasion, by encouraging the disorderly among the passengers to pelt each other with stolen fruit, to tear down the branches of the trees, and insult the peaceable owners and other inhabitants.'

No doubt the lanes of St Martin offered excellent opportunities for some of its more exuberant visitors.

St Martin's most celebrated visitor was the novelist George Eliot. An extensive account of her visit in May 1857 (with her companion, George Lewes) can be found in the Société Jersiaise

67 *Jersey holiday-makers off to France: the sailing of the* Cotentin *from Gorey'. In this picture from the* Illustrated London News *of 18 August 1894, the travellers are well equipped, with brass band instruments and long jacks.* (Illustrated London News)

68 *French tourists at Mont Orgueil, by 'Mars', 1890.*

Annual Bulletin for 1978, and it includes a vivid description of Gorey Harbour where they stayed with the Amy family of Rose Cottage.

> It was a beautiful moment when we came to our lodgings in Gorey. The orchards were all in blossom – and this is an Island of orchards. They cover the slopes; they stretch before you in shady, grassy, indefinite extent through every other gateway by the roadside; they flourish in some spots almost close to the sea.

Like Rooke, George Eliot and her companion were captivated by the 'exquisite' coastal scenery north of the castle. On one occasion, passing through a St Martin cottage garden, she was agreeably surprised by a woman offering them a bunch of lilac and she then 'brought out a telescope for us to see the coast of France, and was extremely obliging, smiling and good'. Which one of our hospitable St Martinais ancestors so impressed the great novelist we shall never know.

By the end of the 19th century, St Martin could boast a surprisingly wide range of hotels and inns, sufficient to satisfy the increasing numbers of tourists arriving, not just from Southampton and Weymouth, but also from France. The *Cotentin*, steaming regularly from Gorey to Carteret, featured in a superb illustration in the *Illustrated London News* of 1894. The Taverners' Register of Licences for 1883 lists 13 licensed premises in St Martin, including the *Royal Hotel* and the *Rozel Bay Hotel*, which are still with us, and a number of others, such as the *Faldouet Inn* (probably the present Les Grandes Rues), which have long since disappeared. *The Moorings*, then named the *British Hotel*, was also licensed in 1883, as was the *Welcome Home Inn*, the *Elphine* being added in 1887.

During the inter-war years, with the beaches and sea bathing promoted as the Island's principal tourist attractions, the family-run tea room became an important part of the service to visitors,

69   *A picnic party at the* Rozel Bay Hotel *in 1875. (Courtesy of Société Jersiaise Photographic Archive, Jersey)*

and St Martin provided some of the best. Archirondel Cottage, then with a thatched roof, was Perrier's Tea Rooms, run by Miss Le Couteur, while further along the bay, at L'Hôpital, the Robin family served teas on trays for the beach. Two tea rooms served Anne Port, the house opposite the beach, now called Seacroft, and another further towards La Crête, run by Mr. Perchard.

Few of these pre-war establishments exist today, but one, Jeffrey's Leap Café, has survived not just the war but also the prospect of total collapse into the bay. Archirondel may have lost Perrier's but has more than made up for the loss with the excellent Driftwood Café, while the pre-war tea rooms at St Catherine's Breakwater, run by Mrs. Amy and Mrs. Marett, have been superseded by the present very popular café. What every one of these establishments provided was service and courtesy and each in its own small way has added to the tourist appeal of the Parish.

Only four licensed premises, *The Castle Green, The Royal, Les Arches* and the *Welcome Inn,* remained open during the Occupation.

The post-war period has seen dramatic changes in the Island's character and topography, some of the worst being the over-development of headlands and bays. St Martin has avoided this trend and has built on its strengths rather than plundered them; the creation of *Château La Chaire Hotel* is one example.

The original La Chaire property was built in the early 19th century by the celebrated botanist Samuel Curtis, who established the beautiful 10-acre grounds and gardens which surround the present hotel. Curtis died in 1860, and he and his daughter Harriet are both buried in St Martin's churchyard. Towards the end of the 19th century, the property was acquired by a Mr. Fletcher, who pulled down Curtis's house and built the present one in its place, a grand house with marble floors and its own private ballroom.

In 1932, La Chaire was bought by Mr. A.V. Nicolle who restored the gardens to their full splendour, but for the period of the German Occupation it remained empty with only one gardener in charge. It was in the years immediately following the war that Major and Mrs. Henry Wigram changed its use to that of an hotel and, apart from a brief period as a private residence, so it has remained, providing the Parish with a fine establishment.

No less important to the life of the Parish has been *Les Arches Hotel* at Archirondel. *Les Arches* was first licensed in 1927, but it is the present modern hotel which, under the generous guidance of Renzo Martin, has provided the Parish not just with an excellent tourist facility but also, for many local groups, an attractive community centre which has done much to ensure the unity of parish life.

It would have been easy in the last two decades for the Parish to have lost, through careless over-development, much of the unspoilt charm which Octavius Rooke celebrated in 1856. It has not and some of the credit for this must go to the Parish's administration. In fact, the two most important tourist developments of recent years, the Parish's campsites, have added considerably to the appeal of a holiday in St Martin.

Beuvelande Campsite, established in 1965 by Stanley and Christine De La Haye, has grown from its initial 300 visitors to over 2,500 in 1998, becoming an AA 4-Pennant Deluxe site and winning Britain's Best Parks Award. Rozel Camping Park, run by John and Joan and David and Heather Germain, was opened in 1975 and developed out of a long-established practice of occasionally allowing visitors to use the farm's fields as a site to pitch tents. Both of these very successful enterprises have made creative use of the Parish's natural amenities rather than abusing them.

Six

The German Occupation 1940-1945

The purpose of this chapter is to describe how the years of Occupation affected the Parish of St Martin. However, as the new millennium begins, many younger people may not know the details of how this desperate period affected the whole Island ...

THE ISLAND'S STORY

The events of the spring and early summer of 1940, when the German forces swept across north-west Europe, by-passing the much vaunted Maginot Line, could hardly have been foreseen in the years immediately preceding the outbreak of war, although many thought that another war with Germany was inevitable. Nor, it appears, were those events generally foreseen much closer to the months in which they occurred. Tucked away safely behind the fleet and the Maginot Line, Jersey, too insignificant to be bombed, was said to be 'the safest place on earth', and as late as March 1940 Jersey was advertised in the English papers as 'the ideal resort for wartime holidays this summer'.

That was written during the period of the so-called 'phoney war' which ended abruptly with the invasion of Belgium, the subsequent evacuation of the British Expeditionary Force from Dunkirk, and the fall of France. Jersey no longer possessed the strategic importance it had enjoyed in the 18th and 19th centuries when the traditional enemy had been France. Indeed Jersey had been the object of attempted French invasions over several centuries.

It had long been recognised that Mont Orgueil and Elizabeth Castle, impregnable though they might have been to the weaponry of those times, could not defend the whole of the Island's coastline and General Henry Seymour Conway, who was appointed Governor of Jersey in 1792 and who had studied the art of fortification, began the project of building Jersey's coastal towers. Later, in the 1840s, the construction of St Catherine's harbour commenced, ostensibly as a 'harbour of refuge' for merchant shipping, but in reality as an anchorage close to France for the British Navy. The works were never completed and only a small section of the second breakwater from Archirondel exists in a rudimentary state.

Those 19th-century works had, of course, become obsolete as defensive fortifications and the decision not to attempt to defend the Channel Islands after the fall of France must have been the correct one. However, Jersey still had a minor role to play before the islands were surrendered and formal demilitarisation took place. After the Dunkirk evacuation, some British forces had been sent to France to try to stem the German advance, but when France surrendered it became necessary to bring back those forces as soon as possible. On 16 June the Bailiff of Jersey,

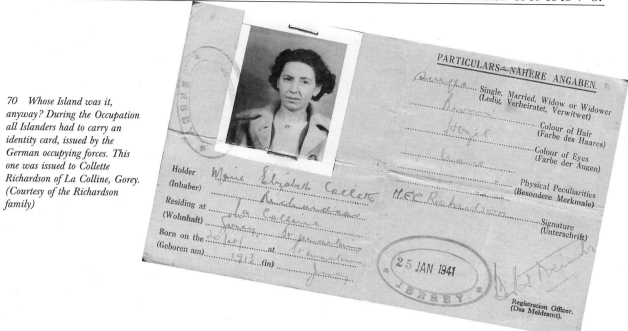

70 *Whose Island was it, anyway? During the Occupation all Islanders had to carry an identity card, issued by the German occupying forces. This one was issued to Collette Richardson of La Colline, Gorey. (Courtesy of the Richardson family)*

Alexander Coutanche (later knighted and subsequently created Jersey's first life peer), asked the Commodore of the St Helier Yacht Club to send as many yachts as possible to assist evacuation of the troops from St Malo. In total, 18 yachts made the passage to St Malo and spent three days ferrying British troops to Jersey. All the yachts returned safely. The decision to demilitarise the Island had effectively been taken in London on 16 June. On 18 June, Jurat Dorey (of Jersey but also representing the Bailiwick of Guernsey) met Home Office officials in London. The formal decision not to defend the islands was taken by the War Cabinet on 19 June and on that day the Bailiff inserted a notice in the *Evening Post* announcing this decision. The Home Secretary agreed that the civilian populations should be permitted to leave if they wished to do so and this informa-tion was telephoned to the islands. In a meeting of the States of Jersey on 20 June, Jurat Dorey said that 'English people might wish to leave but he could not understand why those of old Norman stock who should be rooted to the soil were so anxious to get out'.

The Bailiff, the Crown Officers and the Jurats said that they would remain in their posts and the Bailiff addressed a large gathering in the Royal Square, saying that the duty of the people was to stay calm. That correct advice was easier to give than to follow; Islanders were given very little time in which to make the heart-rending decision to leave or to remain and face an unknown future. The evacuation of those who wished to leave proceeded over the next few days, but most people decided to remain. Cruickshank attributes this to the strength of will of the Bailiff. 'Coutanche firmly grasped the nettle and was never in any doubt as to the proper course. After the initial panic he succeeded in imposing his will on the people. He thought that most should remain, and remain they did. There is little doubt that if he had come to the conclusion that all should go the great majority would have left.' Leslie Sinel's *Occupation Diary* records: 'June 26. Potatoes are being shipped again, but we view the future with anxiety'. That anxiety was fully justified.

The Germans had realised before their invasion of Poland that it might be necessary to occupy the Channel Islands as part of their general strategy, and the need to do so became apparent as their forces moved through France. In June 1940 there was uncertainty as to whether the islands were to be defended, since the demilitarisation decision was not then known to the

71 *Desperate times. The beaches which had been enjoyed by generations of Jersey families for both work and play were now a no-go zone. The 'regrettable incident' occurred at Fliquet Bay when a girl of six stepped on a landmine, after she had been low-water fishing with her family. This notice was published in the* Jersey Evening Post *of 12 March 1941. (Anthony Paines Collection)*

enemy. Aerial reconnaissance showed that in the harbour areas of Jersey and Guernsey there were long columns of lorries which the Germans thought showed the presence of troops to strengthen the islands' defences. In fact, the lorries were carrying potatoes in Jersey and tomatoes in Guernsey. A bombing raid on Jersey and Guernsey was made on 28 June to ascertain whether the strength of retaliation indicated that the islands were, or were not, to be defended. In Jersey, 11 people were killed in this raid, nine were injured and damage was sustained by buildings near the harbour. The uncertainty was not wholly resolved, but on 1 July a Luftwaffe pilot carrying out a routine reconnaissance landed at Guernsey airport. His report that the airport was completely deserted convinced the German command that the islands were not to be defended.

The Occupation of Jersey began with a message, addressed to the Chief of the Military and Civil Authorities, dropped at the airfield early on the morning of 1 July. The message called upon the Island to surrender and to signify surrender by displaying white flags and painting white crosses in prominent positions, one of which was Royal Square. That afternoon a German force arrived at the airport and the Bailiff, accompanied by the Crown Officers, surrendered the Island to the enemy.

So began five years of occupation. The duration of the Occupation and the situation of the Island when Germany (as many then thought likely) won the war could not be predicted. Restrictions on movement and commerce were imposed immediately by Orders of the German Commandant issued on 1 July. Further restrictions were imposed the following day, including an order that 'It is forbidden to listen to any Wireless Transmitting Stations, except German and German controlled Stations'. It is difficult to understand why the Germans, then in a victorious position, thought it necessary to impose such restrictions on information from other sources. In June 1942 it was ordered that all wireless sets belonging to the civilian population were to be handed in to the occupying forces. Many Islanders did not obey that order and secretly listened to broadcasts from England at the risk of severe penalties if their breach of the order was detected.

The most pressing problem for the Island during the Occupation was food, since, although Jersey had exported agricultural products to England, it had been dependent upon imports from

England for other foods. Potatoes could no longer be exported and the Department of Agriculture ordered that four-fifths of the potato land should be sown with corn. The old watermills were brought into use to grind the corn. Sugar beet was planted to provide sugar and a purchasing office was established at Grouville, since France was now the only source of imports. Food rationing was introduced and remained in operation throughout the Occupation. Fishing was restricted, boats being allowed to go only one mile offshore unescorted and two miles with an escort. For a time in September 1940 fishing was banned entirely because of a successful escape, and when the ban was lifted fishing was only allowed out of St Helier. After three escapes, another ban was imposed in August 1943 until security provisions could be strengthened.

A black market flourished, partly supplied by the crews of vessels travelling between Jersey and France who smuggled in goods which could easily be concealed. Barter shops in which goods could be exchanged were established and auction sales became popular. Both these forms of economic activity came to be restricted. Rationed goods were banned from barter shops and newspaper advertisements. At auction sales, certain goods could not be sold at above the controlled price, and later the sale by auction of many goods, including foods, clothing, tobacco and pigs, goats, hens and rabbits was prohibited. By the end of 1944, when all supplies from France were cut off and shortages were becoming serious, all auction sales were banned.

Fuel shortages also became a problem after supplies of coal from Britain became unavailable. Some coal was imported from France, but fuel rationing was introduced. In 1942 the gas supply was cut off at 8 p.m. so many people had to spend their evenings in darkness. The Jersey Department of Labour employed gangs to fell trees for firewood.

Civilian transport was taken under military control and the use of motor cars was restricted to essential uses such as agriculture and milk distribution. The petrol shortage became acute and vehicles of more than 12 h.p. were taken off the roads in 1942.

Fortification of the Islands began in October 1941. Hitler feared that the British might try to recapture the islands for political reasons and ordered that they be made impregnable. This required a large labour force. First, unemployed French labour was brought in, then Spaniards who had been forced to leave Spain at the end of the Civil War, then East Europeans and 1,000 Russian prisoners-of-war. These last were half-starved by their captors and caused a great deal of trouble by getting out of their camps at night and stealing food and even newly-planted potatoes. Finally, men from North Africa arrived. The total number of imported workmen is not known, but one German contractor alone had more than 7,000 men on his pay-roll. The fortification of the islands required not only a very large construction force and vast quantities of materials and weapons but also a large number of troops to man the defences. A German infantry division was kept in the Channel Islands for the whole of the war to defend territory which the British never intended to try to win back.

Some collaboration between Islanders and the occupying forces took place. Some young girls produced illegitimate children with German fathers and some Islanders informed on neighbours who were breaking regulations by, for example, retaining illicit wireless sets. No resistance movement developed as in some other occupied territories. The Island was too small and too heavily filled with German troops for resistance and sabotage to be feasible. The Island authorities necessarily engaged in passive co-operation with the German authorities to the extent that was required to protect the population. There were several escapes and attempted escapes from the Island, some of which ended in deaths by drowning. The number of escapes increased after the Allied invasion of France and the liberation of the adjacent coasts.

News of the use of the 'V' sign in other occupied territories as a gesture of defiance reached Jersey through radio broadcasts and 'V' signs began to appear, to the great annoyance of the Germans who regarded them as sabotage. Later on, in the winter of 1944-45, a stonemason, John Le Guyader, who was re-laying paving stones in Royal Square laid some of them in the shape of a 'V'. Fortunately for Mr. Le Guyader the Germans did not discover this. After the Liberation, the letters 'EGA' and the date 1945 were added to commemorate the Red Cross ship *Vega* which brought food parcels to Jersey in that last hard winter of the war.

In September 1941 the first steps were taken to deport to Germany Jersey residents of British origin. This action was a reprisal, ordered by Hitler, against British action, far away from Jersey, to intern German citizens working in Iran. The Germans made repeated requests for information about British-born residents of Jersey. The numbers, ascertained with great difficulty, showed that the British-born population of Jersey then consisted of 2,733 men over 18 years of age, 2,391 women over 18 and 213 boys and 189 girls under 18. Further investigations revealed a total of 8,166 British-born residents in all the Channel Islands. There was also an instruction that a list should be prepared of all Iranian nationals living in Jersey and, surprisingly, one such person was identified. Hitler wished the deportations to be of a punitive nature, with deportees, including prominent British citizens, being sent to the Pripet Marshes and their property being redistributed amongst Jerseymen of French origin. The proceedings were protracted, and it was not until September of the following year (1942) that the deportations took place. A total of 1,326 people were taken to Germany, most of them for the remainder of the war. Some old and infirm people were returned to Jersey and, as a result of negotiations between the British and German governments (through Switzerland as the protecting power), about 100 Islanders were sent to the United Kingdom on medical grounds in 1944. Further deportations from the islands took place in January 1943 in reprisal for a Commando raid on Sark. (The deportees included the husband of the Dame of Sark, an American by birth who had adopted British citizenship.) Conditions in the internment camps were bad at first, with poor food and inadequate heating, but they later improved.

The worst period of the Occupation for inhabitants of the Island, and for the occupying troops and prisoners, followed the Allied landings in Normandy on 6 June 1944. Islanders could hear the sound of gunfire from the fighting in the Cotentin peninsula and see the smoke from burning towns and villages and they expected soon to be freed. By the middle of August all the adjacent coasts of France had been retaken by Allied forces but for 10 months more the fortress of Jersey remained in German hands and Jerseymen endured the strange experience of being besieged by the British fleet. The ships kept out of range of the guns, but nothing could get in or out of the islands, the intention being to starve the garrison into surrender.

Soon after the D-Day landings, it became obvious to the Germans that the Allied Forces intended to by-pass the islands, but they still wished to maintain their garrisons. How could the troops and the population be fed if supplies from France could not be sustained? Steps were taken

72   D-Day, 6 June 1944. 'The Germans buzzing like multitudinous swarms of bees.' Edmund Blampied illustration from Jersey in Jail, *written by Horace Wyatt. (Courtesy of The Blampied Trustees)*

to reduce the population whilst access to the French ports was still possible. In July, construction workers were taken off the islands because no more building materials would be available to them, and it was proposed that the entire civilian population should be evacuated, except those working on the land and contributing to the production of food. Hitler prevaricated in making a decision about evacuation whilst the shipping routes were still open. By the beginning of September, practically no supplies could be brought in by sea and attempts to drop supplies from aircraft were limited by lack of suitable drop equipment as the islands' airports were too small for the size of aircraft required to bring in supplies. Hitler reluctantly agreed that the British Government should be approached, through the protecting power, and told that food supplies for the civilian population were exhausted and that the German government was willing to permit British ships either to remove civilians or to bring in food.

The British Chiefs of Staff and the Home Office were in favour of the food supply alternative. They thought it would be wrong to remove Islanders from their homes after they had endured years of Occupation and when Liberation was in sight. However the Prime Minister did not share that opinion. In a minute of 27 September he wrote:

> I am entirely opposed to our sending any rations to the Channel Islands ostensibly for the civilian population but in fact enabling the German garrison to prolong their resistance. I therefore prefer to evacuate the women and children at once … it is no part of our job to feed armed Germans and enable them to prolong their hold on British territory.

But by the time the War Cabinet next met, Mr. Churchill had changed his mind. The German government should be told that so long as they were in occupation they were responsible for feeding the people; if they could not, they should surrender the islands.

73 *After D-Day, the Germans believed that a sea-borne invasion of Jersey could come from the coast of France, and the east coast of the Island was promptly fortified. Guns and soldiers proliferated in St Martin. Gorey Harbourmaster, Mr. Godfray, is addressed by a guard. (Courtesy of Société Jersiaise Photographic Archive, Jersey)*

The food shortage in the islands therefore gave rise to legal as well as practical problems. The Bailiff had sent a memorandum to the Germans in August 1944 stating that 'It is an undisputed maxim of International Law that a military power, which in time of war occupies any part of the inhabited territory of an adversary, is bound to provide for the maintenance of the lives of the civilian population.'

However the German Foreign Ministry was of the opinion that international law did not oblige an occupying force to feed the inhabitants of the occupied territory, and there had been instances where occupied territories were supported from elsewhere. (The United States had provided food to Belgium in the First World War and to Greece in the Second.) The German request that the British should feed or remove the population was, the Ministry believed, in accordance with international law.

Large-scale evacuation of civilians (there were 39,000 in Jersey) had by then become impracticable. Moreover, many of them were employed in producing food and providing other essential services for the German troops as well as for the inhabitants. Hitler ruled that there should be no surrender, nor removal of people from the islands, and an investigation by the Germans showed that there was sufficient food to last until the end of the year. There was political pressure in the House of Commons and in the British newspapers for something to be done to relieve the Channel Islands, but on 23 October the Chiefs of Staff also reported that, even if no food was sent to the islands, the civilian population would be all right until the end of the year; they could survive longer with hardship but without starvation. It was decided that no food supplies should be sent from Britain. However, the situation in the Channel Islands continued to

74   The moment of which Islanders had dreamt at last arrived. 'Our dear Channel Islands are also to be freed today,' said Winston Churchill. Liberators mix with the liberated at the former German headquarters. (Photo: Jersey Evening Post)

exercise the minds of the members of the War Cabinet. There were conflicting objectives: one was to sustain the welfare of the civilians; the other was to avoid prolonging the Occupation of the islands by providing food which might be diverted from the civilians to the occupying troops.

On 7 November the German government stated that it was willing to permit food parcels to enter the Channel Islands and that the International Red Cross would supervise the distribution of the parcels. The Red Cross ships would be given safe conduct. Cruickshank says:

> The Germans had won a bloodless victory ... The British Government would now increase the total food supply, and the additional supplies would not have to be carried in German ships. The garrison would be able to prolong their resistance. The Islanders had gone hungry for nearly two months longer than they need have done ...

Sinel records:

> Christmas Day [1944]: weather beautiful – cold and frosty, but bright sunshine ... everyone made the most of this, we hope, the last Christmas under such conditions. Many a sigh of relief was heard when at last the rabbit, fowl or duck made its appearance on the table, for with robberies every night, either by civilians or Germans, one could never be sure what would happen.

Large requisitions of potatoes and cereal had been made by the Germans, which the Bailiff protested was in breach of the Hague Convention.

Nevertheless, requisitions of food continued, and it was not until after Christmas that the S.S. *Vega* arrived at St Peter Port. Islanders had yet to endure some months of Occupation, although the hardship was somewhat moderated by the International Red Cross food parcels, which had been provided by the Canadians.

Cruickshank says:

> The decline and tame capture of the Wehrmacht in the Channel Islands in May 1945 were due in part to the German troops' failure to become efficient market gardeners and peasant farmers. They could never have become completely self-sufficient, but if they had looked ahead they could have put themselves in a position to survive much longer.

The morale of the occupying forces fell to a very low level in the early months of 1945, despite the efforts of the Commanding Officer to sustain it. Hitler committed suicide on 1 May 1945, and on 8 May his successor, Admiral Doenitz, ordered the surrender of all German troops. In a speech Winston Churchill said that 'Our dear Channel Islands are also to be freed today'. At the conclusion of Churchill's speech, the Bailiff raised the Union flag and the Jersey flag over the Royal Courthouse. At last the task of rebuilding Jersey's war-damaged economy could begin.

MY MEMORIES OF THE OCCUPATION

Beatrice Le Huquet was a teacher at St Martin's School throughout the Occupation. Appointed to the staff in January 1929, she finally retired in 1966, after a career spanning 42 years. At St Martin's School, she taught art and French. These are her personal reminiscences of teaching during the German Occupation.

75 *Beatrice Le Huquet (1957) as a St John nurse. She taught at St Martin's School throughout the Occupation. (Beatrice Le Huquet Collection)*

When there were rumours that the Germans would actually invade Jersey, father remembered that grandpa Philippe Le Huquet had a wonderful collection of rifles and pistols, so, determined that these would not fall into enemy hands, he and brother-in-law Bruce Humber motored to St Catherine and walked to the end of the breakwater and threw the weapons into the sea.

One day, I returned from school and my sister told me a German soldier had thrown our washing out of the tray in our wash house and replaced it with some of his clothes. I waited until he returned, and with the appropriate gestures accompanied by a firm 'nein', made him understand that this action was totally out of order. He looked at me and quietly walked out, carrying his dripping laundry. None of the soldiers entered our wash house again.

All schools were ordered to teach German. Many teachers refused, but outsiders who had a smattering of German were installed in the schools. One came to St Martin's School to teach German to a mixed class of 12 to 15-year-olds. This was most unsatisfactory as children from more than one class were involved and this interfered with our routine work and really only the brighter pupils derived any benefit.

Some of the day-to-day arrangements for school became very difficult. Children soon outgrew sizes in boots and shoes. This became quite a problem during the five years of Occupation by the German forces. Some parents, when there were rumours that the Germans might land, foresaw this problem and bought boots and shoes of various sizes while footwear was available in the shops.

This time was very limited as, when the Germans did land, they pounced on all our shops like vultures and sent their purchases to their relatives in Germany. Leather became non-existent and parents were forced to make use of wooden clogs which were made at Summerland. They were just solid wooden soles with a strap across the foot. Children found them painful to wear and preferred to go bare-footed. Blisters and sores were common and difficult to treat as antiseptic creams and suitable lotions were not available from chemists. Salt water was used to keep the wounds clean and help them to heal. Honey was also used if you were lucky enough to have a jar. It is an excellent antiseptic and healer and was in great demand at the General Hospital.

Because of poor nutrition many children and even adults suffered from chilblains. But again nothing in the form of creams or ointments was available. A doctor at the hospital tried an experiment which proved efficacious. Sufferers sat in rows at tables with bowls of very hot water, in which they held their hands, or with hot water in bowls on the floor, into which they immersed their feet. Both hands and feet were held in the water until they became very red. This seemed to have a good effect on the chilblains. Plenty of hot water was available in the hospital as the boilers were kept going by burning tar from the gasworks.

Children who stayed at school for their midday meal did so because the distance to their home was too great and too much for them to undertake because of their poor physical condition. Meals were supplemented by the communal kitchen in Phillips Street run by Miss Fraser, a cookery class teacher. Small dustbins or urns of soup – vegetable, cabbage, or swedes – were distributed by helpers with charcoal-burning vehicles to schools throughout the Island. The children were asked to bring their own bread if it was available, and a bowl, or mug and spoon. Teachers took it in turns to ladle out the soup which was much appreciated by the ever-hungry pupils, especially during the winter.

We had no fires in the schools as suitable fuel was scarce. The children were allowed to keep their coats on in class. The winter of 1944-5 was the worst. It was preceded by a wet and cold autumn resulting in colds, coughs and chilblains. The Education Authority were forced to close the schools as the cheerless and unheated classrooms could not be tolerated any longer.

School materials grew less and less as each week went by. Paper, pencils, pens, writing books, ink and even chalk became scarce so we had to use every kind of material. As an art teacher I encouraged my pupils to use pages of the *Evening Post* on which to paint their subject. Pencils, too, were worn to the smallest stub.

I had a crystal set which I called Joy. I listened to the news every morning, writing down what I had heard on a piece of paper, and then hid it in one of my shoes. As I passed many

German soldiers on my way to school it was rather risky, I admit, but it enabled me to pass on the day's news to my colleagues at school. We met in the staff room as though we were discussing the routine of the day. The latest news was read, so we were well informed about the position of the Allies and the deterioration of the German forces. The scrap of paper was torn into minute pieces and disposed of safely. In order to have a duplicate, I usually wrote the news between the printed lines of a nature book about trees. This book is now in the Jersey Museum but by now the pencil-written words must be nearly obliterated. I hid the book between some of my reference books, thinking the enemy would never find it. Fortunately this was so.

OCCUPATION CHILDHOOD MEMORIES

This account of the war years in St Martin gives a vivid insight into the experience of growing up in a Parish under the control of an enemy force.

I was only seven years old when the war started and 13 when it finished. Looking back, the years of Occupation made a great impression on all young people in the Island at that time.

In February 1940, my father was desperately ill with pneumonia, pleurisy and emphysema. As antibiotics had not yet been discovered he hovered between life and death for six weeks. However he made what appeared to be a complete recovery and he and my mother went off to Alderney for a short convalescence. They returned in haste at a time when people in Jersey were deciding whether or not to evacuate to England. Dad was determined to stay. He stated that if he were to die it would be in Jersey where he belonged. So that was that.

On the day the Germans bombed the Island we were in a field close to the farmhouse digging potatoes – we children were helping to pick the mids and the farm lorry, an old Dodge, was in the lane. As a small child, I hated big bangs. Thunder, fireworks and balloons all terrified me. So when the noise of the German bombers and the machine-gunning and explosions began, I was the first under the lorry with my fingers in my ears, followed by the rest of the family until it all stopped. The enemy landed and, over the following weeks, we learned as children to accept that these very smart, arrogant and strange-tongued soldiers were here and that we had to do as we were bidden or else face severe punishment.

I began my education at Silk's School, a small private school in one of the lanes near the Parish Church. Mr. Silk, the headmaster, was a strict disciplinarian and we learnt our three Rs in the old-fashioned way. At nine years old, I was moved to St Martin's Elementary School, which then catered for all pupils up to the age of 14 years. Both schools were near to my grandparents' home, La Chasse Cottage. They were retired from farming and Grandpa was Connétable of St Martin at the time. La Chasse Cottage formed the dower wing of what we called the big La Chasse, which had belonged to my grandmother's brother before it was sold. The English owners evacuated and the house was empty. It was taken over by the Germans and became their head-quarters for the area. My sister Ruth and I spent many weeks with our grandparents before I was eleven.

A nasty incident occurred during that time and made us very wary of German soldiers. Ruth and I were walking home to La Chasse Cottage for lunch with five other school friends. We were all arm in arm and were chatting and laughing. We were near Gordon Brown's garage and Ruth was on the outside. A very smart German soldier was cycling past and had just gone by when he threw down his bicycle and ran towards Ruth and gave her a mighty slap on her face. Not knowing what it was about, we scattered as fast as we could and poor Ruth was hysterical. My grandfather, as you may well imagine, was furious and immediately went next door to complain bitterly about the incident. We never found out what caused it. Ruth suffered from cold sores and would lick her lips a lot. Whether she did this and the soldier thought she was putting her tongue out at him is anyone's guess. Ruth would never go down that road again during the war, she had been so frightened.

At St Martin's School I worked hard to gain a scholarship to the Jersey College for Girls. We all rode to school on our bicycles whatever the weather and the bikes were continually being patched up. By the end of the Occupation, hose pipe and twisted rope were used for tyres. I well remember old Mr. Silk wobbling all over the road on his bicycle just on the rims. He fell off – much to his embarrassment and our unkind giggling amusement.

At the College for Girls we had a reasonable education bearing in mind the shortage both of books and of up-to-date teaching aids. Many of the teachers who had retired before the war returned to fill in the gaps left by those who had evacuated. It was compulsory to learn German and we were taught by a Miss Le Febvre. She was a gentle person and somewhat deaf, so looking back I am afraid that we were unkind and played all sorts of tricks on her. I feel somewhat ashamed about it all now! However, the college was superbly run and could well be proud of its achievements.

I think I did not miss a day's school except when, at the age of 11, I contracted scarlet fever and was rushed off for a very lonely five weeks' isolation at Overdale Hospital. It was very frightening to begin with as no-one was allowed to come near the hospital. On the first day, I remember a very bad-tempered nurse making me swallow what seemed to be almost raw liver. I was violently sick afterwards, much to her anger. I cried all that night. Thank goodness, there was a very kind young woman in the bed next to mine and she comforted me and helped me settle in. Once I got used to the initial separation I settled in well and made a good recovery. It was so wonderful to be fetched on the Saturday before Easter Day by Mum and my Aunt Lily in her trap. It was a lovely sunny day and the hedges were full of wild flowers. Then, after the Easter holidays, it was back to school. I well remember Slade's buses spluttering up Mont Millais with their huge charcoal burners on the back. We could go faster on our bikes! We played netball and rounders at school and I enjoyed that tremendously. When the war was over the returning girls from the UK beat us hands down at tennis, swimming and hockey. We had a lot of catching up to do.

Because we lived on a farm we were more fortunate than our town cousins when times got really tough, especially after D-Day. We reared chickens and rabbits as well as a few pigs. Mum cooked vegetable soups and casseroles and with our ration of bread we had a reasonable diet. Mum cooked on an old paraffin stove which was placed on stones and heated by faggots of wood. The rabbits were fattened in an old chicken arc, some thirty to forty at a time. My sisters and I spent a lot of time collecting food for the rabbits from the hedges around the farm. When this food ran short in the autumn and winter, there were mid potatoes to use. These had to be introduced very slowly as you could lose rabbits within hours with colic or digestive upsets. Because of the shortage of meat, this was unforgivable.

As people became more hungry and thefts more common, Dad installed trip wires around the farmyard with a wire leading to a bell in his bedroom. One night this began ringing. We all threw open our windows and blew whistles, rang bells and banged tins. The neighbours were woken and all joined in. Soon the night air was reverberating with a mighty din. Dad saw figures running away into the darkness. Whether these were hungry German soldiers from nearby Rozel Mill or starving slave workers (this, I doubt, as we did not see many of these poor unfortunate souls in the north-east of the Island), or even locals, we shall never know. All we do know is that, during the following week the trip wire was cut one night and nearly all the rabbits were taken, as well as a quantity of very green seed potatoes which must have tasted horrible as well as being poisonous if eaten in any quantity. After that, before going to bed every night, we all helped to catch and carry rabbits and chickens into the cider press house which formed the basement of the farmhouse. We then placed sandbags against the door to stop intruders going up into the house from this cellar.

The gun emplacement at Elsingham was only a couple of miles away as the crow flies and when the guns were blasting away at the Allies' planes, the farmhouse, at the top of Ville Brée and only single width at that, would shake and feel as if it were going to fall apart. We children used to get very frightened, and Dad would collect us and take us down to the basement which was quiet and seemed much safer. There was also a gun emplacement in one of our fields looking right over the sea to Les Écréhous and the coast of France. In the lane alongside it there was a bunker and we were all too terrified to venture anywhere near, but we watched from a safe distance as the soldiers changed guard duty.

We kept a sow in the pig sties round the back of the yard but one or two piglets would be fattened in another hideaway away from prying German eyes. When a pig was killed on the farm – somewhere where there would be as little noise as possible – the meat was shared between neighbours and some was salted down. Everyone had their turn. I remember we had a large cold water tap in the cow stable and Dad was washing through the large intestine to make tripe. The smell was horrible and made me feel sick. The following evening my mother cooked a splendid tripe supper for Dad and a dozen or so of his friends. We were sent off to bed but I know that a great game of nap followed the supper, which had been washed down by cider, and carried on well into the night past the curfew hour. Some slept till morning, others melted away along the hedges in the fields back to their own beds.

Our families made carrot tea, dandelion coffee, sugar beet syrup, potato flour and salt from seawater. Dad even grew tobacco and the leaves were hung in the attic to cure. During all this time our many friends and relations from town bought all we could spare in the way of milk, eggs and butter. They never overcharged anyone, however wealthy, for anything they sold. In fact, they gave much away, especially to working-class families who were having terrible problems in making ends meet and feeding their families. In autumn, town friends would walk out to Ville Brée with handcarts to collect wood and twigs for the coming winter cold. They also came gleaning after the oats had been mown and stooked.

Threshing, with the contractor's threshing machine, was a great time. Once again, this was a communal effort, with neighbours working together. They also tried to outwit the German soldier who was on duty checking and counting the bags of grain and managed to hide the odd bag which would then be put away safely, usually in the attic of the home.

As the war went on, the Germans visited the farms regularly, counted the animals and found out how much milk was being sent to the dairy. After D-Day, they began requisitioning some of the cows for slaughter for their own use. They also looked over the horses and asked their ages. We had two farm horses, one Welsh cob, Dolly, and one Clydesdale-type mare, Jess. They were both between the ages of fifteen and twenty years and were in good order and decently fat. The Germans said they would take them for meat and replace them with two heavy hunters. They needed the meat and wanted to rehouse their own horses as they could not import food for them. Dolly was not only a farm horse, she was my beloved and favourite animal. She was black with a white star. We used to harness her up in the farm cart and drive her around everywhere on the farm. Our friends loved this. She was a treasure. I was not told when she was taken away, as my parents realised I would be very distressed. When I knew she had gone and was dead I ran up to the hayloft and hid amongst the bundles of hay and sobbed for hours. I was inconsolable for days and would not speak. Some time after I went with Dad and Uncle Charlie to see the new horses we were to be given at Vermont, St Saviour, and was most surprised to see some very smart young women speaking English riding out with some officers. It was my first contact with collaborators and after what had happened to my little mare I hated these girls even more than I hated the Germans.

For clothing we were fortunate in that we had hand-me-downs from my cousins. This was a tremendous help to my mother. Grandma Billot spent all her spare time mending, darning and patching up clothes so that they were wearable: she always had a needle in her hand when she was sitting down. I am sure her eyes suffered from the very poor light. Candles and smelly carbide lamps were often the only available light, especially during the last two years. After the war, when she was in her seventies she became blind and I feel that all the sewing she did must have contributed to the loss of her sight. We had gloves made out of rabbit fur and, of course, the wooden clogs which we all wore at school. Grandma, as the Connétable's wife, was very involved with the Friendship League which helped anyone in need in the Parish. Collections of vegetables, fruit, eggs and clothing were received at the Public Hall and taken to needy families and old and disabled people. My grandfather was very concerned about the well-being of his parishioners. When the Germans requisitioned bicycles from the Parish, he had to make choices which were very difficult, and made him some enemies. He was also very troubled when the departure of British subjects to camps in Europe had to be arranged. He worked hard to keep back as many people as he could on compassionate grounds and succeeded in several cases. When he was informed that houses and farms were to be searched for guns and firearms, because the Germans did not believe that they had all been handed in, I was at the cottage after school. Grandpa said to me, 'Anne, get back to Ville Brée quickly and tell your father to get the fire out at once. He will understand.' And so, one of my father's treasured possessions, the rifle with which he had won many trophies before the war and which he had hidden in a safe place was slung in haste into the

76 *Most little girls dream of owning their own pony. Anne Billot's beloved Welsh Cob, 'Dolly', was requisitioned by the Germans and slaughtered. (Courtesy of Anne Perchard)*

liquid manure cistern. It was retrieved after the Liberation, all rusted and eaten away with acid. We still have it!!

Our social life centred around the Parish Church and its activities. The priest-in-charge was Canon Wilford. He had retired to Jersey from New Zealand after a lifetime of work in the Christchurch Diocese. He was 'high church' and consequently was not popular with everyone in St Martin, who had always practised a low church form of Anglicanism. However, those of us who were in the Sunday School and choir had great respect and affection for him and we received a wonderful grounding in the Christian faith.

Miss Beatrice Le Huquet was the best Sunday School superintendent anyone could wish for. Mrs. Wilford trained the junior choir in her home once a week after school. The dozen or so young boys and girls who made up this choir and acted as servers developed deep friendships which exist to this day. Whist drives were held at the *Royal Hotel* to raise funds for a Church Hall and these were great fun, especially in winter when we had to get home before the curfew, which was early! We either walked or cycled and I can well remember walking home, in the moonlight on frosty nights, telling each other ghost stories to encourage us to walk even faster! On Good Friday afternoons we would all set off to pick primroses and wild daffodils for decorating the church for Easter. We would sing 'Eternal Father, strong to save' nearly every Sunday and many times German officers would come in and stand at the back looking on. Mr. Hick, a regular churchgoer, would often bring an escaped Russian prisoner who lived with him. Most of us didn't know until the war was over that the stranger in our midst was an escaper. In winter, it was extremely cold in church and we would run briskly at the end of each service to stop our shivering.

During the summer months, after school at St Martin, we would sometimes run down to Archirondel to meet Grandma and Aunty Lily who had driven down in the pony and trap. Archirondel was the only bay we could visit which was not mined, or with barbed wire right to the top of the beach. The only problem was walking back up the hill, which we youngsters had to do as the pony could only carry Grandma and Aunty. Tinsel, the grey pony, was full of spirit and on one occasion, in a hurry to get moving, she reared up and the shafts of the trap snapped. Grandma and Aunty fell out of the back of the trap but fortunately were not hurt, only somewhat shaken and bruised. Meanwhile, the pony bolted up the lane, onto the main road and, with the shafts beating against her sides and flanks, went faster and faster. As it happened, my father was at the Public Hall with his horse and van collecting goods for the Friendship League when he saw this pony bolting past with the shafts still attached. He immediately turned the van around, put Jess into top gear and galloped down to Archirondel where he found us all with no bones broken, just a little shocked! I think this was the last time we went to Archirondel during the Occupation!

Then came D-Day, with squadron after squadron passing overhead and the guns at Elsingham in full flow. At night, from our bedroom windows we could see the skies over France, especially over Caen, lit up with a flickering red and orange glow from the intense bombing and the fires. Everyone wondered how long it would be before we were freed. Little did we realise it would be 11 months before Liberation.

I was 12 now and Dad was recovering from yet another bout of fever. He had made me a crystal set and I was able to copy down the World Service news which was dictated every morning. When anyone called, Dad would give them a copy of the latest daily news. I would also take a copy with me to school and deliver it to elderly friends and relations in town. We also heard the latest songs like 'You are my sunshine', 'Would you like to swing from a star?' and all the Vera Lynn songs which were quite new to us.

The winter of 1944 brought great misery and hunger and the SS *Vega*'s visit with food parcels and flour was a lifeline. Even on the farms we were overjoyed – things were pretty desperate now with us also. There was a shortage of food for the animals and much theft of crops in the fields. The *Vega* brought treats most children could not remember ever having tasted before. The flour ration went to the baker, Mr. Taschke, to be made into the most scrumptious bread we had ever tasted. It was manna from heaven. It was tastier than any cake made from potato flour. Ruth and I queued for the family's ration of white bread at the shop at Rozel Mill. That was our job. The weather was bitterly cold that first time and snow was falling. We walked back through drifts in our farm lane. But we had a feast in store and the cold was of little consequence.

Concerts to raise funds for the Red Cross, in grateful thanks, were held all over the Island. Rozel Rovers Football Club organised a concert in the Public Hall and due to the huge demand for tickets the show ran for six nights instead of the intended three. It is estimated that 1,300 people attended. During the interval an auction was held. Bags of wheat, tins of fruit, even a packet of tea – items hidden since the outbreak of war – raised large sums. In all, the magnificent total of £1,603 was donated to the Red Cross.

Finally, Liberation Day arrived. Dad had a flagpole which was painted and ready for putting up in the front garden. He also fetched out of the rafters the Union Jack which had been hidden there since the beginning of the Occupation.

The old Dodge lorry had been hidden in one of the small sheds with its wheels removed. Because of its age, it had not been requisitioned by the Germans when they first arrived. It was pulled out and made roadworthy. Mechanic friends resuscitated the ancient engine, but there was no petrol to go to St Helier on V.E. Day. However, that did not matter. The radio which we children had never known existed under the floorboards in the pantry was brought out. So that was the reason we were always sent to bed sharp at 8.30 p.m. every night! Dad had listened to the news every evening at 9 p.m. This marvellous wireless was brought out onto the lawn and when we heard Winston Churchill speak, our own Union Jack was hoisted up the flagpole to fly from

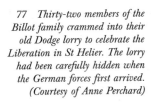

77 *Thirty-two members of the Billot family crammed into their old Dodge lorry to celebrate the Liberation in St Helier. The lorry had been carefully hidden when the German forces first arrived. (Courtesy of Anne Perchard)*

the top of it, proud and free. Looking back over the years this was for me the most important moment of my life. To live in freedom is the most precious thing we have in this world.

We then walked to St Martin's Church for a Thanksgiving Service. It was packed and the emotions ran high with gratitude for a safe delivery from captivity. The following day petrol had been brought for the lorry, and some 32 of us piled into the back of it. We arrived in St Helier and somehow found our way close to the *Pomme d'Or Hotel*. We screamed with joy and happiness as the Tommies marched across throwing sweets to us as they passed. The following days and weeks were filled with glad reunions and news from friends and relatives in Great Britain and abroad as well as with all kinds of celebrations. We looked forward to the future with great excitement and hopefulness with the fervent prayer that war would never again be part of our world.

THE OCCUPATION OF THE PARISH

The following account of the difficulties and trials of the Jersey country Parish of St Martin during the years that it was under the heels of an enemy power gives an insight into the problems faced by most women, in simply trying to keep their families fed and their homes going.

The tale of the difficulties faced during the years of Occupation and the way in which the Island tried to face them is hard to tell. The whole grim picture can best be seen, not so much in diaries or in documents which will become historic, but in glimpses we can catch before the memory of living man has gone. The Church is here to care for both our bodies and our souls. Never before in Jersey had the needs of the body called for greater consideration.

Lack of coal and firewood eventually robbed us of all the amenities of life. French coal which came spasmodically to us was quite unburnable – even when it was not dust. Our quota of logs sometimes amounted to one small piece of wood a day. Kitchen ranges could not be used. A few people were able to buy French stoves of almost dolls-house size. But much of the cooking was done on the top of a five-gallon oil drum, tightly packed with sawdust with a hole left in the middle as an exit for the tiny flame which did the work. This lasted for seven or eight hours. At half time, the potatoes would be cooked and a kettle replacing the saucepan would, before the end, produce boiling water. It wasn't until late in the evening, and then only in the coldest weather, that the majority of us allowed ourselves to have a little fire in our smallest grate. Some had to find refuge in bed, and in their nightmares saw the Germans requisitioning their blankets.

We were never safe in our homes. Constantly, on various pretexts, German officials were at our doors. Now it was the Gestapo searching for a wireless which anonymous informers had told them we possessed. Now it was officers asking us – often very rudely – the number of our rooms, leaving us uncertain about whether or not they were going to turn us out. Now, it was another soldier threatening to report us for some irregularity or other, unless we helped him out of a difficulty of his own. All these visitors used their eyes, and at night would return to steal the rabbits which weeks of care had just made ready for one of the few proper meals we ever had. Beehives were noted and robbed before it was time to take the honey. Fruit trees were stripped and even kitchens were entered and meals just ready to be eaten carried off – saucepans and all!

Ahead were the days when there would be no more butter; when three days in the week they were to be without milk, and when the meat ration was to be four ounces a fortnight. Further ahead were the days when for warmth and cooking we would be dependent upon sticks rooted out from roadside bushes. What troubles came to our women! Everything took so long. The fire would not burn, and when it did it went out as soon as our backs were turned.

It is not easy to write about food. A few did seem to have enough, but for most describing the problem as acute would be an understatement. People went to bed not knowing what they would eat the next day. At times the rations were negligible. We had hoped that our farmers and fishermen would help us out, but everything was commandeered. The sea coast was denied to us, and on the occasions that permits were given for fishing, the Germans met the returning boats and took what they wanted. All that ever reached us in St Martin were a few spider crabs, and then only because our invaders didn't like them.

Towards the end, farmers were not allowed to sell or to give away their produce. Earlier it was sometimes possible to get a few pounds of wheat from those who had already sent in their quota. This we ground in coffee mills. A machine made for coffee beans does not take kindly to grain – often the wheat was mixed with wild oats, which choked the little grinder, so all had to be spread on the kitchen table, and the oats picked out by hand. One old lady became such an expert that when the light failed, she continued her task in the dark, being able to separate the good from the bad by touch.

For those with gardens the staple food was dried beans. One year a wet autumn stopped these ripening, but luckily the season before had been a good one, and those who had used their stocks sparingly found themselves with some to tide them over. But most beans more than a year old become very hard. Although we were told that by soaking in hot water, and by slow cooking, they could be softened, many of us who were not expert enough had to choose between indigestion and hunger.

78 *Monica Amy, who took Holy Orders and became a nun, recounts the difficulties of simple survival in an Island which was under siege. (Gerald Amy Collection)*

Some of the fortunate ones had managed to save up a little invalid food from former days. They kept this for illness, but more often than not, when it was opened, they found that maggots had taken possession. Our extremity can be gauged by the fact that none of this food was thrown away. The fattest of the maggots were removed, but it is safe to say that many others were cooked and eaten.

Before the Red Cross parcels came, things were as bad as they could be. Early in 1945, our bread ration was reduced to two pounds a week, and just before the little food boat came we were getting none. We had ample evidence of our plight on the roads all around us. People who in happier days were best known at cocktail parties could be seen gathering acorns on country lanes. Women who had before knelt only to say their prayers were now kneeling in the fields looking for the few ears of corn the harvesting had left. Little bits of stick protruded from weird baskets fastened onto bicycles which, for tyres, boasted garden hose. Here and there could be seen weary women pushing perambulators, or anything else on wheels, into which they had crammed the smallest twigs.

People who had done magnificent work for the Empire turned their hands to do what they could for the common good. An old colonel, supplied by the farmers with sugar beet, became quite an expert in making syrup – a cold, arduous and back-breaking job. Others used what energy they had in making potato flour. It was a tedious process. Cutting, washing, draining and drying left little time for anything else. To make one pound of flour took about twelve pounds of potatoes. When the day came for potatoes to be no longer available, they turned their flagging energies to making carrot and parsnip tea. From barley they tried to make coffee. They manufactured a sort of Horlicks food drink from sugar beet.

A severe handicap in all these ventures was the lack of cooking utensils. The difficulty of cleaning them was overcome by the use of wood ash – which proved as effective as many pre-war polishes. But in spite of ingenious contraptions there came a time when many saucepans reached the limit of their usefulness. The Island was fortunate in having many mechanics, who helped where they could with such difficulties. Whatever else they saw, our Occupation days really did see great deeds of kindness.

GERMAN FORTIFICATIONS IN THE PARISH OF ST MARTIN

When Hitler ordered that the Channel Islands should be converted into impregnable fortresses, neither he nor the rest of the German high command dreamt that the adjacent French coast would ever be in any other than German hands.

Consequently, they believed that any attack mounted by the British would have to come from the west. This is why the Island's west coast was far more heavily defended than the east. Therefore, like Grouville, the Parish of St Martin can lay claim to fewer concrete works than, say, St Ouen or St Brelade. The fact that the adjacent French coast no longer remained in German hands after August 1944 caused a hasty re-appraisal of the situation but the fortifications built after this date were hurriedly constructed and few remains can be seen.

79   The Bunker at WN Hafen Gorey with its casement for 7.5cm anti-tank gun. The bunker was demolished in 1972 to make way for a coach park. (Michael Ginns Collection)

The biggest bunker in the Parish once stood on Gorey Pier, only to be demolished in 1972. This occupied the area now used for parking coaches and it housed a 7.5cm anti-tank gun. Constructed in early 1944, it covered the harbour area and the northern end of Grouville Bay; ironically enough, the first test shot was fired from the bunker on 6 June, D-Day. Concrete traces of this bunker survive in the angle of the sea wall close to the bus shelter.

No.14 Gorey Pier was not always the innocent dwelling that it now appears to be. Before the war No.14 was a store and in 1944 it was converted into a strongpoint. A close inspection of the window on the ground floor reveals that here was a machine-gun loophole, while on the first floor a 3.7cm anti-tank gun covered the length of the pier. No.14 must be the only flat in the Island to have a reinforced concrete floor with an equally strong concrete ramp leading to the front door; curiously, the latter is at the rear of the building with access from the old Harbour Battery.

At the Harbour Battery there is also a semi-circular concrete machine-gun position, and a mounting for a Renault R35 tank turret which was removed in the 1953 scrap metal drive. All these defences constituted Resistance Nest *Hafen Gorey* (Gorey Harbour), and the troops manning them were quartered in the hotels along the harbour front.

Gorey Castle was one of the medieval fortresses taken over by the Germans immediately upon their arrival in July 1940. At that time the only weapon was a machine-gun mounted at the castle's summit, but later other machine-guns were added as well as an anti-tank gun. However, it was in the coastal artillery role that Gorey Castle played its main part.

In mid-1941, following Hitler's early instructions that the Channel Islands should be fortified, he launched his attack upon the Soviet Union and units of the Army Coastal Artillery moved

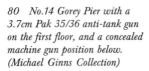

80   No.14 Gorey Pier with a 3.7cm Pak 35/36 anti-tank gun on the first floor, and a concealed machine gun position below. (Michael Ginns Collection)

into Jersey. Three small turrets at the summit of the castle were adapted by the Germans to form Artillery Direction Finding Position No.7 in the round-the-island chain of observation posts. It is interesting to note how the turrets have been cleverly camouflaged with granite to make them blend in with the ancient building.

However, by August 1944 the Normandy coast was firmly in American hands and the east coast of Jersey was thrust into the front line. The main defensive effort of the Germans shifted from the west to the east of Jersey and the Commanding Officer of the First Battalion of Army Coastal Artillery Regiment 1265 moved his H.Q. into the castle. He established himself as *Kommandeur der Kampgruppe Seeziel Ost* (Commander of Battle Group Sea Targets East). Few 'sea targets' ever presented themselves, but probably his busiest night was 8/9 March 1945, when the German garrison in Jersey launched its successful commando raid on the French port of Granville.

At Anne Port, to the north of Gorey, the old sea wall just to the north of the slipway has been raised a few feet with a concrete extension, thus creating an anti-tank wall. A little further north it is worth mentioning that La Crête Quarry, which yields a purple rhyolite stone, was used by the Germans in 1941-2 to provide aggregate for the production of concrete until the stone-crushing machinery broke down and the quarry ceased operations. It is worth noting that any bunker anywhere in the Island which contains La Crête rhyolite must have been built before the autumn of 1942 – the bunker on the slipway at Grève d'Azette (now converted into public lavatories) is a good example.

The uncompleted 19th-century breakwater at Archirondel was also considered vulnerable. Here, the red-and-white 18th-century tower was taken over at an early date and adapted for

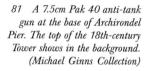

81 A 7.5cm Pak 40 anti-tank gun at the base of Archirondel Pier. The top of the 18th-century Tower shows in the background. (Michael Ginns Collection)

20th-century warfare. Machine-gun positions were built into the old parapet at the base of the tower together with several other concrete modifications. At the landward end of the breakwater, at the side of the recently constructed (1980s) concrete slipway, is a Type 680 casemate for a 7.5cm anti-tank gun which covered the length of beach leading towards the round tower near St Catherine's cross roads. Nearby are the remains of a concrete mounting for a Renault FT 17 tank turret – the mounting was the subject of an experiment by the Liberation forces in 1945 when an attempt was made to destroy the small bunker with explosives. The experiment was not repeated!

A few score yards up Le Mont de la Mare de St Catherine (formerly Waverley Hill) is a turning to the right into a lane known as Les Charrières; here, set into the hedge just after the first sharp left-hand bend, are the remains of Resistance Nest *La Perelle I,* which was armed with machine guns and mortars.

What is known as La Masseline Reservoir was constructed by the Second Company of Engineer Battalion 319 in October 1943. A plaque recording this can be seen halfway down the dam wall, but this is only visible in times of drought when the reservoir is half empty, as it is impressed into the inner face of the concrete wall.

The purple pebbles on the beach by the white Round Tower provided a source of aggregate for the German Army construction troops when they began building the early, light fortifications in the spring of 1941. Stone gathered here was transported right across the Island and can be seen in the concrete of the early defences erected at such places as La Corbière and Le Braye Slip in St Ouen's Bay.

At St Catherine's Breakwater stands Resistance Nest *Mole Verclut.* Running beneath the so-called 'Gibraltar Rock' is a defensive tunnel which supported a Type 670 casemate for a 10.5cm beach defence gun which covered the length of St Catherine's Breakwater. The tunnel is unusual in that it is lined with brick rather than concrete.

82 *The 10.5cm coastal defence gun at Resistance Verclut. The casement was subsequently used as St Catherine's vivier. (Michael Ginns Collection)*

On top of the Rock are the remains of a platform for a 60cm searchlight covering St Catherine's Bay, while higher up, and buried in the undergrowth, is another mounting for a 150cm coastal artillery searchlight code-named *Albert*; this was not installed until September 1944, when the artillery battery near La Coupe, for which it supplied illumination, was moved from Guernsey to stiffen the defences of Jersey's east coast. Other light concrete works are to be seen dotted around the base of the rock.

The footpath which leads uphill from St Catherine's Breakwater to Fliquet is still partially barred by railway lines buried at an angle into the path to obstruct the passage of light vehicles. It doubtless serves the same purpose today as it did in 1944!

The round tower at Fliquet was taken over by the Germans as Resistance Nest *Fliquet*. A draw-ladder leads up to the armoured doorway above road level, and a crawl passage was punched through the base of the tower at road level. Slightly to the north of the tower is a reinforced field-type personnel shelter and machine-gun position, whilst in the garden just across the road there was a 10.5cm beach defence gun in an open position. All traces of this were removed in about 1995.

In the fields that lie between La Rue de la Perruque and La Rue de la Coupe there arrived in September 1944 the 14th Battery of Army Coastal Artillery Regiment 1265 to protect the sea passage between Jersey and the French coast. Known as *Batterie Haeseler* and armed with four 15cm K18 medium field guns, it was installed in field positions of which all traces have long since vanished.

Rozel Bay was well defended but all the fortifications lie in the Parish of Trinity. However, Rozel Mill was taken over as Direction and Range Finding Position No. 6. On the far side of the mill, away from the road, the armoured door is still in position, while at the mill's summit the range markings can still be seen.

83   *A 60cm infantry searchlight, which was installed at WN Mole Verclut in 1944. The Germans feared that this stretch of coastline could face an allied invasion from France. (Michael Ginns Collection)*

At the junction of La Rue des Alleurs and La Grande Route de Rozel a small concrete entrance can be seen in the hedge on the north side of the road. This leads to a small shelter and machine-gun position.

In the angle formed by La Rue de la Fosse à Gres and La Rue des Raisies stood *Batterie Mackensen* which was armed with three 21cm medium howitzers. There are some concrete remains set into the sides of fields and hedges.

Eversley, the large house at the corner of Le Mont de la Mare de St Catherine and La Grande Route de Faldouet, was taken over as a *Truppenverbandsplatz* (casualty receiving station) and named *Posen.*

84   *A defender's view from the casement of a camouflaged 10.5cm coastal defence gun, overlooking St Catherine's Breakwater. (Michael Ginns Collection)*

Victoria Tower, with its sweeping views over the bays of St Catherine and Grouville, was a strongpoint. This was armed with mortars, machine guns, and a 4.7cm Czech anti-tank gun set on a turntable and disguised as a summerhouse. The mounting for this survives, although hidden in the undergrowth, as do several other machine-gun emplacements. The mortar and personnel pits have all been in-filled by the National Trust.

The Tower itself had a 2cm *Flak Oerlikon* anti-aircraft gun mounted on the roof to protect the Freya radar array which was removed from Cancale, on the north coast of Brittany in July 1944 in the face of the advancing Americans, and transported to Jersey on the *m.v. Spinel.* At Victoria Tower, the radar was known as *Funkmessortungsgerät Ost*, or 'Radar Set East'. ('West' was at Grosnez.)

Also near Victoria Tower was the Command and Observation Post for the commanding officer of the Second Battalion of Divisional Artillery Regiment 319. The bunker is still in use as a nuclear radiation monitoring station.

A Jersey Widow's Thoughts At Her Child's Bedside On Liberation Day 1945
Jackie de Gruchy

Let's say a prayer little one
To thank God Liberation's come;
New peace has made this island yours –
Once more you'll dabble un-mined shores:
We'll fish for cabots, run and swim:
These past sad years for you will dim.
But now we'll always play alone –
Your Daddy's never coming home.

Five years have dragged since last we saw
Our Jersey boys, who sailed to war;
Who went from us young men, young dads
To join with England's fighting lads:
Not all will learn their captured isle
At last wears Liberation's smile;
That Freedom anchored in our bay
This shining, sun-washed ninth of May.

You asked, so many times to-day,
'Is *that* my Daddy, gone away?'
And thought you saw friend deportees
Who starve in camps across the seas.
I tried for your sake to rejoice
But found I listened for Dad's voice,
And though I know he is not here –
I searched like you, for his face dear.

When moon's tide smooths barbed wired sand,
Man's work and seasons cleanse the land –
Will Jersey's *thank you* dry to dust?
As her scars heal, will mem'ry rust?
Oh No! 'We will remember them'
Our Jersey eyes won't see again:
Their hard won Peace has blessed this shore
To give us life in full, once more.

*85 'Let's say a prayer, little one to thank God Liberation's come…'.
Jackie De Gruchy, of St Martin, captures a tender moment in verse.
This illustration by her great-uncle, Edmund Blampied, is taken from
a collection of her poetry,* The Way to the Bay. *(Courtesy of The
Blampied Trustees)*

Jackie De Gruchy was born in London during the Second World War, and returned to Jersey with her sister and their mother – who now found herself a young widow – at the end of the Occupation. Her father, a bomber pilot, had been shot down and killed during the hostilities.

A great-niece of Edmund Blampied, she was educated at Mrs. Hilda Ahier's school, Springside, St Martin, where she enjoyed elocution, singing and the piano. She went on to Helvetia House School where she remembers one day opening a new French textbook to find that her great-uncle, Edmund Blampied, had illustrated it. When she explained her connection with the artist, her teacher drily commented, 'well, Jacqueline, my dear, let's hope your French will now improve'.

She married Harold De Gruchy in April 1965 and became a busy farmer's wife, but found time to write poetry between seasons. Her first collection of poetry, *The Way To The Bay*, was published in 1996. It is illustrated using some of the works of her great-uncle.

Just like much of the work of the famous artist, many of Jackie's poems draw upon details and memories from her youth. This poem is a very touching account of how her own mother might have felt on Liberation Day, 9 May 1945, had she not accompanied her husband to England before the Occupation.

1939-1945
A ses enfants morts pour la Patrie
La Paroisse de St Martin Reconnaissante

Amy, George Harvey	Sapper, Royal Engineers	27.12.1944
Bihet, Bernard Joseph	Duke of Cornwall's L.I.	21. 5.1945
Bolitho, Michael Lemprière	Captain, Coldstream Guards	8.11.1942
du Feu, Ronald Henry	Petty Officer, Royal Navy	12.12.1943
Houguez, Snowden George	Private, Hampshire Regiment	26. 6.1941
Johnson, Maurice Gordon	2nd Lieutenant, Royal Irish Fusiliers	16. 9.1940
Vardon, Alfred John	Private, Hampshire Regiment	10. 7.1944

The names of the above St Martinais, killed in action, were added to the central panel of the war memorial.

86   Michael Lemprière Bolitho, grandson of the Seigneur of Rosel, and his memorial in the Manor chapel. (Courtesy of Loveday Bolitho)

Seven

Les Écréhous

PREHISTORIC AND MONASTIC PERIODS

Romantic and inaccessible, Les Écréhous has attracted hermits and recluses to its fascinating but tiny shores for centuries. The British and the French have hotly contested ownership for hundreds of years. Their argument has had as much to do with fishing rights as with sovereignty. An archipelago of rocks and islets lying seven miles east-north-east of Rozel, at high tide the land area is small indeed and only on La Maître Île is there today any quantity of vegetation.

It is hard to imagine how ancient people chose to live there but there is no doubt that they did. Until about 5000 BC, Les Écréhous and Jersey were still attached to the Normandy peninsula. Flowing between them was the estuary of the ancient river Ay. Jersey was probably the first to become an island, with Les Écréhous, lying closer to Normandy, remaining attached to the mainland for a somewhat longer period. It is not possible to determine with any degree of accuracy the exact date of separation, but when a neolithic menhir was erected on La Maître Île the island was almost certainly still part of the Cotentin.

The peat beds adjacent to Blianque Île have yielded neolithic pottery and flints, confirming early prehistoric occupation far below the present high water mark. Evidence that ritual activity took place in this period is provided by the irregular flat slab of stone standing on the edge of the marsh at La Maître Île. It appears to have been deliberately hewn, and is referred to as the orthostat. The menhir is another large stone dating from prehistoric times which was subsequently toppled from its standing position and now lies under the remains of the chapel.

Although Les Écréhous had become islands by the 12th century when a monastery was established, they were certainly of a much greater land area than exists today. Excavations by Dr. Warwick Rodwell in the late 1980s found numerous bones of domestic animals and it is likely that they were grazed there to provide meat for the inhabitants of the monastery. As late as the 19th century, it was reported that Les Écréhous yielded 'a few bales of thin hay', which it would be quite impossible to harvest from the small land area and depleted soil that now exists.

Prior to this 1987-8 expedition there had been only limited interest in exploring the geology and the archaeology of Les Écréhous. The Société Jersiaise organised an expedition in 1928 led by Major A.D.B. Godfray and Major N.V.L. Rybot but their findings were not extensive and only a trial excavation of the old priory was carried out. The results of Dr. Rodwell's expedition were subsequently expanded by further research, and his book, *Les Écréhous*, published in 1996, is acknowledged as the definitive work on the area.

The excavations revealed pottery and other artefacts that indicated a more or less continuous human presence from Neolithic times. Apart from such tangible evidence, there are many other ancient stories of the tenuous hold these islands had on the mainland in times of rising sea

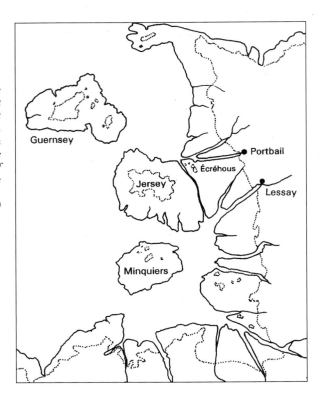

87 An attempt to redraft the Mont St Michel map of 1406. It shows the ancient coastline as it was thought to be before the ninth century and possibly in Roman times. A dotted line shows the coastline of today. The origins of the map are uncertain and its conclusions are speculative. (Adapted from De Potiche, 1891)

levels. There are references in old documents to major incursions of the sea in 541, 603, 709, 1191 and 1214. An ancient map (Fig.87), once in the possession of the monastery at Mont St Michel and believed to date from the ninth century, shows Les Écréhous as still a promontory of the Cotentin, with only a narrow channel separating it from Jersey. This gives some credence to the recurring legend of *La Planche* in which a plank across a stream provided access to Les Écréhous (or Jersey?) from the French mainland.

The name itself is of interest and has its origins in the Scandinavian words, sker-holm or skerjaholm, meaning a rocky island or an island with skerries. It derives from the presence in the islands of the Viking raiders of the Dark Ages. Early documentation includes *Eskerho* (1309), *Ancrowe* (1360) and *Ekerho* (1682). All of these indicate a single island and it was not until 1754 that the plural form used today was adopted. In later years, the excellence of the fishing around the reef resulted in virtually every rock having its own name – usually in Jèrriais – known among the maritime communities of Rozel and Gorey. An example from Frank Le Maistre's detailed toponomy is *L'Êtchièrviéthe*, a rock inhabited by cormorants, derived from the Old Norse *skarfr*. Subsequently, this rock became known as *La Pièrre ès Femmes* as a result of a shipwreck, when the captain put his female passengers ashore, assuming that they would be safe. They were all drowned by the incoming tide and, to this day, fishermen avoid the area at night, claiming that ghostly shrieks can still be heard.

The prehistoric remains discovered on La Maître Île include the menhir and the orthostat, the large flat stones which appear to have had some religious significance, and a variety of pottery sherds and animal bones. In addition, the 1987-8 expeditions collected over 2,300 pieces of worked flint. Most of these date from the Early Neolithic (*c.*4850 BC) and the Early Bronze Age (*c.*1800 BC). This stone does not occur naturally in the area, and confirms prehistoric occupation.

88   The disarticulated burial of a young woman discovered under the Écréhous chapel. It is thought to date from the sixth century. (Photo: W. Rodwell)

One of the most interesting of the archaeological finds was the disarticulated burial of a young woman under the floor of the original chapel building. Not all the bones of the body were included and particularly those of hands, feet and rib cage were missing. The bones were carefully arranged, indicating that this deliberate reburial involved the remains of someone of import. Even radio-carbon dating gave conflicting reports, but the most likely conclusion was that the skeleton dated from the sixth or seventh century. It is possible that this was an early Christian shrine where the remains of a saintly person were venerated and above which the first Écréhous chapel was constructed. The remaining evidence of this chapel beneath the later structures is hard to determine or to date, but it is clear that this was a site of Christian worship possibly as early as the eighth century and certainly long before the construction of the 13th-century priory. The chapel was a simple rectangular stone structure similar to a number of others of the period in western Europe. Whether or not this earlier chapel was still in existence at the time of the establishment of the Priory of St Mary the Virgin subsequent to the 1203 grant to Pierre de Préaux is uncertain. However, the Priory was built on the same site; there were at least two individual buildings, a chapel and a hall of residence, and these went through various stages of development over a period of one hundred years. The Assize Roll of 1323 refers to the house of the Prior at Archirondel: it is likely that the occupation of the Écréhous Priory had had to be curtailed by the inexorable incursion of the sea by this date.

The establishment of St Mary's Priory on La Maître Île is well documented. Pierre de Préaux was a friend of King John and sometime Bailiff of the Cotentin. In 1200 the King granted him 'insulas de Gerse et de Genere et de Aurene' and created him Gardien des Îles. In 1203, he gave the islands to the Abbey of Le Val Richer in Normandy. Two monks and a servant were sent to establish the Priory of St Mary. This must have been a formidable task in a barren land into which the sea was constantly encroaching. As well as building the Priory, providing food and performing their religious offices, the monks had to maintain a light to warn shipping of the surrounding dangers. The chapel was later enlarged and improved and a living hall was built to its north.

In 1309, the Abbot of Val Richer was summoned to Jersey to explain by what rights he held the Écréhous priory, which was partly supported by other properties in Jersey. Even then, he pleaded the poverty of the tenure and it seems that, within the next half century, the monks were spending a large part of their time at a manse at Archirondel. The beginning of the Hundred Years War in 1337 and the infestation of Channel Island waters by pirates can hardly have aided the cause of the tiny Cistercian outpost, which may well have ceased to exist before Henry V forfeited the properties of foreign ecclesiastics in 1415. Writing in 1682, Jean Poingdestre stated 'The small islot of Ekerho had anciently a small Priory ... the Ruins whereof remaine to this day which serve in rainy weather for a shelter to such as goe theither to fish or fetch vraic.'

QUARRYING

Stone was quarried at Les Écréhous and used for building in St Martin during the 17th and 18th centuries. There are numerous quarrying marks on the rocks at the southern end of La Maître Île and it is likely that the Rocking Stone and Le Dent de Marmotière are also relics of past quarrying operations. Écréhous gneiss, although different from the granite found in Jersey, has no particularly fine qualities and it seems strange that anyone should have taken the trouble to transport it across the seven miles of water to Rozel. However, transportation by water was much easier than on the often inadequate roads of those days, particularly for heavy loads of stone.

Écréhous gneiss is easily recognisable, weathering to a pale yellow and having a definite grain, which is not found in the brown and pink granites of Jersey. Its most extensive use is in the 18th-century buildings of La Palloterie and Le Vouest, and it is present in the churchyard wall of St Martin Le Vieux.

FISHING AND THE DISPUTES BETWEEN JERSEY AND FRANCE

After the demise of the Priory, Les Écréhous became Crown property and the buildings may well have been leased to a family as a base for fishing, farming or vraicing. The pottery evidence indicates that La Maître Île was inhabited until the latter part of the 15th century. Thereafter, the islands are likely to have been visited by smugglers and fisherman but sporadic wars between England and France and the activities of pirates prevented any permanent settlement. For various periods, notably in 1646 and 1691, access was prohibited to Jerseymen for security reasons in time of war. This prohibition was primarily directed at smugglers, whose trade included lead for shot and other munitions. Even the Lieutenant-Governor was engaged in the trade, thus attempts to foil it were less than wholehearted.

Although some of the present fishermen's huts date from the 18th century, it was not until the end of the Napoleonic Wars in 1815 that any major reoccupation occurred. On La Maître Île a

89   *A very early photograph of La Marmotière, c.1870. The launch flies the White Ensign and the boys wear naval uniform. It is likely they are cadets from the Royal Naval Training School at Faldouet. The piles of vraic visible in the background would have been the work of Philippe Pinel, a resident of Les Écréhous at the time. (Courtesy of Richard Miles)*

line of fishermen's huts was constructed across and incorporating the ruins of the old priory. On La Marmotière, hut building on a rather grander scale continued spasmodically until recent times and even Blianque Île supported habitations, the older ones of which, built upon shingle, have since been washed away.

The reef has always produced good catches for fishermen, who often stayed on the island for extended periods. They were the main occupants of the various buildings although expeditions to collect vraic during the summer months were also popular. It is unlikely that there was any settled community during the 18th and 19th centuries but there is a historical reference to the fact that Elizabeth Remon sold liquor from an establishment on the islands. This Elizabeth Remon built a cottage on La Maître Île but it was later abandoned.

It was not the limited fishing activities around the islands themselves that caused the long-drawn-out disputes between the English and the French: these were initiated by the far more lucrative oyster dredging business (see chapter 12). After the Battle of Waterloo (1815), which ended the Napoleonic Wars, a new era of peace between Britain and France saw the settlement of disputes at international level by negotiation and diplomacy rather than by confrontation, although on the fishing grounds themselves, more immediate and physical solutions remained the order of the day. Protests by the French government as early as 1819 resulted, finally, in the

90 Extract from the police diary of Centenier George Edouard Noël. On 15 December 1885, Charles Blampied was accused of insulting the eccentric Impôts Officer, H.C. Bertram at Les Écréhous. They were ordered to keep the peace.
(John D. Germain Collection)

signing of the first Fisheries Convention of 1839. This established a division, known as the A-K line, extending from Carteret to St Malo at approximately three miles from the French coast, encompassing the French territory of Chausey. Fishing rights to the east of the line were granted to French fishermen, while to the west was common territory until the Jersey three-mile limit was reached: fishing within this area was reserved for Jerseymen. However, in this agreement no account was taken of Les Écréhous and Les Minquiers and their long-established status as dependent islands of Jersey. This oversight caused continued dispute for the next hundred years, which was only settled by the International Court at The Hague in 1953. During the 1880s there was a flurry of heated correspondence between diplomats on both sides of the Channel: this was fuelled to some degree by the activities of the eccentric impôts officer, H.C. Bertram, who was stationed at Les Écréhous and for a time owned a property there. His efforts at diplomacy included extensive and vituperative letters to French officials; the painting of sign boards on the islands; and threats aimed at the captain of a visiting French government vessel to 'shoot any Frenchman who comes ashore'. After Bertram was sacked, relative peace returned, although it was the habit of Jersey fishermen to cut loose any French pots which they found in the general area of the reef. Matters did not come to a head again until after the Second World War. The Cotentin peninsula was freed from German occupation a year before Liberation came to Jersey and during this period the French took the opportunity to fish Les Écréhous and Les Minquiers as their private preserve. Inevitably, when Jersey was liberated, this situation had to be resolved.

Without royalty, government, politicians or indeed a resident population, Les Écréhous and Les Minquiers can hardly be described as mice that roared. However, they became the centre of world attention and the subject of lengthy legal research when their title was brought before the International Court of Justice. Based upon learned evidence going back to the times of Pierre des

Préaux, the Court ruled that the islets belonged to the United Kingdom and thus to Jersey. Unfortunately, the original brief to the Court was curtailed during the preliminary processes and the matter of fishing rights was still not resolved satisfactorily. By a 1951 agreement, the islets were deemed to be common territory, barring two specific areas, which would be under the jurisdiction of the sovereign power, whoever this was eventually determined so to be. The designated area at Les Écréhous was 'a circle of radius one third of a mile centred on the beacon on La Maître Île'. Much of this area is dry land. Thus this 'right' was of no value and it is hardly surprising that it has not been exercised.

In more recent times Channel Islands fishing disputes have tended to relate to Guernsey, rather than to Jersey, but this has not prevented the French from using Les Écréhous as a convenient venue for publicising their grievances. In 1993, the flag on La Marmotière was removed by a skirmishing party of French fishermen and in the following year there came a major invasion, necessitating the presence of a large force of Jersey police, when the French organised a demonstration on the reef. Apart from the presence of a group of shaven-headed Royalists and neo-fascists, the demonstration was essentially peaceable. Father Gendron, with his Sunday-school class, celebrated Mass on La Taille, probably the first time this service has been held at Les Écréhous in 500 years.

LONG-TERM RESIDENTS AND RECREATIONAL VISITORS

During the late 18th century, it became common for fishermen to spend extended periods on the reef and the majority of the huts were constructed during the following 150 years for this reason. The pattern of life was to spend five days fishing, keeping the catch alive in *nourisses* (floating fish boxes) and to return to Jersey for the Saturday market and a weekend visit to the family.

However, Philippe Pinel made his permanent home on the reef for about 40 years from 1848, first on La Maître Île and finally on Blianque Île. His wife, Jeanne, stayed for a while but the solitude and her husband's drinking and alleged brutality became too much for her and she returned to live in Jersey. Philippe lived by gathering and burning vraic which he then sold to fellow fishermen. He was also an accomplished basket-maker and was renowned for the gift of a basket of dried fish which he despatched to Queen Victoria. In return, Her Majesty sent a seaman's jacket to 'King Philippe of Les Écréhous'. He became something of a celebrity and on visits to Jersey would appear in the St Helier market with his baskets, for sight of which he would charge a fee of one shilling. There are a number of contemporary accounts of parties of visitors to the reef who wanted to pay homage to the 'king'. It seems that these visits called for no small degree of celebration and that, when he was 'officially' crowned, the party lasted for three days. Reginald Raoul Lemprière, Seigneur of Rosel, was a personal friend and eventually purchased from Pinel his hut at Blianque Île. This survived for many years but, being built on shingle, was eventually washed away in the 1950s. Pinel himself, despite having vowed never to return to Jersey, was found very ill on the island in 1896 and was carried against his will to St Helier hospital where he died.

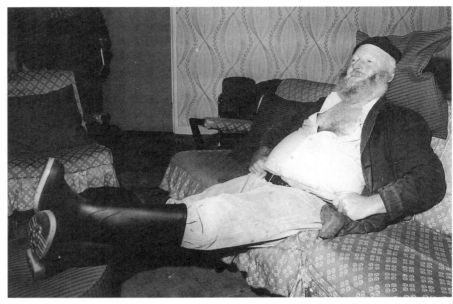

91 *Alphonse Le Gastelois, after he returned to live in Jersey. (Photo: Jersey Evening Post)*

The other long-term resident was Alphonse Le Gastelois. He was a casual labourer who was wrongly suspected of a series of sex crimes which occurred in the eastern parishes during the 1950s. To escape persecution Alphonse accepted employment on La Marmotière, where he stayed for a period of 14 years until 1975. In fact, long before this date conviction of the true offender cleared him of the crimes of which he had been suspected. Nevertheless, he had come to enjoy the solitary life, aided by the generosity of various hut owners. His presence was not appreciated by all and it was alleged by some that his skill as a locksmith gave him access to accommodation and supplies beyond those actually offered. His return to Jersey was precipitated by his being accused of burning down the Trent hut on La Maître Île and, despite acquittal by the Court, he never returned.

In the last years of the 19th century, the expansion of leisure time gave rise to increasing recreational use of the islands. R.R. Lemprière of Rosel Manor was one of the first to build huts purely for holiday purposes and his daughter, Yvonne, eventually came to own a large proportion of all the huts on the islands. The Trent family, which had made its fortune in founding Boots the Chemists, acquired the lease of La Maître Île. Although, by then, Jesse Boot, founder of the family fortune, was too ill to enjoy the short sea trip, his family made extensive use of the island during the summer months.

At the end of the 20th century, recreational use far exceeds fishing as the principal activity on Les Écréhous. During summer weekends, the islands are often crowded with visiting yachts, not only from Jersey but from the new marinas on the adjacent French coast. Nevertheless, there is still peace in which to admire the breathtaking scenery and to relax away from the cares of the busier world such a short distance away. In this modern age, it is a life of pure simplicity: most of the huts make few concessions to 20th- or 21st-century progress. Possibly the words most evocative of a stay on the islands were written by Captain R.J.B. Bolitho:

> What happy memories we have of the children – excited voices and squabbles as they
> messed about the pools and sands at low water catching crabs, shrimps and little fishes.

92 A bathing party at Blianque Île, 1911. Seigneur R.R. Lemprière holds his dog; his wife Clementine stands next to him and to her left is their daughter Yvonne with future husband Harold Robin, who was killed in the Great War. (Courtesy of Tony Watton)

Blue skies, blue sea, rocks and golden sands … hundreds of terns, gulls of course and many many oyster-catchers. As the tide rose the fishermen would return from tending their lobster-pots and wait in their little boats for the moment when there was enough water to moor. The birds driven by the incoming tide seek refuge on the higher rocks, and hold long and noisy committee and general meetings, till darkness quiets their talkings. The sun sets over Sark (20 miles away) painting the sea and sky. Blue, purple and green, red and gold mingle with the blackness of the rocks.

At high water the sea is very close and a mighty tide rushes towards the north, pouring over the rocks in eddies of foam. We try for bass.

The coming of night seems each evening a stupendous act. Completely does the scene change. It's the enormous amount of moving water so near to one that is so impressive. And so to bed. But before sleep there is the eerie noise of little avalanches of pebbles on the steep beach. This continues all night after the tide has gone down, when the pebbles are drying. A sound just as if someone was walking – and it could only be a ghost.

At dawn the tide is coming in, quickly brimming into pool after pool. From the window close to my pillow I can remember mother tern (not 10 feet away) bringing a succession of sand-eels to her babies. Then there are families of oyster-catchers to be tended, also rock pipits busy about getting breakfast. A couple of herons paddle sedately and with startling strike end the life of some little fish.

The sun rises over the coast of France. Carteret light ceases its friendly flashes. We get busy. Boiling water, making tea, breakfast, then fishing for mullet off the rocks at high water. The tide goes down, house work to be done, bathing, boats to be tended, fishing gear to be got ready. Two hours before low water we set forth with hooks and gaffs, nets and baskets, across the rocks and pools perhaps a mile or more to search out lobsters and conger eels from their holes, many of which we have known for years. One by one we straggle back to the house sometimes proud of our catch, happy and perhaps a little tired, each anxious to tell of the exploits and excitements of the day. No one listens.

For those with time to tarry, Les Écréhous remains one of St Martin's magic places.

Eight
The Churches

THE PARISH CHURCH

To judge from the number of chapels it once possessed, St Martin should have been the most religious parish in the Island. As well as the Parish Church, it had the chapels of St Mary and St George in the castle, the chapels of St Agatha and St Catherine in St Catherine's Bay, the Manor Chapel at Rosel, the lonely chapel at Les Écréhous, St Barbe at Faldouet, St Blaize and St Margaret at Rozel, St Etienne at La Quéruée, St Julien where the Fontaine St Julien bubbled by the roadside, St Medard, and the Chapel of Sire Auguste Baudains. Each Sunday morning Mass was said at no fewer than 13 altars in the Parish.

This plethora of chapels dated back to 911, when the Normans accepted Christianity. The knights who had seized the north-east corner of Jersey built stone chapels on their estates. Today,

the only survivors of these medieval times are the Parish Church, the Rosel Manor Chapel, and the unused crypts at Mont Orgueil. During the fervour of this religious heyday the Chapel of St George at the castle was so popular that the government grew nervous in case the fortress was rushed by enemy soldiers disguised as worshippers.

St Martin's Parish Church used to be considered the most important church in the Island. Its endowment was larger than any of the others, and many of its Rectors were Deans. The most powerful of all was Dean Mabon (1514-43), who for a time was Bailiff as well as Dean. He made a pilgrimage to the Holy Land and when he returned built a Chapel of the Holy Sepulchre at La Hougue Bie.

The church still stands at the very heart of parish life, as it has for the whole of the past millennium. The first known record of it is from

93   This granite cross, now located next to the lifeboat slip at St Catherine, dates from the late 15th century. It was probably cast down during the Reformation. (Photo: Chris Blackstone)

a charter dated 1042 in which William, Duke of Normandy (later William the Conqueror, King of England) granted to Cerisy Abbey in France 'the Church of St Martin the Old in the isle of Jersey, its lands and a third of its tithe of grain'. Tithes would only be granted if the church were already established as the Parish Church and, furthermore, it were already considered old, perhaps compared with St Martin de Grouville.

Slowly, over the next five centuries the original small church, on the site of the present chancel, grew into the building we have today, but it has been restored so drastically that it is impossible to date with certainty the various additions.

First the nave was added to the west, and a century later a transept was built making it into the shape of a cross. Then the tower (without a spire) was built. Around this time the wooden roof was replaced by a stone vault. The 14th century saw the south wall of the chancel opened up and the South Chapel (now the Lady Chapel) added. In the next century the south nave was built and the present building was almost complete. An uncompleted chapel to the north of the chancel was started early in the 16th century by Dean Mabon, planned on noble lines, but he died before it was finished. Eventually – after a threat to pull down this unfinished extension by churchwardens who felt it disfigured the church – it was finished to a reduced plan two hundred years later and used to house the militia cannons. More recently, after the cannons had been removed to the parish arsenal, the Mabon extension became the present-day organ chamber and vestry.

The Reformation made a huge impact. Balleine claims that no church in the Island shows fewer traces of the old worship, with altars, stained-glass windows and images all being swept away. All the seats were turned to face the pulpit and the chancel was boarded off to become the parish school. The account book for 1582 begins with the entry: 'Paid to Edward Baudains for sundry missions for the building of the spire, 4 nobles nineteen groats'. However, we cannot be sure that this was the date of the building of the original spire, or the rebuilding of it after it was struck by lightning.

However, this spire did not have a long life. In 1616, on a Sunday morning as the people were going into church, it was struck by lightning and broke off in the middle. Not surprisingly, it caused widespread panic. It was taken as a sign that God's wrath was about to smite the Island, as it was written: 'Judgement must begin at the House of God.' The spire was rebuilt two years later. In 1837 it was again destroyed by lightning, but, when it was rebuilt this time, a lightning conductor was added.

A walk around the outside of the church helps us to understand the various stages the building has gone through. No other Island church has more buttresses than St Martin's. They are numerous, some with pointed tops, some with flat slopes, with three or four levels, different angles, and various colours, all telling their tale of their ages and the building styles of the time. Two of the buttresses bear the date 1754 and were added to stop the stone roof pushing down the north nave wall. Various lintels and blocked up doorways and windows also give away the secrets of time. In 1794 the Ecclesiastical Court gave permission to

94 The handsome sundial donated by George Bandinel, surveillant (churchwarden) of St Martin and Vicomte of Jersey, in 1736. (Photo: Chris Blackstone)

block two doors, since the church had four doors and only two almoners. Whichever doors they stood at, waiting to take the collection, many of the congregation slipped out through the others!

Prior to 1550 and the Reformation, the Church in Jersey was under French church control and a part of the Roman Catholic Church. It was briefly attached (1497-9) to the Diocese of Salisbury in England, but was given by a Papal Bull on St Valentine's Day 1499 to the Diocese of Winchester, an association which remains to this day. After the Reformation the Church in Jersey became part of the Church of England and the living an English Crown appointment. Dean Bandinel's effort to introduce the English prayer book in 1620 failed and under Cromwell it was banned. However, at the Restoration of the Monarchy in 1660 its use was enforced. The Huguenot prayer book was replaced with a French translation of the Book of Common Prayer for Jersey – the last service in French at St Martin's was a Communion service in May 1927.

Twice during the 19th century extensive restorations took place. In 1842 the Rector approached the Parish to restore the church from the Calvinistic pattern it had assumed at the Reformation. The Parish agreed – after two Assemblies, three years apart – 'providing it was at no cost to the Parish'. The parish school was dismantled and removed after nearly 300 years inside the church, and the chancel was restored with a communion table in place once again under the east window. The old granite slabs of the aisle were taken up and placed outside, running west from the main door, and were replaced with tiles. Under these slabs was found the smiling head of a girl saint (now in the Jersey Museum), evidently knocked off during the Reformation. This could have been part of one of eight figures which stood proudly atop the pillars on the spire. At this time the first of the stained-glass windows was put in place.

95 The box for donations to the poor of the Parish is now located in the west wall of the churchyard. (Photo: Chris Blackstone)

Another restoration took place in 1877 and the problem of finance was partly solved by the churchwardens printing bank notes, a popular practice in those days. The bank note printing plates are still in the safe at the Public Hall. The walls were repointed; pews of a uniform design were placed in the church; the west gallery was removed, and a font was placed near the west door. The Seigneur de Rosel undertook the entire restoration of the chancel at his own expense, providing the beautiful reredos, priests' and choir stalls, communion rails and the east window, a font and a lectern. In 1881 a new organ was purchased and placed behind the choir and it is still in use today. A few years later the installation of the remainder of the lovely stained-glass windows began, and these have become the Parish Church's greatest glory. Today only one window has clear glass and this is in the vestry area. This window has a rounded top and may have been part of the transept, making it the oldest window in the building. The outside vestry door frame is similar in style.

Much more restoration and renovation took place in the 20th century. In 1939 the paraffin lamps were replaced with electric light and Lady Trent gave the wonderful statue of St Martin, an ancient wooden carving which she found in the South of France, showing the church's patron saint dividing his cloak to share with a beggar. Other works at this time included the establishment of a Lady chapel; moving the pulpit from the south to the north side of the church; the removal of some pews, and the installation of the treasury, donated by surveillants Stanley De La Haye and John Richard, to show off the church silver. This silver includes:

> A wine cup, six inches high, bearing no silver marks. It does however carry the inscription 'Pour la Paroisse de Saint Martin'.
>
> A wine cup, five inches high, bearing no silver marks.
>
> A wine cup measuring five and a half inches high, with no silver marks, but engraved on the rim of the bowl with a band and three drop patterns and inscribed 'Lorrans Baudains'. This Lorrans Baudains was born about 1545 and died in 1611.

96 *The tombstone of Clement Richardson, shipbuilder, 1793-1878, and members of his family. (Photo: Chris Blackstone)*

> A wine cup measuring seven and a half inches high, with the maker's mark I.G. (the Jersey maker) and inscribed 'Don de Mr. Abraham Horman à l'eglise de St Martin à Jersey 1747'.

At the same time other works were carried out including the refurbishment of some of the windows which were beginning to show the ravages of time.

The lovely church we have today, the oldest building in the Parish, continues to be a lasting testament to the faith which has survived the past two millennia since the birth of Christ. May it continue to bear witness in the coming millennium, not just to the faith of past generations but also to the benefits that faith has brought in helping to order the society which we so richly enjoy, and upon which our Island is so proudly established.

ST MARTIN'S CHURCH, GOURAY

In the early 19th century Gorey was the base for a large and thriving oyster-fishing industry. The immigrant seasonal workforce it employed came mainly from England, and every year from October to May, fishermen and the women who packed for export arrived in St Martin. When these people wanted to worship they trudged the two miles up the hill from Gorey on the rather rough and doubtless muddy roads to attend the Parish Church, only to find that the service was in French and to them unintelligible.

97 St Martin's Church, Gouray, pre-1939. (Gerald Amy Collection)

Their plight prompted the Lieutenant-Governor to provide a room in Mont Orgueil Castle in which divine services could be held. This room proved much too small for the numbers who wished to attend. It was decided to build a chapel in Gorey, at an estimated cost of £845, to accommodate the spiritual needs of the seasonal workers and for the convenience of the local people. Seating was to be for 600, with 300 free pews and 'the rest let for the benefit of the chaplain and the clerk, both of whom shall be appointed by the Rector of St Martin's'.

Building of the chapel began on 19 June 1832 when the Lieutenant-Governor laid the foundation stone on land donated by the Asplet family. The final cost was £800, paid for entirely by voluntary contributions from all over the Channel Islands. On 12 October 1835 'St Martin's Episcopal Chapel of Ease' was consecrated by the Bishop of Winchester.

The attached vicarage was built in 1898 as plans were finalised to make Gouray a 'Consolidated Chapelry'. This came about in 1900 and thus Gouray Chapel was granted its own vicar and independence from the Parish Church. The Ecclesiastical District was created from parts of St Martin's and Grouville parishes with a coastal boundary from Anne Port to Fort William and inland westwards as far as L'Abri Farm.

From its establishment, this fine open-plan and airy building became a thriving church and the spiritual home not just for the people of the village, temporary or otherwise, but also for the residents of the Industrial School at Haut de la Garenne and the Naval Cadet training establishment at Cadet House.

*98 'The male-voice choir' by
Edmund Blampied. (Courtesy of
The Blampied Trustees)*

Sadly, in 1977, for various reasons separate parochial status was removed and a priest-in-charge was appointed from the ranks of the retired clergy – a situation which continues. It is still a thriving church and the church building stands as a proud witness on the hillside above the village it serves, a navigation aid, spiritual and temporal, for those who would use it on land and sea.

ST MARTIN OF TOURS

Sixteen hundred years after his death, St Martin of Tours – the soldier who became a holy man and hermit – still exerts a great and profound influence on the Christian faith and spirituality of the Church today.

The Patron Saint of the Parish Church was a remarkable man, a greatly revered saint known as the father of French monasticism and also the evangeliser of Gaul. Despite living all those years ago we know a great deal more about his life and work than about many others who have followed him, thanks to a rather effusive and flowery biography by Severus Serbicus. As with many famous people, he is remembered best for one deed – in his case, the cutting of his cloak in half to assist a naked beggar. But there was much more to his life than splitting a cloak with his sword.

St Martin was born in 316 in Pannonia (Hungary), the son of a pagan Roman soldier, and was brought up in Pavia, Italy. Because he was a soldier's son he was conscripted into the Roman army and, as a young officer at Amiens in France, he gave half his cloak to a naked beggar. That night in a dream, Christ appeared to him wearing the half-cloak Martin had given away and soon afterwards he was baptised. In 339 he refused to fight saying, 'I am Christ's soldier. I am not allowed to fight.' Accused of cowardice, he offered to stand unarmed between the opposing battle lines but, instead, was given his discharge.

Martin then lived for some time in Italy and Dalmatia, coming under the influence of St Hilary of Poitiers. This encouraged Martin to live as a recluse on an island for a time. Much of his

Christian life was spent in a monastic setting seeking God in silence and prayer. This influence led him, and others associated with him, to found many monasteries.

In 360 Martin was ordained deacon and he began the great pastoral work which marked the rest of his life as a deacon, priest and bishop. He ministered to many people over great areas and often arbitrated in the doctrinal disputes which were prevalent in his time. Martin was a great preacher and evangeliser and he also gained great renown as a healer and wonder-worker.

One of the little-known facts about St Martin was of enormous benefit to the Church. Until the printing press was invented, monks spent much time laboriously hand-copying bibles. At first this was done in capital letters which was a slow and painstaking process. Martin invented a cursive (joined-up) script which speeded up the process considerably and allowed far more bibles to be produced.

Martin was consecrated Bishop of Tours, France, in 372. He continued to live as a monk at nearby Marmoutier where another monastery was established. However, despite his obvious liking and need for the solitary life, his 25 years as Bishop were marked by extensive travels to the remotest corners of his diocese, and beyond, on foot, by donkey and by water. He died at Candes, near Tours, on 8 November 397, while planning yet another journey.

St Martin has two feast days in the Church calendar, an honour given to only a few saints: the first, 4 July, is the date of his ordination and the translation of his mortal remains to Tours Cathedral, and the second, 11 November, is the date of his original burial.

There are, of course, three churches dedicated to St Martin in the Island, the Parish Church, St Martin de Grouville and St Martin, Gouray.

THE ROMAN CATHOLIC CHURCH

In the early part of the 19th century the spiritual needs of 550 Catholics living in and around St Martin were to all intents and purposes ignored.

Most of these people lived too far from the Catholic chapel in St Helier to make attendance there a possibility. It was at least five miles away and they faced a walk of one-and-a-half or even two hours each way to reach it. Together with a service which was one, or even one and a half hours long, most of the country working folk found the time required too great.

In a letter pleading for the establishment of an official Catholic mission in St Martin, nearly 350 French Catholics wrote to the Bishop of Southwark in 1851:

> What shall be said of the domestic servants who make up most of the Catholic population in the Country? Their plight is even more painful. Their non-Catholic masters, full of misguided good-will, would say to them: 'There is a chapel not far from here. Go there if you wish, but we cannot really allow you to have any more time off.' There is also a great difficulty for confessions, communions, and fetching a priest to visit the sick. All this brings harmful results for the life of the Church in this area, and the loss of many souls.
>
> The sick die without the sacraments, and are assisted on their deathbed by Protestant ministers. As there are no churches the workers frequent public houses where they lose health, money and their souls, and bring misery on their families.

9.9   Notre Dame de St Martin and Carteret View. (Original watercolour by Michael Richecoeur)

It ended:

> Herewith, my Lord, is a short sketch of the evil caused by the absence of the Church. A
> Catholic Chapel has been built here uniting all the Catholics. Everything needed to form
> a considerable congregation already exists. All that we ask you to do is send us a priest
> who will remedy all our ills.

The Irish Catholics living in St Martin – brought to Jersey to build St Catherine's Breakwater
– realised their situation as soon as they arrived. Their petition went off at the same time.

Between 1847 and 1855, Catholic services were held in St Martin, organised by Father E.
Hallum who had arrived in Jersey from Bordeaux to convalesce in the gentle climate and sea air.
He stayed with Mr. Philip Falle at Carteret View House on La Grande Route de Faldouet. He did
what he could to minister to the Catholic flock in the east of the Island by building a small chapel,
called Notre Dame de St Martin, and a school next door to Carteret View, and he worked there
in an unofficial capacity for eight years.

Father Hallum wrote his own report which accompanied the two petitions to Bishop Grant
of Southwark. He knew that the two town Catholic clergymen opposed the establishment of a
Catholic chapel in St Martin because they believed it would adversely affect their own congrega-
tions. He said:

> Most of the Catholics living in the country are daily helps or small-time farmers, all of
> them poor, and not having much money to give to the town churches. The other consid-
> eration is that Catholics in the country areas hardly go to Mass at all. Some have not been
> for five and even ten years. Everyone in the Island, whether they be Catholic or Protestant
> agree that the real problem we are faced with is one of selfish interest opposed to the
> interest of the people as a whole. Why should a considerable number of people be forced
> to suffer and be sacrificed for the sake of two individuals, i.e. the town clergy. So it is that
> Protestants rejoice and mock at the way the Church tries to preserve and protect her faith.

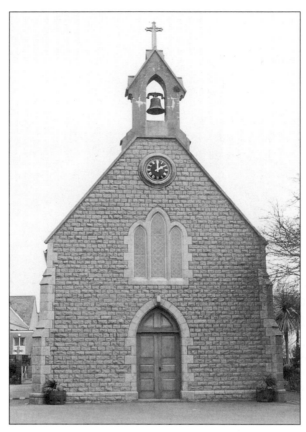

When Father Hallum left in April 1855, he wrote again to Bishop Grant. However, over a year later there was still no replacement for him in St Martin, and his little chapel was not used. In 1856 another petition was sent – this time to the French Emperor, Napoleon III – explaining how the needs of French Catholics were being ignored in the east of the Island. This time there was action, and the petition was sent from Napoleon to the Bishop of Paris and on to Bishop Grant in Southwark. One can only guess at the correspondence that went with it. In the autumn of 1856 Father Joseph Guiramand was named as priest-in-charge of the Catholic Mission of Our Lady of St Martin.

He was 65 and, although advanced in years, indomitable in spirit. He was a former chaplain to the French army, and a Knight of the Legion of Honour. To begin with he lodged at 10 Duhamel Place, St Helier, but life must have been almost impossible for the poor priest making the long daily return journey to St Martin.

By early 1857 he was living in St Martin, and on 2 May he was able to report that work was starting to renovate Father Hallum's Chapel. On 6 September 1857, the chapel was blessed, and became a meeting place for worshippers once again. Quickly, however, it became too small for the growing congregation, and in order to raise money to build a church, Father Guiramand went to France to beg for the necessary funds.

His many appeals were successful, and the new church was built and opened in February 1863. It was dedicated to Our Lady of the Annunciation and Martyrs of Japan. This is the church which stands today, but its name has been shortened for simplicity. The Japanese martyrs might have been dropped from the name, but have not been forgotten. They were a group of Christians who established a firm religious foothold in Japan in the second half of the 16th century, only to suffer severe persecution when they aroused the suspicions of the Japanese. The first persecution took place in 1597, when 26 Christians, including three young altar boys, were tortured and crucified. Later, many thousands suffered imprisonment, torture and death, as the Japanese attempted to extinguish the Christian faith. When 250 years later, Catholic missionaries returned to Japan, they found that thousands of Christians had managed to preserve their faith in spite of the difficulties. Two hundred of the original martyrs were beatified by Pope Pius IX in 1862 and it was against this background that the new church in St Martin was named.

The new Catholic Church was very successful but Father Guiramand was, by now, an old man. As his strength ebbed, the Mission declined. There was no school attached to it to help the cause and children were sent to Protestant schools, where, it was reported, they became the 'prey of heresy'. Father Guiramand was still working there when he died at the great age of eighty-nine.

The French Oblates took charge of the parish in 1884 and set about the task of building up the community with zeal. They established a Catholic school which flourished and the time came when a gallery had to be added to the church to house the large congregation. The French Oblates stayed until 1960 when, with English now the predominant language, the Oblates of the Anglo-Irish province came to St Martin.

It had become necessary to open a Mass centre at Gorey in 1903 and 50 years later, on 20 December 1953, a new church, called Our Lady of the Assumption, was opened in Gorey Village on the site of an old cinema.

The graveyard at St Martin's Catholic Church contains the remains of a celebrity – said to be no less than the grandson of Bonnie Prince Charlie, Charles Edward Stuart. He died while living at St Martin's Terrace, and while he claimed to have royal ancestry, the case appears to be far from proven.

In 1997, the last of the Anglo-Irish Oblates in Jersey died suddenly and tragically. The much-loved Father Eamon Fitzgerald lost his life in a swimming accident at La Coupe and, since then, the parish priest has been a member of the Diocese of Portsmouth. In 150 years, the Catholic Church in St Martin has grown dramatically in membership and support.

101 'A wet Sunday' – crayon drawing from a sketch-book of Edmund Blampied. (Courtesy of The Blampied Trustees)

THE METHODIST CHURCH

Methodism came to the Channel Islands by way of Newfoundland. John and Charles Wesley began their work, which resulted in the founding of the Methodist Church, in the United Kingdom in 1738. However, it took 36 years for their new religion to cross the English Channel and take root in the islands.

The reason for this was fairly simple. There were few social or commercial communications between England and the islands. Not only was the sea a great barrier but the language proved to be a further impediment to communication. The only regular travellers between the islands and England were agents of the government and contingents of H.M. Forces. Jersey did, however, have strong business links with Newfoundland. In 1732 a fleet of 27 locally-built ships crossed to Cape Cod. The main commercial interest was the cod-fishing but the transport of settlers to the Gaspé Coast was also of some importance.

In order to minister to these settlers in Newfoundland, missionaries were sent out from England. Amongst those affected by the missionary zeal of these early Methodist preachers was a Jerseyman, Pierre Le Sueur. He had set up a business in Newfoundland concerned with fishing and curing cod. When he returned to Jersey he brought with him news of the people called Methodists. His message stimulated great interest, and a band of Methodists established itself in the Island. Following this new religion was not without risks. It was necessary for those interested to meet secretly, for the persecution of 'dissenters' became a popular pastime. Early records reveal that the Constable of Trinity had instructed his Parish officials to 'do as you like to the Methodists, provided you do not kill them'.

The work began in the Island under the direction of Robert Carr Brackenbury, the son of an old and distinguished Lincolnshire family. It had been Brackenbury's intention after graduating at Cambridge to take up Holy Orders. He came under the influence of a Methodist preacher and met John Wesley in 1776. He soon became one of his trusted companions and accompanied him on many of his journeys.

The language of the time was, of course, French and it was not easy for an English-speaking man to put his message across effectively. There was a plea from Jersey that a preacher with knowledge of French be sent to the Island, and this resulted in Wesley surveying his band of followers and deciding to send Brackenbury. The year was 1784 and for the first time the name of Robert Carr Brackenbury appeared in the official minutes of Conference, and Jersey was listed at the end of the Stations, being described – with America – as a 'sort of Mission'.

Pierre Le Sueur came under Brackenbury's influence and soon meetings were held in secret in St Helier. As a result of these early enthusiasts, the first chapel was bought by Le Sueur at Havre des Pas. It was a disused Roman Catholic chapel and soon the congregation outgrew the building.

The work spread throughout the Island and Jean de Quetteville, a farmer's son born in the parish of St Martin, decided to concentrate on the people of his own Parish. It is interesting to note that de Quetteville had been educated at Winchester, where his father had sent him as a boarder, and it was there that he heard the Methodists described as objects of ridicule. Although

102 The Methodist Chapel was built in 1851 at a cost of £770. (Photo: Chris Blackstone)

he was by then confirmed in the Anglican Church, he was deeply impressed by their earnestness, and on his return became involved with the early religious revival. The first Methodist services arranged by de Quetteville were held in the courtyard of a house near the Parish Church of St Martin.

It was some years before a purpose-built chapel was consecrated, but in 1820 a building holding 250-300 people was built where Ash Cottage now stands. Ash Cottage is at the entrance to the road where the present chapel is situated. It soon became evident that a bigger building was needed and a new church was built on the present site in 1851. It cost £770 and its popularity meant that by 1891 the chapel was lengthened by about twenty feet. The chapel keeper's house and the Sunday School were later additions.

By that time Jersey Methodism was divided into the English-speaking and the French-speaking circuit. St Martin was part of the latter and the beautifully inscribed Ten Commandments and texts behind the pulpit are a reminder of that period. Much has changed over the years and there are only a token number of French services held today. It is interesting to note that when, in 1787, John Wesley was planning to visit the islands, it was suggested he would do better to preach in French, however inaccurately, than to try to preach in English!

The St Martin Methodist Church serves the needs of the community, as it has done since the foundation stone was laid in 1850, and is a reminder of the early Methodists who struggled against persecution to worship God in the manner of their choosing.

103 Les Landes Methodist Chapel, built in 1883, was closed in 1971 and converted to a private house. (Photo: Jersey Evening Post)

Les Landes Methodist Church was opened as a Bible Christian Chapel on 13 November 1883. It was then a flourishing cause which had been started by Mr. John Cory and Mr. Thomas Tregeagle, two preachers from St Helier. They held open-air services around Archirondel Tower at first and, when the weather was too inclement, they borrowed a room in a cottage (which no longer exists) beside Archirondel beach. One winter Sunday an unusually high tide trapped the congregation in the cottage and they had to wait for the tide to recede before they could get out and go home! Fortunately a permanent site was found when Mrs. Pallot, the mother of Miss Marion Pallot of Les Landes House, who was the Sunday School and day school teacher, offered a parcel of land for a church building. She also gifted the adjoining schoolroom site for their use. For a while Philip Le Gresley was the organist and, after day school, he would rehearse the children at St Agatha where he lived with his parents. Mrs. Le Gresley would provide tea before the choir practised their 'action songs'.

Over the years the small churches suffered a natural decline, and in March 1971 it was announced that Les Landes Methodist Chapel was to close and be offered for sale. Mr. and Mrs. Ransom bought it and transformed it into a family home.

Today the people called Methodist in the Parish of St Martin work with their fellow Christians in the Anglican and Roman Catholic Churches, which is a far cry from the days when they were a persecuted people.

THE ST MARTIN PERQUAGE

It has long been popularly understood that the perquage paths in Jersey were sanctuary paths, offering the opportunity for escape to medieval criminals who could use them to pass unmolested from the Parish Church to the sea.

It was believed that any criminal who could reach the safety of a church would be safe for several days. He could also use this path to pass to the coast, so that he could escape to France. Indeed, Balleine described it as 'a simple way of encouraging criminals to deport themselves'.

This traditional understanding of the perquage has recently been challenged by a St Martin historian, Christopher Aubin. His research has led him to believe that the perquages were nothing to do with sanctuary paths, but were in fact associated with access to the Island's royal mills.

He said:

> The equation of Perquage with sanctuary path has been disproved. That the right of Sanctuary existed is beyond doubt, and that the Perquages existed is also beyond doubt. Sir Edward de Carteret was granted the Perquages and waste lands by Charles II in 1663. They can be traced through Court records and by the sales, by both Sir Edward and his heirs.
>
> The Perquage in the Parish of St Martin started by the spring to the west of the Parish Church. It followed the stream north and east and crossed the Grande Route near Wrentham Hall, before following La Rue des Vaux past La Fontaine Gallie. It then disappears but, presumably, followed the stream and crossed the Commune for the Fief de l'Abbesse de Caen into St Catherine's Valley, where it is picked up again after the confluence with the stream from Rosel Manor. Below the confluence, the stream separates the Communes of the Fief du Roi and the Fief de Rozel. The Perquage ran as far as the planque of the Moulin de la Perrelle and beyond to the sea.
>
> Only two mills are known on this stream, an old malt mill (perhaps the original Rozel fief mill) on the north branch and le Moulin de la Perrelle which was the Seigneurial mill for the Fief de Rozel.
>
> From a study of the Island's Perquages it is clear that they have a connection with Crown Mills. Some mills were Crown-owned and others in private ownership can be shown to have originated in grants from the Crown. Le Moulin de la Perrelle is one of the few exceptions. However, due to the frequent re-granting of the Fief to powerful men during the 13th century and its long sojourn in the then all-powerful de Barentin family, perhaps the exception can be explained.

Mr. Aubin admits that the milling connection might seem less romantic than the idea of sanctuary paths. But for the day-to-day lives of our Jersey ancestors, who were in the vast majority law-abiding, milling was doubtless more important.

But Mr. Aubin's research has uncovered the story of one habitual medieval criminal in St Martin. Thomas Le Seelleur claimed sanctuary in the Parish Church in 1546. He did not, however, escape the gallows by walking down the perquage to a boat waiting to take him to Normandy. Previously, having confessed his guilt to theft, Thomas had been sentenced to be hanged on 29 October 1534. He was lucky, and avoided the gallows. In trouble again in January 1546, he claimed sanctuary in St Martin's Church. Even though guards were posted Thomas escaped, but later gave himself up to the authorities and surrendered his right to sanctuary.

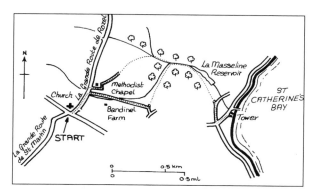

104   The ancient perquage path leads from St Martin Le Vieux to the sea at St Catherine, near the site of La Perelle Mill. (Courtesy of Beth Lloyd)

A wayward character, Thomas was again in trouble in June 1553 for cattle rustling. Again he was sentenced to be hanged. The eternal dangers threatening his soul were enough to convince Thomas to admit to having falsely accused Charles Fraere and Edmond Bertran of the deed. The Court decided to make him an example to others. It ordered that Thomas le Seelleur be hanged till he was dead and that thereafter his body be left hanging till it rot without being given burial. His name disappeared from the records, so it seems that, at last, the sentence was carried out.

105 Stepping stones lead the perquage path across the stream in St Catherine's woods. (Photo: Chris Blackstone)

* * *

Whoever said that the Victorians could not regard a sense of humour as being compatible with religion had not read this tender advice from *St Martin's Parish Magazine* of April 1896:

THE HOUSEWIFE'S CORNER – How to 'cook' a husband.

A good many husbands are spoiled in the cooking. Some wives blow them up as if they were bladders. Others keep them constantly in hot water; others let them freeze by their carelessness and indifference. Some keep them in a stew of irritating ways and words. Others roast them. Some keep them in pickle all their lives. Instead of doing this make, O wife, a clear, steady fire out of love, neatness, and cheerfulness.

Sit your husband as near this as seems to agree with him. If he sputters and fizzes do not be anxious; some husbands do this until they are quite done. Add a little sugar in the form of kisses, but no vinegar or pepper on any account. Spice must be used with great care. Do not stick any sharp instrument into him to see if he is becoming tender. Stir him gently occasionally, lest he lie too flat and close to the kettle and so become useless. Cooked in this way you will find him very digestible, agreeing nicely with you and the children.

During the intervening 100 years, the arrival of feminism has reduced the position of the husband from what could be described as a felicitous ideal!

Nine
The Militia

Because of the vital defensive fortification of Mont Orgueil, the Parish of St Martin often played a major role in the development of the Island's Militia. However, the general evolution of this force very much reflects the history of Jersey as a whole, and of the Island's part in England's quarrels.

There is little doubt that the roots of the Militia coincide with those of the police as a force created for keeping the peace. It was seen as a communal responsibility to which all men of a locality were bound, as quoted from the Carolingian administration (described by Le Huerou): 'The centeniers and dixeniers who dispensed justice in time of peace … were also responsible for leading the people of their jurisdiction to war and commanding them under the control of the Count'.

The first reference to a formal military organisation for the Island appears to be the arrangements made in 1331 for placing the whole force found in the Island under command of the Seigneur de Haubert, de Carteret. This is considered by some as the founding of the Militia. Lists of the garrison at Gorey at this time include such good St Martinais names as Amy, Godel, Laffoley, Messervy, Nicolle and Pallot; all these names are still found in the Parish today.

After the separation from mainland Normandy, Jersey became vital to the English crown as a safe staging port on the line of communications to the remaining Plantagenet continental dependencies of Anjou and Aquitaine. The castle at Gorey was built because of this.

Whether the Island was in a state of war or peace depended upon the dukes and kings to whom allegiance was owed. It was very much in the front line of military activity, and was open to raids and invasions from the French coast. In 1339 we read that:

> Jerseymen appealed to England for protection … but the King had many difficulties and a shortage of money … and considered their duty done in providing 120 men to protect the castle, if larger force were needed the inhabitants must help the defence 'for it is for the salvation of them and their goods'.

Jersey ships and Jersey men took part in privateering up and down the coast, an activity for which the men of St Malo and Harfleur were equally notorious, and it is evident that the role of the Islanders was not merely defensive. In 1377, when France and Castile renewed their alliance, they incorporated within it a dire declaration of intent: 'As England uses the islands as a base for raids upon Brittany they should be entirely depopulated, every house destroyed, every tree cut down and nothing left but blackened desert'.

In all these activities the Jersey levies must have played a prominent part. In 1422, on the accession of Henry VI with the granting of his Charter confirming the Island's liberties and privileges, it was recalled how nobly the people had acted for the safety of the Island. In England,

106   Grenadier of the Jersey Militia, at the time of the Battle of Jersey, 1781. (Courtesy of Janet Ferbrache)

following the death of Henry VI, Wars of the Roses racked the country and Jersey felt the impact.

A fearful consequence of being an outpost in England's wars was the danger of pillage by all and sundry who considered the islands fair game. Edward IV and Louis XI agreed in 1480 that the islands should be considered neutral in any wars between their two kingdoms, and that merchants could use the islands to escape storm and tempest, or for trade, and depart without molestation while the islands remained within sight. This agreement was reinforced by the issue of a Papal Bull by Pope Sixtus IV providing for both spiritual and material penalties: 'Sentence of anathema and eternal damnation (with confiscation of goods) on all who commit such crimes against the islands, or within sight of them as far as an eye can reach.'

In 1549 the French sent a fleet under Captain Francis Breuil (de Bretagne) out of St Malo to Jersey, where they made a landing at Bouley Bay but were beaten back to their ships in a bloody battle at Jardin d'Olivet. It is believed that this is where the Island's Militia fought in brigade formation for the first time.

The Reformation transformed the nature of conflicts in Europe. In France the Edict of St Maur in 1568 banished all Huguenot ministers and made refugees of all who would not subscribe to the supremacy of Rome. The influx of protestants to Jersey brought new ideas and energy in trade.

At the time of the Spanish Armada in 1588 the accounts of Edward Payne, the Connétable of St Martin, reveal that the sum of 16 *ecus* was paid to one Jean Faultrat, who was a member of a prominent Huguenot family in the Island, for an expedition he made to discover the result of the proposed invasion. In the same accounts money was also allocated for powder and lead for the musketeers of the Parish and also for two silver flasks as prizes for their target shooting.

Much of what we know about our Militia in Tudor times is found in the correspondence of Sir Walter Raleigh who was appointed Governor in 1600. An Act of the States, before Raleigh's arrival, revealed that the Royal castles had lacked for maintenance. The States announced: 'Our duty lies in putting our efforts and skill to defend the fortresses … Jean Perrin, Seigneur of Rozel, to have oversight of Mont Orgueil with twelve men above the normal garrison'.

Sir Walter promptly assessed the strategic requirements for the Island's defence. He had come, in the interests of economy, intent upon demolishing Mont Orgueil Castle, but was so struck by its stately architecture and commanding position that he determined to spare it.

107 Sergeant George James Falle of St Martin, c.1860. (Courtesy of Janet Ferbrache)

Raleigh also quickly assessed the details of Jersey's defence, and made it compulsory for the local people to undertake service of 'watch and ward', the basis of militia service, in the Corps de Garde. This guard of 12 local men kept the watch each night, receiving only subsistence of 5s. 6d. each quarter for their trouble. He abolished this practice, putting in place salaried troops, and demolished the guard house outside the gates which had apparently become misused by all sorts and was even used as a butcher's shop.

We know that in 1602 a Spanish fleet of 10 galleons, destined for the Low Countries with 6,000 troops on board, threatened to capture the islands en route. The Militia was mustered and stood to with Jean Perrin, Seigneur of Rosel, in command of the troops of St Martin and St Saviour. We know too that at this time the system of watch and ward was reimposed, beacons were erected and bulwarks repaired. We can only surmise the trouble and strife that these alarms caused amongst the people.

Amongst the precautions taken by the States at this time was an instruction that the Connétables of St Martin, Trinity and Grouville should pay towards the repair and maintenance of cannon at Bouley Bay which were to be manned by men of those parishes and also of St John. Connétables and Captains of each parish were to carry out inspections of all weapons, and boys of 13-16 were to assist the arquebusiers and act as powder monkeys for them.

The report of commissioners Conway and Bird, sent by James I on his accession to report upon the Island's defences, reports the total strength of the Island in 1617 as 2,675 men under arms.

The St Martin company under command of Captain Robert Jacques comprised 210 of which 84 had 'fire weapons' and 126 'short weapons'. This was the largest in the Island, apart from that of Hugh Lemprière of Trinity who mustered 230 men. It was reported then that the arms were exceedingly defective, bills having no iron, only staves, no cuirasses, and too few muskets.

An ordinance was issued by the King reimposing the ancient requirement that there be a 'View of Arms', and mustering and training of the forces twice every year. This was to be taken by the Gentlemen Porters of the castles, to ensure that the officers and sergeants of each company were able to drill their troops. The Gentlemen Porters were professional or retired soldiers employed by the Crown to command garrisons of the King's castles and, amongst these garrisons, Mont Orgueil is named.

There is a written order from the Governor, Sir John Peyton, dated 17 March 1618, to the captains of each parish company, which requires each of them to:

> Apply yourself to your militia duties, now that the manuring and ploughing are done, and to view, train, and exercise the soldiers under your charge upon Monday, Tuesday and Wednesday of Easter week, in time for my View in the Pentecost Holiday: and to change unserviceable weapons of staves, slings, and welsh hooks into fireweapons and pikes so that you may have in every Company of 100 soldiers, 15 Pikes.

As a result of the Commissioners' report in 1622 the parish companies were reorganised into three regiments: the West, North and East Regiments. Each had their own artillery equipment under the command of the parish companies.

In 1625 it was ordered that:

> Ordnance belonging to the Parishes under your Regiment to be filled and mounted, and furnished with powder, bullets, match and linstock, for which the Master Gunner at Mont Orgueil will attend you … and that you cause the Constables to set up the great Watch and Ward through the parishes of your Regiment furnished with able men, and also to erect Beacons.

The Privy Council wrote to the Bailiff in 1626 with further directions:

> to make retrenchements [sic] and defences about the Island to hinder the landing of an enemy: there being by ancient custom a day's work from every family towards repairing Mont Orgueil. To mount such a watch of twelve Islanders each night at Elizabeth Castle as was anciently held before Mont Orgueil. The usual and ancient retrenchments guards and watches upon the avenues and landing places: and to arm the islanders according to the modern fashion of pikes, cuirasses and head pieces, swords, muskets, rests and bandoliers, the abler at their own cost, the poorer at public expense from the wine tax.

In 1643, when Civil War broke out between King and Parliament, Jersey was divided in its loyalties. Feeling in the Island sided with Parliament out of fear that the King, who had ruled without Parliament for 12 years, intended to reimpose the Catholic faith. Islanders recalled the massacres in France which accompanied suppression of the Huguenots. Sir Philippe de Carteret, who was at this time both Bailiff and Lieutenant-Governor, strove to maintain a position of neutrality but felt it was his duty to secure the castles. Parliament despatched their own man, Major Lydcot,

Plate 18. La Marmotière. (Original watercolour by Michael Richecoeur)

Plate 19. A group of shags waits expectantly for the tide to turn at Les Écréhous. (Photo: Michael Dryden)

ST MARTIN LE VIEUX

Plate 20. St Martin gives half his cloak to a beggar. This wooden statue was found in France by Lady Trent, who donated it to the church. (Photo: Stuart McAlister)

Plate 21. One of the glorious stained glass windows in the nave. (Photo: Stuart McAlister)

Plate 22. The parish plate includes a fine silver chalice dating from the 16th century. (Photo: Chris Blackstone)

THE JERSEY MILITIA

Plate 23. An officer of the 2nd or North Regiment, Royal Militia, Island of Jersey, c.1850. (Jersey Museums Service Collection)

Plate 24. This Jersey militia standard of the 2nd, Royal or East, Regiment hangs in St Martin's Church. (Photo: Chris Blackstone)

Plate 25. 'Carolling'. This watercolour by Edmund Blampied displays the humour apparent in so many of his works. (Courtesy of The Blampied Trustees)

Plate 26. 'Hauling out at St Catherine's Breakwater.' This early, and previously unpublished, crayon drawing was discovered recently. (Courtesy of The Blampied Trustees)

108 Jersey Militia at camp, 1906. Anley Richardson (seated, right) survived military service but was killed by a bull on his farm at North Lynn in 1948. (Courtesy of Maurice and Nancy Vautier)

as Governor and ordered the arrest of Sir Philippe. Despite the fact that members of the de Carteret family commanded 10 of the 12 companies, the Militia gave their support to Lydcot, but Sir Philippe avoided capture, and his garrisons in Mont Orgueil and Elizabeth Castle, supplied by boat from St Malo, were able to hold out.

In August of that year Sir Philippe died and his nephew Captain George de Carteret became Bailiff and Lieutenant-Governor. With this appointment Charles sent a letter in which he pledged to 'maintain the Protestant religion in the island as in the days of Elizabeth'. With the benefit of these assurances and an aversion to rule by Lydcot, opinion moved again in favour of the King. Seizing the moment, de Carteret raised a small force in St Malo and, landing at Gorey, received the submission of the local seigneurs. The Parliamentary Governor had no power without the Militia and, realising this was lost, Lydcot fled to Guernsey and so to England.

On 30 January 1649, the King was executed by order of Parliament. On confirmation of his death de Carteret ordered the proclamation of the 19-year-old Prince of Wales as King, and ensured that all public officials and every member of the Militia not only swore, but also signed, the oath of allegiance.

In September the young Charles II came to Jersey, and with him over three hundred followers who needed housing and hosting. De Carteret moved out of his quarters in Elizabeth Castle into Fort Charles at the other end of the Island, and for five months over that winter the penniless young King held Court in the Island while his courtiers and advisers planned his return to the throne. The King retired to Paris and lived as a pensioner of the French king.

Jersey was soon at war again. France was now by far the most powerful nation in Europe, under direct control of a King who was a sincere Catholic with a vision of France styled in the mode of Charlemagne and Saint Louis.

The effect in Jersey was again to bring the Island onto a war footing. Word from Paris suggested that Louis' first act would be the recovery of the Channel Islands to the French crown. Sir Thomas Morgan, a true soldier, was appointed Governor. Balleine tells us: 'Sir Thomas has 4,000 foot and 200 horse well equipped. He is camping in the fields, resolved to die in defence of the Island.'

Philip Falle, writing in 1734, describes a report that the great Marshal de Turenne, under whose command Morgan had fought in the Netherlands, had dissuaded his government from undertaking any invasion for so long as the Island was commanded by Sir Thomas,

> Who was not a man to be frightened, or deterred by any superior force that could be brought against him from making a desperate defence: but would sacrifice himself with all his people sooner than give up a place committed to his Trust. By what he had been seen to do in Flanders it might be guessed how he would behave on an occasion like this. Such an obstinate resistance would cause too much blood to be shed on both sides.

Sir Thomas grouped the parish companies into three regiments and a troop of horse. He equipped the men in scarlet coats like Cromwell's troops. It was Morgan who also brought control of the parish artillery pieces under a central command for he appointed a Comptroller of Artillery. These artillery pieces, *robinets*, mostly small bore, had been in the possession of the parishes and maintained by them for many years. Morgan was undoubtedly a man of abrasive character, 'very sharp and peremptory'. The Connétable of St Martin experienced this direct approach when he protested at the Governor's illegal importation and sale of 60 hogsheads of cider at Mont Orgueil. The Governor threatened that he would 'lay him by the heels'.

The threat from France diminished, but the Militia undoubtedly benefited from the highly professional attention applied to it. Sir Thomas transformed the trained bands of the 12 parishes into 27 companies, the West Regiment with nine, the North ten, and East with eight. The whole, with a troop of horse of about sixty, consisted of about two and a half thousand, allowing 14 files to each company. The Northern Regiment, encompassing St Martin, was therefore the largest force.

When William acceded to the throne, and James fled to France, Jersey was once more an outpost in war with France. Her privilege of neutrality – which had to some degree protected her against blockade and allowed freedom to trade – was lost. William would not tolerate trading with the enemy and issued a proclamation banning any trade in French products. Such a prohibition naturally created a market and, as the price of lead differed between the Island and the mainland, a thriving black market was established on Les Écréhous where men from Normandy and Jersey met to make their trade. The Lieutenant-Governor, a civilian and merchant, was himself involved in this trade and granted passes for movement. Indeed it is reported that the Connétable of Grouville, a Major of Militia, Charles Le Hardy, who had stopped a boat bound for the reef with such a pass, had his commission revoked.

The 18th century was one of much conflict in Europe as the protestant and republican regimes in the Low Countries allied through William with protestant England in their possessions overseas.

In Jersey, the Code of 1771 shows that there were then four regiments of infantry, the North-West, North, South-west and East, each with their own colonel, lieutenant-colonel, and major. The numbers of their captains and subalterns varied with the number of companies. The North or 2nd Regiment was formed from the parishes of St Martin and Trinity and found eight companies, each with a captain, lieutenant and ensign, and in addition a captain and lieutenant with the artillery.

With France's entry into war with England in 1778 to support the American colonists in their rebellion, Jersey once more became a front line outpost. England's response was again to license privateering through Letters of Marque, and Jerseymen took full advantage of such authority.

In the 1781 invasion of Jersey, the 2nd, North Regiment would have been called out by the alarm cannons being fired throughout the Island. Its precise part in the action is unclear but it is interesting to read the account given by Lieutenant-Colonel William Lemprière, who commanded the North Regiment. In a letter dated 13 February to his father Charles Lemprière, he wrote about the part taken by his younger brother Thomas, who was shown in the list of casualties as an aide-de-camp, who suffered a wound which he received in the Market Place:

> The very instant that my brother heard that some of our troops were forming at Gallows Hill, he immediately went to join them. The 95th Regiment was not yet arrived: and he went at the desire of the commanding officer of the 78th to hasten the march of the St Martin's Division, who for want of orders had marched towards Grouville, having heard that some of the enemy were in those quarters. As soon as he returned he found Major Pierson at the head of the 95th, to whom he offered his services. During the whole time of the action my brother kept near the Major, and on horseback, to be ready to carry any messages or orders. He was only two or three yards from the Major when he was killed. Towards the close of the action, which seemed to last but ten minutes … my brother advanced almost as far as the Pyramid, to endeavour if possible to ascertain amidst the noise and confusion, what that meant. And there he received a shot, which entered at the right shoulder and passed nearly through the centre of the back. The officers of the regulars allow that he displayed marks of great courage but that he certainly exposed himself more than prudence required.

The letter also raises a matter of military nicety in a time of great formality in matters of military procedure:

> Our Lieutenant-Governor gave out in public that the Militia were to put themselves under the command of the Regulars – which compelled the Colonels of Militia to resign, and would have caused total dissolution of our Militia had not he very soon recalled his orders, on which the Colonels reassumed their commands as before.

It is also interesting to note his thoughts about the collection made amongst his colleagues to help the victims of the battle. The sum totalled 8,000 livres from which it was proposed that each widow should have three *louis d'or*, with two for each child. The badly wounded would have five *louis* while those with slight wounds three only.

The state of the Militia depended greatly upon the vigour of each successive Governor. General Don was in power from 1806 to 1814. Don was by training a Royal Engineer, although he had commanded an infantry battalion in Jersey during Gordon's governorship, and as such was expert in the technicalities of modern warfare. It was he who developed much of the military infrastructure which remains part of our heritage today. On his arrival he found Lieutenant-Colonel John Le Couteur already in place, since his appointment as Inspector of Militia by General Gordon in 1799. These two men wrought great things for the Militia's discipline and efficiency over the five-year period of their collaboration up to the time, in 1811, when Le Couteur was promoted to the rank of Major-General and posted to Ireland.

Don had drill sheds built in every parish to ensure training could still be carried out even in the most inclement weather; in St Martin the drill shed was on the site of the present Public Hall. He had found only one battalion which he considered fit for service and persuaded the States to fund these sheds at a cost of £2,400. He reported in November 1807 that in each parish a division of Militia now exercised each Sunday for two hours before divine service but this practice was discontinued in 1810.

With the victory at Waterloo and the end of the war against Napoleon disarmament commenced. The Jersey Naval Station at Gorey was discontinued and the garrison of regular troops withdrawn from Mont Orgueil.

The Militia in peacetime tended towards the social rather than the martial arts. In Jersey there continued a regular garrison, which not only brought welcome business to the commercial classes but also much social intercourse to the gentry. It was in London in 1831, supposedly at the dinner table while paying his respects to the King to whom he had been appointed ADC, that General Le Couteur is said to have persuaded William IV to grant the title 'Royal' to the Militia in Jersey.

Peace lasted but a short time. In France, revolution occurred in 1830 and tension was raised again. Victoria Tower was constructed in 1837, soon after the Queen's accession. It was built to the Martello design, with a moat and drawbridge as opposed to a raised doorway and removable steps, and was intended not only to cover Anne Port bay but also to deny enemy access to Mont St Nicholas from which Mont Orgueil could have been threatened by enemy attackers.

An 1840 report states: 'The defence of this Island very materially depends upon the fine, loyal, spirited and well organized militia.' But most of their muskets were old and unserviceable. There were guns which were worn out and it was recommended that they be replaced.

Le Quesne, writing in 1856, describes the Artillery in clear and glowing terms:

> The Militia Artillery is a fine Corps. It consists of six Batteries forming a force of twenty-four nine-pounders and eight howitzers. The men are picked men (for the most part they possess real property). The batteries are by law attached to their respective regiments but rarely appear with them but are commanded by the Lieut-Governor as a regiment under a Colonel of Artillery, performing their manoeuvers as a body. The artillery is horsed, the horses paid for from commuted service funds. The militia guns, from the reformation until 1844 were kept stored at the west end of each church – proclaiming the truth that defence of our country is a sacred and religious duty. The guns were removed from the churches, on the grant from the Government of new clothing and new powder guns for the militia, in 1844, to Arsenals built by the States.

109   *The band of the Second, or East, Regiment, c.1910. (Courtesy of The Lemprière Collection)*

110   *No.2 Company, Royal Militia of the Island of Jersey, mobilised in 1914/15. (Gerald Amy Collection)*

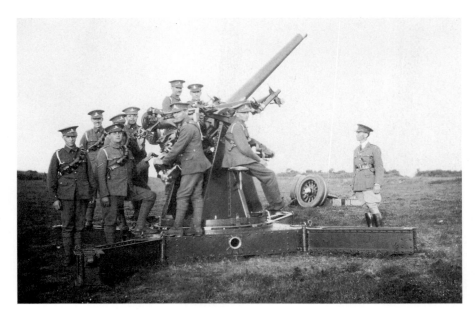

111   Anti-aircraft gun section, commanded by Lieutenant Vivian Richardson at Les Platons camp, 1926. (Courtesy of the Richardson family)

The science of war was also transformed during this period through great advances in the capabilities of weapons and of communications. Great strides had been made in the forging of iron and then steel with resultant changes in weaponry. These advances impacted upon this Island in the standards of organisation and technical expertise demanded by the UK government in return for the financial support they provided.

Queen Victoria's Diamond Jubilee in 1897 saw the Militia represented by a contingent in the Empire parade in London. Contingents from every corner of the Empire marched through the capital demonstrating the wide variety of races and creeds which formed that common weal.

Between the wars, there was in the Island, as in the UK, a belief that the spectre of war had been put to rest. In 1921 the Militia was reduced to a single regiment which received new colours on 26 July 1925, the old colours of the 2nd, or East, Regiment being laid up in St Martin Church on 2 August. In 1929, following the Government's withdrawal of financial support, service in the Militia ceased to be an obligation on all and became purely voluntary, resulting in a significant reduction in strength to 250 men.

With the rise of fascist forces in Germany, the Militia was once again mobilised for the defence of the Island. Following Dunkirk and the fall of France in 1940 the Island was demilitarised, and virtually the whole force, 11 officers and 193 men, volunteered to serve in the British forces, leaving the Island on the requisitioned potato boat S.S. *Hodder*.

In the UK they formed the nucleus of 11th (Royal Militia Island of Jersey) Battalion of the Hampshire Regiment under command of Lieutenant-Colonel H.M. Vatcher M.C., T.D. Men from St Martin included Winter De Gruchy, later to be Connétable during the 1980s, Ronald du Feu, who lost his life in the hostilities, Henri Whitel, and Clarence Whitley. Total losses of those who left the Island on 20 June were eight killed, six wounded and four prisoners-of-war.

In 1946 following the war the Jersey Militia was disbanded. Some years later National Service ended. Jerseymen had not been subjected to National Service, but might volunteer. A *projet* was brought to the States proposing reconstitution of the Militia but this was heavily defeated. With this defeat those who supported the concept of reviving the Militia abandoned their cause

112   Units of the Jersey Militia march through St Helier in January 1939. (Courtesy of The Lemprière Collection)

and the ceremony in 1954 at the Town Church – at which the colours were laid up – appeared to be the end of a distinguished story.

But 30 years later the Militia was reinstated. The UK government requested a contribution from the Jersey government to help reduce the costs of the defence budget to the taxpayer. The States agreed to establish a Squadron of Royal Engineers as part of the Territorial Army at the Islanders' expense. The Squadron was formed in October 1988, and the title of 'Royal Militia Island of Jersey' was approved by the Queen. The Militia provided a Royal Guard for her visit to Jersey in 1989.

The role of the Squadron, originally that of a Field Squadron, was changed in December 1991 to that of support for the RAF Harrier force. Shortly afterwards the Squadron took over the new TA Centre converted for them by the States at La Collette and named after one of Jersey's famous sons, Lieutenant-Colonel Ferdinand Le Quesne VC. The Squadron's new Honorary Colonel was another of Jersey's famous military commanders, General Sir John Wilsey. He rose to the very pinnacle of the British Army as Commander-in-Chief before his retirement in the last decade of the 20th century. In 1995 the Squadron was granted Privilege by the States, an honour designed to equate to the traditional Freedom of the City granted to units elsewhere.

The Municipality

THE PARISH ADMINISTRATION

At the heart of life in St Martin lies the parish administration. At its head is the Connétable, who is elected by an Electoral Assembly and sworn in at the Royal Court for a three-year term of office. Sometimes there is more than one candidate for the office, and on these occasions an election must take place, with the same procedures being followed as when there is an election for Members of the States.

The Connétable is supported by two procureurs du bien public who are elected by an assembly of principals and electors to keep an eye on finances and the running of parish affairs. These officers are also sworn in at the Royal Court and serve a term of three years. There is also a Comité Paroissial, a committee consisting of the Connétable, the two procureurs, the Rector, the churchwardens, the Parish Deputy, and the three centeniers. These officers are not sworn in as a committee, but serve in an advisory capacity.

The Parish also relies upon a Roads Committee (Comité des Chemins), which consists of five officers: the Connétable, the Rector and three parishioners elected at a Parish Assembly and

113   On 1 March 1989 the Parish presented certificates to 44 former officials, including Connétables, procureurs du bien public, Honorary Police and members of the Roads Committee. Former Connétable, Winter De Gruchy, holding a certificate, sits in front of his successor, Stanley De La Haye. (Photo: Jersey Evening Post)

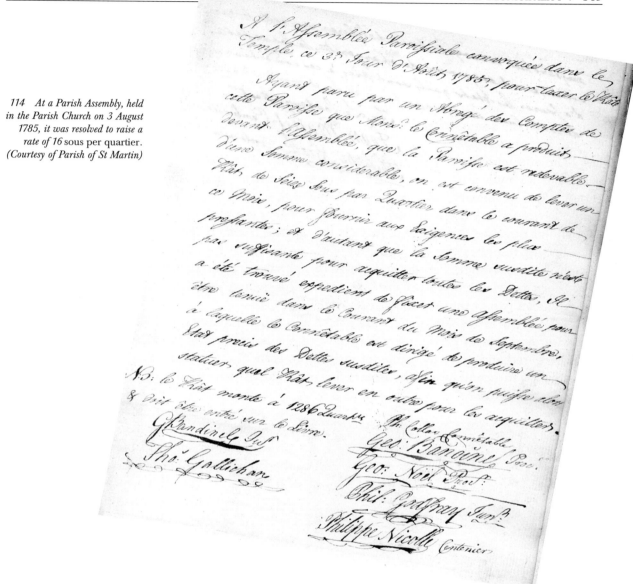

114 At a Parish Assembly, held in the Parish Church on 3 August 1785, it was resolved to raise a rate of 16 sous per quartier. (Courtesy of Parish of St Martin)

sworn in at the Royal Court to serve a term of office lasting three years. This committee is respon-sible for the upkeep of Parish by-roads, ensuring that they are properly cleaned and swept, and resurfaced when necessary, and that the drains are maintained and kept clean. The Roads Com-mittee is also responsible for the employment of roadsweepers; for the regular collection of refuse and for the Visites du Branchage. These must be arranged twice a year in July and September: trees must be cut by landowners or tenants to give a clearance of 12 feet over a road and eight feet over a pavement, the hedges must be cut and the cuttings cleared away. The Roads Committee is supported by the Roads Inspectors. Each vingtaine has two inspectors, giving a total of 10 for the whole Parish. These officers are also elected at a Parish Assembly and are sworn in at the Royal Court to serve a term of three years. In the past they were responsible for calculating and paying the wages due to the road-sweepers in their vingtaine, on behalf of the Roads Committee. They were also responsible for reporting any road repairs which might be necessary, or problems with trees and branchage. Today, however, the job of calculating the wages for roadsweepers, when it has been necessary to employ them, is done in the Parish Office. There is now one full-time employee in the administration who is employed by the Roads Committee and is responsible for the upkeep of the roads.

The administration of the Parish is based upon an annual cycle. In January, the property schedules for rates are sent out and have to be completed and returned by the middle of the month. Also in January, licences must be renewed, including dog licences and *port d'armes*, or shot-gun licences. A large number of driving licences are also due for renewal in January, although this is not an annual event. In 1994 the law was changed and the licences of those passing their driving test after that date must be renewed five years from the date of issue. In the same month, Sunday Trading Permits and Places of Refreshment Permits are also due for renewal.

February, March and April are busy months for the rates assessors, and the assessment committee sits on two or three evenings each week.

In May the assessment notices are posted and the committee sits for seven consecutive days to answer any queries parishioners may have on the assessment of their property. The draft rate list is prepared and made available for inspection. Franchise forms are sent out, usually with the assessment notice, and have to be returned, completed, by the end of June. On 31 May the Parish financial year ends.

115 *This roadside sign at the bottom of Les Landes Hill commemorates those responsible for the road's reconstruction. (Photo: Chris Blackstone)*

In June and July franchise forms for voting are received and processed. The electoral list is prepared and made available for inspection, and the preparation of accounts takes place, ready for the Parish Assembly which is held to fix the rate. Also at this time the estimates of the proposed requirements for the next financial year are prepared. After the Assembly has fixed the rate for the current year the rate demands are prepared and posted.

In August and September the rate payments are collected. According to the Rate Law these must be paid within two months of the rate being fixed. This is followed by the preparation and printing of the rate book.

In the past the collection of parish rates was the responsibility of the vingtenier and until recently there was one parish whose vingteniers still performed this duty. In October, the vingteniers in St Martin sit for those who wish to perpetuate this tradition. After this, parish rate reminders are sent and a few weeks later names of defaulters are sent to a debt collector and, if necessary, taken to court.

In November and December, the property schedules are prepared ready for posting in early January.

These are the annual tasks which must be carried out in order to keep the Parish running smoothly. There are other matters which come under the parish administration, including welfare claims, issuing firearms certificates, the hire of the Public Hall and any work required by the honorary police. There are also, from time to time, Parish and Electoral Assemblies to be arranged to consider such matters as requests for liquor licences, the election of parish officials and any item requiring the decision of the principals (ratepayers) and electors of the Parish. The notice for an Assembly must be posted in the parish box at the church to cover a Sunday and must give a minimum notice of 48 hours prior to the Assembly.

Every six years arrangements must be made to receive a Visite Royal. On this occasion the members of the Royal Court visit the Parish to inspect the parish books. The Parish must also find three or more matters upon which the Court can be asked to give a judgement. For instance there may be a tree which the administration feels is dangerous and should be brought down, but the owner disagrees. In this ceremony, which is steeped in ancient ritual, the Royal Court will make its decision, and lawyers can be invited to make representations on the site.

Every three years there is an election for Members of the States. The term for a Deputy is three years and for a Senator six years.

As well as these considerable duties, the administration is responsible for the upkeep of all the Parish properties.

ST MARTIN'S PUBLIC HALL

In 1877 each of the parishes of Jersey was offered £2,000 by the States to build themselves a Parish Hall. In St Martin, a Parish Assembly was duly convened and parishioners met at the *Royal Hotel* to consider this matter.

The Assembly instructed the Connétable to invite tenders for a two-storey building, but when they came in, the Parish was not satisfied with the tenders it received. This was a major obstacle, and 10 years passed before the Parish received an offer of £75 towards the cost of the new building from the Rector of St Martin, the Reverend Le Neveu. The money had been given by friends of St Martin's Church Sunday School towards the cost of the erection of a public hall on the condition that the Sunday School should be held in it on Sunday mornings. As a result, St Martin's is the only parish to have a Public rather than a Parish Hall, although St Helier also differs from the norm, having a Town Hall.

New plans were drawn up by the architect, Hammond Rush, with an estimated cost of £300. This scheme was eventually adopted, and the Public Hall was built. In the past 100 years it has been refurbished and extended several times.

In April 1954, under Constable Henry Ahier, a Parish Assembly approved plans to extend the building to provide administrative offices for an estimated cost of £2,233. In 1971, during the term of office of Constable George Le Masurier, the offices were again extended, adding centeniers' offices and an office for the Connétable. 1987 saw the collapse of the hall floor when the leg of the

116 *The plaque commemorating the building of the Public Hall. The image of St Martin was presented by Ransom's Garden Centre in 1980. (Photo: Chris Blackstone)*

piano fell through it. The hall and committee room to the rear of the stage were then totally refurbished and the hall reopened by the Bailiff of Jersey, Sir Peter Crill, in 1988.

The main office was renovated and improved in 1991 by Constable Stanley De La Haye. His successor, John Germain, authorised a further extension to the offices and the redecoration of the hall in 1997. This was major work; the new extension included three offices for the honorary police, toilet facilities for the disabled and a small kitchen. Use was made of the roof space, providing two large committee rooms. This time the work cost £180,000 – 600 times more than the cost of building the original hall. The extended building was officially opened by the Bailiff of Jersey, Sir Philip Bailhache, in 1997.

117 *The Public Hall has always been a popular venue for social events. At this meeting of St Martin's Ex-servicemen's Association in the 1930s. Colonel Stocker (President) stands in front of the police batons. On his right is J.T. Amy (Secretary). Electricity had not been installed and the lamp is fuelled by acetylene. (John Le Seelleur Collection)*

Those generous supporters of St Martin's Parish Church Sunday School in the 19th century would be pleased to know that a thriving Sunday School still meets in the Public Hall each weekend.

PARISH FINANCES

'The Connétable is responsible for the preparation of accounts which show the general balances of the Parish and its income and expenditure for each financial year'. This is set down in the Report of the Auditors to the Principals and Electors of the Parish of St Martin. The Connétable is also responsible for keeping proper accounting records and, together with the procureurs du bien public, 'for safeguarding the assets of the Parish and hence for taking reasonable steps for the prevention and detection of fraud and other irregularities'.

Although much public expenditure is now centralised in the States of Jersey, there are still important and significant items that are funded through the parishes. St Martin's financial year ends on 31 May and, for 1998/9, a total expenditure of over half a million pounds was budgeted. The three largest items of expenditure are roads and properties at £160,000, public welfare £145,000, and general administration £95,000.

The responsibility for roads and properties involves the upkeep of roads in the Parish, other than the main roads, which are maintained by the States. Roads maintenance is under the supervision of the Comité des Chemins which appoints inspectors in each vingtaine. In the safe at the Public Hall, among many other historic records, are the minutes recording the activities of this Comité well back into the last century. The responsibility for the collection of refuse costs the Parish £45,000 per annum: a sobering thought, when taking empty bottles to the glass bin!

Parish Welfare includes a number of responsibilities and much of the allocation of funds is under the personal supervision of the Connétable. Grants are made to assist with nursing home accommodation, for fuel, for medical and dental treatment, to the unemployed and to the aged and infirm. However, able-bodied men seeking assistance may well find that they are required to help with road maintenance work.

Over the years, there have been a number of charitable bequests to parish funds, including the Don Gruchy (the gift of Mrs. Jeanne Gruchy in 1848), which funded the Clos des Pauvres, a field leased out, the income of which is added to welfare funds. These bequests are administered as part of *Charité* by the *surveillants* (churchwardens). The *surveillants* also administer the *Trésor*, which is the fund for church maintenance, and also pays the sexton and graveyard worker and maintains the graveyards. The 'H' Trust, an anonymous bequest, which is administered by the Connétable and procureurs as trustees, provided the Parish's first sheltered housing.

In recent years, a Sheltered Housing Fund has been set up to provide accommodation for the elderly of the Parish. In the financial year 1977/8, £50,000 was injected into this fund. A plan was devised to build additional housing adjacent to that already existing at Le Court Clos. Along with the Housing Association, this is seen as a worthwhile enterprise to care and provide for parishioners and to support the entity of the Parish as a community.

Apart from rentals, bank interest and small receipts from 339 licensed dogs, 90 holders of *un permis de port d'arme* (shotgun licence), and sale of *bannelais* (road sweepings auctioned to farmers as

118 The Parish note or Billet used about one hundred years ago to fund major projects. This was more akin to a loan security than a true bank note. (Courtesy of the Parish of St Martin)

119 The parish rates register of 1784. The Lemprière family appear as the largest landowners, but the Richardsons, Mallets, Noëls and Nicolles are also featured. (Courtesy of the Parish of St Martin)

fertilizer), the bulk of parish expenditure is funded from the annual rate assessment. The property schedules are distributed at the beginning of the year to every property holder, requiring them to give details of their properties and particularly any changes during the year. These schedules are duly assessed by the committee of 'Experts', who agree what they consider to be a fair market rental value of the property. As a guide, they use States Housing Department rentals and, in recent years, there has been an initiative to rationalise rates Island-wide. The figure arrived at by the Experts, after making due allowance for repairs, is divided between the owner's *(foncier's) quartiers* and the occupier's financial responsibility. For 1998, the total rate assessment amounted to 22,426,357 *quartiers.* The greatest assessment at 223,947 quartiers was for *Les Arches Hotel,* with Rosel Manor in second place at 166,143. At the other end of the scale, a number of people are charged at 60 quartiers, giving rise to a rate charge of £1.20, for small areas of garden, which encroach from their properties in neighbouring parishes. Possibly the smallest individual property is an outhouse at Les Écréhous, assessed at 261 quartiers and liable to an annual rate of approximately £5.20.

After the rating lists have been completed, it is the responsibility of the Connétable, advised by the accountants to the Parish, the procureurs du bien public and other officials, to decide the rate per quartier to be recommended to the Parish Assembly. Each 1p of rate will produce a revenue of about £225,000 and it is usual to try to equalise the actual annual charge, as far as possible by transfers to and from reserves. The rate is set by the Parish Assembly, usually in July of each year.

Were it not for the huge amount of time and effort given unstintingly by the Honorary Police and many others who serve the Parish on a voluntary and unremunerated basis, the costs of administration would be very much greater. The total administration of our community of about 2,300 electors and their families is run by only three paid personnel. Parish Secretary Helen Blampied has worked at the Public Hall for 16 years and has held the secretaryship since July 1994, when Clifford Robins retired. Her duties include all the day-to-day accounting; the Parish's accountants, Alex Picot & Co., only attend annually to prepare accounts and budgets and to carry out an audit. The procureurs du bien public are elected for a three-year term and act as advisors to the Connétable on matters of financial policy; however, they are not involved in the routine administration of accounts.

The close contact which the parishioners have with parish administration through the assemblies, the community feeling engendered by the many social events centred on the Public Hall and the personal attention of the Connétable to parish welfare all make for a simple and efficient administration. The fact that this is entrusted to a few dedicated employees, backed up by many voluntary workers, ensures that parish funds are administered efficiently and without the bureaucracy which has become notorious in many larger public bodies.

THE HONORARY POLICE

The story of the Honorary Police in St Martin naturally follows the development of policing in Jersey in more general terms. The definitive roots and origins of our police system are lost in the mists of time but some examination of those origins is appropriate to this short history.

For centuries the whole basis and structure of our parish society in Jersey has rested upon the position of the Connétable for local administration, including most significantly policing of the parish. The title Connétable itself probably originated in Roman times and was certainly used in Charlemagne's Frankish administration. At this time the Connétable or *Comes Stabuli* was one of three principal supporters of the King. The *Senechal* or steward was responsible for administration of the royal household including the treasury. The *Boutillier* was responsible for provisioning, and the *Comes Stabuli* for transport and the horses.

120 The crest of St Martin's Honorary Police. (Courtesy of the Parish of St Martin)

In time this role became one of military organisation and command so that by the 12th century the title had become used far more widely throughout Europe to denote any person in a position to command men, as the word 'commander' is used today.

But the role and responsibilities of the Connétable date from earlier times than this. The principle of local collective obligation for communal security prevailed throughout Europe and the arrangements made were similar in every land. Every man was enlisted at the age of puberty into a social and military unit responsible for local protection against vagabonds and wandering bands, and for more general service in defence of the kingdom under the command of the Count. The Assize of Arms laid down in statute by Henry II in his continental lands as Count of Anjou by which title he was hereditary Senechal of France, and of Touraine, and as Duke both of Aquitaine and of Normandy, and later also in England, which required men to hold weapons and armour according to their rank, was a redefining of existing practice rather than any new policy decision.

Throughout Europe too, the peoples of a village or burgh were required to report to the Count's officers at quarterly Assemblies or 'Assizes' to show that their communal obligations for care and maintenance of the land they tilled, and the ditches, paths, roads and bridges on those lands, had been fulfilled, and also to report any who had offended against the law. These reports, known as *presentements*, were made at the relevant court on behalf of the village by the *Chief Pledge* and it is this role, undertaken in earliest days by different families by rota, that has developed over the centuries into the position of Connétable as the personification of the parish responsibilities that remain in Jersey today.

As with all institutions, changes in practice and terminology occurred as time passed, but in Jersey the changes did not follow those in the Kingdom of England. When the King of France, Philippe Auguste, deprived his vassal, John, King of England, of his Duchy of Normandy in 1204 the Channel Islands remained loyal to John in a watershed decision which initiated our Island autonomy, and at the same time freed many vassals of their powerful overlords. It may be that the term Connétable, as applied to the principal man of the Parish, was introduced in Jersey at this time, as it was in England. There, in the expectation of invasion following the loss of Normandy, at a council which met at London in January 1205 under that great public servant Hubert Walter, the whole kingdom was organised into one gigantic commune for home defence, controlled by Constables appointed in every hundred and borough 'for the defence of the kingdom and the preservation of the peace'.

121   The Officers of St Martin's Honorary Police, 1998.

M.D. Blampied   M.S. Noël   S.D. McAlister   C.S. Hornby   C.S. De La Haye   C.G. Pallot
(C.O.)   (C.O.)   (C.O.)   (C.O.)   (C.O.)   (Vingtenier)

M.F. Gotel   M.O. Stevens   S.J. Frank   J.M. Gindill   D.A. Dunne   M.B. Le Couteur   A. Phillips
(Vingtenier)   (Vingtenier)   (C.O.)   (C.O.)   (C.O.)   (Vingtenier)   (C.O.)

S.J.M. Perchard   M. Lees   J.B. Germain   N.G. Le Cornu   J.G. Poole
(Vingtenier)   (Centenier)   (Connétable)   (Centenier)   (Centenier)

(Photo: Stuart McAlister)

The autonomy which arose from the separation from Normandy is clearly demonstrated in the fact that the Statute of Winchester of 1285 and the Justices of the Peace Act of 1361, both of which formalised arrangements for law enforcement in England, had no place in Jersey. This divergence in practice between Jersey and the English realm bears examination.

The Statute of Winchester, a milestone in the development of policing in England, reaffirmed the principle of local responsibility for policing a district by setting out in statute three ancient measures, 'watch and ward', 'hue and cry' and the 'assize of arms'. They first provided for a nightly watch at each gate of any walled town between sunset and sunrise for which all men of the town were rostered by the Constable for regular duty. The 'hue and cry' raised against any fugitive must be pursued by the whole population on pain of punishment, and the 'assize of arms' required every man from 15 to 60 to have 'harness to keep the peace', varying with rank from a bow and arrows to 'horse, hauberke and helm of iron'. Constables of each Hundred Court were to make inspection of arms each half year.

The Justices of the Peace Act gathered up elements of earlier systems, varying with location, and cast them into a statutory mould common throughout the kingdom, marking transition in England from the feudal means of peacekeeping to a system based upon a working partnership between the Justice and the Parish Constable.

While the Statute of Winchester was directed to localising the means of law enforcement the Justices of the Peace Act tended to centralise the authority by which the system worked, under the hand of the King by whom the Justices were appointed. The higher status of the Justices – they were often Lords of the Manor to which the Constable made his *presentements* – meant that the Constable tended to become the 'Justice's man' and to act merely as his executive.

That these statutes were not applicable in Jersey does not mean that they did not reflect Island life. The practices upon which the Statute of Winchester were based were of ancient origin and being common throughout Europe would have existed also here.

The significant difference in Jersey was that the position of Justice of the Peace was not put in place. Where in England the parish now took a diminishing role with increased emphasis upon the Shire Court and centralised legal practices, here the administrative role of the parish burgeoned, quite separate from feudal functions, and the position of Connétable evolved into one of major importance in the Island with a voice in the Assembly of the States.

While the Connétable was the personification of his parish in all things, his policing role was carried out on his behalf by his centeniers. As with the Connétable, the chronology of this arrangement and the origin of the title are lost in time. It is however clear that the term is analogous with that of centurion in the Latin tongue, with its pedigree traceable in civil administration to 500 BC, when Severus Tullius, sixth King of the Romans, transposed the military organisation, a 'centurie' – a company of 100 men commanded by a centurion – into the civil administration, with his reorganisation of the Roman municipality into six classes each comprised of several 'centuries', each of which in war must provide 100 fighting men.

The title, if not the identical role, can be traced from Rome through the romanised barbarian tribes of northern Europe into the combined military and civil administration of Charlemagne's realm, of which Jersey was at least nominally a part, and of which we read in Le Huerou's *L'histoire des Institutions Carolingiennes*: 'The centeniers and dixeniers who dispensed justice in time of peace in the centaines and dixaines into which the country was divided were also responsible for leading the people of their jurisdiction to war and of commanding them under the control of the Count.' We also find in Wharton's *Law Lexicon* (1902) the centenier defined as: 'Petty judges, under sheriffs of counties, that had rule of a hundred and judged smaller matters among them.'

We know too from A.C. Saunders *Jersey before and after the Norman Conquest of England* that the title was applied in Jersey at least from the time of Edward III, for he states:

> The Commissioners … in July 1331 heard the Islands claim to their ancient rights & privileges … It was decided that, instead of a Provost as in former days, each Parish should be

122 *Extract from the police diary of Centenier George Edouard Noël. On 13 July 1880 Pierre Jouanne was fined six shillings and had to pay a further three shillings for damage to a wheelbarrow. Details of the offence were not given. (John D. Germain Collection)*

in the charge of a Constable, assisted by Centeniers and Vingteniers, and the whole of the men placed under the command of the Seigneur de Haubert, de Carteret.

We can therefore be confident that, whenever it was instituted in Jersey, the office was intended to provide assistance to the Connétable in his command of the men of the Parish in defence of the Island and enforcement of law as is set out in the oath of their office.

The title of vingtenier can be traced similarly to the same period, and constable's officers were originally referred to as 'sermente' or 'sworn men' and comprised those individuals who were sworn as members of the 'enditement' or jury of preliminary enquiry, which from the most early times had attested to matters of fact in local affairs. Le Quesne quotes from Le Geyt that the procureur du roi could not commit a man to prison 'sans ajoint ou soufissant endite'. He states that records from 1574 indicate the number of sermentes forming the endite was only six, that they heard the evidence out of court and that the arrest was made upon their report. Their policing role and limitations upon their jurisdiction, until the law of 1974 swept away all common law differences between ranks, was defined clearly by the *Loi Assemblées Paroissiales* (1804) which stated:

> Each Vingtenier within his vingtaine and in the absence of the Connétable and Centeniers … shall have the power and be responsible to see kept the peace … and have the right to be assisted by the Constable's Officers and shall seize disturbers of the peace and take them to the Chief of Police of the Parish.

Historical record specific to St Martin is relatively scarce; however, there are some landmarks in the evolution of our parish police which must be recorded here. During the Middle Ages the principal place of imprisonment in the Island was Mont Orgueil Castle and it is said that it is this which justifies the Crown upon the St Martin crest. Le Quesne describes how prisoners were escorted from there to the Court House in St Helier by a guard of halberdiers whose duty it was also to attend any floggings or executions. The halberdiers were all freeholders of St Martin, Grouville or St Saviour, and in St Martin every freeholder on the Queen's Fief was bound to furnish a halberd. In St Martin the number was estimated at over one hundred, while Grouville and St Saviour together found only thirty.

On 18 October 1806, at the suggestion of General Don, the States agreed that each officer of police should be issued with a baton or *enseigne d'office* for easy identification of their authority. These batons carried the Royal arms on one side with those of the Island, and all surmounted by a Royal Crown. The batons were introduced following a fracas in St Martin with oystermen when soldiers sent to support the Connétable failed to recognise the centeniers at the scene of the disturbance and took them for members of the trouble makers. These batons went out of general use and have now been replaced by the officers' badge and warrant card. A number of batons are still owned by the Parish and are displayed at the Public Hall.

During this period there was much political in-fighting between the Laurel and the Rose factions. One prominent point of conflict was related to the fact that members of the police had early in the century been introduced to the voting roll by virtue of their office and were seen to have undue weight in the Parish Assembly. At a time when the franchise was limited to those paying a certain level of rate such influence when directed at the rating of individuals could manipulate the electorate significantly. Fierce political argument and manoeuvring was widespread, of which it was reported in the *Royal Channel Islands Almanack and Guide Book* in 1842:

> The natives themselves are divided into two factions or parties, the Laurel or high, and the Rose or low party who hate each other more bitterly than do rival actors or singers. They seldom intermarry, seldom salute each other in the public ways, and carry their mutual animosities into every transaction of their lives, legislative, judicial, municipal and private.

In 1834, on the retirement of Connétable Philip Godfray, his relative François Godfray, a young and dramatic firebrand who was prominent in the Laurel faction and who had just been ousted from the office of Connétable in St Helier, seized the opportunity presented by the vacancy in St Martin and was elected Connétable here, defeating Thomas Messervy by 64 votes. Elected again in 1838, Godfray served a second term but lost the support of the Parish as a result of the saga of the Oystermen's Revolt.

The States had laid down new beds in Grouville Bay which they controlled by strict regulation of dredging seasons. On 9 April 1838 the Gorey fishermen set out for the beds before the designated date and were pursued by Godfray who ordered them to turn back. Despite being threatened and jeered at, and abandoned by his own parish police, he took the names of every boat involved and the next morning himself arrested several of the ringleaders. Undeterred, the fishermen again raided the oyster beds four days later, but on this occasion the Connétable had at his disposal a regular battalion of foot and the St Helier battalion of militia with their artillery pieces, all under the command of the Lieutenant-Governor himself. When a final appeal to the good sense of the oystermen failed, Godfray ordered the guns to fire warning shots which soon brought the revolt to an end. Despite this gallant excursion in defence of the law, Godfray lost the confidence of his parishioners and he was defeated by Thomas Messervy at the next election in 1841.

Messervy faced a further election challenge in 1844 from Thomas Laffoley which he won, polling 177 votes to the latter's 140 votes. The loser immediately protested at a number of irregularities, claiming that a considerable number of voters should not have been included in the rate list, that others were under age, and that Messervy had employed bribery and threats to sway the

123   Chef de Police George
Gaudin, c.1845. This portrait is
by P.J. Ouless, much better known
for his seascapes and marine
paintings. St Martin's Church
can be seen through the window.
(Courtesy of Richard Miles)

vote. The Inferior Number of the Royal Court heard the case the following month, ruling against Laffoley, but he appealed to the Superior Number and, failing there also, to the Queen's Privy Council. While this process was going on the Connétable was unable to renew his oath of office and the administration of the Parish and its representation in the States was carried on by successive Chefs de Police. Finally, after 18 years, in 1862 Laffoley withdrew his appeal, freeing Messervy to take office; being now an old man, he was permitted by the Royal Court to step down and a new election was ordered.

Also during this period, from about 1847 to 1856, work was being carried out on the construction of the breakwater at St Catherine and the number of centeniers in St Martin was increased from two to four to deal with the influx of about five hundred workers, many with their wives and families, and the problems which they inevitably created. In his book *The Harbour that Failed* William Davies quotes several examples of such problems:

> On Monday afternoon four of the workmen and a boy presented themselves at the house of Centenier Sohier, while only the women were at home, and insisted upon having something to eat. The women, all terror, gave them bread and butter, and they then demanded potatoes which were also given, and the fellows then decamped.

> At Mrs. Mollet's pub in St Martin a few Jerseymen were quietly supping their ale when five or six workmen entered and commenced an attack on the Jerseymen. Mrs. Mollet's nephew was roused from his bed to assist in quelling the fracas and he was hit in the mouth with a stone, breaking five of his teeth.

> In 1850 a drunken quarrel occurred at St Catherine which ended in one of the oystermen drawing his knife and stabbing a workman from St Catherine within an inch or two of his heart.

It was during the Victorian era that change came apace to Jersey and to the police system. For almost 300 years the Island had been allowed to go its own way, not without excitements but certainly with little impact upon its internal administration. This was the Age of Reform in England where, in 1829, the Metropolitan Police Act had swept away the system of parish constables and empowered the Home Secretary to appoint 'a sufficient number of fit and able men' who became known as the New Police. Pressure arose in Jersey for reforms on the English model, voiced most loudly by Abraham Le Cras in pamphlets, books and newspapers, and supported by representations of English residents, who were already now, following the Napoleonic Wars, breaching the earlier isolation of the Islands in pursuit of low taxation, and who found strange what Jerseymen took as customary usage.

In 1847, arising out of these representations, a Royal Commission was appointed to enquire into the administration of justice in the Channel Islands and their critical views may be summarised in the following extracts from their report:

> The first objection is that the functions of the police are so distributed that the authority of the several officers is confined to districts unnecessarily small ... no reason appears to exist for confining the authority of any police officer to the particular vingtaine or parish.

> The next objection is that the police is made up of persons whose principal business is not the discharge of the duty imposed by their character as police officers, and who do not act under the constant superintendence essential to a well organised system.

> Another result of the imperfect organisation of the system is that there are no places appropriate to the temporary confinement of persons apprehended. By law the parties can not be placed in prison without a magistrate's warrant: the consequence is that the police officers have now only the alternative of violating the law or themselves providing proper places of custody.

> A further objection arises from the officers being involved in what are in this Island called political disputes ... In every parish there is a strong police and anti-police party. The elections of officers of police are the occasions for eager party conflicts.

> Mr Le Sueur ... suggests three remedies: an improvement in the law on rating, appointment of a magistrate for immediate adjudication on minor offences, and the institution of a paid night watch.

The Commissioners agreed with Mr. Le Sueur as to two of the remedies, the appointment of a magistrate and a night watch, but considered a revised rating law insufficient to eliminate political manoeuvring. They recommended a paid police force, independent of the parochial assemblies, having power to act throughout the Island, while Connétables, centeniers, vingteniers and constable's officers should lose their policing role while still being elected as before. In making these recommendations the commissioners quite evidently misunderstood the ethos behind the traditions of honorary service, for they commented with astonishment: 'We were indeed assured by one of the most active centeniers that he served for the love of his country; but it will not be reasonable to calculate upon such a motive in general as an inducement to undertake the duties of a police officer.'

This view can be compared with that expressed by Le Quesne, who wrote in 1853 in his *Constitution of Jersey*:

> If we consider it from a higher point of view we shall find much to admire by its encouragement of independence of character. The desire of acquiring the esteem and confidence of our neighbours and countrymen should be cultivated, as it rests on moral qualities and leads to good. Whatever encourages this feeling is of benefit for the results cannot be achieved except from the possession of good qualifications. Now the spirit of the institution of the police system as it exists in Jersey is not to be sought solely in its adaptation to the purpose of detecting and preventing crime, but in its incentive to manliness and virtue.

The States were reluctant to implement the changes proposed and the English government threatened to legislate directly. There was considerable support for the proposed measures also amongst more eminent Jerseymen. A 'New Police Committee' was formed and in 1850 the Seigneur of Rosel, Philip Raoul Lemprière, presided at a public meeting convened at the *Temperance Hotel* in St Helier for the purpose of adopting a petition to the States for the immediate enactment of more effective measures for the protection of life and property. Signatories included many prominent Jersey names such as Clement Hemery, Rear-Admiral George le Geyt, Lieutenant-Colonel J.M. Simonet of the 4th Militia Regiment, Philip Le Brocq, Charles Le Cornu, Le Couteur Balleine and the Reverend A. Le Sueur, Rector of Grouville.

Eventually the States passed laws which met the greatest concerns, providing for a Police Court, Petty Debts Court and a paid force of police to assist the Connétable of St Helier, while avoiding the direct influence of the Crown in their operation. It was from the *Loi Centeniers et Officiers de Police* (1853) and *Loi Police Salariée* (1853), that the present dual system of parish and States of Jersey police forces has developed.

The position of the Honorary Police has been subject to further pressures during the second half of the 20th century. Changes in transport and communications have opened up the formerly somewhat closed society of parish life. Changes in employment from those principally connected with the land to those more common in cities have widened the horizons of people beyond the boundaries of the parish in which they live. The pattern of policing duties has changed too. Motoring offences now account for a high percentage of police activity, while drug offences and other modern-day crimes once undreamed of have made an impact. With these changes an increasing need for sophistication in policing methods brought even greater reliance upon the skills and resources only available through a trained professional police force in the enforcement of law and prevention of crime.

Following the 1939-45 war and constitutional changes of 1946, the *Paid Police Force (Jersey) Law 1951* was enacted, which extended the provision of paid assistance for Connétables to the whole Island, vesting the administration of the Jersey Paid Police Force in the Defence Committee and making the expenses a charge upon the general revenues of the States. This law extended the area within which the force was permitted to operate, in support of the Connétable of each parish, to the whole Island, but categorically reserved the responsibility for the investigation and prosecution of offences which were to 'remain exclusively within the competence of the Attorney General and the Honorary Police'. In 1960 the name of the force was changed to The

124   *A smart turn-out by the Honorary Police to welcome Prince Edward in 1935. Stanley De La Haye is at right rear and next to him is John Noël Germain. Centre front is Percy Journeaux who stood for election as Connétable in 1935. (Courtesy of Stanley De La Haye)*

States of Jersey Police and the word 'paid' deleted throughout the law as being a derogatory term.

In 1971, following a general increase in crime and the emotive situation caused by the hunt for the 'Beast of Jersey', the States commissioned Mr. R.G. Fenwick, H.M. Inspector of Constabulary, to carry out an inspection of the Force and to report upon its relations with the Honorary Police. The Defence Committee accepted many of the recommendations made, but presented its own report, with the Connétables' support, to the States which passed the *Police Force (Jersey) Law 1974* which, as amended, remains in effect today.

The appointment from England in 1982 of a Chief Officer of the States Police Force, Mr. David Parkinson, led to a period in which the practices and principles of policing in the Island were subjected to close scrutiny and critical appraisal. The high professional standards of this officer combined with his ignorance of the customs of the Island soon created a damaging conflict with the Connétables in whose hands all responsibility for policing had been vested. These conflicts were not reduced by the fear that his proposals, and those of H.M. Inspectors of Constabulary, who supported him in their inspection reports, were directed to imposing English practice in the Island. During the 12 years of his office, relations between Honorary and States police initially sank to a low level. However, as time passed the reforms initiated inside the States force became acceptable to most members of the Honorary Police, to whom it became self-evident that their own procedures and practices must change also to meet the demands of good practice. The need for a single source of response to changing practice, rather than 12 separate and different responses from the parishes, and the inability of the Connétables to act together in consensus, led the Centeniers Association to take the lead in Island-wide consultation, consideration of options and representation of the consensus views of the Honorary Police, both in discussions with other agencies and in a self-regulatory role. This initiative in many ways saved the honorary police from self-destruction in conflict with the requirements of modern policing which it was evident must be implemented.

Much of the debate during this period was carried out in the deliberations of working parties set up by the States. The Sir Godfray Le Quesne working party which considered the provision of judicial services in the Island reported in October 1990, making recommendations in relation to the centeniers' and Connétables' role in presentation of offenders before the Courts. The recommendation that the role of the Magistrate should be changed and that Centeniers be required to prosecute in an adversarial manner has been resisted by their Association and has not been adopted in full. It is likely however that the concerns expressed by this working party will be met in other ways including the option for the Magistrate to sit in an adversarial role in some more complex cases and for Crown Officers to prosecute such cases before him.

A further working party was appointed in 1991, chaired by Sir Martin Le Quesne, to examine the recommendations of his brother's committee as they affected policing in the Island, the working of the Police Law of 1974, and the relationships between the States and Honorary Police. The committee, which was formed from representatives of the agencies involved, included the Deputy for St Martin, Terence Jéhan, and Centenier Maurice Lees. This committee made certain recommendations relating to public access to the policing process, including the establishment of an independent Police Complaints Authority, but owing to the chairman's ill health its work was cut short.

As a result, in January 1995 the States authorised the Defence Committee to commission yet another working party to make a full and thorough review of the policing system in Jersey and this, consisting of four distinguished residents of Jersey, was appointed under the chairmanship of Sir Cecil Clothier, a distinguished English QC, who had been chairman of the Police Complaints Authority in England and was also a member of Sir Godfray Le Quesne's committee.

This working party reported in July 1996 recommending the retention of the Honorary Police but removal of the Connétables from policing duties, the establishment of a Police Authority, and a hierarchical control of honorary officers through an appointed Chief Officer. A further recommendation was for enhancement of the centenier's role at Parish Hall Enquiries with expansion of jurisdiction and authority to make findings of guilt, rather than merely dealing with admitted offences. Significantly, there was no recommendation that responsibility for charging of offenders should be removed from centeniers and vested in the professional force, as had been recommended by successive H.M. Inspectors of Police in their periodic reports on the States Police; this was based on the principle that what works should not be changed.

The Centeniers Association, which had taken a prominent and positive position in its representations to the working party, considered some of these recommendations to be unwise and likely to prove destructive to the voluntary spirit upon which the honorary system depends. They considered in particular that, while Connétables should have no policing role, the territorial connection to the Parish was fundamental to the system and that honorary officers should still operate in the name of their Connétable. Similar considerations dictated that a single hierarchical Chief Officer as a commander was inconsistent with the ethic of voluntarism which rests upon the individual integrity and personal judgement of each officer and his election by the people of his locality.

While welcoming recommendations for enhanced Parish Hall jurisdiction, the Association considered that a power to make a finding of guilt would be a step too far, as this would change the status of the Enquiry to that of a Court with a resultant requirement for representation, press reporting and undue panoply of the law. This view was echoed by the Attorney-General who then began to examine ways to achieve the objective without such drastic change of context. The Defence Committee, understanding these concerns and others expressed within the Island, accepted the report in principle but decided upon a further working party, involving the agencies affected, to consider which recommendations should be implemented and in what manner. In the event, the proposals made by the Defence Committee to the States accepted the concerns expressed by the centeniers, agreeing that the role of Chief Officer should be vested in the Chairman of an Honorary Police Association, combining both existing bodies, who would be responsive and accountable to the membership in decision making. The processes involved in these decisions continue as we go to press. However it would appear that the evolution of our honorary system has successfully passed through a significant point of change and will be well placed to continue to provide as beneficial a service to the people of the Island as in the past.

It is a characteristic of the honorary system that many men serve where their forebears served before them. This may be seen in the lists of Connétables, centeniers and other officers (Appendix 3).

125 Visite du Branchage, 1998. Parish Secretary Helen Blampied (left), Rector Lawrence Turner (right) with Connétable, Procureurs and other members of the Comité des Chemins. (Photo: Stuart McAlister)

That this is not a recent phenomenon may be seen from the notes inscribed by Edward Durell, Rector of St Saviour, in his 1837 edition of Philip Falle's *Account of the Isle of Jersey* of 1694, by which he corrected, expanded and enhanced that work. Therein appears Note 118, which comments upon Falle's observation that family names are mostly Norman, some Breton and a few English, from King John's time downwards:

> The writer of this note has before him a Copy of a Record from the Assizes of the English Exchequer of the 21st of Edward I of some Assizes held in Jersey on St Clement's Day, the 23rd of November, 1292. This Record is a mere muster roll of names and is so far curious, that it contains the names of many of the families that still exist in Jersey ... [As to the *Jurati de Harrel*, or *Jurates of Heriot*] Each of the twelve Parishes had six ... The surnames that are still in this Island are ...St Martin – *Ahier, Noel, Pallot*

These names can still be found today, not only in the list of electors but also in ranks of honorary officers. Charles Ahier was centenier from 1887-99, Philip Ahier from 1920-9 and Henry Ahier from 1946-50 and then Connétable from 1950-63. Josué Noël is shown in the 1887 rate list as an ex-centenier and three separate Noëls figure in the lists of officers who have served since the war. The Pallot family have provided as centeniers, John 1893-8, John George 1905-20 and Clifford George 1929-46. Other old Jersey names which figure repeatedly include those of the present Connétable, Germain, Billots, De Gruchys, De La Hayes and De La Mares, Le Couteurs, Le Masuriers and Le Seelleurs, Perchards, Renoufs and Richardsons. Old Jersey families are not the only ones to provide adherents and many officers today are first or second generation Jerseymen (and women) who appreciate the value and virtue of the system.

PLANNING AND DEVELOPMENT

Most of the people who live in St Martin have little doubt that it is Jersey's most beautiful parish. This may be a highly biased point of view, but in comparison with the rest of Jersey, significant areas of the Parish are still unspoiled, reflecting both the importance of agriculture and the rich vein of historic events which have taken place over the centuries in this corner of the Island.

However, parishioners should also acknowledge the fact that, in planning terms, the Parish has enjoyed a degree of protection not enjoyed by other, more urban areas. It was not until after

World War II that the States became aware of the need for some centralised control over changes to the environment and development within the Island. No strategic policy was set down until the Barratt Plan of 1961 which introduced a positive planning approach to control development.

In 1966, following the Barratt Plan, the new Island Development Committee prepared a Village Development scheme for St Martin which considered a number of areas to be suitable for residential development. These included the triangular area west of the Parish Church, which was identified for shopping and parish amenities; the grounds of the house Neville Holt; an area behind the Public Hall for dwellings on septic tank drainage, and two areas to north and south of Chasse Bandinel for consideration for future residential development when sewers became available.

The IDC of 1981 commissioned a further study to address their mounting supply and demand problems and in 1987 the States approved the IDC's Island Plan. The Plan was intended to protect and enhance the environment and heritage of the Island, and to make provision for reasonable development over the following years. The Plan designated areas of land zoned for approved uses which included the Built-up Area, Green Zone and Agricultural Priority Zone. The Parish of St Martin was categorised as a zone of Agricultural Priority, with extensive areas around the coastline as Green Zone. In addition, the Plan identified a number of Sites of Special Interest, both in St Martin's historic buildings, and in its other environmentally-important areas.

The publication of the Island Plan did not put an end to all malpractice and over-development, and there have been many public battles. These included plans for Haut de la Garenne, which have still not been resolved, and a famous argument over plans to build a car park on a beautiful and unspoiled meadow in Rozel which, after acrimonious public debate, were defeated.

Jersey's rising population has brought unrelenting pressure on land and soaring property prices. Low-cost housing has become ever harder to find and pressure for development to meet the insatiable demands for housing has increased. In 1989 the President of the IDC advised the Connétable that his department would be carrying out a study of the St Martin's Village settlement area in order to identify sites suitable for residential development, and he asked that a small committee of parishioners be appointed to help with the task. The Connétable, Stanley De La Haye, nominated the Parish Deputy Henri Dubras, architect Nigel Biggar, Michael Richecoeur, and Centenier Maurice Lees.

The study report which the sub-committee produced in the following year reviewed the Island Plan provisions, and the needs and aspirations of the people of St Martin. Its objective was to continue development of the village while conserving specific buildings and enhancing the village character. Recent developments were reviewed, the existing village was appraised, and proposals were set out for conservation measures. Also, areas in which housing development might be permitted and measures for improving traffic and community facilities were suggested. The study identified five small areas in which housing development might be deemed suitable, and suggested the Parish adopt a target, over the next 10 to 20 years, for 60 low-cost houses to be built to cater for the needs of pensioners, newly-weds and families who might otherwise have been forced by market prices to leave the Parish.

The 'St Martin's Village Conservation & Development Plan' was finally presented to the States and received approval in December 1993, effectively creating a village envelope within

126 The commemorative plaque at La Rue De La Haye. (Photo: Glenn Rankine)

which development might be permitted. It had been decided that any development should be carried out without charge to the rate-payer, and for that purpose a housing association should be formed.

The trustees, or members, included Connétable Stanley De La Haye, chairman, Centenier Maurice Lees, secretary, and former Parish Deputy Terence Jéhan, treasurer. The declared object of the Association was to assist in the provision of residential accommodation for people having a close connection with the Parish.

During 1994 the process of planning and development application went forward. The Association emphasised in its applications to IDC that it wished to ensure that the rural ambiance of St Martin should not be spoiled. The concept was for a traditional-style development using materials which, as far as possible, would give the look and feel of traditional rural Jersey buildings. Construction work started in May 1994 and the project was completed on time and within budget, so that the new residents could move into their homes on 7 June 1996. On that day, the development's new road, La Rue De La Haye, was formally named and a commemorative stone unveiled.

PARTY POLITICS

By the 18th century, pent-up feelings throughout the Island about injustice, dissatisfaction with the realisation of many abuses in the legal system and the great need for reform could no longer be contained. In 1714 the States attempted to reform the monetary system which, in trading with the French and the English, greatly disadvantaged the thrifty farmer and the hard-working labourer compared with the wealthy inhabitant. Dissatisfaction with this serious state of affairs witnessed the burgeoning of political parties. There were also riots, mainly concerning the price of bread. *The Code of Laws 1771* which, for the first time in history, codified the laws, meant that no man need be in ignorance of his rights. Two political parties emerged, the Charlots (Conservatives) led by Charles Lemprière, Lieutenant-Bailiff at the time, and the Jeannots (Liberals) led by John Dumaresq, who wished for the betterment of their fellow Islanders. They were later called the Magots, a derogatory slang name given them by the Charlots but which was adopted. By the 1830s the parties called themselves the Laurel (Conservative) and Rose (Liberal) parties. The bitter controversy between the two factions sullied local history for many years and quarrels and decisions were decided, unhappily, on the grounds of party rather than by merit.

François Godfray, after beginning his illustrious political career as Connétable of St Helier, was Connétable of St Martin from 1834 to 1841. He received his legal education in Paris and his political rise on his return to Jersey was rapid. He was one of the major players in the political arena. Godfray epitomised his party, the Laurel, and took an important part in his party newspaper *Le Constitutionel*; the Magot paper was called *La Gazette*. He came from a privileged middle-class background and was labelled 'the Baron of Bagatelle', a name referring to the fact that he owned 17 fiefs in his lifetime and enforced his feudal rights with the full power of the law. He was labelled by some as an unreasonable man, yet his willingness to represent rural interests, however unpopular they were in town, brought him much rural support.

Rural and conservative St Martin continued to be a Laurel-dominated hot-bed for much of the 19th century, whilst urban and liberally inclined St Helier remained loyal to the Rose. These parties were not parties in the sense of political organisations with an official structure and a coherent body of ideas. Rather they represented groups of people who identified with each other on a personal level, the allegiances often the result of family affiliations. The personalities of the leading politicians were more important than ideas. The policies and general attitudes were remarkably similar and, without the newspapers, it would be difficult to distinguish Rose-dominated parishes from Laurel ones. The importance of the parties lay in their ability to politicise the parishioners of even the most distant of the rural parishes, to the extent of each party having a separate tavern; in St Martin, the *Royal* and the *Crown* on either side of the Parish Church!

Between 1800 and 1850, the result of one in every six elections was challenged in the Royal Court. In St Martin from 1844 to 1862, because of disputed results, the Chef de Police was obliged to serve in a dual capacity as active policeman and head of the Parish. In 1840 the States attempted to settle the problem of parishes being left unrepresented during the course of long court cases, by allowing officers elected by the majority to be sworn in immediately and fulfil their obligations unless it was ruled otherwise. 19th-century Connétables usually served two terms – six years. Party dominance was clearly carried through the Connétable and virulent parish politics were a reflection of this power, as were the desires of the local factions to obtain control of the Parish Assembly. However, massive corruption and perversion of justice did not result from this oligarchic rule and, when talking about abuse in the parish system in the 19th century, we are really talking about favouritism rather than oppression.

A Crown-appointed commission in 1847 caused both party politics and the rural/urban confrontation to subside, showing a concern to project a united front for the betterment of the Island and to enact some reforms. But by 1852 this general truce had been too much for that most political of parishes, St Martin, whose parishioners continued to contest elections with traditional vigour. The new Island-wide elections for Deputies in 1857 generated very little political rancour, but at elections for Connétable every possible device was employed to bring electors to the poll or to keep them away. Canvassing would involve offering cider and spirits to bribe potential supporters. Electors of the opposite party would also be tempted with alcohol and when, as was intended, they became drunk, they would be taken off to Les Écréhous to stay there till the election was over! Other ruses involved bribery and promises of land tenure and goods. On the day itself, bands paraded, the supporters wore favours, and chairs, decorated with laurel or florally ornamented, were locked secretly away until the result was announced. Then came the victory procession. The band led the way to the hostelry, either the *Crown* or the *Royal* and there were

127 Five Deputies of St Martin: F.J. ('Bob') Hill (1993-), Raoul Lemprière-Robin (1969-78), Helen Baker (1978-84), Henri Dubras (1984-90), Terence Jéhan (1990-3). (Photo: Stuart McAlister)

speeches which, as time wore on and the drinks flowed, were delivered with much fervour and increasing eloquence.

The bitter rivalry which divided the Island's population for 100 years was abandoned at the end of the 19th century. Since then, party politics have played no major role in Jersey government.

In 1935 there had not been an election for Connétable in the Parish for 31 years and so enthusiasm ran high when Deputy Charles Philippe Billot and Centenier Charles Percy Journeaux both declared themselves for the vacancy created by the resignation of Mr. Thomas Renouf De Gruchy. Interest was intense for many weeks beforehand and the Parish was scoured continuously by both sides in the search for voters. Persuasive arguments in favour of each candidate were the order of the day. On polling day 484 voters passed through the booth. The poll closed at 2.25p.m. and an hour later the result of the count showed that Mr. Billot (colours – blue and white) had won by the slender majority of 12 votes. Loud cheers by the Billot supporters greeted the result. He was carried shoulder-high to his committee room in a spacious annexe attached to Mr. Ching's premises near the telephone exchange. His health was duly honoured and he delivered an address wherein he heartily thanked all who had supported his candidature. Mr. Journeaux (colours – red, white and blue), who had run him so close in what was described as a very good sporting contest, met his supporters in his committee room at the *Royal Hotel* and he too thanked all who had honoured him with their votes.

Three years after, however, Mr. Journeaux decided to challenge Mr. Billot yet again and once more there was intense interest in the progress of events. When the poll opened on the morning of 6 December 1938, many residents from outlying areas were present and stayed on to await the result. This was declared at 7.45p.m. to impatient electors and friends in the Public Hall and hundreds outside. Mr. Billot was again returned but with the larger majority of thirty-seven. Shouts of 'good old Charlie' followed by scenes of unprecedented excitement and enthusiasm took place. Community singing of songs such as 'Alouette' and 'Vive La Campagnie' led by the 'Parish dustmen', with their decorated parish dust-cart finding special favour, made for a memorable evening with much cheering for the victor's best-known supporters. Standing on a table in

POST. WEDNESDAY, DECEMBER 7 1938

"BILLOT" IS ST. MARTIN'S CHOICE

CONSTABLE RE-ELECTED AFTER KEEN FIGHT

CONFIDENCE IN "THE OLD DOG"

the school room, which was used as a committee room, Mr. Billot was evidently very touched by the congratulations and expressions of confidence showered on him. He promised to carry on and do still better in the years to come. He was happy that confidence in 'the old dog' remained and that his efforts in keeping up the traditions of our forefathers, to hand on to our children, had been recognised. He also thanked all the ladies and especially his wife for having been of tremendous support and then asked for three cheers for the gallant loser.

There has not been an election for Connétable since. There have been some very intense elections for Deputy between very interesting candidates and, despite all the regulations imposed now, St Martin still lives up to its reputation for loving elections, especially the parochial variety. These are always entered into by both sides with vigour and enthusiasm and, in most cases, good-natured rivalry but, until the result is declared, with all-out canvassing on behalf of the candidates.

128 'The Parish Dust-cart' gave light-hearted and enthusiastic support for Charles Billot in the 1938 election for Connétable. (Jersey Evening Post)

129 'Canvassing'. A watercolour and ink drawing by Edmund Blampied. (Courtesy of The Blampied Trustees)

Eleven
Farming - The Staple Industry

FARMING

Farming has been at the very heart of life in the Parish of St Martin, as far back as when records began. However, it is not clear how or exactly when the first farmers started. It is known that by the year 9000 BC Neolithic man was moving from the Near East westwards over Europe, and had reached France and the Iberian peninsula by 4000 BC. The Channel Islands were gradually separating from the mainland of France to which they had been joined in the heavily forested land mass of Eurasia. Some of these Neolithic people settled along the shore lines, fishing for shellfish from simple boats and hunting and trapping wild animals such as deer.

Pioneer farmers such as these could well have settled in what is now Jersey's south-eastern coast, which was low-lying and had rich soil. These early people began to domesticate goats, pigs and cattle: man the hunter was becoming man the farmer. They wore animal skins and made linen garments from flax which they grew. Farming for them was very different from farming today. Farmers now know that the land must be cherished and recognised as a very precious, irreplaceable commodity; farmers then adopted slash and burn policies, which meant that every few years they would move on to the closest virgin area, because their over-exploitation of a place had diminished its resources.

The Island was a refuge in times of conflict over the years prior to Roman colonisation. This brought for the next 400 years a period of peace and prosperity. However, this was again followed by a period of tumult, when barbarian invaders frequently attacked, making the expansion of farming impossible anywhere in the Island.

It was only during the first half of the 10th century, when the Islands came under the control of the Duchy of Normandy, that conditions improved sufficiently for farmers to be able to clear and settle in large areas of the Island.

The feudal system was introduced by the Normans. Through this, Jersey's Seigneurs had considerable authority within their fiefs – land which had been bestowed upon them by various overlords and kings. This land was an acknowledgment and reward for loyalty, and in exchange certain duties and obligations were expected. In Jersey, the Seigneur did not own the freehold for the land, but held rights over those who lived on his fief. Rozel was the largest fief in the Parish of St Martin and the small family-owned farms on this fief kept a yoke of oxen to draw a cart and help with ploughing, a cow or two for milk and butter, and a few sheep for wool and mutton. The wife made most of the clothes from the wool which was spun at home. Enough wheat and rye was grown to provide for a year's supply of home-made bread and for tithes for the church. Cider made from fruit from the farm's apple trees provided drink. Bees supplied honey for sweetening and mead, as well as wax for candles. Even though the farms were freehold, it is known that

130 Grain was grown in St Martin from earliest times until after World War II, when the land was put to more profitable uses. This picture shows the Cabot family's threshing machine busily employed near St Martin's Arsenal in 1954. (Courtesy of Ronald Cabot)

sheep, corn and cattle were given to the Seigneur in return for living on his fief. Carting the Seigneur's hay, collecting vraic for his land and mending the roads were also part of the duties.

An enormous privilege in those feudal days, when men were regarded merely as serfs, was the grant by King Henry VII of an ample charter to Jersey, one article of which secured freedom of trade to enable Islanders to dispose of their goods peaceably. He fixed Friday

> As the weekly market day for all sorts of victuals and other necessaries for the said Captain and soldiers of the said Castle, to be held in front of or near to Mont Orgueil Castle and that sheep, oxen and such victuals, shall be sold at such a price, as heretofore, as by Justice has been ordered and shall hereafter be ordered in such case at a reasonable price.

Rabbits were introduced into England by the Romans. From then on and during the Middle Ages rabbit meat was an important source of food. Garennes (warrens) were established and to have permission for one was a privilege. Haut de la Garenne was a royal garenne which provided meat for the castle occupants. The area would have been managed by a keeper and there was strict surveillance which allowed no-one but the keeper and his staff to hunt and trap the animals. Poaching was strictly prohibited and the punishment for offenders severe. As late as 1807 an Oak Apple Day Festival for the Island's gentry was held on the King's warren to commemorate the restoration of the monarchy in 1660. Children celebrated by wearing oak leaves to school, a custom which was followed into the 20th century.

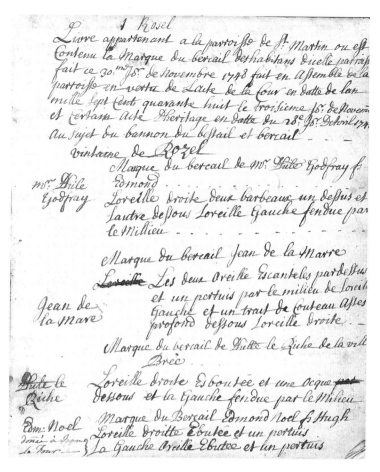

131 *Each farmer's sheep were identified by a unique mark, a* marque de bétail. *These were described and listed in a book, dating from 1748, still in existence at the Public Hall. (Courtesy of the Parish of St Martin)*

Jersey's rich soil served the farmers well. In Tudor times it was recorded: 'Wheat being sufficiently abundant for both the isles do utter great quantitie of'. Export of surplus grain to France was not uncommon in good years. As every tenth sheaf was tithed to the church, this rich harvest was of enormous financial benefit, and, until the Reformation, tithes from St Martin went to the great Abbey of Cerisy in Normandy. No doubt this drained wealth from the Island, especially as the Rectors were also appointed by the parent abbey from France.

Cottage industries developed on the smallholdings and a cash economy developed, based initially on the export of knitted goods to the mainland. This brought extra money into the households. The tradition of knitting began as early as the 1500s, possibly introduced through Protestant refugees from France where intricately-patterned stockings were a speciality. To supply this thriving industry sheep rearing was very important, although as time went on wool was imported to keep the industry flourishing. The sheep were a hardy breed, which developed some unusual characteristics through being isolated, up to six horns being recorded on some animals. They fed generally on the common land, and also on enclosed areas under cultivation, where the medieval right of *banon* permitted animals to forage freely from the end of harvest until the next ploughing season.

However, as more and more land was enclosed they were restricted to the poorer common land – the cliffs and slopes where they were confined by either hedges or walls to graze between

132 Reginald Raoul Lemprière, Seigneur de Rosel, with a young heifer in the manor garden c.1920. (Courtesy of Derrick Frigot)

the sea and the fertile land above. Some of these ancient hedges and walls still exist today, among the few remaining monuments to this period in the Island. Generally, however, the sheep were neglected and badly managed. This system was called *du Bercas d'Falaise* and was still in operation at the beginning of the 20th century. Records kept by the Roads Committee of the Parish of St Martin in 1748 make interesting reading, describing the identification of the different farmers' animals. Called *Marques de Bétail*, they were very crude ear marks on the animals used as a means of identification: *un quanteau* meant cut on the slant; *pertuis* was a hole; *teste* was the head; *ocque* meant a notch; and *ébouté* was the term to describe taking the tip off the ear.

Le Moulin de la Perelle (au Foulain) at St Catherine was a fulling mill, which stood on the site of the present Mill Farm.

During the 1500s an increasing population resulted in the planting of many more cider apple trees. There was a market in England, and merchants exploited this new commercial opportunity. There were great advantages – no duties to pay and shipping was cheap. Cider and knitting became important cash crops, and the growing of wheat faded out. This caused great concern to the government, which was worried about the risks involved in having to buy wheat from outside the Island, and the church, worried about the loss of tithes. The church managed to recoup its position, however, by imposing a tithe on the number of apple trees under cultivation.

By the late 1700s, one quarter of Jersey's arable land was taken up with apple orchards, most extensively in the Parishes of St Martin, St Saviour, Grouville and St Clement. In 1801, the Reverend François le Couteur (Rector of St Martin, patriot and expert on cider) estimated that the people of Jersey drank up to a million gallons of cider each year, and that three-quarters of a million gallons were exported per annum. The orchards needed shelter from high winds and protection from intruding animals, and so these fields were enclosed by high banks, on the top of which blackthorn was planted. This made the small roads of the Parish feel like paths in a maze. Cider apple trees were also planted on the tops of these banks and, as they were not in fields, escaped the payment of tithes. Farmers went to the considerable expense of installing their own apple crushers and presses in purpose-built sheds, truly indicative of the smallholder's character. They obviously preferred to be self-sufficient in business, and although two factories were built, both failed.

The knitting industry was effectively killed off by the Industrial Revolution in England, and sheep farming petered out when it was overtaken by the more profitable businesses of cattle export and early potatoes. Côtils for growing these potatoes were cut into the land on east- and south-facing slopes where previously sheep had grazed.

133   *Life was hard for farmers working at the turn of the 20th century, but there were lighter moments. 'The Joy Ride', a drypoint by Edmund Blampied. (Courtesy of The Blampied Trustees)*

From the 1830s, again owing to the Industrial Revolution and a new emphasis on good road and canal building, and also a realisation by farmers in Somerset and Hereford that conditions were very favourable for apple growing there, the number of gallons of cider shipped to the mainland each year decreased very quickly. For a while, the export of cider was replaced by the apples themselves, as huge quantities were sent to the new cider factories in England. But the ageing orchards were no longer replaced and only enough cider was made to quench the thirsts of the Breton workers who helped during the potato and hay harvests until the early 1950s.

So, some fifty years after the demise of the knitting industry, the cider industry also came to an end.

But there is a legacy of the apple-growing industry of Jersey and St Martin. Black Butter is a concentrated jam, made from cider and sweet apples with sugar, lemons, liquorice and other spices, such as nutmeg and cinnamon, which were added at the end. Traditionally it was made in small quantities at home over a hearth fire, but it could also be a huge communal effort with families or whole neighbourhoods getting together to make from 250 to 300 lbs at a time. Two to three days would be spent peeling as many as 42 hundredweight barrels of apples, which at the same time gave a wonderful opportunity for catching up with all the news and gossip and singing all the traditional songs. Then, on the big day, when all the preparation was done, the hearth in one of the outhouses would be lit with small branches and fuelled with long, thick logs to produce a fierce heat. A large brass *bachin* with 20 gallons of cider would be put on the *trepis* in the late afternoon and the liquor would be reduced by half. Apples would then be added (up to 22 half-hundredweight barrels of sweet peeled apples and two of Bramleys) throughout the night, and during the following day. Two men would stir the mixture the whole time to prevent it from sticking to the bottom and burning. The accordionist would have played and much singing and dancing would have taken place with lots of recently home-brewed cider to quench the thirsts of these industrious people. When all the apples had been absorbed into a thick creamy brown

134 Mr. W.C. Renouf of St Martin, setting off from La Ville Brée with potatoes for shipment. (John Le Seelleur Collection)

mixture, 28lbs of sugar, 24 chopped lemons, 1lb grated nutmeg, 1lb cinnamon and 3lbs of mixed spice were added along with sticks of liquorice. All was tasted and stirred well together. Then the *bachin* was lifted off the hearth by many strong arms and the lovely aromatic mixture potted up to make some 300lbs of *nièr beurre*, stored in earthenware glazed pots of all sizes for use during the winter months.

During the Occupation years, Black Butter was made whenever possible in the autumn. It was not quite the same, however – few things during the Occupation were. Sugar, lemons and spices were unobtainable, but liquorice and saccharin (for sweetening) were bought from chemists such as Croix de Lorraine and Stone's in St Helier. The preserving quality was not good but it did not have to last long. It was eaten quickly! With the curfew in force, everyone involved stayed on site and *une séthée de nièr beurre* must have lifted the spirits for many days after during those unhappy times.

Black Butter is still made, but more by clubs and societies for fund-raising purposes. The St Martin's Methodist Church has for many years made a large amount of Black Butter at Le Côtil, Faldouet, and more recently at Summerville, Rozel. It has proved to be an excellent fund-raiser and a traditional social occasion for church members and their friends. Apples are collected from anyone who may still have trees, and when there are shortages, fruit has been imported from nearby Normandy.

Jersey is perhaps best known for two things – the Jersey Royal potato and the Jersey cow. St Martin has some of the earliest – and therefore the most valuable – potato land in the Island. The full potential of the early potato was first appreciated in the late 1800s, when farmers realised the profits which could be made. Their minds turned to finding more land which was suitable for their cultivation, and they began grubbing up and working suitable patches of soil, especially those with a southern aspect and close to the sea, where ground frosts were very rarely experienced.

This is how the very steep slopes at St Catherine and Gorey were developed. At St Catherine, Thomas Le Seelleur owned all the land going down to the bay until 1845. When the Breakwater was built a road was needed from Gorey to service it. As the price demanded by Le Seelleur

135   *Philip Ahier (1856-1941) at Seymour Farm with his family. (Courtesy of Donald Ahier)*

was too high, a compulsory purchase was used by the Crown. When the scheme was abandoned he bought the land back. He realised the potential of this area for very early potato production and it is known that he was often seen grubbing up the gorse bushes by moonlight.

These côtils are now considered some of the earliest in the Island and are very productive and profitable. The Gorey côtils changed owners twice in the last 14 years of the 20th century. On the first occasion they were sold for £65,000 (£6,500 per vergée), and then five years later at £120,000 (£12,000 per vergée). Heady prices, even in modern days! Today, a tractor and winch plough are used to work the côtils, but one hundred years ago men were paid piecework to dig them over with a spade. George De La Haye, of La Falaise, Fliquet, with a friend to help him, dug 14 vergées in one year – an amazing feat. Because of their steep slopes, côtils are expensive areas to work, but the price paid for this premium product is high, and it is usually well worth the effort. Today, very early potatoes are still mostly dug by hand with a five-pronged fork. Pickers follow, sorting out the crop into 'ware' and 'mids', handling them very gently, as they can easily be damaged by tools or machines.

French author Pierre Galichet, writing in 1912, in a book entitled *Le Fermier de L'Ile de Jersey*, gives a fascinating insight into the life of one of St Martin's most respected farmers, Philip Ahier of Seymour Farm, Gorey.

Philip's grandfather had earlier sold his farm to live in St Helier and work in commerce. His father, however, returned to farming and bought a farm, just at a profitable time, when the price of cattle for export was going up, and the Jersey Royal potato was becoming popular.

Philip gained interest and experience as a child and young man working on his father's farm. He also ran a small farm of his own until he had earned sufficient capital to sell it and buy something larger and better. This was Seymour Farm, an excellent farm of 70 vergées, well above the average size. The land was very fertile and there was good pasture on the exposed slopes toward the sea.

Philip Ahier was very proud of his ancestry, which could be traced back to the early 15th century. He married at the age of 22 and fathered eight healthy children. Because of the laws of

136   Mr. E.G. Buesnel of St Martin, with his box cart, harvesting swedes.

inheritance, through which the eldest son would receive the property, two younger sons emigrated. One remained, sickly with tuberculosis, and was nursed at home, while another worked on the farm for a wage. The eldest son was renting another farm until his father retired, when he knew he would take over the farm. Of the three daughters, as yet unmarried, one worked at home to help her mother (no other house help was employed) and the other two went to St Helier to work as seamstresses. By 1912, Philip was a highly respected breeder and judge at the Royal Jersey Agricultural and Horticultural Society's shows. He sold animals to the USA as well as to the UK and received £125 for a cow, a top price at that time. He had a herd of 11 cows and five heifers. The sale of cattle provided his main profit, although milk sales were also very important. His average yield was 10 litres per cow per day, although he did have some cows giving 20 litres per day when freshly calved. He did not keep many bull calves as he considered the milk was too expensive to rear calves for veal.

Philip Ahier grew 30 vergées of potatoes, producing 6,000 lbs per vergée. The potatoes were followed by second crops of mangolds, carrots, turnips and swedes, harvested from October to December. These were used to feed the cattle during the winter months. He did not grow outdoor tomatoes as many other farmers did; he preferred to excel in what he did best, cattle and potatoes. He bought in as little as possible, preferring to grow as much as he could to save on costs. As the cattle were bred solely for sale and milk there was little meat for the kitchen, so a few pigs were reared annually, fed on peelings, kitchen waste, potatoes which were not good enough to sell, and root crops. Nothing was wasted, therefore the cost to the household budget was minimal. Tea, coffee, sugar and a small amount of wine were the only groceries bought. The family made its own bread in the large oven in the shed in the yard. They were very proud of this, as it kept them self-sufficient.

Breton workers came over for the potato-digging season. During these very busy months they earned more than they would have done at home. They also accepted less comfortable surroundings than other people in Jersey. They fed themselves but were provided with cider. On the farm, fertilizer came from farmyard manure and vraic from the nearby bay. Only lime was bought in, a necessary neutralising agent in the highly acidic soil.

Seymour Farm was just a short distance from Gorey Village and close to the Jersey Eastern Railway Station. The house was modern and not of the style of older granite farmhouses. The living quarters were on the ground floor and simple but comfortable. A large glass-faced bookcase containing encyclopedias, good editions of the classics, and books for children took pride of place in the large living-room. On the walls proudly hung photographs of bulls and cows which had won show prizes. Along the windows of the first-floor bedroom area ran a long covered balcony, making the house somewhat Italian in style. In front of the house was a prettily planted

137 A young Jersey girl with her charges. Edmund Blampied illustration commissioned for the reverse of the Occupation 10s. note. (Courtesy of The Blampied Trustees)

flower garden with a small glasshouse in which the sickly youngest son spent most of his time. A little further on was a prolific *jardin à potage.*

Leaving the house on the right, one entered the large farmyard. A long building contained the cattle stables and shed for ploughs and implements. The first floor was used for storing grain and seed potatoes. Another shed contained the cider-press and alongside it a lumber-room where the Breton workers were housed during the potato season. The shed with the bread-oven was also there.

At very busy times, farmers worked communally to help one another, and ate together. Otherwise the home was a very important place where most spare time was spent. Apart from belonging to associations such as the Police Honorifique, the Royal Jersey Agricultural and Horticultural Society, or a church with its meetings and services which would be enthusiastically and well supported, little other entertainment was sought. Close family units existed with all their strengths and, no doubt, their weaknesses, too. Little communication took place with other residents, either in St Helier or in the Parish of St Martin, who were not farmers. This way of life would begin to change slowly after the impact of the Great War of 1914-18.

The Jersey cow was in demand for export to the rest of Great Britain as early as the 1700s. Visitors to the Island were attracted to the graceful, small, brown cow with very rich milk, and farmers were obviously attracted by the great strengths of the breed – its large milk production and its economical use of pasture. There was also a great shortage of cattle in the UK due to the ravages of the dreadful cattle plague, rinderpest.

As demand increased, cattle were shipped over from Normandy in large numbers. They were pastured for a few months in the Island then sold at market in St Helier as Alderneys (as all C.I. cattle were known, due to the fact that the last port of call was Alderney and the ships were called Alderney Paquets). French cattle escaped excise duty in this way as Jersey was not a foreign country. The French economy was in a bad way following the Napoleonic Wars and this proved a valuable and lucrative loophole. Rozel Bay was much frequented by French boats which sailed over with loads of livestock. As late as 1812 it is known that cattle were still being brought over in contravention of a 1789 Law, introduced to strengthen and safeguard the Jersey breed by banning the importation of all live cattle. No doubt many St Martin farmers made a lot of money working with farmers from Normandy by pasturing their animals before selling them on. Acts were again passed in 1826, 1864 and 1878 when the trade finally stopped.

138 'The lovely things said about a 'orse when it's up for sale!' Edmund Blampied. (Courtesy of The Blampied Trustees)

The first Agricultural Society in Jersey was founded in 1790 by the St Martin's Rector, Reverend François le Couteur, but, unfortunately, it foundered in a short time. Forty-three years later, in August 1833, steps were taken by the Lieutenant-Governor of the day and important gentlemen farmers to form an agricultural and horticultural society. By the end of the year King William IV had graciously bestowed his patronage on the newly founded Royal Jersey Agricultural and Horticultural Society.

The most important step forward for the breed took place in 1866, when the herd book was formed to register officially all animals. The first bull registered was 'Dandy' belonging to Mr. James Godfray of St Martin. The breeding of good Jersey cattle became an integral part of Island life, and its importance resulted in many parishes forming their own breeding and showing societies. In 1894 the Comice Agricole de St Martin was born. It was to play a most important part in the social life of the Parish.

In Rozel Vingtaine, St Martin, in the 1920s, there were 55 small family-run mixed farms. The average size of a herd was eight or nine cows with three or four followers and maybe one bull. Animals were all tethered, and were rugged in winter. They were milked by hand, mainly by the daughters of the family. Butter was churned and sold at the weekly market in St Helier. Pigs and chickens made up the menagerie and were fed on grain and leftovers. Jersey talljacks were widely grown, as were mangolds, turnips and swedes after potatoes, for use in winter when the grass no longer grew. Hay was conserved for winter feed by mowing with horses or manually

139 'Bouquet's Dreaming Dazzler' of La Poudretterie, Rozel, the most sensational sire the island has ever bred. Sire of eight Island Supreme Champion cows, winner of silver and gold medals and 27 progeny titles. (Courtesy of John Pallot)

140 'Ansom Designette' was a gift to Queen Elizabeth from the R.J.A.and H.S. in 1978. Her breeder, Anne Perchard of La Ferme, is pictured with the Queen during her visit to Jersey that summer. (Courtesy of Anne Perchard)

with a scythe (mostly by Breton workers, who were paid piecework). This was intensive manual work, and the hay was turned by hand with hayforks and put into haycocks or on mushroom-shaped granite stones so that vermin could not attack it. When the hay was ready for the loft, it was made into *bottes*, loaded onto vans, and thrown into the loft and stacked. Oats and wheat for animal feed, and bread, were also grown and harvested. Ricks were built in farmyards. Threshing, in the late autumn, was a communal effort with a huge meal to finish the proceedings in the farm kitchen of the farmer concerned. Some cider apple trees remained and cider was still made for the labourers and the family. Some farmers also bottled cider to be kept for special occasions, but this could be a tricky business with corks flying out with mighty bangs, if the cider had not been bottled at exactly the correct time. It was rumoured that the state of the moon played its part in determining when bottling should take place!

On these smallholdings fifteen to twenty vergées of Royal early potatoes were grown. They were planted by hand following a horse and planting plough, then weeded and harrowed by hand, banked up (ridged) by a horse pulling a scarifier and banking hoe, then sprayed with a hand-pumped knapsack sprayer using copper sulphate or dust. Again, it was labour-intensive work.

Breton *paysans* would come over for the digging, usually in family groups of three or four. The accommodation provided for them was very basic. They would live and cook in one of the outhouses. Some would even sleep in the hayloft. They brought their salt pork with them and this, cooked with bread and soup, washed down by litres of farm cider, formed their basic diet. They would harvest on average half a vergée per day – this was achieved by one member of the team digging with a fork, one shaking the haulms and putting the potatoes in rows, and one picking up the potatoes into two wicker baskets, grading the larger potatoes and the mids. The farmer would load the full barrels onto his horse and van, or his lorry (by the '30s some farmers had motorised transport), and go off to the weighbridge in St Helier, to take his turn in the queue and sell his load at the best price to a merchant. During the waiting time for packing in one of the stores on the Esplanade or Commercial Buildings, farmers got together to discuss the prices and the markets, to gossip and to put the Island to rights.

Farmyard manure and vraic were used on the fields. At Gorey, during the autumn and early spring storms, vraic would be loaded and carted up to the farms between the tides. Black sand from St Catherine known as *la vaase* was a valuable commodity, and was carted away to enrich poor land. As the sand area on the beach was very soft, farmers had to watch very carefully that their carts did not sink. Small loads would be taken up from the beach to the road and loaded onto bigger carts.

Part of the duties of farmers and proprietors since feudal times had been the upkeep of the roads. It was still the duty of ratepayers to honour this commitment until the Second World War, when the roads were surfaced. Annually, each farm had to provide a man with a horse and cart (if the farm was large, then two men with two horses and two carts) to transport stone and repair the roads. Ratepayers who were not farmers had the option of giving a day's work or paying for someone else to do it.

The 1930s arrived and the years of the Great Depression. Times became hard. Because of high unemployment in the UK, men were brought over from there to work in the potato season

141   The Le Seelleur family harvesting the bumper potato crop of 1911 at Le Villot. (John Le Seelleur Collection)

in place of the Bretons. Many stayed over, married Jersey girls and integrated into society. Those who found potato work too hard returned to the mainland.

On 1 July 1940, 10 months after war had been declared against Germany, the Island was occupied by the enemy. Farming changed radically and food for the Island's population was the only priority. Fertilizers were virtually unavailable and crops were wheat, oats, potatoes, sugar beet, carrots and beans. Cattle, pigs, chickens and rabbits were reared for meat. Beans, an unusual but useful crop, were threshed at Jardin d'Olivet, Trinity, by John Cabot in his threshing-machine, which had in the past been used for corn. The first beans were all split, but fortunately an adjustment was made to the machine, with a better result. As the months went by, meat became more scarce and cattle, pigs and even horses were commandeered for slaughter. The barter of food for goods became commonplace. Some farmers sold at black market prices and made a lot of money. After D-Day times were harder still, especially for the lower-paid people. Rations were meagre. Gleaning took place after harvest and small handcarts were wheeled out to pick up kindling wood from the lanes and hedges for the coming winter. It was all very difficult.

When at the beginning of 1945 the Red Cross ship *Vega* arrived with its first cargo of precious food, the Parish farmers went down to the harbour with their horses and vans to collect and bring back the parcels to the Public Hall for distribution.

Then, within six months, the longed-for Liberation Day arrived and farming again took its traditional place in the Island's economy.

Cattle, potatoes and tomatoes were in great demand in the UK, and tomatoes were grown on many farms where they had never been grown before. Cars, tractors and modern machinery were bought from the excellent profits made during those lucrative years. Horses were replaced by little grey Fergies for ploughing, with single-row Brabant ploughs, and for pulling, with Farley trailers, but were still used for planting the potato crop.

Sons and daughters of farming families joined the Jersey Young Farmers' Club, giving them the chance to hear talks on scientific advances in farming; to debate, to socialise and to travel. This was a tremendously exciting step forward both in education and social life after the repressive restrictions of the Occupation.

142 *A gathering at Rozel Campsite in 1969 to celebrate the 50th anniversary of the Jersey Young Farmers Club. (Jersey Evening Post)*

Then, in the early 1950s, the bubble burst and only tomatoes grown on suitable land, and of the best quality, found a market. More and more farmers started to grow a second crop after potatoes. In the 1960s especially, cauliflowers were grown on a large scale, with daffodils, calabrese and lettuce also in cultivation. But St Martin did not see a large-scale development of glasshouses as happened in some other parishes. On the dairy farms, milking machines were replacing human hands, which was enormous progress both in the speed of milking and in the hygienic quality of the milk. Winter crops were important in keeping staff gainfully employed in the slack months during the potato cycle of standing (October to December), planting (January to March) and lifting (late April to July).

Costs generally were rising. Labour, imported fertilizers and other agricultural commodities were all rapidly becoming more expensive, and to keep pace annual turnover on farms had to increase, too. The French workers, now finding gainful employment in their own country, were no longer interested in coming to Jersey to work on farms, and it was sometimes difficult to find replacement casual labour. First Italian and then Portuguese workers, mainly from the island of Madeira, began coming over to work on contracts organised through the Jersey Farmers' Union,

143 *'Carting potatoes, Jersey', an early pen drawing by Edmund Blampied. (Courtesy of The Blampied Trustees)*

and provided the required workforce. It is important that the contribution of the Portuguese agricultural worker is not underestimated. The husband and wife teams have proved themselves to be hardworking, diligent and almost irreplaceable.

The low tax status of the Channel Islands encouraged overseas banks and finance companies to set up in Jersey and Guernsey. The entry of the UK into the Common Market also meant that there were no longer tariffs for produce from other European countries, and the Jersey farmer has faced increasing competition in the market place. Older farmers, finding that their children did not wish to follow them, often left the industry. The young people were not attracted to their parents' lifestyle, and this meant the family farm was often sold to rich immigrants who found the houses most desirable residences after modernisation. Jersey's young men and women who would, in the past, have followed their parents into farming, joined the new high-paying finance industry instead. The influx of merchant banks, stockbrokers, firms of accountants and tax consultants provided a new and important source of prosperity to the Island, easily superseding both farming and the once buoyant tourism as Jersey's biggest industry.

Farming's contribution to the Island's gross national product took a nose-dive. And so it continued until the late 1990s, when it was estimated that the farming industry accounted for only four percent of the Island's GNP.

To survive modern financial pressures, small farms were combined and integrated and family partnerships and companies have been formed. Mechanisation and modernisation of all aspects of the industry have taken place including economies of scale and management techniques which would have flabbergasted our forbears. These techniques have proved to be the only means for agriculture to remain viable in an increasingly competitive market-place. World goods arrive on UK supermarket shelves daily by air, as well as by sea and lorry from Europe. Over 80 per cent of the Island's crops are now sold to the major supermarkets in the UK. The protocol and assurance schemes demanded by them have taxed the minds of even the most able farmers.

144 Mechanical harvesting of potatoes in 1998. On the côtils, this work is still done manually. (Courtesy of Anne Perchard)

145 *Farming was very different at the turn of the last century. Life was lived at a slower pace, as this pastoral scene above St Catherine clearly illustrates. (Gerald Amy Collection)*

However, the men and women now left in the industry are highly trained and motivated. They hope to cope with any situation with vision and true Jersey determination and aim to work to ensure a viable living for themselves and their families.

It is amazing to realise that there are now only 14 full-time farms in the Parish, whereas 60 years ago there were around two hundred. Four of these remaining Parish farms have cattle, with about four hundred and fifty milking cows between them. The area of land used for farming has changed very little but techniques have altered dramatically, in line with other world economies. St Martin is a beautiful rural parish with a tradition of producing good custodians of the land. Long may this continue. God bless the plough!

146 *'Linden Hall Sybil' of La Ferme with her offspring. Fertility enhancement produced multiple embryos, which were then transferred to surrogate mothers to bring to term. (Courtesy of Derrick Frigot)*

COMICE AGRICOLE DE ST MARTIN

The Comice Agricole de St Martin was founded on 1 March 1894. Its purpose was to improve and strengthen the breed of Jersey cattle and other farm animals, and to improve general farm management. It is a reminder of the days when farming was the Island's greatest industry, and when the breeding, showing, and export of Jersey cattle was such big business that whole farms could be bought from the proceeds of the sale of a single animal.

The St Martin Comice had its roots in the Comice Agricole du District du Nord, which had been formed by the inhabitants of both Trinity and St Martin in 1863. This association, under the chairmanship of the Reverend William Lemprière, Seigneur of Rosel, set out the rules and procedures to be followed in establishing cattle shows. Twenty-nine rules were made, with a scale of points to be awarded to bulls, cows, heifers, horses and pigs displayed at an annual show to be held in May, with prizes awarded to the animals which were 'approaching almost perfection and those who attained good cultivation and general farm management'. Subscriptions were five shillings, and there were 64 members.

Both shows and meetings were usually held at St Martin's Arsenal, and competition became very keen and hard-fought – any infringement of the rules brought penalties. In 1869, a Mr. William Alexandre had to forfeit his third prize in the yearling bull class because it was found that he had arrived at the show after the stipulated time. Mr. Richard Blampied had to forfeit his first prize when he admitted contravening Article 24 of the rules, and had not made his bull available to all members for six months, at 2s. 6d. per cow.

In November 1873, 27 members signed a requête asking for a discussion on dividing the Comice du Nord into a St Martin's District and a Trinity District. The decision was close, but it was decided to carry on in its amalgamated form. However, separate parish classes were established within the Comice, and sweepstakes introduced. St Martin was the stronger parish and the desire to establish an independent entity remained. Again there was a vote on establishing two separate Comices and again it was defeated. However, it would appear that St Martin was not prepared to accept the result and the Comice Agricole de St Martin was formed, with a total of 79 founder members. Not all St Martin breeders left the Comice du Nord, however, and some still carried on showing in Trinity. But it was obvious that the number of entries from St Martin was diminishing each year. In 1899 there was a complaint that it was unfair that the few remaining St Martinais members should share half the prizes.

It is known that the Comice du Nord continued until 1910, when it finally changed its name to La Société Agricole de la Trinité, applying to hold joint shows with St Martin. This was readily agreed and thus the two parish societies were reunited.

The years 1894 to 1910 were the boom years of the Comice and this is probably what inspired the organisation to petition the States of Jersey in 1898 for an Act of Incorporation, which was sanctioned by Her Majesty, widening its power and entitling the Comice to own property.

Not only were the cattle and horticultural sections flourishing, but the Comice became the centre of parish activities and social life. Sir George Clement Bertram, Bailiff of Jersey, became a

147   *Comice Agricole de St Martin at Rosel Manor in 1905. (John Le Seelleur Collection)*

148   *Comice Agricole de St Martin. The Centenary Year Committee, 1994. Left to right, standing: Mr. J.F. Jehan, Mr. W.C. Renouf, Mr. F.M. De Gruchy, Mr. S.G. Luce, Mr. H.J. De Gruchy, Mr. D.P. Becquet, Mr. R.J. Perchard, Mr. J.R. Renouf; seated: Mrs. Anne Perchard, Mr. C.W. Renouf, Mr. G.A. Richardson, Mr. T.R. De Gruchy, Mr. J.G. Pallot, Mr. G.C. Richardson, Mr. J.B. Germain, Mrs. Paulette De La Haye. (Courtesy of Comice Agricole de St Martin)*

patron. The Reverend George Balleine was president, and the Comice entered exhibits in the Battle of Flowers and succeeded in winning the trophy in 1907. The records of that year recorded: 'The Comice passed a vote of thanks to Captain C.B. Nicolle, and the ladies and gentlemen who took part in the Comice Float at the Battle of Flowers, winning the first prize and cup. It was decided to present the ladies with a gold brooch bearing the date and initials of the Comice.' Do any of these brooches still exist ?

Although the Comice took an active interest in all aspects of farming life in St Martin, the breeding and exhibition of the Jersey cow was the greatest interest in those early years, and still is today. The export markets worldwide of Jerseys were undoubtedly at their best during the first quarter of the 20th century and the 10 years following the second World War. These were very profitable times for the sale of thousands of cattle and the Comice Shows were the major show-case for the promotion of the Parish's top quality animals to buyers from around the world.

In 1994, a most successful day-long Centenary Show was held at Rosel Manor (where else?) with a superb cattle show and many other displays and attractions, all celebrating the event in true Jersey carnival style.

However, while there were 79 members when the Comice was founded, there are now only four herds of cattle in St Martin, all in the Vingtaine of Rozel, with about 470 milking cows between them. There has been a gradual demise of small mixed farm holdings, and a change to large specialist farm units. Ever increasing costs and the greater profitability of cash crops has diminished the number of cattle breeders. Without a flourishing export trade, the future of the parish cattle shows is not promising.

However, should the pendulum swing back, St Martin can still boast a nucleus of keen and expert cattle breeders ready to take advantage of any developments which might lead to a resurgence of the interest and enthusiasm which has been the hallmark of the Comice Agricole de St Martin for the past 106 years.

149   *'Tired workers'. Etching by Edmund Blampied, 1914. (Courtesy of The Blampied Trustees)*

Maritime St Martin

SHIPBUILDING AT GOREY AND ST CATHERINE

A farmer working his côtils above St Catherine's Bay in the early summer of 1850 would survey, as he paused from his labours to gaze out to sea, a scene very different from that which appears today.

The bay is empty of pleasure boats bobbing on their moorings, but there are ships at anchor, including some sail-assisted steam-powered vessels. Half-a-mile to the north, the new breakwater intended to provide a 'harbour of refuge' is thrusting out to sea (Fig.153). On the beach below the coastal tower, a ship is nearing completion on the stocks of the newly established Le Huquet shipyard. She is a cutter of 60 tons, to be launched on 10 July and named *Louisa*, built for George Asplet of Gorey and to be captained by Abraham Asplet. Further south along the Bay, close to Archirondel Tower, are the remnants of earlier yards of Edward Le Huquet (closed in 1847) and of Vardon & Le Huquet (closed in 1841). The slip beside St Catherine's Tower will not be built for another 40 years and there is no sea wall. The beach looks, apart from the absence of the *Louisa*, much as it appears in the picture by Ouless completed a few years earlier, showing vraic gatherers at St Catherine's Bay (Fig.167).

Further down the coast, Gorey is not yet the hive of shipbuilding activity which it will become over the next 20 years, but already there is some building there. Philip Le Sueur's yard near Fort Henry has been working for five years and Jean Vardon's since 1842. Earlier, John Fauvel had built on Gorey Pier but he built only four vessels over a 16-year period.

The earliest record of boatbuilding in Jersey relates to events within the Parish of St Martin. It occurred when Mont Orgueil Castle was besieged by Yorkists in 1468 during the Wars of the Roses. The siege lasted for 19 weeks and provisions were running short so the defenders of the castle began to build a boat to obtain fresh supplies. Realising that the sounds of the carpenters' hammers would be heard by the attackers, the construction of a second boat was begun in full view of the enemy, work on both boats being undertaken at the same time, so that the sounds of the two lots of hammerings were mingled. In this way the boat intended to be used for foraging was completed whilst the other was only half-built. Treachery, however, was afoot and a Jerseyman working within the castle fired an arrow bearing a message that two boats were being built, the one in view being a mere decoy. With this forewarning, a close watch was kept and the intended supply boat was captured as soon as it was launched.

The antiquity of the craft of boatbuilding all over the world demonstrates that the necessary skills can readily be acquired, and small seafaring vessels must have been built in Jersey long before the incident at Mont Orgueil. Jersey people have fished in local waters for centuries and their boats would not have been bought outside the Island. There was a sufficiency of timber in

the Island for boatbuilding and medieval fisherman would not have possessed money to purchase their vessels elsewhere. Locally owned vessels are known to have been involved in the Newfoundland trade from the latter part of the 16th century (Jean Guilleaume is credited with bringing the first cargo of fish from the Newfoundland grounds in 1596) and there seems no reason to doubt that experience gained over many years in the construction of small fishing and coastal vessels would, by that period, have enabled Jerseymen to build ships of around one hundred tons, the size required for voyages to Newfoundland. John Cabot reported in 1497 that the fishermen of Normandy and Brittany were fishing the Newfoundland banks and it may well be that these early fishermen included some from the adjacent Channel Islands.

The construction of a vessel of 280 tons, the *Elisha Tupper*, launched into St Aubin's Bay near the mouth of St Peter's Valley in June 1789, may be regarded as heralding the substantial shipbuilding industries which were to develop in the Channel Islands during the following century. The *Elisha Tupper* was built under the direction of a Jerseyman named Janvrin, a merchant of the Island who was active in the Newfoundland trade, but was named after a Guernseyman who was one of the shareholders in the enterprise and also a merchant engaged in Newfoundland business.

A few other vessels of similar size to the *Elisha Tupper* were built in Jersey over the next 25 years, but 1815 marked the real beginning of that short period of about sixty years during which major shipbuilding industries in Jersey and in Guernsey emerged, flourished and declined.

Some statistics illustrate this remarkable episode in Jersey's industrial history. The Jersey shipbuilding industry was considerably greater than that of Guernsey. Between 1815 and 1879, 881 vessels were built in Jersey, totalling 101,638 tons; the number of vessels built in Guernsey during the same period was 300 with a total tonnage of 39,382. The peak year of construction for the two Islands together was 1864, when the production of wooden sailing vessels from Channel Island yards was equivalent to 5.9 per cent of the total tonnage built in UK yards. The decline of the industry was almost as rapid as its growth. During the 1870s fewer than 10 ships were built each year compared with more than 20 during the previous decade.

151   A schooner in the final stages of construction at Gorey. (Courtesy of Société Jersiaise Photographic Archive, Jersey)

What circumstances gave rise to these developments? Although ships had been built in Jersey for a very long time, most locally owned vessels had been built in England or had been seized as prizes in time of war. However, after 1783 the demand for shipping in the Channel Islands began to increase. A.G. Jamieson in *A People of the Sea* says that perhaps this was partly as a result of the general stimulus given to British shipping after the American Revolution. In 1775 more than a third of the British merchant navy vessels were of American construction, but after the revolution those vessels were excluded from trade within the British Empire. The resulting shortage of tonnage began to be met in part by shipbuilding in the Channel Islands, starting with the *Elisha Tupper*.

The impetus given to shipbuilding in the Channel Islands was not sustained during the Napoleonic Wars when many of the Newfoundland trade ships were built in Canada, and vessels taken as prizes from the enemy were plentiful and cheap. Nevertheless an indirect consequence of the wars was to give an economic advantage to Channel Island builders.

During the wars, the British Government had sought to encourage trade between Britain and Canada by imposing a duty on the importation of foreign timber into Britain. British merchants had agreed to develop that trade only on the condition that the duty would remain in force after the wars, but the duty did not apply to foreign timber imported into the Channel Islands. Shipbuilders in the Islands could therefore bring in timber from northern Europe more cheaply than British builders. In addition, Jersey had an economic advantage over its rival shipbuilders in Guernsey in the form of lower costs and lower wages, with the result that a vessel could be built

152 A view of the shipyards on the Gorey waterfront. (Courtesy of Société Jersiaise Photographic Archive, Jersey)

and equipped in Jersey for about £2 per ton less than in Guernsey. It was reported that the brig *Hope*, constructed in Jersey in 1832, was '... built of oak, copper sheathed and well found, with provisions for six months and a month's advance to the crew – cost at sea £14 7s 6d per ton. In comparison, the brig *Lily*, built at Guernsey in 1840 – cost at sea just under £18 per ton.'

The Jersey industry was concentrated in St Aubin's Bay with yards stretching from what is now the Esplanade to First Tower. The yards in St Martin at St Catherine and at Gorey, the latter extending south along the bay into Grouville, were however, of substantial importance. Appendix VII contains details of the St Catherine and Gorey shipbuilders and the vessels they built, with tonnage, rig and owner. The Appendix has been prepared from information provided by Alex Podger from official Registers and from lists in John Jean's two books, *Jersey Sailing Ships* and *Jersey Ships and Railways*. The Appendix shows E. Le Huquet and Vardon & Le Huquet as the earliest to establish yards at St Catherine, each launching a vessel in 1837, and J. & T. Le Huquet as much the largest builder, with 46 vessels to its credit. Many of these were fairly small cutters, but some schooners and brigs in excess of 100 tons were built. Even today a stump of wood from the Le Huquet yard occasionally emerges from the shingle near the inshore lifeboat launching slip.

The Gorey builders were eventually more numerous than those of St Catherine and built more ships, probably because access to the beach was easier and the yards were closer to the village where many of the craftsmen lived. Nowadays, with the sea lapping the wall at high tide from the Common to the harbour, shipbuilding at Gorey seems impossible. However, as Godfray's (1849) map shows, there was no road along this stretch of the coast and in old photographs ships can be seen under construction close to the steep slopes below Le Mont de Gouray. Between them, the Gorey builders built a total of 122 vessels. Francis Picot, the largest builder at Gorey, built 44, but that was two fewer than J. & T. Le Huquet built at St Catherine. Charles Aubin and Philip Bellot each constructed 24 vessels. The largest ship built at Gorey was the *Gazelle*, of 242 tons, built in 1864 by Francis Picot. Jean Vardon's yard at Petit Portelet behind Mont Orgueil is shown in Fig 150. A fountain erected by the Public Works Committee near the harbour

153 The boat-building shed at Elmore, St Martin. Capitaine Philippe Le Huquet (rear), his son Philip John (right), and Philip Le Seelleur. (Beatrice Le Huquet Collection)

commemorates the Gorey industry, the base of the fountain resembling the keel of a ship on the stocks, with the names of some of the vessels built at Gorey inscribed on it. The fountain was designed by C. Warren and sculptured by L. Chataignere.

The names inscribed are:

West Side	East Side
Vivid	Rapid
Zephyr	Milton
Excelsior	St Peter
Morning Star	Charlotte
Storm Bird	Belladonna
Advance	Albatross
Supply	Rambler
Hero	Union

John Jean has provided the writer with some further information about the connections of local shipbuilders with the Parish of St Martin. George Asplet gave the ground upon which Gouray Church was built. Philip Bellot married Ann Starck and they lived at Albion House at Faldouet between 1891 and 1914. John Picot was born in the Parish in 1833. He lived at Fairview, Gorey, and died in 1917. Clement Richardson married Susan Le Huquet and they lived at Rozel; he named the first boat he built at Flicquet *Susan*. Their gravestone in St Martin's churchyard is shown in Fig.96. Another Richardson, John, was a small builder at St Martin. In 1846 he built a cutter of 15 tons which had a very long career under many owners, the first of whom was John Richardson himself. Having been sold to an English owner in 1930, she was later bought by the writer Hilaire Belloc who named her *Yacht of Jersey* and sailed her in the English Channel. The vessel disappeared from the Register in 1955, 110 years after she was built. Thomas Le Huquet emigrated to New Zealand, where he continued to build ships.

Although the 1860s saw the height of Jersey's shipbuilding industry, the causes of its subsequent decline were already becoming apparent. In a speech in December 1867 Daniel Le Vesconte said that the prospects for Jersey shipbuilding were not good because wooden ships were giving way to ships of iron or of iron and wood, for the building of which a great deal more capital investment would be required. Moreover, sail was beginning to give way to steam. Le Vesconte thought that a more practical proposition for the Island in the changing circumstances was ship repairing which had always provided work for the Island shipwrights. However in the event his hopes were not fulfilled as the necessary drydock facilities were not constructed. Gradually, the Island's shipyards went out of business but those which survived the longest were the yards at Gorey and St Catherine.

ST CATHERINE – THE HARBOUR THAT NEVER WAS

St Catherine's Bay in the Parish of St Martin is distinguished by an impressive and grandiose Victorian military building project of stunning proportions. It remains a project rather than a finished work. What exists today, a breakwater stretching 2,300 feet out to sea, is only a fraction of what was intended. It protects the anchorage at St Catherine from northerly winds, and it is a popular venue for walkers and fishermen. Otherwise it stands useless, admittedly splendidly useless, a monument to military folly.

Defensive fortifications from earlier times which survive in a pristine state are by their very nature unproven. No one knows how effective they might have been because no one bothered to challenge them. The world is full of such monuments to the depth of the military purse (the British one at that) in locations scattered around the Empire on which the sun never set.

That said, many fulfilled their brief and provided the necessary place of safety and even the springboard for a counter attack. But many were seen at the time as follies – monuments, it has been said, to the tendency of admirals and generals to plan for the wars they fought in their youth rather than the wars which might have to be fought by the next generation – and in the Parish of St Martin, lies one of the biggest follies of them all. It started life as a vainglorious piece of military planning that those not in London, where the idea originated, could see at the time (they have since been proved right) was ill-thought out and ill-researched stupidity on a grand scale.

The late William (Bill) Davies, in his book *The Harbour That Failed*, tells a story of ineptitude, acrimony and excessive over-spending on a project known to be useless long before it was abandoned. He also outlines the effect of all this activity on a peaceful community in the north east of Jersey. The decision to abandon was welcomed with relief, he writes. Residents no longer needed to dread for the safety of their womenfolk or their crops and, in no time at all, the coastal strip flanking St Catherine's Bay settled down to rural peace despite the occasional attempts of late to rally support for a marina in the bay on the basis that 'half the work has already been completed'.

How did such a colossal piece of engineering work, costing the British Government £250,000 in the mid-19th century, taking four or five years to build, never actually completed, and finally abandoned as a white elephant by its projectors, come to be erected?

Officially, at least, the construction of a harbour at St Catherine was designated a 'harbour of refuge'. With the growth in power and prosperity of Great Britain there was a call for its merchant

154 *The building of St Catherine's Breakwater was news not just in Jersey. Engraving from the* Illustrated London News *of 11 September 1852 (Illustrated London News)*

fleet to have areas to ride out storms and rest, waiting for the right conditions to sail again. But it was more than natural forces which were causing concerns to the wealthy ship owners and indeed to the Government. Britannia might well be ruling the waves at that time, but the gunboats and the warships also needed respite. The existing dockyards were unable to accommodate the growing fleet which could not stay at sea for ever; it needed constant provisioning and, as the times changed, coaling.

Meanwhile across the Channel the ancient enemy, France, was rebuilding and enlarging harbours from Dunkirk to Brest. Cherbourg was developed to the extent that it was seen as a potential threat to the south coast of England. What were the French up to? If they were going to 'try it again' then once more control of the sea and in particular the English Channel would be indispensable and the Channel Islands were seen as vital elements in the British line of defence. Ships on station in the Channel Islands, it was argued, might be able to harass a French force intent on invasion. This argument was developed later in a much more sinister way and the harbour of refuge, Bill Davies suggests very strongly, could well have become something rather different.

A petition was sent to Queen Victoria by the States of Jersey on 26 August 1840. The petition contained 12 clauses, of which four are relevant to this subject:

> That though your Majesty is now in a state of peace and alliance with France the States, reflecting on the mutability of human affairs have seen, with considerable anxiety, the gigantic affairs which have been made on the opposite coast for the enlargement and the fortification of the Ports of Cherbourg, Granville and St Malo and on the immense mass of offense which these places will possess in time of war.

> That there is at present no harbour about the Island where ships of the line might be stationed with sufficient security or steam vessels be kept afloat at all times.

That such a harbour would, moreover, offer a refuge in stress of weather to the British squadrons of observation on the neighbouring coasts of France.

That a convenient spot may be surveyed and selected on the north coast of the Island and that a harbour and breakwater may be constructed where armed steam vessels might be constantly kept afloat.

Owing to an unfortunate confusion in the transmission of replies the petition was not acknowledged until 8 November 1840, when the Lords of the Admiralty wrote: 'The subject is one whose importance will continue to engage their lordship's attention.' But this did not stop the States pursuing their anti-French policy and suggesting in December 1840 that Sir William Symonds, Inspector-General of the Royal Navy and a man who had lived in Jersey and knew its feeble defences, should act as an intermediary between the two governments, and that the UK Government should construct a port at Bouley Bay.

Had this been done, there is every possibility that a good harbour might have been built there. But it was not. Between 1841 and 1846 there was a period of *entente cordiale* between the English and the French. This was wrecked by The Spanish Marriage Question in 1846, when the Queen of Spain and her sister both married allies of the French King. This was seen by Victoria and her firebrand Prime Minister Lord Palmerston as a very real threat and led directly to the building of the Breakwater.

The English may well have been suspicious of the French, and the feeling was certainly reciprocated. When works at Alderney and Jersey started, the French Government registered a protest. Military developments in the Channel Islands could only have sinister implications it was thought and, as Bill Davies argued in his book, those fears were not entirely misplaced.

No one disagreed about the strategic significance of the Channel Islands. There was no argument that Jersey was badly placed to withstand a French invasion should one occur and military thinking favoured a French landing on the south coast near Noirmont. But St Catherine is not well placed to intercept a southerly attack from France, which was deemed the most likely direction. So why was St Catherine's Bay chosen? By 1842 the British Government had set up a separate investigation into the state of the Channel Islands in terms of defences for trade and commerce. On that committee was Captain (later Admiral Sir) Edward Belcher whose ideas and recommendations carried great weight in Government, yet that body's work and its recommendations do not feature in the later 1844 report. Stranger still, work at St Catherine started in 1847.

Whatever the reasons for this apparent ignorance, on the part of the left hand, of what the right hand was doing, scant regard seems to have been paid to warnings about St Catherine's positioning in repelling an attack from the south. The fact that low seas and high rocks on a line from Seymour Tower to the French coast would cut off the harrying force was dismissed. Indeed Belcher asserted, against all odds, that a deep water channel existed from north to south and he stubbornly pushed his choice of St Catherine through at Government level even though no less than three admirals favoured Noirmont.

The Admiralty commissioned James Walker – a renowned civil engineer – to review the findings of the Commission and, based on a few visits, he did so. Subsequently his company was instructed to make immediate purchases in Alderney and Jersey to enable the construction of Le

Braye and St Catherine's Breakwaters. The French might well complain about the intentions behind the construction of a harbour at St Catherine, and they had a point, for hawks such as Belcher certainly saw it as a possible springboard from which to invade France and attack Cherbourg from the rear, thus giving support to any future British naval blockade of the French.

There can be no doubt that the British Government was in deadly earnest, for between March and June 1847, lands and farms in St Martin measuring 600 vergées were bought up, and on 28 June 1847 the *Jersey and Guernsey News* reported that work had started at St Catherine's Bay that very day. 'Fifty men were pulling down trees near Archirondel Tower. One hundred additional men are expected next week. Two vessels have arrived laden with tools, railway sleepers, etc. One is in Gorey Harbour and the other is moored off St Catherine's.'

French protests were diplomatically convenient to divert attention from their own programme of enlarging fortifications. But they had no reason to worry. Neither Belcher, nor Walker and nor, through them, the Admiralty, took any notice of other opinions expressed, particularly concerning the effects of currents and tides, and St Catherine's quickly silted up. The lack of any progress – beyond some essential preliminaries – of the southern (never completed) Archirondel arm and the effect on the water flow caused by the building of the northern (surviving) Verclut arm, proved the doubters right. It soon became apparent that there was simply not enough water in the proposed harbour to contain a fleet, be it offensive or defensive. The bay now has anything up to two fathoms of water less than it had 100 years ago.

Work stopped at Archirondel in 1849 and the scheme of a huge pier extending some 4,500 feet out to sea before turning north another 1,100 feet to form the proposed 500-feet wide harbour mouth remained a dream in an Admiralty file. If completed, it would have been over two and a half times the length of the existing breakwater of 2,300 feet. As it was, the cessation of work to the south speeded up the development to the north and, at the same time, hastened the inevitable abandonment of a project which everyone could see was leading nowhere. Tactically, looking only at a map, St Catherine might well be an ideally located base from which to launch an invasion of France, but a harbour without water is not the best place from which to do it.

The expenditure grew and the serious concern which grew with it eventually had to be admitted in public. As Bill Davies writes: 'A ludicrous situation arose whereby the bay started to shallow at the same time as naval ships grew in stature and, consequently in draft. St Catherine's Bay always was doomed to failure as a harbour; nature had taken care of that.' Finally, the project was abandoned but there remained the problem of what to do with the surviving and useless arm. True it carried a lighthouse, but that was only necessary because of the existence of the breakwater itself; this was finally finished in 1855 with the light being placed on it in 1856.

So what was delivered for the princely sum of £234,235 16s. 0d., exclusive of the purchase of land and property? It was not a harbour of refuge since it was open to south-easterly gales. Nor was it a satisfactory naval base because there was not enough water and any ships, which might have been stationed there, could not have operated satisfactorily to the south. Notwithstanding all the foregoing, it was a provocation to the French.

All in all it was an expensive folly and on 23 February 1876, after some twenty years of haggling and (very successful) stonewalling tactics, the States of Jersey, who had resisted the

*155   St Catherine's Breakwater from Fliquet Bay. An engraving by
Rock & Co. of London, 1866.*

Government trying to sell them the Verclut arm 'at a proper valuation', accepted St Catherine's Breakwater as an outright gift. Even then there were doubts, for no one wanted to accept responsibility for the upkeep and maintenance of a structure that, it was acknowledged in Jersey as well as in London, seemed to have no practical purpose whatsoever.

The effects of the construction were more than political and financial. The folly and the mistakes could be buried in the files in London but the presence in Jersey of so large a force of workers could not pass unnoticed. What would have been a substantial minority in St Helier, bringing with it a raft of social problems, was one thing, but in the peaceful rural parish of St Martin the effects of numbers of workers and dependants – variously estimated at well over 1,000 at peak levels – was dramatic.

Contemporary reports brought forward this editorial from the *Jersey Times* in February 1848, arguing the need for a paid town police force.

> A gang of half drunken fellows, belonging to St Catherine's Bay Works, were rolling about and shouting in the very heart of town, and endeavouring to force open the doors of any house in which they descried a light; and this between midnight and one o'clock in the morning, with no police officer of any description to interfere and put a stop to their ruffianism.

And later in the same month: 'We are sorry to hear that depredations are nightly committed in the parishes of St Martin, St Saviour and Trinity by some scoundrels supposed to be employed at St Catherine's Bay.' There followed reports of people being waylaid, threatened and robbed, farmhouses found food missing, women 'even in broad daylight' have loaves of bread taken from them and 'the owners of vegetable gardens and fields around St Catherine's also feel a nuisance for scarcely a vegetable can they keep; the depredations are carried on so far as even milking cows in the day-time'.

There were attempts to do something for the immigrants even if they were reported as 'indigent Irish people whose whole wardrobe consisted of a few rags in which they were clad'. In June 1851 there was a report which stated: 'A sermon was preached on Sunday, the 8th inst., at the Chapel, St Catherine's Bay by the Rev. Jas. Le Maistre in aid of the St Catherine's Bay Sunday School, when the sum collected amounted to £4.0.0d.'

156 *The lighthouse keeper's cottage at St Catherine's Breakwater. In front of the cottage is 'The Pebble', a piece of Rozel conglomerate rock, referred to in chapter 1. (Gerald Amy Collection)*

With the benefit of hindsight it is easy to see how a workforce of some five hundred with dependants dumped in a near inaccessible location would have no option but impinge on the peaceful life of the Island whether they searched for food, drink or pleasure. It was simply too large a group to assimilate. They were evidently regarded with great suspicion, and there were several reports in the local press of unpleasant and threatening behaviour. These were repudiated in a letter to the *Jersey Times* by the company's resident engineer, Mr. H.T.W. Neville.

Even so there are reports, in 1851, of an event which quite understandably shocked the public sensibilities of the time. The *Jersey Times* carried a report of: 'A disgraceful scene in which two unfortunate women, stripped to their waists, were induced upon a pitched battle, and seriously mangled each other in the presence of spectators; two brutes in the garb of men, acting as their respective seconds.'

However, it is hard to believe that a hundred and fifty years ago a firm of contractors would have been so solicitous about the welfare of their workers as Messrs. Jackson and Bean were for the years in which they were responsible for building the Breakwater. They brought over their own surgeon-doctor, who was called in whenever an accident took place. There were many accidents, and he was kept busy. In September 1849 there was also an outbreak of cholera in St Martin, with nine deaths occurring among the 33 cases. Dr. F. Padmore of St Helier, was called in to help treat the sufferers, and when the outbreak was controlled he was presented with a gold watch and chain by the colony of workers. A nearby house was converted into a small hospital where injured workers could receive immediate attention, and was also used as a clinic for the children of the workforce. This building at St Catherine is still called L'Hôpital today. A school was established for the fifty or so children of the workforce. One pupil was so intelligent that his higher education was paid for by the Seigneur of Rosel. In the evenings, the schoolroom was used as a sort of social club, and the members of the St Catherine's Harbour Works Brass Band (initiated by the workers themselves) practised and gave performances.

The contractors also organised a savings bank where, it is said, 'sums of money as low as sixpence are received from the workmen'. And finally the contractors also thought about the spiritual needs of the workforce and erected a chapel. This is probably the building now known as La Chapelle in the lane running parallel to the Pine Walk.

So, has the story of St Catherine's harbour ended? Maybe it has quietened down for a time, but the sight of a long breakwater jutting out to sea for no apparent purpose has inspired many to find a use for it, and there have been suggestions of land reclamation, marinas, and other associated development. Perhaps they will never be started for much the same reason as the great harbour was never finished. St Catherine's Bay – beautiful St Catherine's Bay – is in the wrong place.

ST CATHERINE'S LIGHTHOUSE

The first lighthouse, a cast-iron tower, was erected at the end of the breakwater in 1857. The light, 60 feet above high water level, was a paraffin wick burner giving a fixed white light of 100 candle-power with a range of 10 miles. Although replaced by a double-wick burner in 1906, the method of illumination remained the same until the light was extinguished at the outbreak of war with Germany on 3 September 1939. Indeed, the same unit was relit in June 1945 and was only replaced by a more modern system in 1950. This was an acetylene flashing light with an increased range of 11½ miles at 585 candle-power.

The lighthouse keeper from 1936 to 1953 was John Francis Marett, whose widow still lives at La Frênaie near La Chasse. She remembers the often frightening task of lighting the lamp undertaken by her husband who had to negotiate the length of the breakwater in the face of gales, breaking seas and driving rain.

The light was electrified in 1973 and soon after the old tower was replaced with the present galvanised trellis structure. Happily, the original 1857 tower has been preserved and now can be seen outside the Maritime Museum in St Helier.

157 St Catherine's Lighthouse, c.1935. (Courtesy of William Renouf)

158 The 'rig' at the Royal
Naval Training School, Faldouet.
The dormitory building, which
now forms part of Seymour Farm
is behind. (Courtesy of Société
Jersiaise Photographic Archive,
Jersey)

THE ROYAL NAVAL TRAINING SCHOOL

Little is known about the Royal Naval Training School. There are old photographs showing the masts and all the rigging of a ship set up in the garden of a house in Gorey, now known, appropriately enough, as The Old Cadet House. This house, which stands off the track leading up to the Victoria Tower, was the quarters for officers and staff. It is believed that some of the boys lived in a typical mid-Victorian naval building, now known as Seymour Farm, nearby. When this property was bought in 1908 by the father of Captain F. Ahier, there were no internal communications on the first floor, and the family had to climb up an outside staircase and walk along an open verandah for access to the rooms.

There was a reference to the Royal Naval Training School in the *British Press and Jersey Times Almanac* for 1863, saying: 'This school was founded in the early part of 1860 by Captain Philip de Saumarez RN, under the superintendence of Commander C. Burney RN, commander of the *Speedy*, Master, Mr. W. Pawley. Thirty boys are educated and trained as pilots and thirty in ship drill.'

The 1869 edition of the *Almanac* reported: 'There is a complete staff of schoolmasters and seamanship and gunnery instructors. One hundred and fifty boys are yearly trained there for the Royal Navy in all branches of a young seaman's duty.'

However, some mystery still surrounds the training school. It seems unlikely that it could have been a genuine Royal Naval establishment because there has never been a reference to it with the prefix H.M.S. as is normal with naval shore training schools. Also, Commander Burney was not appointed solely for duties at the school, but, according to the Navy Lists of the time, to H.M.S. *Dasher*, 'additional for Training Establishment at Gorey'. Strangely too, the Gorey school

159 Seymour Farm, 1998. The architectural details reveal its former use as a naval dormitory. (Photo: Chris Blackstone)

was not mentioned in the obituaries of either Captain de Saumarez or Commander Burney. However, Philip Ahier recorded that the States of Jersey had begun to provide funds in 1836 'towards the building of the Naval School at Gorey'.

THE OYSTER FISHERIES

Balleine describes Gorey as 'The Village the Oysters Built'. Despite its imposing Castle, Gorey was on a slow spiral of decay from the end of the 17th century until the beginning of the 19th century. The oyster boom made Gorey what it is today.

In 1685 Dumaresq wrote: 'At the foot of the Castle is the most ancient harbour in the Island. There is an old decayed pier, where such small boats as use the neighbouring coast of Normandy resort.' By the beginning of the 19th century this had gone beyond decay, and had completely disappeared. Paintings of the castle in 1802 and 1815, by Serre and Tobias Young, show no trace of the pier.

There had always been an oyster bed not far from shore. Even prehistoric man had liked oysters, for oyster shells have been found at La Hougue Bie, and the beds off Gorey were fished throughout the Middle Ages. Both the French and the English fished closer to home and there was a limited export of Jersey oysters to England. The export trade increased after 1797 and, despite a French law passed in 1785, the English started to arrive soon afterwards to exploit the extensive beds off Chausey, only one to three leagues from the French coast. By 1810, a regular oyster fishery had been established in Jersey, chiefly to supply the merchants of the chartered oyster companies of Kent and Sussex, although Essex dredgers continued to be the largest contingent of non-Jersey vessels in this new industry.

Gorey was the favourite base, and so the States of Jersey rebuilt Gorey Pier between 1816 and 1817, at a cost of £16,000. Oyster dredgers were based in other harbours too, and more piers, intended to provide protection for the oyster fleet, were built at Bonne Nuit, Rozel, La Rocque and Bouley Bay. The harbours on the north coast were used primarily by vessels fishing the Carteret

160 *A Royal Navy gunboat alongside Gorey Pier. Several of these vessels were stationed at Gorey, on fishery protection duties during the second half of the 19th century. They were 135ft, composite-built vessels driven by a 650hp engine and carrying four breech loading guns. HMS Mistletoe of the Albacore class was probably on station the longest. She was built in 1883 and sold out of the service in 1907. (V & A Picture Library)*

area but also took the overflow from overcrowded Gorey which remained the principal base. By the 1830s it ranked as the third most important port in Jersey after St Helier and St Aubin.

The dredgers landed their catch in the harbour, the oysters were sorted and packed, and then they were shipped in fast vessels to England where they were laid down in Kentish – or other beds – for fattening, before being sent for sale in London. The whole operation was carried out as swiftly as possible, so that the oysters would not start to decay. Also, the landing, sorting and shipment of oysters was done as much as possible in the cool of the dawn or the evening, or even at night, so that the precious shellfish were not subjected to the full heat of the day.

After the peace with France in 1815, the industry grew rapidly. The first big boom came in the 1820s and early 1830s, when on average 100,000 tubs of oysters were sent to England each year. In 1822 the industry relied upon more than 300 vessels, manned by over 1,500 British seamen. In 1834-5 catches fell dramatically and did not recover until the 1850s. The trade had great benefits for the Island economy. The sorting and packing of the oysters gave work to nearly one thousand poor people in the eastern part of Jersey, and 'the circulation of a considerable sum created greater activity in the operations of the general commerce of the Island'. Oysters were so cheap in Jersey that they were served free at all hotel meals.

The competition for oysters caused serious diplomatic incidents between Britain and France. The French were hostile to what appeared to be a British monopoly of the oyster beds, especially when, after 1819, English and Jersey dredgers fished closer and closer to Granville – even to within cannon shot of the fort there.

The diplomatic incidents were in reality part of a broader diplomatic scene in that the concept of territorial waters and exclusive fishing rights was being explored in relation to the North Sea fisheries. The British did not exercise a monopoly of the oyster beds – there was an intrinsic difference in the ways oysters were fished in as much as the British way was a general open season whereas the French regulated the fisheries by specific banks. To the French fishermen the behaviour of the British was outrageous as not only were they dredging what they regarded as French oyster beds but, more often than not, they were doing it in the restricted season.

The British Government was forced to offer compensation after incidents occurred in which British oystermen (mostly English rather than Jerseymen) raided the French coast, bent upon the destruction of French fishing gear, and clashed with a French warship. The Lieutenant-Governor of the Island was directed to order English and Jersey boats not to fish within one league of the French coast. This did little to appease the French, however, as they had demanded that British oyster boats should not come within two leagues of their coast.

Further clashes took place in 1822, and the States of Jersey complained to the Privy Council about French harassment. In May of that year, British warships arrived in the waters between Jersey and France, but they were intended as much to curb British aggression as to discourage hostile action by the French. Diplomatic negotiations were opened between the British and the French governments over the problems of the oyster beds and, in a gesture of conciliation, the British Government in 1824 ordered that British vessels should keep out of a zone extending two leagues from the French coast in the disputed area.

This no doubt mollified the French fishermen, but the members of the British fleet were far from happy. On the morning of 14 March 1828 near Chausey an English fisherman, John Smith, was killed when boarding the cutter *Favourite*, under command of a French prize crew, after being arrested by the French naval vessel *Goëland*. The States of Jersey again complained to the Privy Council about the hostile conduct of the French, but the complaint was rejected. The British Government, embarrassed at this apparent sabotage of its attempts at a diplomatic solution, condemned the actions of the English and Jersey oystermen.

The oystermen entered the 1830s in discontented mood; the two-league limit was an unwelcome restriction. The British warships stationed at Gorey did as much to curb the activities of the

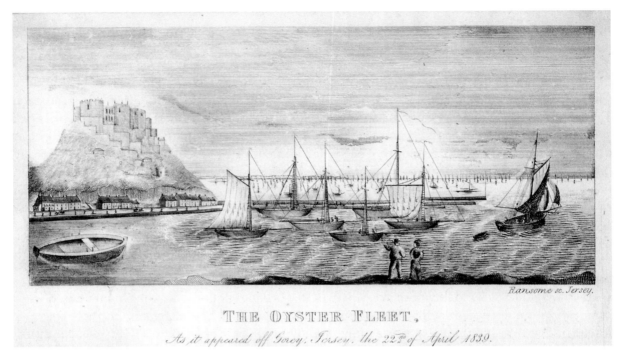

THE OYSTER FLEET,

As it appeared off Gorey, Jersey, the 22nd of April 1839.

Ransome sc. Jersey.

161 'The Oyster Fleet as it appeared off Gorey, Jersey, 22nd April 1839'. (Courtesy of John De Veulle)

British fleet as the French. By the middle of the decade catches were falling, and the collapse of the industry seemed imminent.

The States of Jersey took decisive action. It moved to control the industry and restock the oyster beds; which were already suffering from over-fishing. An Act of May 1834 imposed new regulations, and an inspector equipped with a cutter was established at Gorey to enforce them. Between 1834 and 1837 the States spent nearly £4,000 on regulating and encouraging the industry.

The Jersey government had laid down new beds in Grouville Bay in an attempt to boost the industry. These had to be carefully preserved until they were ripe for dredging. But the oyster fishermen were reckless and by no means law-abiding. In 1838, around 140 boats raided the forbidden beds. The Connétable, Mr. Godfray, tried to get the fishery protection cutter *Cracker* to take him after the oystermen but was refused so he took the States cutter, *Inca*, along with the two Inspector of Fisheries assistants, Mauger and Payne, and four naval ratings from the *Cracker*. Rather than the ring leaders he arrested Thomas Ahier, the captain of the first boat he came to; George Vardon was arrested for inciting his crew to throw the Inspector's assistants overboard and Henri Bougourd was arrested for resisting arrest!

On 12 April the oystermen raided the beds again, and this time the Connétable asked the Lieutenant-Governor for help. He marched out at the head of a company of the 60th Regiment of Foot, the 4th Regiment, St Helier Battalion of the Royal Jersey Militia. A couple of cannon balls brought the boats back to port, and 96 more skippers were arrested and later fined by the Royal Court. The only casualty of this Battle of the Oyster Shells was the Lieutenant-Governor, who caught a cold and died of pneumonia some weeks later. But the action did bring the oyster fleet to heel, and forced the industry to accept that it was under Jersey's control.

International negotiations resulted in a new agreement over fishing rights: the British should have exclusive rights within three miles of the coast of Jersey, and the French should exercise similar rights off the coast of France, the area in between being open to both nationalities. The exception was an area east of a line from Cape Carteret on the Cotentin Peninsula to Pointe de Meinga near St Malo on the north coast of Brittany, including the Chausey Islands. Here the British accepted that the French had an exclusive zone extending six miles off shore.

The British and the French governments also agreed to a closed season for fishing, from May until 31 August, but little attempt was made initially to enforce it. This was despite the presence of the inspector of the Jersey oyster fishery at Gorey, and a British gunboat in the port.

After the boom of the 1850s, however, the position changed dramatically. Partly because of smaller catches in Jersey, the British fleet had searched further afield for oysters, and had found new beds in deep water in the English Channel, between Cherbourg and Dunkirk. These beds were easiest to fish in the summer and yielded good catches. The French intervened to put a stop to this new deep-water industry, and demanded that the British Government should enforce the closed season for fishing. There was much argument about whether the closed season had ever been intended to apply to waters outside Jersey, but British law was confused, and after agreeing to the French request to enforce the ban, a new law was passed to clarify the position and the British oyster-fishing industry was more strictly controlled than ever before. From this point, the Jersey oyster fishery went into rapid decline.

The mid-1850s saw the industry's greatest boom. In 1856 there were 256 boats manned by 1,300 seamen, exporting nearly 180,000 tubs of oysters worth £35,000. In addition, more than 11,000 pints of stewed oysters were exported by the canning factory, which had been set up in Gorey in 1837. By 1860 there were only 165 boats still fishing, exporting around 98,000 tubs. The collapse accelerated, and in 1863, a mere 46 boats produced 9,800 tubs of oysters worth just £3,000. Why had the rot set in?

The decline was not peculiar to Jersey, although in Jersey it was very much more serious than in the Channel ports. The demise of the industry was examined by several parliamentary committees, which identified three possible and conflicting causes:

1.   Oysters suffered a natural periodic decline in their reproductive capacity.

2.   Over-fishing and failure to observe the closed season had depleted stocks.

3.   The closed season – a conservation measure – had actually resulted in the failure of the oysters, because the previous constant dredging had prevented weed accumulating. Weed was now choking the young of the oyster.

The 1866 Sea Fisheries Committee rather hesitantly laid the blame at the door of the first option. An added factor was the French fishermen's determination to extend their exclusive zone. British dredgers were chased away, while French vessels were allowed to dredge indiscriminately, even taking the small oysters which the 1843 rules declared should be thrown back.

But whatever the reasons for the decline, the rapidly diminishing catches of the 1860s soon forced the Jersey oyster fleet to go elsewhere. Sadly, in 1871, the inspector of the Jersey oyster fishery made his last report. He noted that only six boats had been employed in that year, and

162 *The oyster trade brought much growth and prosperity to Gorey. This late 19th-century photograph shows Mrs. Cartwright's* Taunton Inn *and Park's ship chandlery. (John Le Seelleur Collection)*

only 1,200 tubs of oysters, worth £600, were exported. The glory days had ended and the Jersey oyster industry was clearly moribund. It had, however, left a permanent imprint on the south-eastern corner of the Island.

THE NEWFOUNDLAND TRADE

In the cemetery at St George's Cove on the coast of the Gaspé peninsula there is a monument bearing the dates 1819-1972 and the following inscription:

THEY CAME ON THE SEA

FROM THE CHANNEL

ISLANDS OF GUERNSEY

AND JERSEY

BESIDE THE SEA

THEY BUILT HOMES

CHURCHES AND SCHOOLS

FROM THE SEA

THEY LIVED

AND BY THE SEA

THEY REST

This is a lasting memorial to Channel Island settlers whose family names are to be found on the gravestones in cemeteries around the Gaspé coast and whose descendants bear those names today. They include family names which are familiar in St Martin.

The first inhabitants of this region around the estuary of the St Lawrence River were North American Indians whose ancestors crossed the land bridge between Siberia and Alaska at an unknown date and, over countless generations, eventually made their way to the eastern seaboard

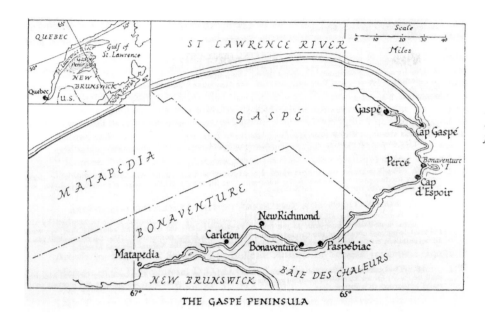

163 The Gaspé, at the mouth of Canada's St Lawrence River, was one of the biggest settlement areas in the western hemisphere for Jersey seamen and traders.

THE GASPÉ PENINSULA

of the continent and the Gaspé peninsula. They were called the Micmac, a tribe of Algonquin-Huron stock. Gaspé is a Micmac name, said to mean Finisterre. This, says Marguerite Syvret, is one of the many affinities Gaspé has with Brittany in history and legend.

It has been suggested that the Phoenicians, who were great voyagers and traders, discovered the continent, and that their unrecorded stories of that distant land may have been the origins of the legend of lost Atlantis. However there is little doubt that the Vikings were the first to cross from the other side of the ocean and to establish a settlement on the coast. They had settled in Iceland and Greenland before the year 1000 and there is a romantic story that around 1020 an Icelandic merchant named Thorfinn Karsenfi spent a winter with Eric the Red at the latter's Greenland home. There he met, and subsequently married, a beautiful widow named Gudrig, whose late husband had frequently travelled from Greenland to western lands, and during the long winter evenings Gudrig related the tales about those lands which she had learned from her husband. Thorfinn resolved to journey himself to those parts and in the following spring he mounted an expedition of 160 persons to explore them. Reaching the coast, they turned towards the south and came across the remains of a Viking ship that had been wrecked years before. They sailed on to Gaspé Bay and to what is now the Baie des Chaleurs, where they established a settlement. The following winter was a hard one, and they sailed further south to the Hudson River where they traded with the local Indians. However a quarrel with the Indians developed and the expedition returned to the Baie des Chaleurs. The settlement was later abandoned and Thorfinn returned to Greenland. Several centuries would pass before there were again European settlements on the coast.

Fishermen from Jersey had discovered the rich fishing grounds of the Grand Banks south of Newfoundland by the 16th century and probably earlier. They had fished far north in Icelandic waters and tradition says that on occasions they had been driven westwards by north-easterly gales and had found the fishing grounds within sight of Newfoundland. John Jean writes (*Jersey Sailing Ships*) that John Guilleame is credited with having brought the first cargo of Newfoundland fish to Jersey in 1596, and in following years Jersey vessels regularly set out for the fishing grounds

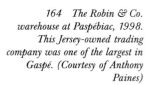

164 The Robin & Co. warehouse at Paspébiac, 1998. This Jersey-owned trading company was one of the largest in Gaspé. (Courtesy of Anthony Paines)

each spring, returning in early autumn. The small vessels used for these voyages wintered at St Malo because little shelter was available in Jersey.

Canada was at that time a French possession. The Gaspé peninsula had been claimed for France by Jacques Cartier, whose expedition set out from St Malo in 1534 seeking a north-west passage to China. That circumstance did not, however, prevent Jersey boats from fishing in Newfoundland waters. The annual voyages to the fishing grounds led to the establishment of permanent settlements, first on the east coast of Newfoundland, then on the southern and western coasts of the island and finally, in the late 18th century, on the Gaspé peninsula itself. It is difficult for us who live today in the comfort and security of St Martin to imagine the courage and fortitude of the fishermen who sailed over the Atlantic Ocean in quite small vessels, and of the families who followed them to set up homes in that far-off territory.

The first permanent settlers on the peninsula were the French (known as the Acadians) who had settled in Canada during French rule, and fishermen from Normandy and Brittany, but they were soon followed by people from Jersey. It was only three years after the Treaty of Paris ended the Seven Years War with France in 1763 that Charles Robin, a young man of 23, first went to Gaspé. His employers, Robin, Pipon & Co., already had establishments in Newfoundland. After great hardships in the early years, Charles Robin built up an enterprise in Gaspé, based at Paspébiac, which dominated economic and domestic life on the Gaspé coast for 150 years. With the setting up of these businesses on the coast, the migratory pattern of fishing gave way to a resident fishery, although ships still overwintered in the Channel Islands before carrying stores to the settlements in the spring for the next fishing season. They also brought the craftsmen needed for maintenance of the fleet – carpenters, sailmakers, coopers, blacksmiths and other artisans. The young apprentices were bound for four years at the end of which they received the sum of £120.

There was a great demand for fish from the Catholic countries of Europe and South America which led to the creation of a complex export trade from the Newfoundland fishery. That trade demanded considerable managerial and organisational skills and required the importation to the settlements of almost all the goods and equipment that were necessary for the catching and preservation of the fish, the maintenance of the fishing fleet and the sustenance of the residents and crews. The cod catches were brought ashore for gutting and salting and then dried on the beaches until they were ready for shipment. By the mid-19th century the 'cod trade triangle' was well established. The first leg of the triangle was the outward voyage from the Channel Islands to the fisheries with stores and passengers. The second leg was the shipment of the cod, either eastwards to Portugal, Spain, Italy and other European destinations, or to the Caribbean and South America. After the sale of their cargoes the ships returned to their home ports with goods from the countries they had visited: for example, coffee and sugar from the Caribbean and South America, fruit and wine from the Mediterranean countries, and manufactures and metals from England. Thus, almost as a by-product, the cod trade developed a general sea-going carrying trade making Jersey, for a short period, a centre of commerce, and bringing considerable wealth to many Jersey merchants. The signs of that prosperity can still be seen in the so-called 'cod houses' – fine residences built by merchants with their profits from the cod trade and its ancillary activities.

Just as the shipbuilding industry declined for reasons outside the control of the Island, so external economic and political changes weakened the Newfoundland trade. A final blow was the failure of the Jersey Banking Company in 1886. This failure resulted from the mismanagement of Philip Gosset, who was both manager of the Bank and Treasurer of the States. Thereafter the Island's economy revolved again around agriculture and tourism, some commerce and, more recently, finance.

VRAIC

Jersey is not the only place in northern Europe where vraic has been used for centuries to fertilise and improve the texture of the land; but nowhere else has this product of the sea been so widely used and appreciated. So highly has it been prized that detailed rules have been made, and strictly enforced, to preserve the harvest by preventing over-cutting of the weed and the consequent depletion of the crop. An old Jersey proverb is '*Point de vraic, point de hautgard*' (No seaweed, no corn stacks).

Vraic was, and is today, most extensively used in the coastal areas of the Island and particularly in the east and west. The reason why it is less used in fields on higher ground away from the coast is not the seemingly obvious one that vraic is heavy to transport (although it is) but that vraic spread on the land cools the soil and those fields of heavier soil are not warmed by the spring sunshine as are the côtils of St Martin and the lighter soils of St Ouen. The use of vraic declined with the introduction of chemical fertilizers, but a drive around the St Martin's coast in September still shows many fields and côtils spread with vraic, to be ploughed in later in preparation for the planting of Jersey Royals.

165 Vraicmen, *dry point by Edmund Blampied. (Courtesy of The Blampied Trustees)*

166 'The seaweed harvest in Jersey *c.*1860'. *A certain amount of artistic licence is evident in the etching, particularly in the location of the buildings. The tower on the beach beneath Gorey Church is particularly interesting!* *(John Le Seelleur Collection)*

For centuries, Les Écréhous have been a favourite and important centre for the cutting of vraic. This industry encouraged the building of huts on the reef, especially when the value of burnt vraic ashes as a fertilizer was discovered, because it was easier to burn the vraic on the spot than to first carry it home. An extensive level platform was created there among the old priory buildings for laying out and drying vraic before it could be burned. G.R. Balleine, writing in 1951, tells us that a fisherman named Philip Pinel built himself a cottage on Blianque Île in 1848, in which he lived for nearly fifty years, surviving off fish and burning seaweed to ashes. He built up a flourishing export trade to Jersey, and came to be known as the King of the Écréhous.

In 1935, Marett wrote: 'About half a league to the North West of this Bay [St Catherine's], there is a small creek called Rosel, where the Islanders keep several boats both for fishing and for going to Ecreho, there to fetch such sea-weed as they burn and manure their land with.'

The historian Philip Falle wrote somewhat lyrically about vraic. After describing it as 'a Weed more valuable to us than the choicest Plant cultivated in our Gardens …', he wrote:

> Tis gathered only at certain times appointed by the Magistrate and notified to the People by the public Cryer on a Market-day. There are two Seasons of cutting, the one in Summer, the other about the Vernal Equinox. The *Summer Vraic*, being first well dried by the Sun on the Shore, serves for Kitchen and fewel in Country-houses and makes a hot glowing Fire; and the ashes, which are carefully preserved, serve for Manure. We hold them equivalent to a like Quantity of Lime. The *Winter Vraic* being spred on the Green Swerd, and after buried by the Furrows of the plough, 'tis incredible how with its fat unctuous Substance it meliorates and fertilizes the earth, imbibing itself into it, softening the Clod, and keeping the Root of the Corn moist during the most parching Heats of Summer. In

167   Vraicing scene at St Catherine, P.J. Ouless, c.1850. (Courtesy of Anthony Paines)

stormy weather the sea does often tear up from the rocks vast Quantities of this useful Weed and casts it upon the Shore, where the glad Husbandman gathers it, and proper Officers attend to seeing it distributed in just Proportions.

John Le Seelleur, who farms the family property Haye Hogard and some of the Rosel Manor land, gives a more prosaic but more scientific description of the qualities of vraic and the reasons why he continues to apply it to his land. It contains trace elements such as manganese, magnesium and iodine. Jersey soil is not rich in the former elements, and iodine seems to be active against eelworm. The weed contains small crustaceans and molluscs which provide calcium – another substance in which Jersey is lacking. The weed builds up humus which is drawn down into the soil by earthworms and, in general, land which has been treated with vraic produces healthier plants. Carting and spreading vraic is heavy work and costs about £80 a vergée. The old method of using horse-drawn carts, so familiar from many of Edmund Blampied's lithographs, has given way to tractors hauling large high-sided trailers carrying twenty times the load of the old carts. Tractors with front-loaders have replaced the men with forks seen in the Ouless painting of St Catherine.

There are two kinds of vraic: the *vraic venu* or *vraic de marée*, which is the weed torn from the rocks by the waves and washed up along the shore, and *vraic taillé* which is harvested from the rocks with a sickle. The distinction was important because whilst *vraic venu* might be collected from the beaches at any time, the harvesting of *vraic taillé* has been subject to regulation for several hundred years, at first probably by custom but later, from the early 16th century, by legislation. The laws were codified by the *Code of Laws of the Island of Jersey, 1771* and have since been amended many times. The *Code* contained particular rules for some of the western parishes, as indeed have

168   Vraic drying on the beach at St Catherine, 1909. (Courtesy of Tom Marett)

subsequent enactments. For the east coast it provided that 'in accordance with custom' summer vraic could not be cut over more than one tide. Generally, the *Code* prohibited gathering vraic before sunrise or after sunset on penalty of a £10 fine. The present law, whilst still containing special provisions relating to the western parishes, permits the cutting of vraic from 1 February to 30 April between sunrise on Mondays and sunset on Saturdays. However the practice of cutting vraic from the rocks did not survive the German Occupation of the Island and today it is the *vraic venu* which is gathered for the fields.

Collecting and carting vraic was heavy work in which the farmer and all his family, including the womenfolk, would participate. William Plees, writing in 1817 with reference to *vraic venu* said '… even in the midst of winter, whole families, comprising men, women and children of both sexes, are seen raking together the highly-prized boon of Nature, and sometimes breast high in water; vraicking, like a Catholic holiday, suspending other secular employments'. Especially during the cutting of the *vraic taillé*, sustenance was needed during the day and was provided in the form of the traditional vraic cakes (small buns containing currants or raisins and flavoured with spices and peel), boiled pork, a large keg of cider and a smaller one of brandy. Formerly, suppers would be held at the end of the season with singing, dancing and other amusements, but this custom appears to have declined during the 19th century.

Many farmers, particularly those living near the coast, combined farming with fishing and the use of boats to collect vraic from distant rocks is of great antiquity. The Assize Roll of 1309 records that three St Martinais, with 24 other men, went to Les Écréhous to collect vraic and that on the return journey the boat overturned and many were drowned. Balleine recorded in 1951, 'under the queer law of deodand the boat that had caused the accident was sentenced to be confiscated for murder'. In 1844 another St Martin tragedy occurred with the wreck of the *Laurel*, a cutter which had been built at St Catherine in 1824 by John Le Huquet. The following account of the tragedy is taken from *Stories of Jersey Seas, of Jersey's Coast and of Jersey Seamen* by Philip Ahier:

On Monday morning, July 30th, 1844 this cutter, captained by Mr. John Pallot, left Gorey Harbour with nineteen persons, which included three women, all bent on gathering seaweed. Reaching to the windward side of La Conchière, the most outlying rock in Grouville, the captain dropped anchor and allowed it to touch his vessel. It was a lovely day at the time, otherwise, so we are told, it would not have been placed in that position.

In the afternoon, however, there began to blow a strong west-north-west breeze, accompanied by squalls of rain. About 2 o'clock, as soon as the cutter had been refloated, and at the moment when the crew and passengers were about to get under weigh, a strong gust of wind thrust the vessel upon the rocks in its vicinity, causing it to spring a leak and eventually to sink.

Messrs John Pallot (Capt.), Francis Amy, John Coutanche and Edward Le Vesconte, jnr. in their small boat hastened to remove several persons on to the neighbouring rocks, promising them that they would return to fetch them before the incoming tide reached them. They left one man and one woman, Mr. Carrel and Mrs. Romeril, on the cutter. These two now took refuge among the shrouds, reckoning to be rescued later on.

Folks living on the sea coast had seen what had happened and it was discerned by telescope that the six persons who had been placed on La Conchière had formed a circle by holding each other's hands.

Mr Philippe Marie, an experienced Grouville pilot, was prevailed upon by the folk at La Rocque to get to La Conchière with all possible speed. He left La Rocque Harbour with his son, Mr. Jean Marie and Messrs Elie Gaudin and John Picot, as soon as he could get his boat afloat at about 5 o'clock. But before they could get to the tragic spot, the six persons on La Conchière were swept by a huge wave from off the rock and were drowned.

Pilot Marie then proceeded to the cutter, where they saw the two persons who were clinging to the shrouds and who had been in that unenviable position for three hours. When she saw the pilot boat coming to her relief she flung herself into the sea, thereby hoping that she would be rescued, but she sank to rise no more. Mr. Marie and his crew strove hard by means of ropes to save Mr. Jean Carrel, but in vain.

One of the men placed upon the rocks by Captain Pallot jumped into a small boat, but it was hurled against the other rocks, smashed to bits by the force of the seas and its occupant drowned.

It was not known how long the five other persons placed amongst the rocks remained there, if it was a lengthy period their position became perilous. They must have seen that the rising tide would engulf them and their suspense must have been terrible while they were awaiting relief. Captain Pallot ultimately rescued them and brought them to shore, but they were completely exhausted when they were landed at Gorey Pier.

Mr Thomas Le Seelleur and four other persons who were also vraicing in the vicinity did all they possibly could to come to the assistance of those who were still clinging to the rocks, but the sea was so tempestuous that they could not approach them, although they threw overboard the vraic that they had collected and were rowing for more than one hour. They had the mortification of seeing several persons drown, one after the other.

A detachment of sailors from H.M.S. *Sylvia* with many civilians aboard set out from Gorey Harbour where they were stationed in an endeavour to be of assistance, but their trip to La Conchière proved fruitless.

The toll of this tragedy was that 14 persons, including the three women, were drowned, and only six were saved. The Laurel was refloated on August 2nd 1844 and towed to Gorey Harbour, where it was found to have suffered considerable damage. The bodies of those drowned were washed ashore at odd times, the last being that of Mrs. Falle on September 25th 1844. At each inquest Capt. Pallot was absolved of any blame and the verdicts were "accidental death".

A subscription list was opened for the benefit of the widows and orphans resulting from the tragedy and yielded £250, which was divided amongst the families affected.

The States of Jersey voted sums of money to Mr. Philippe Marie and to the others by way of compensation for any losses incurred as a result of their going to the assistance of the Laurel.

Vraicing could be a dangerous business.

ST CATHERINE'S LIFEBOAT

Jersey has had an inshore lifeboat since 1968. Initially, the boat was funded by members of St Helier Yacht Club and the St Helier Lifeboat crew, and was stationed at St Helier Harbour.

In 1969, the Royal National Lifeboat Institution (RNLI) took over responsibility for the inshore boat and a 15ft D-Class inflatable lifeboat was stationed at St Catherine in an old German bunker behind the viviers. This lifeboat, which had a single engine and was operational in summer months only, was launched by the crew pushing the boat on a trailer down the slip. So damp was the interior of the bunker that snails and slugs had to be removed from the boat – and the crew's oilskins – prior to launching.

Early in 1983, sea trials were carried out with a 17ft twin-engined C-Class inflatable lifeboat. As a result of the success of these trials, in the early part of 1984, the new C-Class lifeboat *Sebag of Jersey*, funded by a generous donation from the Clarkson Trust, was established in a purpose-built station alongside the sailing club at St Catherine.

The local RNLI honorary secretary of that time, Harbourmaster Captain Ronald Taylor, asked Assistant Harbourmaster Frank Jeune to run the St Catherine Station, and with a crew of around fifteen local volunteers the boat operated 24 hours a day, all year round. During her time at St Catherine between 1984 and 1990 she was launched on service 111 times.

During one service, in October 1985, the lifeboat was damaged during a search of the rocky waters off La Rocque in thick fog. Whilst repairs were being effected by the RNLI in Cowes a relief D-Class lifeboat was stationed at St Catherine. The following week, this lifeboat was involved in the rescue of six French sailors after their yacht, *Ixtlan*, hit rocks and began sinking off Seymour Tower. With the tide falling, the helm had to negotiate the lifeboat between the rocks to reach the stricken vessel and find space on board for the extra passengers. Cramped enough with four crew, the lifeboat ended up carrying 11 people to safe water where the St Helier Lifeboat was standing by. The rescue, which lasted five hours, was reported in a national sailing magazine.

On another occasion, in 1987, the lifeboat was called out to search for two women after they failed to return from a ride across Grouville beach in fog. They were found, with their horses, almost two hours later on Seymour Tower where they had taken refuge from the rising spring tide. Leaving one crewman with them, the lifeboat returned to Gorey for blankets and other provisions to see them through the night before the next low tide when help arrived from the shore. It took a major night-time operation, involving diggers and tractors building a ramp over the steps to the tower, and covering it in a carpet of straw bales, to coax the horses back down, and they finally reached safety 33 hours after their ordeal began. This rescue led to several stories

169   C-Class lifeboat Sebag of Jersey *leads her successor, Atlantic 21* Jessie Eliza *during sea-trials. (Jersey Evening Post)*

– and cartoons – in the national press. It was lead story on ITN's national lunchtime news bulletin on the day of the rescue.

The operational range of the St Catherine Lifeboat is not restricted to the east coast of Jersey. Services have taken the lifeboat across to the French coast on various occasions, including a five-hour-long service to tow a boat back from just off Le Senequet, 20 miles south east of the station. After the 1987 Sark to Jersey rowing race, the lifeboat ended up towing a different speedboat back to Sark. The crew received a few quizzical looks when they walked into the bar at the top of the hill, in their drysuits, in search of fuel and a drink before the trip back to Jersey!

It was the extended range and duration of services carried out that prompted the RNLI in 1989 to carry out sea trials with a new class of lifeboat. In October 1990, an Atlantic 21 was stationed in a new larger boathouse built near the tower in St Catherine's Bay. Initially the relief fleet boat *Lions International* was based at the new station until, in October 1991, the station's own lifeboat *Jessie Eliza* came on service.

The Atlantic 21 was developed by the RNLI in the late 1960s and proved to be an economic method of handling rescue work requiring a fast launch and passage to a casualty, along with the ability to work close to rocks or in shallow conditions. The lifeboat, which is seven metres in length, is a rigid inflatable, the hull being made of glass reinforced plastic. The crew of three is seated on a console unit which contains VHF radio, compass, controls, a GPS navigation system, first aid kit and other equipment.

In the event of a capsize, a crew member activates a gas bottle which rapidly inflates the bag on a roll-bar assembly above the engines. Within a few seconds the boat rolls upright and the engines, which are made inversion proof, can be restarted. In 1996, the twin engines on *Jessie Eliza* were replaced with more powerful 70 hp engines providing speeds of up to 34 knots. Les Écréhous could be reached in just 15 minutes from launching and Grosnez, on the north-west corner, in only half an hour.

One of the more memorable rescues carried out in *Jessie Eliza* was of a surfer on New Year's Day in 1994. By that evening the wind had picked up to a gale force 7–8 and the helmsman recalls watching from his home as the waves came over Gorey Pier and into the harbour producing spray which rose up and over the houses. Moments later his pager went off – cries for help had

170 Atlantic 21 Jessie Eliza, *a rigid inflatable, capable of speeds to 34 knots. (Jersey Evening Post)*

been heard by the police off Plémont. The lifeboat launched at 2136 into a sea of white water. The conditions were so bad that during the launch the whole rig, comprising tractor, trailer and lifeboat, was pushed up the beach by the breaking surf and the boat almost capsized out of the trailer. The 12-mile passage to Plémont was hampered by the heavy, confused seas. Strong winds, violent rain and hail showers reduced the visibility to less than twenty yards.

They finally arrived on scene one hour later but were only able to locate the surfer after hearing his cries for help. Having pulled him from the sea at 2250 it emerged that there was actually another person in the water in the area. Having landed the first surfer on the beach at Grève de Lecq the lifeboat returned to the scene, searching out beyond L'Étacq, joined by the St Helier Lifeboat, before being recalled at 0130. The lifeboat returned to the scene with a fresh crew at first light, 0730. The search was called off after the pilot cutter *Ronez* found the second surfer clinging to his board near St Aubin's Bay.

In recognition of the courage of the crew that night, senior helmsman Nigel Sweeny was awarded 'The Thanks of the Institution' on vellum, and the two crew members, Paul Richardson and John Heyes, were presented with framed letters of appreciation. The helmsman was also presented with the Walter and Elizabeth Groombridge Award for the most meritorious service performed by the crew of an Atlantic 21 that year.

The ability to manoeuvre the Atlantic 21 class lifeboat in shallow water was highlighted by the rescue of a boy stranded on a rock, again off Plémont, in April 1996. Conditions on this occasion meant that the lifeboat was on scene within 15 minutes of launching. With a two-metre swell breaking over the rock he was on, which was surrounded by other smaller outcrops, the only approach was via a narrow gulley. The crew dropped anchor and with seas breaking over the lifeboat and only three feet of water under the keel, the helmsman, Bruce Ferguson, veered the boat down (reversed) towards the rock to reach the boy and carry him to safety.

On Easter Monday, 1995, the lifeboat assisted in the rescue of 300 passengers from the crippled ferry *St Malo* after she struck rocks off La Corbière.

The longest service the lifeboat has carried out was on a Sunday in March 1996 at the end of a busy weekend in which there had been a service on the Saturday afternoon followed by an engine change and a major pre-arranged exercise the next morning. The lifeboat was launched at 2135 on that Sunday night to search for an overdue fishing vessel and returned to station at 0130 before being launched again at first light, 0530. There were two crew changes and refuelling stops, in bays around the coast, during the day and the boat finally arrived back on station at 2030. During the 19-hour service the lifeboat ended up more than 15 miles offshore, south-west of La Corbière Lighthouse. Sadly, only wreckage from the missing fishing vessel was found.

The St Catherine's Lifeboat station is manned by 12 sea-going crew and two launcher/mechanics, all of whom live close to the station and are dedicated volunteers. The first woman joined the crew on active service in June 1995. On standby 24 hours a day, 365 days a year, the crew are called by a pager system and are prepared to drop everything immediately to ensure that the lifeboat is launched as quickly as possible – on average within 10 minutes.

During the period from commissioning to the end of 1998, the St Catherine's Atlantic 21 lifeboat was launched on service 180 times. The lifeboat has proved a fast and versatile means of enabling the crewmen and women of the RNLI to provide assistance to vessels, divers, swimmers, surfers and many others in difficulty anywhere around the coast of Jersey.

GOREY REGATTA

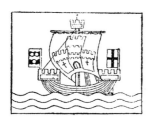

Gorey Regatta is a significant part of Jersey's heritage. Apart from the war years, the Regatta has taken place annually for almost 150 years. It started when the oyster-fishing industry was in its heyday, with the working oyster dredgers and their crews competing for prizes offered by the merchants of the industry. But whereas the oyster is now rarely found living naturally in local waters, the Regatta is still firmly placed in the Island's yachting calendar.

Gone is the fleet of dredgers, the shipyards that built them, the dredgermen, ships chandlers, sailmakers, blockmakers, blacksmiths, and everything else that went with the oyster industry. Gone too are the shops that sold liquor – so numerous that it is said that almost every house on Gorey Pier and on the adjacent hill sold gin at 1d. a glass. But the Regatta has survived, a reminder of those heady days when the population of St Martin was swelled by the hard-sailing and hard-drinking oystermen.

The dredgermen handled their sailing boats expertly. They had scant respect for the local officers of the law and often defied them. When the Regatta time came, competition was intense and sailing displays really worthwhile.

Competitors were not in the least averse to damaging each other's gear, either cutting halyards or attaching a bucket to the keel of a rival. As a precaution, a member or more of a crew would remain aboard the previous night to keep guard. The racing was not without hazard, and in 1926 the committee awarded £2 to the crew of *Jubilee* in appreciation of their services in saving S.R. Perchard and Mr. Faudemer, the crew of *Mavis* which had capsized and sunk during the sailing of the 5th Event. Mr. Perchard obviously was not disheartened by this disaster, as the following year he and *Mavis* won their race.

Apart from sailing, there were rowing and sculling races and side shows. Competitors enjoyed pillow fights sitting astride a greasy pole suspended horizontally above the water.

The actual racing would invariably go well. But it was usually followed by much drunkenness and inevitable brawls arising out of the rivalry between the crews. Indeed, it seems that this tradition had still not entirely died out when in 1953, a report of the annual dinner stated: 'Unfortunately at one time immediately following the speeches, things tended to get rather out of hand and some members were guilty of unseemly behaviour. Jumping crackers and cannon crashers were thrown under the tables and many of the ladies present were considerably alarmed.'

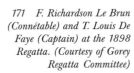

171 F. Richardson Le Brun (Connétable) and T. Louis De Faye (Captain) at the 1898 Regatta. (Courtesy of Gorey Regatta Committee)

172 Gorey Regatta Committee, 1922. Photograph taken on the Duke of Normandy *which was rented by the committee at a cost of £3. (Courtesy of Gorey Regatta Committee)*

The fisher folk would turn out both themselves and their boats in the finest trim they could manage for Regatta Day. All the crews would wear woollen caps in their own distinctive coloured pattern, with a long tassel and a pom-pom at the end.

Fishing boats from all round the Island would come to Gorey to compete in the Regatta. In those days sailing was almost the monopoly of the professional sailor and fisherman. Today the survival of sailing rests entirely in the hands of the enthusiastic amateur. The spectators too were usually connected with the fishing trade or the fleet of dredgers. They were intensely interested and very knowledgeable about the boats, their crews and the racing.

Racing probably started on an informal basis, but it was well established by the latter part of the 19th century and it is generally accepted that 1852 was the official formation date. Certainly, by 1899 the regatta was well established, and with it a multitude of events including 'duck hunt after live ducks'. Any attempt to revive this particular sport today would probably fall foul of the law. Similarly, the 1929 event, 'backward race for ladies', might not find favour with the politically correct generation of the 1990s.

In the years before World War II many fine French fishing vessels would compete in their own special races and their performance was always a great treat for spectators. In 1926, the prizes for the *entente cordiale* race for French fishing boats were increased to a total of 900 francs. However, as the rate of exchange was then 170 francs to the pound sterling, this may not have been a sufficient incentive to ensure the continuance of this particular event.

There is a strong tradition of service. T. Louis De Faye, who was Captain in 1898, held the post until 1934 and served on the committee until his death in 1937. P.N. Richardson was vice-president in 1927 and his sons, Denys and Vivian, both served as regatta captains. The patrons and sponsors included R.R. Lemprière, Seigneur of Rozel, T.B. Davis of the schooner yacht *Westward*, and Sir Jesse Boot (later Lord Trent). The Boot family held the lease on Maître Île at Les Écréhous and their boats, *Jesse* (recently restored by the Jersey Museum Service) and *Florence* were regular scratch competitors.

In 1946, the Regatta resumed after the Occupation. Before World War II there were two yacht clubs at Gorey: Gorey Yacht Club and Gorey Castle Yacht Club. Today, Gorey Boat Owners Association may be seen as their successor. After the end of the war Lieutenant-Commander Denys Richardson, the captain, managed to restart the Regatta despite the practical obstacles, including the fact that the former headquarters, the *British Elfine Hotel*, was ruined in the Occupation. On 22 August 1946, some 20 boats were able to take part in the competition, only 15 months after Liberation.

Today the yacht racing is still well supported with many vessels coming from St Helier and a major influx of dinghies from St Catherine's Sailing Club. Many of the trophies date back to pre-war days and are keenly contested. The kind of fierce rivalry which still exists is documented in the records of the protest committee. Although protests are usually heard immediately following the Regatta, there have been several instances of a prolonged and acrimonious correspondence and appeals made to the Royal Yachting Association. Indeed, after the 1964 Regatta, the protest procedure in one case was not settled until May 1966. This was relatively civilised compared with the correspondence which followed an incident in 1961. The strength of feeling in this case harked

173   A poster advertising the 1899 Regatta. (Photo: Robin Briault)

174 *Yacht* Stranger II *racing in 1925. (Gorey Regatta Committee)*

back to the rivalry among those 19th-century oystermen. The correspondence from the captain of the protesting yacht to the chairman of the protest committee described the judgement as 'farcical and misguided' and the chairman himself as 'hazy and biased'. The reply condemned the protester's letter as 'unfortunate if not insulting' and 'contemptible', and described the gentleman himself as 'cowardly'.

Although this was an isolated incident and an exception to the usually relaxed and good-natured conduct of sailors and officials, it does show that the yachtsmen of Gorey take their sailing seriously.

175 *A mixed class racing shortly after WWII. The nearest boats are Falcons, previously of Gorey Castle Yacht Club. The helmsman of F7, on port tack, appears to have allowed his knowledge of the racing rules to become a little rusty during the wartime absence! (Jersey Evening Post)*

ST CATHERINE'S SAILING CLUB

St Catherine's Sailing Club has helped to encourage the development of many of Jersey's expert amateur yachtsmen. For nearly fifty years it has provided a base to which families have brought their young to gain experience of dinghy sailing and racing in a supportive friendly environment.

The club was formed at a meeting held at St Martin's School on 11 March 1953. C. Robins was elected president and the annual subscription was set at 5s. for seniors and 2s. 6d. for juniors.

The first race took place between *Blue Jacket*, a La Rocque fishing boat, and *Elsie*, described as a 'very fast looking Bermudan sloop'. Racing in the early years was organised from the tower alongside St Catherine's slip.

It was not until 1956 that the club acquired its own premises, renting from the Harbours and Airport Committee the old carpenters' shed near St Catherine's Breakwater for £2 per annum. In the early days the facilities were somewhat primitive and included a starter's hut precariously mounted on scaffold poles. Water supplies for the canteen (surprisingly not 'the galley') were obtained from rainwater catchment via a buried tank. This supplied many a cup of beverage without ill effect until investigation of the tank disclosed the floating, decomposed remains of several rats and other small animals.

The club has always been particularly family-oriented and great importance is attached to race training and general sailing instruction for children. This has meant that the club has also concentrated on safety. One of the club's major expenses has always been the provision of adequate guard boats. Their value was demonstrated when a freak thunderstorm devastated an evening's racing, capsizing the entire fleet. All the crews were brought ashore safely, but one Topper could not be brought back. It was eventually recovered from the French coast – remarkably unscathed. In the early days, guard boats were summoned by displaying a large orange board from the clubhouse; this has now been replaced by VHF radios.

The club joined the Royal Yachting Association in 1957, changed the title of its senior officer from 'President' to the more usual 'Commodore', and adopted a burgee featuring the shield of St Martin superimposed on St Catherine's Wheel. By 1960, the early lug-sail dinghies had given way to class racing in Enterprises, Scorpions and Mirrors. Race meetings were organised with a variety of other clubs, including Cercle Nautique of Carteret, St Thomas' Hospital, and RAF Thorney Island. A regular competition has also been held against teams from Guernsey and Alderney.

In 1970 the carpenters' shed was completely rebuilt. It was further extended in 1980 into a fine modern clubhouse with all the required facilities for race organisation and social functions.

There has always been a wide range in the types of dinghy sailed, and the fleet has varied from year to year as boat design has progressed. But Mirrors have stood the test of time and are still among the most popular of the classes, providing an ideal and economic start for younger members. Fireballs, which were popular some years ago, have more recently been superseded by more modern boats such as Streakers, Toppers, Lasers and Isos, which comprise most of the present fleet.

176 *The clubhouse provides a good vantage point from which to watch the racing in St Catherine's Bay. (Courtesy of John Newcombe)*

The club has hosted a number of national events, including a competition for Streakers in 1991 and the Topper European Championships in 1985.

In 1998 the Island Games came to Jersey and members of St Catherine's Sailing Club were involved in both sailing and providing race officers in various capacities. The club was also represented in the extensive planning stages leading up to the Games. The club proudly records that its members took a gold in the Laser Standard Class and a silver in the match racing for yachts.

Members have travelled to various venues, including Holland and the Baltic, to compete in National and International events, acquitting themselves well and showing the Jersey flag and the St Catherine's club burgee. Sailing has been an occupation in Jersey since time began. St Catherine's has helped ensure – in more recent years at least – that people learn to sail in safety and with fun.

GOREY CASTLE YACHT CLUB

Gorey Castle Yacht Club was formed shortly before World War II, in 1937 or 1938, and did not survive the hostilities. During its brief existence, it established a class of wooden, clinker-built dinghies described variously as Falcons or Weymouth One Designs which were sailed from Gorey. They were all named after birds, such as *Kestrel* owned by Colonel Christopher Riley, the club commodore. These were very safe, steady boats and ideal for instructing cadets.

Andalusia Richardson, Colonel Riley's daughter, remembers fondly the instruction given by Colonel Dyce of Maufant Lodge, Vice-Commodore: 'He was a dour man and a hard taskmaster but taught us well the intricacies of sailing, which made it enjoyable the remainder of my active life.' She also recalls that she and her brother John were never allowed to bicycle past St Martin's Church on Sundays dressed in 'boating clothes'. This was for fear of offending parishioners who could not know that they had worshipped earlier elsewhere. Bicycle bags carried a change of clothes, while they accepted the discipline of 'thought for others' without question.

The clubhouse was established in a room above the *Elfine Hotel* on Gorey Pier and equipped with crockery bearing the burgee and colours of the club. It is questionable as to whether they had a liquor licence to the detriment of the hotel bar!

Towards the end of her long and sartorially notorious life Mrs. Dyce gave to Andalusia some items of GCYC art nouveau crockery and a brooch. This was in gilt and red-and-white enamel depicting the vice-commodore's burgee and valued by her as a gift from her husband. Andalusia donated these items to the Jersey Museum.

After the war, the remaining funds of the club were donated to St Catherine's Sailing Club.

GOREY BOAT-OWNERS ASSOCIATION

The Gorey Boat-Owners Association was inaugurated on Sunday, 23 November 1963 after Albert Able and others had called a meeting of the owners of boats moored in Gorey Harbour.

Their object was to ascertain whether there was sufficient interest to form an association for the benefit of all concerned, as it had been felt for some time that the interests of harbour users could be enhanced by the formation of such a body.

Pat Gruchy was its first chairman and Tony Chamier (later to be Constable of Grouville) became vice-chairman. Colonel Herbert Stevenson, Maurice Le Cuirot, Alfie Le Fèvre, George Langdon, E. Falle and G. Le Gresley served as committee members. Captain R.J. Bolitho and Advocate Denys Richardson were invited to become patrons and, later in the life of the association, Jurat William Hamilton and Mr. R. Le Carpentier were honoured in a similar manner.

The *raison d'être* for the association was to protect the interests of its members and to act as a pressure group to obtain better facilities in and around the harbour. It was felt that such an association would be better able to negotiate with the Harbour Office than individual boat owners. Accordingly the committee set to work to improve facilities, though initially their requests were of a rather modest nature. An application for a power point was made (the chairman remarking that he hoped everyone would use it) and in 1964 this was followed by one for a 'hygienic toilet' for visiting yachtsmen. These early requests serve only to remind us just how much the association has achieved to date.

During 1964, the threat of a marina development in Gorey became very real – a group of developers was buying property in the area and submitting plans to the relevant committees of the States. These involved creating 386 berths of which 205 would have been for vessels up to 25 feet. At the other end of the scale there were to be 15 berths for those between 70 and 100 feet. The depth would be maintained at eight feet throughout the marina.

The membership, once aware of the size of the project and of the proposed cost of keeping a boat in the marina, decided to oppose the scheme. The committee was advised by Advocate Richardson and his brother Mr. Vivian Richardson, and the latter accepted the task of being the association's spokesman at a public meeting held in the Town Hall on 15 February 1965. At a packed meeting the proposal to build a marina was heavily defeated and subsequently withdrawn

177 The Channel Island 22 is the most widely used boat in the GBOA. (Courtesy of Hugh Fauvel)

and the association owes a huge debt of gratitude to the committee of the time and in particular the Richardson family for the successful outcome of that meeting.

In its early days the association took on the task of rescue work in conjunction with the Harbour Office. Certain boats were designated for this purpose and fuel supplied by the authorities. Assistant Harbourmaster Frank Jeune, who lived near the harbour, was authorised to use these boats for rescue work and they were involved in many searches off the Island's north and east coasts.

The demand for better facilities grew, and soon the association was pressing the Harbour Office for a depth gauge, storage space on the pier, use of the crane, a telephone box and a pontoon. Many of these facilities have since been provided by the authorities.

By 1966 the association had more than 60 members. The annual subscription was ten shillings and the use of the power point two shillings and sixpence. The crane was made available to members and Alfie Le Fèvre was authorised by the Harbour Office to operate it.

The social side of the association began to develop and suppers were held in conjunction with the Combined Boat-Owners' Association. One of the first rallies to Portbail was held on Sunday, 13 July 1971.

With the growth of the membership and the increasing commercialisation of Gorey came the problem of car parking on the pier. Many meetings were held between the committee and the Harbour Office, but to no avail. Three-hour parking was introduced much to the dissatisfaction of the boat owners. This problem remains – although rather worse by now than in 1971.

Today the association is thriving with a membership exceeding two hundred. Its activities include rallies to Les Écréhous and France, support for the RNLI, Channel Islands Air Search and the Jubilee Sailing Trust and social activities (including some for children). Its primary aims are still to provide better facilities, and also to promote good seamanship and safety at sea. None of these things would be possible without the efforts of those far-sighted boat-owners back in 1963.

The Community

Ma Pâraisse
Par Amelia Perchard

Ch'est St Martin, qu'est ma pâraisse,
Ou'est qu'mes anchêtres pour bein longtemps,
Ont vêtchu tous dé péthe en fis,
La vie paisibl'ye dés bouans vièrs temps!

Sa côte si belle est l'envie d'tous,
Dé Gouâré, jusqu'au fond d'Rozé,
Lé bleau briselames dé Ste Cath'rinne,
La pointe d'la Crête, la Baie d'Flitché!

Ses miles dé ruettes, bordées d'fossés,
D'bleaux bouais, et d'muthâlles dé granni,
Qué nou trouve partout lá pâraisse,
Donnent à tout l'monde divèrs pliaîsi!

Lé vièr châté si ordgilleux,
Comme j'savons, car san nom nos l'dit.
Monté en garde comme dé tout temps,
Si formidabl'ye sus san rotchi!

L'églyise auvec san haut cliochi,
Toutes ses f'nêtres dé vèrre couleuthé.
Ou'est qu'nou trouve la fouai et la paix,
Dans s'n înmense trantchillité!

Y'a eune municipalité
Qui n'aime pon viae trop dé changements;
Et tâche dé garder not' pâraisse,
Eune pliâche speciale pour nos d'scendants!

Amelia L. Perchard (née Noël), born in 1921 in St Martin, has lived in the Parish all her life and is one of the Island's acknowledged experts on Jèrriais. It was her first language, and she has been competing in the Norman-French section of the Jersey Eisteddfod since the age of eight. Over the years she has written numerous poems and plays for both junior and adult competition. One-act plays written by her and entered in the Eisteddfod for the Parish of St Martin have won the 'Les Enfuntchis Trophy' 11 times in 16 years. She has also translated and adapted many songs, Christmas carols and hymns into Jèrriais. She is a member of the Don Balleine Trust, has been a member of l'Assembliée d'Jèrriais since its formation in 1951; and is now a member of the recently formed 'Parler Normand et Jèrriais'.

ST MARTIN'S BATTLE OF FLOWERS ASSOCIATION

The Battle of Flowers is a unique Jersey institution which is stepping into the new millennium with as much enthusiasm as it enjoyed when it began in 1902.

178 Amelia Perchard in the 1960s, wearing the wedding dress of her great-grandmother. (Courtesy of Amelia Perchard)

The first Battle was organised to celebrate the coronation of King Edward VII. Such was its success that it has continued every year since – interrupted only by the two world wars. Until the 1960s it was dominated by floats entered by individual families, and the flowers were pulled off during the parade and hurled down onto the crowds of spectators. In more recent times the Battle's premier exhibits have come from the parishes of the Island and leading clubs and associations, and the practice of dismantling the floats has come to an end – largely because of increasing concerns about the likelihood of someone suffering serious injury.

Support for the Battle waned for a time, but it is now possibly stronger than ever, and St Martin has established an impressive record of success in the competition among the floats.

St Martin's Battle of Flowers Association was established in the 1960s. It first entered the Battle in 1968 under the chairmanship of Bill Perchard. Many people still involved today will remember some of the spectacular floats and the ever-growing chassis, until the decision was taken to restrict their size.

Between 1979 and 1988 St Martin was absent from the Battle, but the parish's presence was re-established when Peter Germain set up a new committee. The first float was 'Spirit of the East' designed by artist Michael Richecoeur, a resident of the Parish. Bob Pallot then took over the leadership of the team and took the Parish on to win the Prix d'Excellence in 1997 with 'Coral Calypso'.

In more recent years the chairman has been Percy Gicquel who, with designer Nancy Thelland, has shown that the Parish is capable of producing some excellent floats.

The energy and community spirit which goes into the production of any large Battle of Flowers float is a remarkable thing. St Martin's entry is no exception. The main committee, the band of flower growers, the Diamond Club weeders, the army of people who turn up to help cut and stick, the dancers and costume-makers, the refreshment team, the builders, welders, engineers and electricians – all of them take part in a huge community enterprise which culminates in two parades which now take place on the second Thursday and Friday in August.

Not only does a Battle of Flowers float need people, it also needs a place. The need for a suitable venue is paramount and the construction of a 40-foot float requires plenty of space. The

179 *'St Martin's Car' which won second prize in the early 1930s. (Gerald Amy Collection)*

Parish has been lucky over the years to have received help in finding a venue from the Le Couteur and Perchard families.

The base of the float is a specially-modified old tractor. Two iron girders approximately 35 feet long are attached to the tractor, with a platform resting between. Wheels are changed to ensure that the float conforms to height restrictions. Each year the float is stripped back to its foundations before rebuilding begins. In the last decade, power steering has been added to make the job of navigating the float a little easier.

The flowers required for each year's entry have to be ordered before the end of January. About 14,500 stems of different colours – usually mostly chrysanthemums, as it was found that they last longest and are most suitable for the job – must be ordered from a commercial grower. Asters in four different colours are also grown; these are planted by volunteers in a field in the Parish which is donated rent-free for the purpose and are tended by retired volunteer residents of St Martin.

About a quarter of the float is usually decorated using harestails. These are ordered from the UK, dyed in various colours, and are prepared as early as possible. These grasses can be stuck onto the float well in advance of the parade itself, and 'harestailing' – undertaken by a group of volunteers – usually goes on for several months.

Building the float itself is overseen by engineers; small sections are often built separately and joined on later. Building materials include plywood, metal, chicken wire, cardboard and polystyrene. Once the framework is complete, the whole structure is covered in papier mâché and painted in the appropriate colours to be used as a guide for placing the flowers later.

Fixing the fresh flowers in place starts on the Monday of Battle of Flowers week. For three full days and nights the building shed sees feverish activity, carrying on until the early hours of the Thursday morning – the day of the Battle itself. During this week food is provided to the construction team by another band of volunteer helpers.

On the big day itself, the float is manned by over a dozen people wearing costumes specially designed to complement the theme of the float, and made by dressmakers in the Parish.

Such is the enthusiasm for the competition in St Martin that a junior entry was established in 1995 and they have already won several trophies.

180   Nancy Thelland with a friend. Many of the displays are now constructed from polystyrene, which is very light and easy to shape. (Nancy Thelland Collection)

181   Decorating the floats takes many hours of work: Dorothea Coombs, Cliff Manning and Garnet Perchard are part of a dedicated team. (Nancy Thelland Collection)

182   Beware of hungry fish! Pauline Perchard appears unconcerned. (Nancy Thelland Collection)

Over the years, St Martin has won many major trophies:

1971	The Bees' Wedding	Prix d'Excellence
1972	Dragon's Festival	Prix d'Honneur
1973	Melody Time	Prix d'Honneur
1975	How!	Prix d'Honneur
1978	Dutch Treat	Prix d'Excellence
1988	Spirit of the East	
1989	Hurray for Hollywood	Grand Prix de Paroisse and Illumination Award
1990	Teddy's Toytown	Animation Award
1991	James Bond	4th in class
1992	Flying Down to Rio	Carnival Award
1993	Russian Rhapsody	Prix d'Honneur
1994	Cirque de Magique	Illumination Award
1995	Flight of Fantasy	Prix d'Honneur and Illumination Award
1996	Totem	Best Set Piece and Illumination Award
1997	Coral Calypso	Prix d'Excellence, Best Animation & Inter-Parochial Awards
1998	Night on the Tiles	Prix d'Excellence

St Martin's Juniors have won the following trophies:

1995	Magic Dragon	Prix de Mérite, Fully Floral, Best in Class Awards
1996	Enter the Emperor	3rd in class
1997	The Guard of Atlantis	
1998	Catastrophic	Most Humorous, Fully Floral, Best in Class Awards

THE SCHOOLS OF ST MARTIN

One hundred years ago, there were at least seventy private schools in the Island. Many of these were in isolated country communities, where it was easier to send small children to a local 'dame school' with a few pupils, rather than enforce lengthy, twice-daily perambulations across a parish to a central school.

Even in these larger, central schools, there were still difficulties with the transition of language in the early years of this century. While there was pressure from the education authority to use English as the principal language in school, many of the visiting inspectors wrote their reports in French.

St Martin's School

A Parish Assembly was called in February 1897 to consider what St Martin should do to fulfil the requirements of a law passed in the Island three years earlier. The Law on Primary Instruction,

183 A receipt for school fees for Le Seelleur children in 1907. (John Le Seelleur Collection)

which took effect from 25 January 1894 placed a burden upon the parishes of Jersey to provide a place of education. But in St Martin, no school existed in the area of the Parish Church.

The Parish Assembly resolved to proceed with the building of a school for boys and girls and a committee was charged with finding a suitable site, negotiating a price, preparing plans and specifications, and estimating the total cost.

The committee moved swiftly and, three months later, another Parish Assembly was held to consider their recommendations. The Connétable and procureurs du bien public were authorised to pass a contract to buy three vergées of land, which formed part of the field known as 'Le Jardin du Shed ou Grand Jardin' from Mr. Charles Pallot, fils Jean. The agreed price of the land was £153 sterling, together with the cost of the erection of a wall to divide the field. The Assembly voted the sum of £500 to cover the costs of the transaction and authorised the circulation of one pound notes guaranteed by the Parish. This production of bank notes was a common occurrence in those days. They were reimbursable at the rate of £100 per annum.

Correspondence and plans went to and from Whitehall over the next two years and it was not until 13 July 1899 that the Parish Assembly accepted a tender submitted by Messrs. Springate and Baker – builders based in Gorey – to build a school for a sum of £2,836 10s. The Assembly voted the sum of £3,000 for the purpose and it was agreed that the work should be completed within 12 months of the agreement being signed. It was also decided to ask the States' Education Committee to bear half the cost, which amounted to £1,543.

A Commemoration Stone was laid in October 1899 in the presence of Frederick Richardson Le Brun, Connétable, and various other dignitaries. A silver trowel was presented to the Connétable bearing the following inscription: 'Présenté à F. Richardson Le Brun, Gent, Connétable de St. Martin, à l'occasion de la pose de la pierre commémorative de l'École Paroissiale, Le 19 Octobre, 1899.'

The commemoration stone itself was placed above the main door of the school and carries the wording:

18 St. MARTIN. 99
ÉCOLE PAROISSIALE.
F. RICHARDSON LE BRUN.
CONNÉTABLE.

184   Mrs. De St Paër, wife of St Martin's School's first headmaster, with the elementary class, c.1910. (John Le Seelleur Collection)

A small lead sealed safe was placed behind the stone containing a time capsule – a collection of documents, coinage and postage stamps. This included the *Almanack of Jersey Times and British Press* of 1899; copies of the Acts of the Parish Assemblies relating to the new school; *le Règlement sur enseignement de la Langue Française*; the rates list – *la Liste du Rât de la Paroisse de St Martin* – for 1899; English postage stamps, worth from ½d. to 1 shilling; and various silver and bronze coins of the years 1874-99.

After the ceremony, the Connétable entertained the committee which had carried the responsibility for planning the new school, and other friends and dignitaries, in the committee room of the Public Hall.

The Parish School opened on 1 October 1900 with 59 pupils. Within two years, this number had nearly trebled. In those early days, the school was not without its difficulties. The first headmaster, Mr. Charles De St Paër, reported 'Many scholars are not conversant with English'. The inspector's report the following year advised that the managers should be strongly advised to maintain a strong staff in 'this new and difficult school'. There was no explanation of the nature of the difficulties, but language differentials, agricultural absenteeism and the inheritance of the immigrant labour for St Catherine's Breakwater may all have been contributing factors.

In 1910 The Rector, G.P. Balleine, who also acted as *correspondent* (supervisor) for the school, was particularly damning and reported that: 'the children are irresponsive and inarticulate under oral examination and generally indisposed to active mental effort'. On the other hand, the *examen français* of the same year awarded 31 'excellent' certificates and 55 'bien'. This contrast possibly provides an interesting insight into the individualistic approach to language in St Martin at that time. Certainly, the 1916 report on the infants' class that 'all speak French' would not be applicable today.

In 1902 the school closed for the celebration of the Coronation of Edward VII, with the school band heading the procession. Day holidays for other events seem to have been a regular feature and these included not only Battle of Flowers, Gorey Regatta and St Martin's Horticultural Show, but also the 1912 'airoplane' race from St Malo to Jersey. From early days, pupils entered the Jersey Eisteddfod, with the school choir several times, winning the Donaldson Shield in the 1920s.

The St Martin's School log book records that Beatrice Le Huquet took up her duties as a teacher on 13 September 1920. She was formally appointed to the staff on 5 November 1928 after attending Salisbury Training College. She retired from teaching in 1966 after 46 years' service to the school. Not content with this, she then worked for a further 25 years as a St John Ambulance nurse at Jersey General Hospital. A number of other teachers gave a lifetime of service to the school.

In the 1930s the Parish School absorbed not only the boys from Faldouet School but also those from Dr. Barnardo's home at Teighmore. This initially caused great disruption. The Report for 1932 recorded:

> During the year, the school has entirely changed in character. It is no longer a typical rural school, catering for the needs of a scattered Parish, but a composite institution representing many different types of children. The transfer of the senior boys hitherto educated at Dr Barnardo's Homes, and at the Jersey Home, is a step in the right direction. It liberates the boys from their circumscribed surroundings, brings them at an impressionable age into closer touch with children whose antecedents have been more fortunate than their own, and it helps to erase the stigmata associated in the public mind with charitable institutions. On the other hand the sudden influx of boys from the two homes has plunged the school into great difficulties. Not the least of these difficulties is that the balance as between the sexes has been upset and there are now 168 boys as against 84 girls on the role.

At the same time, the teaching of the junior boys at The Jersey Home, including those transferred from Barnardo's, came under the general supervision of St Martin's School. Many of the Barnardo's boys came from the Stepney orphanage and a report of their prowess was extremely critical. 'Out of a total of 73, only 36 are of normal capacity, whilst 25 are described as dull and backward and 12 as mentally unfit.' It seems that there was a measure of relief at St Martin's School when Teighmore was closed in 1933.

On 29 May 1940, school closed for the annual potato-digging holiday. But this year was special, and it was reopened prematurely, to determine the numbers of children evacuated from the Island. On 8 July the school log reported laconically: 'attendance poor owing to unsettled conditions following Occupation of Island by German forces'.

The following year, an official request for names of those students whose parents wished them to learn German elicited four names out of a total enrolment of 172. As the War progressed, there were increasing absences due to lack of footwear. Many resorted to wooden clogs and repairs were carried out with old tyre covers. The food shortages had a great effect on school life. It was deemed wise to curtail sporting activities and, rather more strangely, but for the same reason, a directive was received that caning on the hand was forbidden. In 1943, instruction in German became compulsory for children of 12 and over and, on at least one occasion, the headmaster was summoned to report on progress to the German authorities. Lunchtime soup was provided for the children, but as the war progressed it became impossible to obtain fuel to heat it.

In 1946, 46 boys from the former Faldouet School were assimilated without problems. Four years later, His Majesty's Inspector concluded his report saying: 'The children are alert, obvi-

185   *Staff of St Martin's School, 1920. Beatrice Le Huquet (left front) went to England for training soon after. She returned to the school, where she continued to teach throughout the Occupation, retiring in 1966. (Beatrice Le Huquet Collection)*

ously happy and well cared for. This is a good School and an active community.' Although clearly much has changed at St Martin's School during the fifty years following that report, one thing has not. It is still a happy school in a strong Parish.

St Martin's (Quéruée) School

A school log book covering the period March 1900–October 1920 is held at St Martin's School, into which it seems the Quéruée school was amalgamated. It appears that this school catered for younger children but there is no evidence to suggest where it was located. Just like many other country schools, there was major absenteeism at the time of potato planting and on several occasions the school closed completely for three or four weeks in February and March. When school resumed after the summer holiday in 1917, the log reported: 'Attendance this week has been very low owing to a great number of children being still employed in agricultural work'. Indeed, as late as 1940, the country schools closed for the month of June for the potato-digging season. The children of the millennium-end, transported to school in their parents' air-conditioned automobiles, live a life far removed from that of their great-grandparents for whom agricultural labour took precedence over 'book-learning'.

   In March 1919 it was reported that there were 197 registered pupils at 'Ecole de St Martin, Centrale et La Quéruée'.

St Martin's Collegiate School

Also known as 'Silk's Academy', the school was founded in 1905 by Mr. William E. 'Pop' Silk, who ran it until he retired in 1948. Mr. Silk was a dedicated teacher and is remembered with respect by his former pupils. The day before he died at the age of 86, he told his daughter, 'I have never wanted to do anything else but teach, this was my life'.

   The school was started at Clairval, Gorey. Writing on a postcard view of Clairval soon after, Mr. Silk said, 'This was taken in 1906. I have since extended the premises – I keep a limited number of good class boys (35).'

186 *Silk's Academy at* Clairval *in 1906. The pupils then numbered around thirty-five. (Courtesy of Beryl Crimp)*

187 *Mr. W.E. Silk with St Martin's Collegiate School football team, 1948. The school closed when Mr. Silk retired later that year. The pupils were referred to as 'silkworms' by the students at St Martin's School. The two schools shared intense rivalry. (Courtesy of Gerald Le Cocq)*

By 1911 the school had outgrown its premises and moved to Springside House. A number of parents requested that their daughters might attend the school and it became co-educational. There were approximately fifteen boarders at Springside, including a number from France, but Mr. and Mrs. Silk found that this was more than they could cope with comfortably and, in 1920, after another move to Les Alpes, the number of boarders was reduced in favour of an increased number of day-pupils. At this time, the name 'St Martin's Collegiate School' was adopted. The school built its own premises in La Longue Rue in 1933. It remained open throughout the Occupation but the *Jersey Evening Post* recorded that the 1941 celebration of the headmaster's birthday was the first time in the school's 36 years that the pupils had been unable to provide a present. 'But,' said the article, 'it did not deter them from clubbing together… and expressing their good wishes in prose and verse on a handsome illuminated vellum artistically designed and written by an old boy of the school, Mr. C.W. Springate, and read aloud by the head pupil, R. Le Boutillier.'

When the school closed in 1948, a number of the pupils transferred to De La Salle College, which was better known as The Beeches at that time.

Springside

Springside School came into being in 1923, opened by two imaginative and intrepid sisters, Mrs. Hilda Ahier and Miss Linda Le Seelleur who were ably supported, especially in the teaching of French, by their mother, Mrs. Elizabeth Le Seelleur. Among its first three pupils was Stanley De

188 Springside School Eisteddfod choir, 1953, with Miss Le Seelleur and Mrs. Ahier. (Courtesy of Graham Crosby)

La Haye, a future Connétable of the Parish, and numbers gradually grew to a maximum of about twenty. The pupils usually moved on at about eleven years of age. The school had an excellent reputation, partly because it sought to inculcate real values into the minds and hearts of its pupils, and also because it included music, elocution and dancing – taught by Miss Jeanette Boielle – in its curriculum at a time when this was not altogether common. It was rare indeed when Springside School pupils were not among the prizewinners at the Jersey Eisteddfod.

The school closed in the 1960s, following the death of Miss Le Seelleur.

Les Alpes (Miss Touzel)

Better known as 'Touzel's', this school was located initially in Grouville. All the classes took place in one large room. Elsie Touzel continued to teach until she was 90 and was mentioned in the *Guinness Book of Records* as the teacher with the longest known period of service. She was born in 1889 and started teaching at the age of sixteen. She set up her first school at Les Fonds, Fauvic and moved to Les Alpes near St Martin's Church in 1933. At its peak, the school had as many as fifty pupils and Miss Touzel herself taught languages, history, science, shorthand, typing and book-keeping. The school continued until 1977, when a broken hip forced Miss Touzel to give up full-time teaching. She continued with private tuition for a further two years until she was ninety. Among her pupils were John Germain (1929-36) and his grand-daughter, Carol-Ann Germain, who credits Miss Touzel with being a major influence in her acquisition of eight O-Levels.

Elsie Touzel typified the dedicated 'dame-school' teacher. They were the backbone of country education until improved transport made consolidation of small schools a practical proposition. Speaking of her in 1981, Margaret Le Brocq, a pre-World War I pupil, said 'She was a great disciplinarian and would not stand any nonsense from any of us. But I think she taught us so well that we had a better start than many children.'

189 Miss Touzel (92) rings the bell for former pupils, Centenier Frank Lucas (1929-36), Margaret Le Brocq (pre WWI), Carol-Ann Germain (1976-9) and John D. Germain (1921-9). Her teaching career spanned 74 years, 1905-1979. (Photo: Jersey Evening Post*)*

Faldouet School, Upper and Lower Divisions

This was not a separate school as such, but established the education of the boys at Teighmore (Barnardo's) and Jersey Home (Haut de La Garenne). Its records start in 1917, the senior school for boys of 11 and over being conducted at Teighmore and the Junior School at The Jersey Home for Boys. It continued until 1946 when the senior boys were transferred to St Martin's School.

St Martin's Catholic School, Berni Centre

When Father Larose came to Jersey in 1884 he was keen to establish a school as soon as possible as it was felt that Catholic children then being sent to Protestant schools were the 'prey of heresy'. The Catholic school started with 10 children in December that year in a room in the presbytery. Numbers grew quickly to 80 and every room in the house was turned to school use, so much so that Father Larose had to move out.

The school was closed by the States in 1911.

Lynton Private School, Rue des Marettes

The school was started by Miss Perchard and was later run by Mrs. Edith Blampied (née Springate). It had at least 20 pupils during the Second World War and closed soon after the war ended.

Greenhill House School, Les Landes

This school, which operated in the early years of the century, had a reputation for being strictly administered. It was run by a Miss Olive Martin (later Mrs. Du Feu), assisted by a Miss Whitley, and had as many as 40 pupils.

The National School

This school was located on the Gorey coast road in the building which later became *The Welcome Inn*. The headmaster was a Mr. Taylor, assisted by Mr. Coker and Miss Sybil Le Cocq. The school closed during the 1914-18 war.

190   Miss V.W. Martin with pupils of Greenhill House School, and Chloe the dog, c.1918.

Crown Stores School

This building, known previously as *Pallot's Hotel*, became a school for a short period.

Rozel School / Rosel Manor School

Located on Rue des Alleurs, this school was opened in the 1880s. One of its first teachers was Thomas Stent, who was born in 1865; his father was a gardener at Rosel Manor. Thomas must have shown early promise, as his education was paid for by the Seigneur. The family returned to Lancashire, but Thomas subsequently answered an advertisement to teach at Rozel School and so returned to Jersey, marrying Emily Mollet of St Martin in 1890. Thomas progressed from Rozel to Headmaster of St Luke's School in St Helier, where he taught for many years. Among his pupils at Rozel was Edmund Blampied, who obviously developed an affection for his teacher. For many years afterwards, he sent drawings to Mr. and Mrs. Stent each Christmas.

191   Christmas wishes sent to Thomas Stent and family in 1934 by former pupil Edmund Blampied. (Courtesy of Richard Stent)

192   The Happiest Days of Your Life? Pupils of St Martin's Elementary School present a pageant as part of the 1937 celebration of the coronation of King George VI. (Photo: Jersey Evening Post)

Beechside (Miss Cooper)

This small school operated at Rozel in the early years of the century. It is reported as having only five pupils.

Rozel Mill (Miss Vardon)

Miss Vardon's school had seven or eight pupils and operated for a mere three years from 1926.

School for Young Ladies at Elmore

This school, held at the Le Huquet family home, was in existence in 1898, as shown in a surviving brochure. However, this tells us little beyond the fee structure, which was 8s. 6d. per term for pupils under 10 years of age and 10s. for older girls. Extras were: 'music 15s.' and 'use of piano for practising 2s. 6d.' It is reported elsewhere that the teacher was a Miss Renouf and that the school closed before the 1914-18 war.

JÈRRIAIS IN ST MARTIN - THE LANGUAGE SHIFT

Twenty years ago, 300 people in the Parish of St Martin still spoke Jèrriais. It is impossible to say with any certainty how many still speak the Island's mother-tongue today.

193 French origins. (Pen drawing by Sasha Bellamy)

Until the beginning of the 19th century, English was to all intents and purposes a foreign language in Jersey. It was known to those who had commercial dealings with England, or who had studied there, but its progress was much slower in St Martin – and the other rural parishes – than it was in St Helier and the built-up areas along the south coast.

Where St Martin differed from the other country parishes was in the effect of a huge influx of English-speakers in the 19th century. These were the people employed in the building of St Catherine's Breakwater and in the flourishing oyster trade at Gorey. Both these industries brought many English-speaking people to the Island, and their stay – albeit temporary – must have had some impact on the spread of English in the Parish. When the building of the breakwater came to an end and the oyster trade collapsed, the population dropped dramatically, by 32 per cent. We can safely assume that most of this reduction in population involved English-speakers returning to the mainland, but they departed having had a great effect upon St Martin, principally in the Gorey area.

Elsewhere in this book, we examine the varied imprints left upon St Martin by both the building of the breakwater, and the oyster fisheries. This chapter addresses the effects these projects had on the language. Apart from Gorey, the local farming community probably went on much as it had done for centuries. By the middle of the 19th century, most of them would have spoken some English, but it was not generally their first language or even their second. French was the language of church and chapel, as well as of the legislature and the law courts; Jèrriais was the language of the home.

Teaching at Rosel Manor School was still in French in 1875, but English became the language of instruction when compulsory schooling was introduced towards the end of the 19th century. St Martin's École Élémentaire opened in 1900. The introduction of schooling in English must have been an important factor in the anglicisation of the country parishes, although many children appear to have started school knowing no English. There is an entry in the log books of St Martin's School for 5 October 1900 recording that 'Many scholars are not conversant with English'. As late as 1951, at least one pupil – now a teacher – was in that same situation when he started school. There are stories about teachers forbidding children to speak Jèrriais. They no doubt thought they were acting in the children's best interests but this policy must have had a long-term negative impact on the continued use of Jèrriais. Until the Second World War, however, Jèrriais was still widely spoken by most of the native-born inhabitants of the Parish, including some with English-sounding surnames like Richardson (a prominent St Martinais family) and Manning.

The rot began to set in after the war, when some children started refusing to speak the vernacular which their parents used. In other cases, parents started speaking English to their

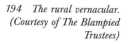

194   *The rural vernacular.*
(Courtesy of The Blampied Trustees)

children, although they still used Jèrriais themselves. No doubt there was a feeling that in encouraging their children to speak English, they were being more progressive and fashionable, and enhancing their future prospects. Unfortunately, the vernacular was generally held in low esteem even by those who spoke it, since both French and, increasingly, English, had greater prestige. This lack of respect for the vernacular only began to have a serious impact on its use in the last fifty years. The 1989 census (the only one which requested information about Jèrriais), showed the number of people in the Parish who declared themselves speakers of the vernacular to be 300 out of a total population of 3,271, or 9.2 per cent. This was slightly lower than in the parishes of Trinity and St John (12.2 and 13.4 per cent, respectively). Why were fewer people in St Martin using it? Probably because of the long-term effects of the breakwater workers and the oyster fishermen in anglicising the Gorey area.

The damage has been done and few, if any, young people are native speakers of Jèrriais. But a strong desire to preserve the language is manifesting itself. Only time will tell whether anything significant can be salvaged by classes in Jèrriais, whether they are taken on a voluntary basis or as part of the school curriculum. Given the inability of the schools to produce any great competence in French, hopes should not be pitched too high.

It is, however, time that we examined the salient characteristics of Jèrriais. This poses a few problems. Firstly, although it is grammatically, and to a lesser extent lexically, uniform, there are surprising phonetic variations in it, considering the relatively small size of Jersey, which make it difficult to describe its sound-system in a simple way. The main division is that between east and west, but within these areas, there are many local variations: Dr. Frank Le Maistre, on the map included in his *Dictionnaire Jersiais-Français,* distinguishes by name six different varieties of Jèrriais – those of Les Landes, l'Étacq and La Moye in the west, and Mont Mado, La Rocque and Faldouet in the north and east. The area round Rozel, partly in Trinity and partly in St Martin, is also pinpointed, though not mentioned by name. The local Jèrriais of Rozel is characterised by differences in the quality of its nasal vowels *în* and *ain/ein,* which are more open than elsewhere in the

195 *'A veritable game of French and English'. An argument in St Helier's fish market, as depicted by the* Illustrated London News, *11 August 1894. (*Illustrated London News*)*

Island. A second particularity of St Martinais is referred to in a poem about Jèrriais written in 1875 by Philippe Langlois. According to him

> A St. Martin i' disent *veze*
>
> Faisant de l' *r* un *z* comme en *peze*.

The more usual pronunciation of these words is *véthe* 'indeed' and *péthe* 'father'. In his *Dictionnaire Jersiais-Français*, published in 1966, Dr. Le Maistre noted that this pronunciation was still heard in the Faldouet area: 'Cependant, les gens de Faldouët diront encore de nos jours *péze, méze, vésité, etc*, pour *père, mère, vérité'*. This was written over thirty years ago, possibly on the basis of even earlier contacts, and it has unfortunately been impossible to find any people whose Jèrriais is still characterised by this particular St Martinais trait – or even to find anyone who remembers hearing it. There probably is someone in the Parish who still uses the *péze, méze* forms – but for how much longer ?

Before attempting to describe some of the features of Jèrriais in St Martin and elsewhere, I must mention a second, and related, difficulty: the notation of sounds. The use of a purely phonetic script, favoured by linguists in scientific journals, is not a practical proposition in a work of this kind, though it permits much greater accuracy. I shall therefore follow the practice of local authors, which is to write Jèrriais according to the spelling conventions valid for French, with some modifications designed to cope with sounds that do not occur in French. Thus *th* represents the sound of *th* in English *mother*, *tch* that of *ch* in English *chat* and *dg* that of *dg* in English *hedge*. There are other significant differences between Jèrriais and French that are not made as clear as these. Jèrriais retains differences between short and long final vowels: thus, whereas Fr. *pieds* is pronounced in the same way as *pied*, the Jèrr. plural *pids* ends in a long vowel, not the short one of *pid*. Jèrriais has retained five nasal vowels, with *fin* or *pîn* pronounced differently from *faim and pain*. The letters *ê* and *ô* do not correspond to their French equivalents either: except in St Ouënnais, words like *bête* or *côte* are pronounced like English *bait* and *coat* – i.e. as diphthongs. Eastern Jèrriais (EJ) has a number of other secondary diphthongs, particularly ones affecting the long *eu* of words like *deux* 'two', which is pronounced like Engl. *die* in the north-east. The La Rocque vernacular even has (perhaps one should now say had) nasal diphthongs in words like *c'mînse* 'shirt'.

Among distinctive consonantal features are the retention of an aspirated *h* in words like *hanque* 'hip' and *hache* 'axe', and the general replacement of [k] and [g] sounds by *tch* and *dg* where they were followed by the front vowels *e*, *i* and *eu*: hence (for example) *tcheu* (Fr. *coeur*), *tchînze* (Fr. *quinze*), *tchue* 'vat' (Fr. *cuve*), *dgèrre* (Fr. *guerre*) or *dgider* (Fr. *guider*).

The most unusual developments are those affecting *r*. Where it survives, this consonant is pronounced with the tip of the tongue, not at the back of the mouth, as in Parisian French. In many environments, however, it has been replaced by other sounds: any *r* that was originally intervocalic has generally been replaced by *th* (cf. *péthe* 'father', *mouothue* 'cod', etc.), but also by *z* as well as *th* in words like *maqu'se* (also *maqu'thé* and *maqu'ré*) 'mackerel'. As we have seen, St Martinais (probably that of Faldouet) is said to have been characterised by a greater use of *z*, while that of Trinity has a more frequent retention of *r*, and St Ouënnais has a distinctive tendency to introduce *th* into words which never contained an intervocalic *r* (e.g. *méthon* 'house'). Where *r* was brought into contact with certain consonants, it took the form of those consonants to produce a series of (pronounced) double consonants, as in *pot'tie* 'pottery', *hrod'die* 'embroidery', *fauch'chie* 'hay-making', etc. This has created differences such as that between *j'pâlais* 'I was speaking' and *j'pâl'lais* 'I would speak' (Fr. *parlais* and *parlerais*).

Typical phonetic features of the northern forms of Norman (to which Jèrriais and Dgernesiais belong) are the retention of Latin *k* and *g* in words like *cat* 'cat', *caud* 'hot', *vaque* 'cow' or *gardîn* 'garden' (cf. Fr. *chat, chaud, vache, jardin*), and the differing development of Latin [k] and [ti] before the vowels *e* and *i*, which have generally changed to a *sh*-sound in Jèrriais, as opposed to the *s*-sound of French (cf. Jèrr. *chent, chendre, Chent'nyi*, but Fr. *cent, cendre, Centenier*). Another typical Norman feature was the failure of the diphthong *ei* to differentiate further to *oi*, which in modern French has ended up being pronounced as [wa]. This accounts for the difference between (for instance), Jèrr. *mais* 'month' and Fr. *mois*, or *vaile* 'sail' and Fr. *voile*. A feature of some varieties of Norman – including Eastern Jèrriais (EJ) – is the retention of an earlier diphthong *au* in words like Jèrr. *caud* 'hot' (pronounced like English *cow*) and *haut* 'high', as well as in plurals such as *j'vaux* 'horses', whereas the Western vernaculars (WJ) typically have a diphthong pronounced like the *oe* of Engl. 'hoe'. A feature that is observed sporadically in Norman – the retention of an initial Germanic *w-* as *v-* rather than *g-* (earlier *gw-*) is attested in a few words like *vaule* 'pole' (Fr. *gaule*) or *vitchet* 'wicket-door' (Fr. *guichet*).

Many of the features of Jèrriais date from a more recent period – although the 17th-19th centuries are not all that recent. In many cases, these secondary developments are paralleled by ones in Lower Normandy. One is the development of *l* in consonant groups like *pl- bl-*, *cl-* and *gl-* via *ly-* to *y*, as in *pliein* (pronounced as *pyein*) 'full' or *blianc* (pronounced as *byan*) 'white'. Another – probably earlier – feature of many Norman vernaculars, including Jèrriais, is that '*ll*' in *mouillé* has normally become *l* in words like *famile* 'family' and *file* 'girl, daughter', where it has regularly reduced to a *y-* sound in French (*famille, fille*).

This clearly does not cover all the interesting features of Jèrriais phonology – that would demand a whole book – but it is time to touch on some of the other characteristics that make it so different from Parisian French, particularly in EJ.

Like other forms of Norman, Jèrriais has preserved a number of borrowings from Old Norse that never penetrated into French: e.g. *flyondre* 'flounder', *haut* 'tope' (a kind of dogfish), *gradile* 'currant', *han* 'galingale', *hôgard* 'stackyard for corn', *tro* 'trough'. It has also retained many archaic words or senses that have disappeared from modern French: *couôrre* 'to run', *couôtre* 'to sew', *êcache* 'crutch' (Old Fr. *eschace*), *êpart* 'flash of lightning', *feuntchi* 'to singe, to smoke' (Old Fr. *fungier*), *garce* 'girl', *mârri* 'angry', *muchi* 'to hide' (Old Fr. *mucier*), *oui* 'to hear', *souler* 'to be in the habit of', *toûtre* 'to cough', etc. etc. Other words have developed senses that are rather different from their French equivalents: a *cliôs* is a field, a *camp* (the Norman equivalent of *champ*) is a strip of land, a *fôssé* is a hedgerow, not a ditch, and a *hèrnais* is a box-cart, not 'harness', which is *la graie*.

Most modern technical terms are borrowed from English, and pronounced as in English, but some borrowings are obviously not recent, because of the modifications that they have undergone: cf. *bliatchîn* 'blacking, boot-polish', *bosque* 'bin, trough' (from Engl. *box*), *capeur* 'copper for boiling clothes', *dgêle* 'gale', *gelesses* 'braces' (from dialectal Engl. *galluses*), *goteur* 'gutter', *tchil* 'kiln', etc.

There are some lexical variations within the Island, mainly between east and west. The bee is known variously as a *môque* (western *moûque*) or *bourdon à mi/myi* (honey fly), and by a few in St Martin and Trinity, as an *ain* (a word derived from Latin *apis*). The acorn is a *gliand* in EJ, a *tchênelle* in the west. Stairs are *d'grés* in EJ, but a *leveé* in WJ. 'To plaster' is *causer* in EJ, *pliâtrer* in the west (the plasterer is consequently a *causaix* in EJ, and a *pliâtreux* in WJ). 'Manure' is *conré* in EJ, and *fumyi* in the west. The 'missel-thrush' is a *trâle* in EJ and a *herbette* in WJ. A roof is a *couvèrtuthe* in St Ouënnais, but a *lief* elsewhere – and so on.

196   Lingua franca, AD 2000.
(Pen drawing by Sasha Bellamy)

There is not enough space for much discussion of the grammatical forms and syntax of Jèrriais. We can, however, note general similarities between them and the more conservative Norman vernaculars of the Cotentin and the Basse-Normandie. Confusingly for French-speakers, *j'/jé* is used as the equivalent of Fr. *nous*, while *nou* is the equivalent of Fr. *on*. As in Old French, the equivalent of the French plural pronoun *ils* is *il* (from Latin *illi*). The endings of the *passé simple* tense have been largely regularised, as in Normandy, on the model of the *-ir* verbs (e.g. *j'allis*, *j'marchis*, etc.), which has helped this tense to remain one in constant use, whereas it has fallen into disuse in colloquial French. Third person plural forms ending in *îtent* are not general on the mainland, but are found in Haguais (spoken in the north-west of the Cotentin peninsula), which has many close ties with Jèrriais. The usual endings of the first and second person plural of the imperfect and conditional tenses are *-êmes* and *-êtes* (e.g. *j'avêmes/ous avêtes* 'we/you had'), which also have near parallels in Old French and in modern Norman vernaculars.

The linguistic situation in St Martin at the millennium is unfortunately one of the near total triumph of English, although there are still some of those 300 Jèrriais-speakers around. Unfortunately, the younger ones are mainly in their fifties, and no-one knows of any children learning it at their mother's knee – so it is only a matter of time before the only Jèrriais that survives will be that learnt in classes of various kinds. For those who see Jèrriais as the most distinctive surviving element of Jersey's individuality, that is scant consolation.

THE ST MARTIN BANDS

There was a wealth of musical talent and enthusiasm in the Parish in the early part of the 20th century, as we know that at least four different bands existed. This was no doubt due in part to the necessity for the folk of those days to make their own entertainment, but it also helps to illustrate the great strength of the social life of the Parish of St Martin. Little is known of these bands, other than from the reminiscences provided by Beatrice Le Huquet of the Fife and Drum Band, which was led by her father.

Captain Philippe Le Huquet was the founder, in 1909, of the **St Martin's Fife and Drum Band**. This group of men practised each week in the greenhouse of the Le Huquet family home, Elmore, and staged regular performances. The major event of their year was Guy Fawkes night, when the band would march around the Parish, playing their instruments, always finishing at Rosel Manor where they would perform for the Seigneur before receiving suitable refreshments.

Philippe Le Huquet and his brother Thomas were shipbuilders and ran the family yard at St Catherine, where they built 44 vessels – some of them were small cutters, but others were schooners and brigs of over 100 tons, constructed for the Newfoundland trade. Philippe, who was born in 1856, also had musical talent, and he wrote the scores and composed music for the Fife and Drum Band. He played a very active role in the life of the Parish, and was also a churchwarden towards the end of the 19th century. His band was a prominent feature of the social life of the Parish in the early years of the century, and it played a significant part in the Parish's peace celebrations of 1919. The Band's activities came to an end when Captain Le Huquet became ill in the mid-1920s.

St Martin's Brass Band is recorded in several fine photographs dated 1908. There is also a picture of its members marching at the head of the procession in the 1919 peace celebrations. This may or may not have been the same band later styled the **United Brass Band,** a picture of which hangs in the Public Hall. This band was affiliated to the Wesleyan Guild and the Slade and Le Seelleur families were among its members. It is believed to have ceased activity sometime in the early 1930s and its remaining funds were used to purchase new hymn books. The Reverend

197 *St Martin's Fife and Drum Band at Rosel Manor, c.1909. Capitaine Philippe Le Huquet is the bearded gentleman in the front row. (Beatrice Le Huquet Collection)*

198 *St Martin's Brass Band of 1908, a happy and informal group. (John Le Seelleur Collection)*

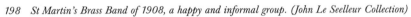

ST. MARTIN'S UNITED BRASS BAND
CIRCA 1925

199 The Brass Band of 1925 adopted uniforms and a more serious countenance. It had a Wesleyan affiliation. (Courtesy of the Parish of St Martin)

Back Row L to R: G. Noel, J. Ecobichon, P. F. Misson, W. Matson, W. P. Le Seelleur, Chas. Noel, Cliff. Noel, C. Gallichan
Centre Row L to R: H. Ahier, R. Gallichan, C. Newell, S. Le Gresley, G. W. Ching, G. Dawes, A. Whitley, D. C. Le Seelleur
Seated L to R: G. Slade, E. Slade, P. Noel, J. Pallot, A. Tech, P. Quenault
Connétable Bandmaster
Presented by G. A. Ching, Ash Cottage, 1982.

David Le Seelleur remembers the instruments being stored in his parents' attic during his childhood. *The Jersey Methodist* records a concert held on 10 March 1921:

> The stage was most elaborately decorated and whoever was responsible for the work had most certainly put all his (or her) heart into it. Somebody had evidently searched the Island and explored many veins for talent, and the fare provided was excellent. The band and male voice choir rendered great service. The banjo, as usual, provided most enjoyable items, and a trio rendered with spirit, humour and musical talent fairly brought the house down, and the President had to relax from the sternness and rigidity of the 'no encore' rule, which he did with a smile as he had done for the banjo duet.
>
> Bandmaster Tesh received a token of the men's respect and gratitude in the form of an enlarged photograph of the band. Our President in a few words made the presentation, and thanked all friends who took part in the organising of the concert and who supplied the items of the programme.

The band played at bazaars, fêtes and church events Island-wide and also paid at least two visits to Guernsey. Possibly the highlight of its career was a performance given for King George V when he visited Jersey in 1921.

In the latter part of the 1930s, there was another fife and drum band, much larger than the earlier one of Philippe Le Huquet, but only a photograph survives and nothing is known of this band other than that J.T. Amy was at one time bandmaster.

200   *The fife and drum band of the late 1930s. John Thomas Amy was bandmaster but little else is known of this band. (Gerald Amy Collection)*

ST MARTIN'S OLDE TYME MUSIC HALL

St Martin's Olde Tyme Music Hall began on Saturday, 3 December 1968. Mrs. Sophie De La Mare and her family and friends were at Eden Chapel to see the Youth Club production of Olde Tyme Music Hall, under the chairmanship of Harold De Gruchy. What a show it was!

Sophie was so impressed by what she saw that night that she asked Harold if he would contemplate doing the whole thing again at St Martin. He was only too pleased, and in April 1969 the very first show was staged at St Martin's Public Hall. It was the result of a great deal of hard work by the very talented De La Mare family and their friends, and much planning and pre-production work at Sophie's home, L'Abri, St Martin.

Harold De Gruchy was the chairman of this first production, and he was supported by three talented musicians: Alan Mollet on piano, Wilson De La Mare on double bass, and Barry De La Mare playing the drums. The production team consisted of Sophie and her grandson David De La Mare, who went on to have a successful career as a producer, staging shows at *Swanson's Hotel*, St Helier, and also in Bournemouth.

The final night of this first production – *Music, Melody and Mirth* – brought only one complaint from the audience. They wanted more. So, by popular demand, Sophie De La Mare put on three more shows at the Public Hall in 1970, 1971 and 1973. By this time, people flocked from all over the Island and still the unlucky ones had to be turned away. On the last night of the 1973 production Sophie and David De La Mare asked the cast if they would come with them to St Helier. And so the production went to town, and in October 1974 played to capacity audiences at the Opera House. The move was logical. The show had proved so popular it had outgrown the Public Hall, but putting on a production in St Helier was quite a challenge. Nevertheless the hard work paid off. The *Jersey Evening Post* on 25 October 1974 reported enthusiastically that St Martin's Olde Tyme Music Hall was 'an extravaganza of music, melody and mirth.' Yes, they had come to town,

201   St Martin's Olde Tyme Music Hall presents Roaring Twenties *in 1974.*

and the Opera House was to become their regular home for the next 22 years. It had become well and truly established in the Island's social calendar. Since its inception it had been run on a very informal basis by members of the De La Mare family, but as the organisation grew it was felt that the burden of responsibility should be shared by others, and that the whole thing should be placed on a more formal footing.

A meeting at the *Hotel Savoy* on 4 December 1974 was attended by large numbers of supporters, organisers and well-wishers, and it was unanimously decided to form a society, of which the main aim should be to preserve and foster the spirit and traditions of Olde Tyme Music Hall and to continue to produce shows, the proceeds of which should go to charity. The first officers of the society were elected:

Chairman: Wilson De La Mare, Secretary: Dennis Perrin, Treasurer: Roselle Perrin

Committee: Monica Noel, Dinah Pallot, Pam Pallot, Mrs. Harold De Gruchy, David De La Mare, Ken Fox and Stephen Geary.

The first charity to receive a donation was the Jersey Blind Society, which benefited to the tune of £500 – the proceeds of the 1975 production. For the next 22 years the Opera House stage echoed to the sound of music, melody and mirth, entertaining thousands of people, who all came to love the unique personality of Olde Tyme Music Hall.

Sophie De La Mare continued to support the society, becoming the Honorary Life President. Her help was tremendous, inspiring many a producer, and she was always on hand ready to give advice or support. The members of the society have never forgotten their commitment to those less fortunate than themselves and over the years have raised £50,000 for local charities.

Similarly, they have never forgotten their debt to Sophie De La Mare, a great lady who created St Martin's Olde Tyme Music Hall and who gave music, melody and mirth to the Island.

THE ST MARTIN TAPESTRY

The Parish of St Martin has retained a strong sense of community which sets it apart from some of the more urbanised parishes in Jersey. The Occupation Tapestry was a wonderful community project which was undertaken by all 12 parishes of the Island. However, in St Martin the experience of producing it was enjoyed so much that, on its completion, the team felt that they would like to start again, this time producing a tapestry panel illustrating St Martin itself.

A design was chosen depicting familiar landmarks and work began in June 1995. It was carried out by 23 members of the Parish and took a year to complete.

The first stitch was placed by Connétable John Germain and the last by the wife of the Lieutenant-Governor, Lady Wilkes. All parishioners were invited to place a stitch and groups of children from St Martin's School added theirs, too.

Such a large tapestry requires expert stretching and mounting, and this was carried out by the Textile Conservation Trust at Hampton Court before its return to the Island for framing. It was completed in time to take pride of place in the newly-extended and refurbished Public Hall, which was officially opened by the Bailiff, Sir Philip Bailhache, in 1997: the completed work now hangs there for all to see and admire.

St Martin's Tapestry
30 May 1995–21 June 1996

Designer and Co-ordinator: Nancy Thelland

Helen Baker	Patricia Myers	Jacki Godber	Rhona, Lady Guthrie
Betty Herivel	Helen Horton	Alice Laverick	Clare Blair
Anne Billot Paines	Gladys Vautier	Alexi Yates	Barbara Le Troquer
Helen Blampied	Patricia Clarke	Amelia Perchard	Caroline Garthwaite
Pauline Perchard	Nicky Greenwood	Annie Richardson	Margaret Poole
Ann Watkin	Fiona Yates		

GOREY FÊTE

Gorey Fête started life as St Martin's Gymkhana. It began in 1948 to help raise money for St Martin's Parish Church and, in particular, to pay for interior repairs. The first president was the Reverend E.C. Lemprière, Mrs. Roselle Bolitho was chairman, Mr. Jack Richard was secretary, and Mr. Stanley De La Haye was the treasurer. In 1988 Mr. De La Haye took over as chairman and he continues in the post to this day.

That first Gymkhana was held in the grounds of Rosel Manor, and – unlike today – equestrian events were the main feature of the day's entertainments. Although it was successful enough to be repeated for about five years, escalating costs became prohibitive and the Gymkhana was discontinued in 1953.

In 1954 the Constable of the Parish, Mr. H. Ahier, held a meeting with a group of parishioners, and it was decided to restart the event, but to widen its appeal and turn it into a Parish Fête. It

202 Divers at Gorey Pier, c.1905. At that time, the fête formed part of Gorey Regatta. (Gerald Amy Collection)

was also decided to move the venue to the harbour at Gorey, in the hope of attracting more people.

Both these decisions were proved to be the right ones as, since then, the Gorey Fête has continued annually with increasing success and popularity. Since 1993 it has established itself as the largest parish fête in the Island, attracting about 8,000 people through the turnstiles each year. Nowadays, funds raised at this event are shared among various local charities and over £50,000 has been handed out in this way.

A typical Fête takes place on a Thursday at the end of August. Gates open at 10.30a.m. and close at 11.45p.m.: visitors can enjoy a variety of events throughout the day, with a Grand Carnival Parade headed by a marching band, a bonny baby competition, fairground rides, a spaghetti-eating competition, and a yard of ale drinking competition. The stalls spread all around the Pier, and stringent traffic control is required to take care of the crowds and cars. Other popular events which have been successful year after year are a grand fireworks display and a disco with dancing continuing until close to midnight, when the Fête closes its doors for another year. This has proved to be a winning formula, with old-fashioned fairground fun and more modern attractions designed to appeal to young and old alike. The beautiful backdrop of Gorey Castle and Harbour complements the occasion – the biggest social event in the calendar of St Martin.

JUMELLAGE

The idea of Twinning or Jumellage originated after the First World War when English towns, eager to effect a reconciliation with the rest of Europe, sought to establish formal links. Since then countless twinnings have been established worldwide in order to create a greater awareness of different countries through sporting, educational, social and cultural ties.

For a number of years many people in St Martin had wanted to establish a twin town but it was not achieved without much discussion. Sometimes finding a long-lasting partner can be difficult. This was very much the case with St Martin's passage to its eventual Jumellage.

203 The twinning ceremony between St Martin and Montmartin sur Mer at Mont Orgueil, 24 May 1997.

In 1984 the late Connétable, Winter De Gruchy, sought Parish approval to link St Martin with St Sauveur le Vicomte. There were fears about the potential benefits, sustainability and possible cost of the venture, and at a well-attended Parish Assembly the debate was lively and passionate, culminating in a vote with only 14 people in favour, and 50 against.

Ten years later the newly elected Parish Deputy, Bob Hill, gathered support for a self-funding twinning association to be established. Meetings were held with the criterion of seeking a twin in Normandy with a similar background to St Martin. With great assistance from John Denize an ideal twin was found in the form of the Commune Canton de Montmartin Sur Mer.

The Commune de Montmartin Sur Mer consists of a collection of 12 small villages with a total population of around three thousand. It is a rural part of Normandy, situated between Carteret and Granville and tourism and farming form the backbone of community life. Individually many of the villages were in danger of losing their identity through the migration of villagers to the cities, but through the formation of the Commune or Canton much of the area's rich heritage will be retained. The opportunity of establishing an official twinning was warmly received by parishioners in both communities.

Once links between St Martin and Montmartin had been established, they both formed committees to raise funds and organise visits. The exchange of visits afforded many parishioners the opportunity of learning more about one another and of the benefits that would follow, should an official twinning be arranged.

On the evening of 27 February 1997 there was another well-attended Parish Assembly. Again lively debate ensued but on this occasion the proponents were better prepared. A self-funding association would not require injections of cash from the Parish coffers. The proposal, which was seconded by Olive, Winter De Gruchy's widow, was adopted by 47 votes to 17 and arrangements were undertaken to organise an official Twinning Ceremony. Mont Orgueil Castle was chosen for this and on Saturday, 24 May 1997, a party of 30 French people representing the 12 villages which form the Communauté braved unseasonably high winds and waves when they travelled to Gorey. They were collected from the harbour and transported to the Public Hall for breakfast, which included Jersey Wonders, before going on to the castle for the ceremony.

Some 140 people attended, and the association president, Deputy Bob Hill, in his speech of welcome, likened it to a marriage ceremony – but a ceremony which united two communities rather than two individuals.

The Bailiff referred to the event as not only an historic day but also a friendly one. 'We in Jersey are proud of our Norman heritage,' he added 'and it is right and fitting in this modern world that our roots and our long-standing links with our neighbours should not be forgotten.'

The Charter bringing the twinning into formal effect was signed by St Martin Connétable, John Germain, and Dr. Olivier Beck, Conseiller General du Canton de Montmartin sur Mer, in the presence of the Bailiff, Sir Philip Bailhache, and M. Pierre Aguiton, Président du Conseil Général de La Manche.

Deputy Hill said:

> Saturday May 24th 1997 was a truly memorable day for St Martin. The Twinning link, although still in its infancy, is based on a firm foundation through the formation of an industrious St Martin Jumellage Association. It is a self-funding organisation committed to fostering relations between the two communities. The committee has run several fund-raising activities and the benefits of the twinning link should become even more apparent in the years to come. It is a means of strengthening our own feeling of community and, as time goes by, to involve all generations and walks of life in a community effort of friend-ship, within our Parish and extending across that short stretch of sea to Montmartin.

ST MARTIN'S FOOTBALL CLUB

St Martin's Football Club is the oldest in Jersey and might well be the oldest in the Channel Islands. It was already experiencing success in 1894.

Although Grouville formed a football club 10 years earlier than St Martin, it was disbanded in the 1930s, although later reformed. The St Martin club has kept going, a record unbroken even by the war years.

The enthusiasm for football was generated in the early days by the militia. In 1919, the St Martin's Football Club colours were black and amber, the colours of the Hampshire Regiment, in which many Jerseymen served. These Hampshire militiamen included Mr. Jack Amy, a man who was to breathe new life into the club in the years after the Great War, when he was elected club captain in November 1919.

Throughout its history the club's colours have changed many times. The first photograph shows a plain coloured strip which may have been dark blue. In the early years the club secretary was Mr. W.E. Silk, the headmaster and owner of St Martin's Collegiate School.

St. Martin Football Club 1894

C. MOLLET   J. W. MESSERVY   J. FEREY   J. DUVAL   T. STENT   H. FALLE   C. P. BILLOT
E. GRUCHY   J. MOLLET   T. GREY
J. G. PALLOT   A. STOCKER   W. MOLLET

204 The first recorded football team in St Martin. Thomas Stent taught at Rozel School. Charles Billot and John Pallot both became Connétable and the former also served as Deputy. (Courtesy of St Martin Football Club)

In 1930 the club turned its attention to the problem of transport. Sometimes matches were played in St Brelade or St Ouen, and Mr. William Le Seelleur was paid £3 for using his lorry for team transport. It was not unusual for players to cycle from Gorey to St Ouen wearing football kit – football boots tied to the handlebars – play the whole game, then cycle back to Gorey.

By 1932, the game had become popular among business people and it was decided to form the Saturday League, for the benefit of those who worked through the week but had Saturdays off. The traditional Jersey Football League played its matches on Thursday afternoons. The new league started in the 1933-4 season, with enough clubs to form three divisions. Only two years later St Martin won their first honours in the Saturday Football League, winning the 3rd Division. This was a welcome turnaround in the fortunes of the club. The 1932-3 season had been a financial disaster, with the annual report showing a deficit of £15 13s. 1d. To cover what was thought of as a huge loss, the treasurer, Mr. Silk, topped up the account out of his own pocket. There is no record of his being reimbursed.

The winning trend continued. The annual report for the 1936-7 season read:

> Our greatest achievement for many years in the history of this Club was the winning of the Le Riche Open Cup. In this victory we had to beat Ryans F.C. who are champions of the Saturday Football League Division 1. Their team is composed of Jersey Football League Division 1 Thursday players and included two of that year's Muratti players. We also won the Trinity Shield. I can safely say that our team for 1936-37 was the best that ever represented St Martin.

This was signed by O.W. Pallot, the honorary secretary. The club felt that it was time to change the colours again, and they reverted to black and amber. However, the club only possessed

205   The highly successful team of 1943-4.

10 shirts and one goalkeeper's jersey. The substitute had to be photographed in a khaki-coloured shirt, and it was hoped that it wouldn't be too noticeable in black and white.

At various times the club has been grateful to farmers for the use of their land. The Renouard, De Gruchy, Baudains, Richard and De La Haye families had all helped during the years, as had the Seigneur of Rosel and the Parish authorities. At the start of the 1937-8 season, Mr. Renouard of Rose Lea Farm told the club that he must change the field he had made available to them. The new field had a terrific slope of approximately ten feet between the two pairs of goalposts and it was not favoured by visiting teams. However, it was the best the club could manage and the captain winning the toss usually elected to play uphill in the first half, saving the downhill advantage for the second. Under the present rules for pitches, it would be deemed unfit for play.

At the start of World War II, the club lost most of its players. At least six first team regulars joined up and the club secretary also had to leave his post to serve his country. But the 1940-1 season saw a revival. For the first time in the club's history non-natives and non-residents of the parish were admitted. It became apparent that some of them came from the town areas hoping to make friends in the country who might supply much-needed vegetables. One sadness of this season was the loss of Colonel Stocker, one of the club's stalwarts who had served in the First World War and survived, only to be killed tragically by a German vehicle while walking down Hill Street early in the Occupation.

The Occupation years were successful for the club. It won the Division 1 Trophy in 1942-3 and again in 1943-4. It won the Le Riche Cup in 1943-4 when a crowd of 2,000 watched at the FB Fields.

Three of the first team players, Snowdon George Houguez, Ronald du Feu and Alfred Vardon, were killed in the Second World War. Four months after the Liberation, in September 1945, it was decided to revert to the former club rules restricting membership to natives, residents of the Parish, and formerly registered members. This immediately deprived the club of some excellent players who wanted to join in the success of the St Martin Club. Seven years later this rule was rescinded, allowing non-natives to represent the Parish once again.

In 1949 the Saturday Football League considered a complaint about the club's strip. At that time they wore black with amber collars and cuffs, and it was claimed that the colours were confusing for linesmen, who couldn't tell the difference between St Martin players and the referee. The club was ordered, by a majority vote, to change its pattern of shirt, and they chose the same colours in a quartered design.

The 1950s and early 1960s were successful years for St Martin's Football Club. In 1953-4, the club won Division 3 of the Saturday Football League; in 1956-7, it won Division 4; in l960-1, Division 3; and in 1963-4, the Trinity Shield.

In 1968 the club initiated a number of joint activities with Oaklands F.C., and many of the Oaklands players greatly assisted in the social life and administration of the club. This was also the year that Mr. S.J. De La Haye provided a new playing field which offered the players the luxury of hot showers. However, there were drawbacks. During the summer the field was used as a campsite and players sometimes found tent pegs half buried in the ground. A local bomb disposal officer was called in to clear as many as he could find, making it a much safer pitch.

The first formal appointment of a player-coach was made in 1969. Before that, anyone wanting to sign on had been able to start kicking a ball without proper training and coaching, learning the rules as they went on. Now the training was more organised and it appeared to reap great rewards. In 1970-1, St Martin won Division 3. In the following year it won Division 2, and the year after, in 1972-3, it won Division 1. This was the most successful run that the club had experienced in its history.

The St Martin's Club still does not have its own field. Although it would very much like to have a home of its own, the search has proved unsuccessful. Home matches are played at St Martin's School. The teams have enjoyed success in recent years: in 1976, the club won the Trinity Sports Shield, in 1997 the W.J. Collins Memorial Trophy, which is particularly notable because it is a Guernsey trophy, played for each year between clubs in both Islands who are not competing in the Jeremie Cup. In the final of the latter competition, St Martin, Jersey beat St Martin, Guernsey.

ROZEL ROVERS FOOTBALL CLUB

Rozel Rovers Football Club was formed in 1943, to encourage sport for the young men of the vingtaine of Rozel. Its first general meeting was held on the new pitch – a field lent to the newly formed club by Thomas Billot of La Ville Brée who became its president for the first 16 years. The meeting consisted of 20 young men, eager to get the club going and have good sport.

Plate 27. 'Zebre's Dazzling Zenith', champion bull of St Martin, owned by John Pallot of La Poudretterie Farm. (Courtesy of John Pallot)

Plate 28. 'Lynn's Dairy Lady.' Supreme Champion of St Martin, spring 1984, exhibited by Colin Richardson of North Lynn Farm. (Courtesy of Gerald Richardson)

Plate 29. Flying Foam, *a schooner of 160 tons, was launched at J. & T. Le Huquet's yard at St Catherine on 4 July 1879. Her first master was Philip Noël. She was wrecked in 1937. (Courtesy of Martyn Chambers)*

Plate 30. The brig Escape *in a fresh breeze, by P. J. Ouless, 1866. She was built by J. & T. Le Huquet at St Catherine in 1861 and was owned by G. N. Le Quesne. (Courtesy of Bonhams & Langlois)*

Plate 31. The New Generation – Reception Class at St Martin's School, September 1998. (Photo: Jersey Evening Post)
From back row to front, left to right: Tracy De Oliviera, Alana Rondel, Tania Franco; Matthew Le Brun, Matthew Perchard, Matthew Le Gallais, Russell Lewis; Sophie Le Bon, Emma D'Orleans, Emily Heald, Claire Garnier, Freya Little; Claire Williamson, Rachel Maindonald, Stephanie Devine, Natalie Dixon, Harriet Little, Ryan Shuttleworth, José Vieira, Rufus Scholefield

Plate 32. 'Fair Jersey Girls'. This Autochrome postcard from Edwardian times promoted the healthful benefits of Jersey. (John Le Seelleur Collection)

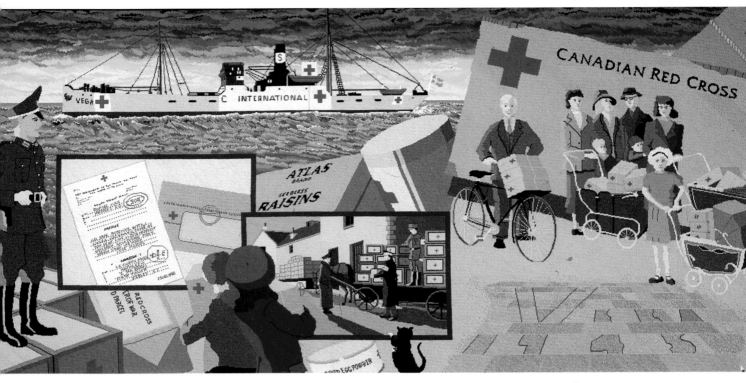

Plate 33. Section of the Liberation Tapestry embroidered by parishioners of St Martin. (Jersey Museums Service Collection)

Plate 34. The St Martin Parish tapestry. (Nancy Thelland Collection)

The new club was quickly affiliated to the Saturday Football League, and the 1944-5 season began with a visit from Trinity F.C. The home team lost by one goal. The last game of the season was against a team picked from St Martin's F.C., who were mostly first division players. St Martin won by two goals to one, the game being watched by a crowd of over three hundred. A collection of £42 was taken and given to the St Martin's Red Cross Fund. The club did much to help the Red Cross during the difficult final episode of the Occupation, including organising a highly successful fund-raising concert at the Public Hall. It is interesting to see that the subscription fee for the club in those Occupation years was either six shillings and fourpence-ha'penny or three German marks.

In the club's second official season, they finished second in Division 3. The minutes of the AGM held later that year were candid: 'We were unlucky in losing several of our players at the beginning of the season, but I believe we should have been at the top of the league; how we lost the two games against Trinity remains more so a mystery as it was thought by all concerned that they would be our easiest team to beat.' By then the subscriptions had gone up to five shillings for seniors and one shilling for juniors, 'or more, to those who could afford it'.

In the 1946-7 season, there was much debate about whether to open the club to a wider public, but it was decided to keep the register of members to the natives and residents of Rozel. Of the eight teams competing that year in Division 3, Rozel finished fourth having played 14 games: won six, lost seven and drawn one.

The players were wearing a white strip and, although some wanted to change to coloured shirts, it was decided to stay as they were – post-war coupons made it almost impossible to obtain the coloured shirts they wanted. By the time they reached the 1948-9 season, the club was fielding two teams. At the end of the year, the minutes recorded: 'The past season can be described as successful from a sportsman's point of view. No trophies won, but all league engagements fulfilled.'

By the time the 1951-2 season arrived, it was decided – after much lengthy debate – to amend the club's rules. The original rules stated that the object of the club was to encourage amateur football throughout the vingtaine. In the new rules the words 'throughout the vingtaine' were omitted. The following year, members debated whether to amalgamate with St Martin's Football Club. The motion was unanimously defeated, and the Rovers were firmly established as an independent entity.

For most of the 1950s the club was successful in the First Division of the league, reaching third place. The second team was also doing well in the Third Division. In the 1959-60 season, the club had difficulties:

> The last year has probably been the most difficult one for the club since it was founded in 1943. The committee knew at the start of the season that we were not strong enough for the First Division but the Saturday Football League thought differently. Great credit is due to the players for turning out regularly when most of the time the result was a foregone conclusion before the game started, and also because they accepted defeat without a moan. Our teams finished bottom of the First and Third Divisions respectively.

Back in the Second and Fourth Divisions, the club played on. In 1962, the St Martin's Club made another bid to amalgamate with the Rovers. The message went back: on no account did Rozel Rovers wish to amalgamate with them.

206 Deputy Bailiff Vernon Tomes opens the new clubhouse in January 1989. (Photo: Jersey Evening Post)

For the next 10 years the club played in the Second and Fourth Divisions, but the membership was thriving. From 1945 until 1958 the club had used a field lent by Arthur Corson of Cottage Farm and later played at FB Fields. There were increasing anxieties to find a ground of their own and in April 1972 a special meeting was called to discuss the purchase of available land at Le Couvent in St Lawrence. Field 503, measuring 7 vergées, 26 perch was for sale for £450 per vergée. It had been found for the club by Hedley Jehan, one of the club's founder members, who had always followed the matches with interest.

The first team managed to get back into the First Division for a couple of seasons in the 1970s, and a junior eleven was formed. They were now established in a blue and white strip, and in time for the 1980-1 season changed from blue and white hoops to blue shirts with white sleeves.

The record of minutes from the first 50 years of the club reveal a general disappointment in its level of sporting achievement. The report for the 1986/87 season said: 'The club appears to have developed into a social club, with the playing of football matches a necessary interruption and, as a result, the club has had a very bad season on the field of play, while social events have been a tremendous success.' Two years later, a new clubhouse costing £45,000 was built at the ground by Denis Satchwell with the help of many players and club members. It was financed by the issue of 10-year bonds which have all now been repaid. It replaced the original timber clubhouse built in 1974 and was said to be the envy of every other club in the Island, but the official report rather ruefully reflected:

> We now need to throw the image of being a small happy club into being a large happy club. This will only happen if everyone puts the effort in that they have done this year. We now have the basis of a very successful club and with extra players to strengthen our squad for Division 1 we will be there to stay this time and kill the reputation of certainty to come straight down to Division 2.

Sadly for the Rovers, this confidence was misplaced, and the following year they were back in Division 2. The demotion only lasted one season and the club moved on to some of its most successful years. Although it has not yet won the First Division, over twenty team trophies have been gained since 1990. The club fields three senior teams and junior teams at under-14, under-16 and under-18. The Le Couvent ground has excellent facilities and hosted several of the matches for the 1997 Island Games.

Rozel Rovers has always been a close-knit community since it began during the Occupation. The Corson and Richardson families, among others, have been involved with it since the very beginning. Arthur Corson, who had been a founder member, an excellent footballer, and a vice-president, died in 1997 and his widow Lucie presented the Arthur Corson Memorial Trophy in his memory. Rozel Rovers and St Martin's F.C. compete for it each year, prolonging the friendly rivalry between the two clubs. The first match, in 1998, resulted in Rozel Rovers winning 3–2.

LA PRÉFÉRENCE, ST MARTIN – The Vegetarian Home for Children

La Préférence Children's Home in St Martin was in many ways well ahead of its time. Children there followed a vegetarian regime, long before such an idea became fashionable. Perhaps more importantly, it provided a homely environment for children who found themselves alone in the world, when other organisations providing a similar service did so in a very different style.

Flora and Sydney Walden always dreamed that one day they might run a children's home. When they finally achieved their ambition, their project became a model which was followed later in the 20th century by other homes in Jersey, enabling children in care to enjoy a more natural and homely existence rather than the more traditional, institutional style of upbringing.

The Waldens came to Jersey after Sydney had been seriously injured in a street accident. He was forced to spend nearly a year in hospital after which the couple left England to live in Jersey, so that he could recuperate more easily.

Barely in her fifties, Flora Walden was the breadwinner. With her family growing up around her, she agreed to run a vegetarian guest house. They bought a small property by the sea in Gorey, which they ran successfully for two or three years.

Early in 1951 a vegetarian children's home that had existed for many years in Liverpool closed down. It left many of the children there homeless and two of the small boys had a father who lived in Jersey. His wife had left him and he could not care for the boys himself. He told Mr. and Mrs. Walden of his predicament: the boys had been brought up as vegetarians and he had no one to turn to. In addition, an eight-year-old girl from Liverpool, whose parents had deserted her, was with them. As the summer season had not started, Mr. and Mrs. Walden agreed to take all three children and foster them, but it was not easy. Very little money came from any source to support these children and the father of the two boys was unemployed.

The Walden family had troubles of their own and Mr. and Mrs. Walden found themselves bringing up their own grandchildren as well. By 1952 the number had increased to six children and it was difficult, if not impossible, to try to run a guest house as well.

By this time the Waldens had made a number of friends and contacts in the vegetarian movement. Approaches were made to vegetarians in Britain to try to gain financial help.

Towards the end of 1952, when the Jersey Medical Officer stepped in and condemned the little house at Gorey as being unsuitable as a foster home, Mr. and Mrs. Walden turned once more

207 *La Préférence soon after its purchase in 1953. (Courtesy of La Préférence Home)*

to their friends for assistance. Several generous and influential Jersey residents came to their rescue, but this still was not enough to finance a children's home. One of those who gave considerable advice was the late Dr. Florence Sexton, herself a vegetarian with much experience of nutrition, especially during the German Occupation, and she became a valued friend.

They searched for a suitable property and they eventually found an old rambling house that had been empty for a year. It was almost derelict, with a garden like a wilderness, but they were offered a nine-year lease. It was in St Martin, rather far from the sea, and needed a great deal of repair and decoration. The agonising choice had to be made between running a guest house or a children's home, and the children eventually won the day.

Early in 1953, with some help from local people and financial support from vegetarians in England, the old house began to take shape as a sanctuary for needy and under-privileged children, who streamed in. The name of the house, appropriately enough, was La Préférence.

In March 1953, the Walden family moved in. They persuaded their son and daughter to help them, increased the number of children and wrote to interested people and vegetarians for financial aid. Mrs. Walden registered herself as a foster mother and all seemed set fair, but not for long. They were beset on all sides by difficulties, prejudice, bad luck with repairs, lack of water (sometimes in summer the well dried up and they had to rely on rainwater), staff sickness and lack of funds.

In May 1953, armed with a £20 cheque from a well-wisher and a bank mandate, a small committee was formed in London under the direction of the late Mr. Sydney Hurren. He became the honorary treasurer, with Mrs. Helen Brown as honorary secretary. Dr. B.P. Allinson, Mr. Cyril Oliver, Mr. Ronald Lightowler and other well-known vegetarians became associated with the Home and gave moral support and valuable advice. The Home gradually expanded and overcame many of the obstacles and was recognised as a worthwhile and valuable project both in Jersey and elsewhere.

In May 1957, Mr. Walden died suddenly in the garden he had worked so hard to improve. Mrs. Walden laboured on with 16 children under her care at the time.

In 1962 the lease ran out and the owners offered the house to Mrs. Walden for sale, but funds were insufficient and it was not until the timely arrival of two legacies and an anonymous gift of £3,700 that anything approaching the necessary figure was forthcoming. After several months of uncertainty the house was finally purchased. About this time the Home was also granted official status as an English charity by the Charity Commission so that covenanted subscriptions, free of income tax, could be given to aid it.

It is difficult to believe that in 1960 the water supply came from inadequate wells which often dried up in summer and that all cooking was done on an old-fashioned Aga cooker. There was little or no heating in the upstairs rooms and only coal fires in the draughty lower rooms, while the cess-pits were grossly inadequate for the increasing family. Yet the occupants managed to be happy and the youngsters remarkably fit and well, as visitors have testified.

After a number of years of frustration, disappointment and hard work, the rooms were well heated, all cooking was done by gas or electricity and a new well was sunk more than 60 feet down in the garden, reliably producing hundreds of gallons of sweet water per week. The drainage too was vastly improved and the children were able to play happily on a well-laid lawn.

Over the years, local residents began to take interest and even to ask questions concerning vegetarian food and the children's upbringing. Even as late as 1962, to run such a household as a family unit was unusual in Jersey as children's homes were more often large and institutionalised. Mrs. Walden's evident success at this venture prompted surprise and even criticism, though the happy, healthy children in the Home gave convincing proof of the efficacy of her methods. Nowadays, family group homes are quite common and the segregation of boys and girls is not allowed, so that her persistence and courage in the early days were more than justified. La Préférence was approved and registered by the States Education Committee under its *Children (Jersey) Law, 1969* as a 'Voluntary Home' and was able to accept up to 20 children in residence.

The Vegetarian Children's Charity which held the residual funds from the old Liverpool home gave financial aid over the years, except for a short period when a new home was opened in the Liverpool area, but when it closed, the support for Jersey increased and a much closer link was forged between the two bodies.

Mrs. Walden's grand-daughter, Christine, and her husband, Desmond Lagadu, came to live in the Home to help Mrs. Walden and when, in 1971, she retired as Housemother, the Lagadus were appointed as Houseparents by the executive committee. Mrs. Walden decided to visit several of her children who had emigrated to Australia and enjoyed being with them so much that she has stayed there ever since.

The children who came to the Home were orphans, abandoned by parents or from broken homes. They often needed emotional support. Many were sent by the Jersey Children's Department; others were lodged by parents, who may have been unable to cope with their children for a period because of family problems. Most of the children stayed for a long time and some were there from babyhood. They stayed until they felt that they were able to cope with life and often moved out into a home of their own in their late teens. The executive committee insisted that the Home should strive to be a real home and not an institution. Children were not told to move out at a particular age and could stay as long as they wished. The record was held by a boy who stayed until he was due to marry at 25 years of age.

The Home prepared the children for life and, at the same time, it was run on strictly vegetarian lines. When the time came to leave, some children would follow the vegetarian ethic while others would revert to eating meat. La Préférence found that most of the children readily accepted a vegetarian diet and, indeed, thrived on it. The organisers prided themselves on the health of the children and believed it compared well with other children in care. Visits to the doctor were said to be few and far between and the children's attendance record at school was excellent. Every effort was made to minimise the disadvantages the children had suffered and to ensure that they received as good a start in life as possible.

ST JOHN AMBULANCE

The first St John Ambulance division was formed in Jersey in 1928 with Dr. Florence Sexton the officer in charge. This was a nursing division staffed by women members. The ambulance division for men was formed five years later in 1933. The duties of the brigade were many and varied and their familiar uniform was seen at sports meetings, fêtes, sand races, hill climbs, and places of entertainment as well as at most official functions around the Island. In addition St John Ambulance nurses worked at the General Hospital and often escorted patients to and from the hospital here and to hospitals in England.

The brigade played an important part in the Island's life during the German Occupation. In 1940, members were on duty to care for victims of the air raid on Jersey, Red Cross letters containing news of bereavements were delivered to relatives by members of St John and, when the Red Cross parcels arrived, the distribution and safeguarding of them was entrusted to the brigade. On Tuesday, 6 February 1945, 1,343 food parcels were distributed around the Parish of St Martin.

209   Cadet Officer Beatrice Le Huquet leads St Martin's No.5 Nursing Cadet Division in a march-past at St Mark's Church, 1950s. (Beatrice Le Huquet Collection)

The new headquarters in Midvale Road were completed and occupied in 1951, the foundation stone having been laid in 1950 by Countess Mountbatten of Burma.

On 10 May 1937, a women's first aid class started at the Wesleyan schoolroom in St Martin with lectures given by Dr. B.V. O'Connor and class secretary Margaret Messervy, and on 25 June it is recorded that there were eight successful candidates in the first aid examinations. These classes moved to St Martin's Public Hall in January 1939. During the war, parish working parties were set up, those in St Martin under Mrs. G.M. Billot.

The No. 5 Cadet Nursing Division was formed in October 1947 and registered in February 1948. The weekly meetings were held in St Martin's School. Beatrice Le Huquet, who had passed her first aid examination in 1939, joined the St John Ambulance Nursing Division at the St Martin's branch inauguration and was responsible for the female cadets, who at first came from St Martin's School, but later included girls from outside. Miss Le Huquet progressed from the rank of Cadet Officer to Officer (Sister) in the Order and finally retired as Area Staff Officer and Officer in Charge of No. 5 St Martin Nursing Cadet Division in 1973.

The boys' section was established in 1949 under Superintendent Frederick Beadle. Deputy Bob Hill and present Commissioner John Gavey were among the first cadets.

In 1949 Miss M.M. Messervy was authorised to organise first aid classes at St Martin but it was reported that 'some difficulty' had been experienced in obtaining the doctors required to act as lecturers and examiners – this is a problem which still exists today.

The St Martin Division had long needed premises of its own and set up a committee to raise funds. Money was raised, much of it by the cadets' parents, using the slogan 'be a brick and buy a brick'. A plot of land was bought for £275, with substantial financial help from Mrs. Bradford Martin in memory of her two sons, who had been killed on active service in the Far East. The foundation stone was laid by Connétable Ahier on 15 March 1962. The building and its furnishings cost a total of £4,800.

And so, on 6 April 1966, six years after the idea was first aired, the new Neville Holt Hall for the St Martin Division was dedicated by the Rector, the Reverend F.O. Brackley. The Lieutenant-Governor, Vice-Admiral Sir Michael Villiers, officially opened the Hall and Lady Villiers unveiled the plaque. The Chairman of the Council of the Order of St John for Jersey, Major-General Neville Hind said: 'I feel sure that this hall will be in good hands and will be used not only for the work of St John and its cadets in particular, but for all those who have shown what faith, hope, and charity can still do in St Martin'. It is noteworthy that when Harold Hudson, who originally owned the plot of land, died in the 1990s, he willed the cost of the land back to the division.

In 1987 the boy and girl cadets (11-16 year olds) combined their classes, meeting on Friday evenings, and the badgers (6-10 year olds) were established; these groups along with the adult members now became known as St Martin Division. A wide range of subjects is studied including radio communication, cookery and nutrition, caring home skills, child care, animal care, communication with the deaf and blind and fire-fighting.

The cadets take part in competitions against the other three Jersey divisions, with inter-insulars against Guernsey and also regional competitions. The Channel Islands are part of the UK southern region, which includes Surrey, Sussex, Kent, Guernsey and Jersey. Teams which win those regional heats go forward to the UK finals. An annual parade and church service takes place each summer.

At the time of writing the St Martin Division is thriving, under the Divisional Superintendent Susan Pugsley, her two divisional officers and the newly appointed nursing officer. There are 30 badgers, 22 cadets and 10 adults. St Martin can also boast having produced the Cadet of the Year for both 1998 and 1999.

ST MARTIN'S WOMEN'S INSTITUTE

The St Martin's Women's Institute was formed in 1949, the first meeting being held in the Public Hall on 26 October. There were 41 members and the president was Mrs. Roselle Bolitho, vice-president Mrs. O'Connor, secretary Mrs. Anthony, treasurer Mrs. Calder. The annual subscription was 3s. 6d.

Throughout the years, the Institute meetings have been held once a month in the Public Hall. If the hall was closed for some reason, then another venue would be found. Members have enjoyed many varied and interesting speakers and also social times when they have organised their own entertainment.

There has always been a keen interest in singing, dancing and drama and as a result the members have had great fun organising concerts and pantomimes and have enjoyed entertaining other institutes and residents of old people's homes, as well as their own members. They have frequently won trophies at Federation drama events and their entries in the Eisteddfod have been very successful. The Jersey Theatrical Club Bowl has been won on more than one occasion.

Joining with some of the members of Trinity W.I. members formed a successful singing group for several years. St Martin's W.I. members are keen participants in handicrafts and flower arranging and, over the years, have produced many beautiful and imaginative items which have won trophies in various competitions, including the Eisteddfod and craft and produce shows.

The W.I. has always been renowned for its organising and catering skills and has taken great pride in supplying helpers and food for many Federation and Parish events.

Sport, including walking, swimming, tennis and badminton, has featured in the lives of many of our members. The Institute had a darts team for several years and one or two keen members recently tried their hands at abseiling.

210   A happy meeting at St Martin's Public Hall. (Courtesy of St Martin's W.I.)

Regular visits to the theatre have been enjoyed, as well as visits to places of local interest. During the summer months, day trips to France or the other islands are organised and, over recent years, localities have included Bayeux, Caen, St Lô, Coutance and Villedieu des Poelles, leaving by boat from Gorey for Carteret. These have become so popular that husbands, friends and members of other Institutes go along, too.

Many members have attended residential courses at Denman College and have learnt new skills. Delegates from St Martin's W.I. have attended National Federation meetings and many lasting friendships have been made.

After hearing about the plight of displaced persons in camps in Europe during the 1950s, the Institute members adopted Frau Akki and her family. She was an Estonian lady with a son and daughter in a camp in Germany. Regular parcels were sent to the family containing clothing, wool, chocolate and other necessities. The association with the family continued for many years, until Frau Akki and her son died. Their daughter had learnt English and continued to make contact through Mrs. E. Whiteside and they eventually met in England a few years ago and the friendship continues to this day.

Some of the projects undertaken by the Institute include providing the teak seat at the entrance to St Martin's Cemetery in May 1971, planting trees in the Pine Walk at St Catherine in March 1974, and planning and planting the garden at Le Court Clos.

PAST PRESIDENTS

1949-55	Mrs. R.Bolitho	1956-58	Mrs. E. Whiteside
1959-61	Mrs. R. Brown	1962-63	Mrs. Holmes
1964-65	Mrs. Able	1966-67	Mrs. E. Senior
1968-69	Mrs. P. Thornton	1970-71	Mrs. O. Clarke
1972-73	Mrs. E. Senior	1974	Mrs. Rowbotham
1975-76	Mrs. R. Brown	1977-79	Mrs. M. Robson
1980-82	Mrs. D. Podger	1983-85	Mrs. S. Whitehouse
1986-88	Mrs. Coupland	1989	Mrs. J. Chaplin
1990-92	Mrs. J. Thomson	1993-95	Miss M. Owens
1996-99	Mrs. K. Richardson		

THE GIRLS' BRIGADE

The Girls' Life Brigade was first established in Jersey before World War Two. It was when the Island was returning to the normality of peacetime, after the Liberation, that the Girls' Brigade sent an officer, Miss Major, to Jersey to organise a training course. As a result of her visit a Company was formed in St Martin in 1946. The first Captain was Margaret Dorey, the Lieutenant was Mazel Slade and the Company was known as 6th Jersey, St Martin's.

The Brigade has strong connections with the church, but is inter-denominational. Its motto is: 'Seek, Serve and follow Christ'. Members work to a multi-faceted programme which includes spiritual, physical and educational service.

In 1967 a combined band was formed with the Boys' Brigade, the St Martin's 2nd Jersey. With the help of Brian Snell and Alan Shipton they practised every Monday evening until they were ready to play at events. They took part in the Battle of Flowers for eight years – the girls wearing white blouses and red skirts and the boys red shirts and white trousers. The 6th Jersey takes part in all Girls' Brigade district events, as well as staging an annual parade for Liberation Day and a Remembrance Parade in St Martin. The Captain of the 6th Company is Muriel Cobden.

THE BOYS' BRIGADE

The Boys' Life Brigade was established in St Martin by Gordon and Muriel Cobden in 1965 because, while the Girls' Brigade was thriving at St Martin's Chapel, there was no similar organisation for the boys of the Parish. Alan Colback was Captain of the Life Boys at Wesley Grove. Mr. Cobden started teaching volunteer boys but as there were not enough members to form a company he went to Haut de la Garenne and managed to recruit enough new members there to form the 2nd Jersey Boys' Brigade, which was registered as a company in the Jersey Battalion. They took part in many sporting events, and enjoyed great success. They won the Brigade's five-a-side football trophy for 11 years without losing a game against any other company. Along with the girls, the 2nd Company attends Founder's Day Parades at Les Frères, the Parish Remembrance service, and the Liberation Day parade. The present captain is Gordon Cobden.

ST MARTIN'S DIAMOND CLUB

Set up in 1983 as a self-supporting group, the St Martin's Diamond Club for the over-60s meets on the first Thursday of the month in the Public Hall.

The first President was the late Connétable De Gruchy; the current president is Rodney De Gruchy. There are over 80 members.

At the AGM in April suggestions are put forward for speakers for the meetings – there is always a very wide range of topics. There are also organised trips to the theatre, an annual carol service, a summer coach outing, an annual dinner and a Christmas party.

ST MARTIN'S FLOWER CLUB

St Martin's Flower Club was established by Kathleen Robinson in 1968 and she was its first chairman. At that time The Jersey Flower Club had a waiting list of over 200, so this second club was set up to cater for those in the east of the Island. Members meet in St Martin's Public Hall on the first Wednesday of each month, except for August. The membership stands at about sixty.

At each meeting there is a flower demonstration and seven times each year a visiting demonstrator is invited from England. The demonstrator is shared with Jersey Flower Club, thereby halving accommodation and travelling expenses, and occasionally a day school is organised for enthusiasts. The club visits two private gardens each July.

A themed competition is held each month for which a trophy and points are awarded. The member with the most points at the end of each year is presented with a special trophy, donated in memory of past members, and retains it for one year.

The club also provides flower displays for many of the charity functions held around the Island.

* * *

211 *This Edmund Blampied cartoon shows that St Martinais do not eschew the pleasures of life!*
(Courtesy of The Blampied Trustees)

ᒣourteen
Natural History

BIRD LIFE

Given its hospitable climate and varied landscape, it comes as no surprise to learn that a little over 200 species of bird regularly share and enjoy a strong and seasonal association with Jersey. At almost any time of the year, many of these species eagerly take advantage of the fields, gardens, woodlands, seashore and the coastal headlands which are so abundant in the Parish of St Martin.

212 *The honey buzzard, an occasional visitor from France.*

In addition to all these rich and productive habitats, the Parish also provides an extra natural dimension in the rugged form of the offshore reef of Les Écréhous. What makes the Parish of St Martin even more attractive to certain birds is its proximity to the Normandy coast. This ensures that, when the right wind and weather conditions prevail, many uncommon species – the honey buzzard is an excellent example – temporarily slip across this short stretch of water, to the delight of local ornithologists.

Within the Parish, the open fields and hedgerows and the private gardens, both large and small, support all the common and familiar species of birds. It is particularly during early spring, however, that they announce their presence with the sweetest and strongest of song. The strength and beauty of these all-encompassing melodic bursts are best appreciated during the breaking of a May dawn in the woodland of Rozel. This rich and beautiful area, more commonly known as St Catherine's Woods, is the largest of Jersey's woodlands still open and accessible to the general public. The age of the woodland can best be reflected by some of the tree species – the presence of both the ancient yew and the sharp-fruited medlar, for instance. A little before the darkness of night slips away, the first cock robin reasserts his territorial rights with fulsome song. Moments later he is quickly joined by other woodland choristers such as the song thrush, the blackbird and the tiny Wren. These are the real early risers, each of them eager to stake their claim on what has become their very own, and intensely well defended, piece of real estate. As the daylight strengthens,

213 *The shy 'mouse-bird' or Short-toed Treecreeper.*

chaffinches, great tits, blue tits, chiffchaffs, blackcaps, wood pigeons, collared doves and, a summer visitor from the continent, the turtle dove, all vocally rise to the special occasion of the dawn chorus. Even the tiny 'mouse-bird' – the common, yet extremely shy, short-toed treecreeper – eventually lends its thin contact call to the grandness of the woodland overture.

Other birds present in Rozel woods have no need or desire to become part of this choral activity. The great-spotted woodpecker and two of Jersey's resident birds of prey, the kestrel and the sparrowhawk for instance, have neither the sweetness of voice nor the need to defend a territory to make any vocal contribution. Yet another woodland bird which has now sadly disappeared from Jersey's countryside is the rook. This member of the crow family once received the undivided attention of the Reverend W. Lemprière who, in the mid-1850s, attempted to introduce a small flock of them into the woodland at Rozel. Despite achieving the daunting task of making and siting a set of artificial nests, the birds apparently declined his invitation to take up their new residences and promptly disappeared.

Not too far away from this delightfully popular woodland is the long arm of St Catherine's Breakwater. This finger of granite, pointing as it does towards the coast of Normandy, provides an excellent vantage point for watching all kinds of sea life. While many types of sea bird frequent the vast open waters beyond the breakwater, other smaller shore birds find an abundance of food amongst the rocks and gullies at Fliquet Bay. By far the most numerous of the seagoing birds are the shags: small, bottle-green cormorants which nest annually along the Island's steep north

214   The great-spotted woodpecker.

coast. These large, heavy birds are frequently seen, either singularly or in large flocks, flying south beyond the breakwater towards the shallow feeding grounds of Grouville Bay. Gannets, the largest and whitest of all sea birds, also appear off the breakwater during the summer months. These powerful sea birds nest on Alderney's offshore stacks but are often tempted to feed along Jersey's north-east coast. St Catherine's Bay, incidentally, also enjoys the company of bottle-nose dolphins, the Island's favourite sea mammal. A considerable proportion of local dolphin sightings reported annually are from this Bay. Grey herons, oystercatchers, turnstones and, a fairly new

215   The herring gull, a notoriously aggressive and vociferous scavenger.

arrival to the Island, the little egret, are also often encountered sifting for food along the rocky gullies to either side of the breakwater.

During the months of summer, St Martin's offshore reef, Les Écréhous, provides food and shelter to a large number of bird species. Not only does the reef support its regular breeding inhabitants such as common terns, cormorants, oystercatchers, great black-backed, lesser black-backed and herring gulls, its geographical position is also of significant importance and benefit to a multitude of small, migrating birds.

With such a diversity of land and seascape, it is easy to understand why the parish of St Martin encompasses and treasures all that is best in wildlife and wild places.

WILD FLOWERS

Many rare and unusual wild flowers grow in the varied habitats of the Parish of St Martin.

Grass-poly, *Lythrum hyssopifolia,* is the rarest. A low hairless annual with tiny pink flowers, it is not easily seen. It is known to be hardy, but its powers of survival must indeed be tested where it is found near St Catherine's Breakwater. Close to the large rock known as Gibraltar it survives yachts being parked on it and people walking all over it. David McClintock recorded: 'It is very rare, persisting only in Jersey'.

In her *Flora of Jersey* Frances Le Sueur wrote:

> Grass-poly, a rare species in Britain, has been known at St Catherine's Bay since 1841 when it was collected from there by the Rev. W.W. Newbould. The quantity varies considerably from year to year, as Attenborough noted as far back as 1917 – which was a good year for it, as was 1982. *Flora Europea* states that it needs disturbed and seasonally flooded ground, and this it has at St Catherine's Bay. Babington (1839) recorded it first from Grouville, and it was collected there again in 1894. Mrs. E.M. Whiteside found it in 1967 in a field at St Martin, and it has since appeared nearby in a garden, which is a most unusual habitat.

A delightful rarity is the **Jersey Fern**, *Annogramma leptophylla*, **du ou d'la capillaithe**. It is our only annual fern and very small – about three inches high – and grows on the side of rocky banks. *Flora of Jersey* states 'Jersey Fern does better after a hot summer and mild wet winter. It was particularly fine and luxuriant in all its stations in the spring of 1978 when two mild wet winters followed the 1976 summer which was one of the hottest and driest on record.' It was perhaps this which enabled Miss F.M. Evans and Mrs. E.M. Towers to rediscover it in St Martin after an interval of more than thirty years. In 1972 the Jersey Post Office issued a 3p stamp featuring this treasure.

216 Cow parsnip or hogweed is abundant alongside Parish roads in summer.

Four-leaved All-seed, *Polycarpon tetraphyllum*, has a title which describes itself. Although very common in Jersey where many people are continually pulling it up from their gardens, botanists from Britain are always interested in this plant, which is only found there in the south-west.

A favourite flower is the **Autumn Lady's Tresses**, *Spiranthes spiralis*. This is a small orchid – no taller than six inches. The flowers, which are fragrantly almond-scented, spiral round on their stems, which no doubt accounts for its name. They are very often found in churchyards and are a joy to see in the new churchyard, and the old one too, at St Martin's Parish Church.

From April onwards the **Three-cornered Leek**, *Allium triquetrum*, **d'l'as sauvage,** flourishes abundantly along the hedge-banks and roadsides. Although it is found in the south-west of England it is rare in the rest of Britain. The drooping flowers are beautiful white bells with a green stripe and there is an excellent illustration by Pandora Sellars in the *Flora of Jersey*. Some people imagine it is a white bluebell and pick it, only to be dismayed by the smell and understand why another name for it is **Stinking Onions**. The stem is one of the distinguishing characteristics, and is not round but triangular.

A particularly charming flower is the **Pencilled Cranesbill**, *Geranium versicolor*, which was originally a plant of mountain woods in the eastern Mediterranean and may well be a garden escape from many

217 The yellow flag, common in St Catherine's Woods.

years ago. It was first recorded in Jersey in 1832, and was found in six different Jersey parishes in the last century. It occasionally grows in hedge-banks and is uncommon, growing from nine to 15 inches tall with pale pink flowers delicately veined in purple.

Many of the rarities are very small and in order to see them properly one must be able to get close: try a prone position or simply get down on your hands and knees. Another small, but beautiful and unusual, plant is the **Jersey or Sand-crocus**, *Romulea columnae*, **des genottes**, which is only one to two inches high. Its small, star-like blue flowers can be found from the end of March until mid-April, or even later. The leaves are very thin and curly and not easily seen in the grass. David McClintock advises: 'They are no good at all in normal English gardens,' and Frances Le Sueur said: 'The first mention of it was in the late 18th century when Captain J. Finlay wrote to Sir Joseph Banks on 27 February 1787 telling him of it in Jersey, and describing it.'

Another rarity is the **Mossy Stonecrop**, *Crassula tillaea*. This is tiny, only about an inch long. It starts off green but develops into a brilliant red. It grows along the retaining wall at Archirondel Tower and survives the constant trampling there.

In addition to these unusual plants there are very many common ones which, although they may not have the distinction of being rare, nonetheless delight us, and help to add to the beauty of St Martin.

There is the **Cow Parsnip** or **Hogweed**, *Heracleum sphondylium*, **d'la bénarde**, which abounds. This can be a nuisance in the garden but lovely by the roadside and other places. It is not the very similar **Queen Anne's Lace**; that is *Anthriscus sylvestris*.

The **Yellow Flag**, *Iris pseudacorus*, **du bliajeu**, is often found flourishing in or near the patches of water which exist in the Parish. Its brilliant yellow flowers are most attractive, and they provide a wonderful splash of vibrant colour in the summer months at places such as St Catherine's Woods.

Winter Heliotrope, *Petasites fragrans*, **du pas d'âne** is found on many roadside banks. The leaf looks like **Coltsfoot**, and while it has an insignificant-looking flower, its delicate scent is a great pleasure in winter.

An interesting plant is **Japanese Knotweed**, *Polygonum cuspidatum*, which can grow to six feet. Do not introduce it into your garden – it will take over.

Pennywort or **Navelwort**, *Umbilicus rupestris*, **des cratchillons**, is found all over Jersey, thriving in the roadside walls which are among the Island's uniquely beautiful features. This plant has round fleshy leaves with a hollow in the centre and the flowers are green spikes.

218 The foxglove, source of digitalis, a frequently-used medicine.

Everyone knows the **Foxglove**, *Digitalis purpurea*, **dé l'ouothelle dé brébis**. Its tall spikes of bright pink flowers are common in woods and banks. The leaves contain digitoxin which produces digitalis used to treat ailments of the heart.

A most useful book is the *Pocket Guide to Wild Flowers* by David McClintock published by Collins. It would need to be a big pocket but it contains a great deal of helpful information.

This article was not written by a botanist, but by an elderly parishioner who has loved wild flowers all her long life and has learned so much from the Botany Section of the Société Jersiaise. She joined this Section in the '60s and, with Miss F.M. Evans, searched in St Martin for the flowers which were to be identified for the *Flora of Jersey*.

THE SQUIRRELS OF THE WOODS OF ST MARTIN

The red squirrels of St Martin are important for two reasons. The first concerns the squirrels themselves. Throughout the mainland of Britain, these appealing creatures are under threat. Since the end of the 19th century, their number has been decimated by the grey squirrel, which was imported from its native North America in 1876. Although the exact mechanism by which grey squirrels replace red squirrels is not understood, it is known that wherever grey squirrels thrive, red squirrel populations almost always disappear. In Jersey, the appealing red squirrel lives undisturbed by such a threat, as the grey squirrel has never been imported to the Island.

The second reason concerns the ecological health of our rural Parish. Red squirrels are a flagship species, whose presence indicates the health of the whole woodland environment in St Martin. They are a powerful indicator of the richness and diversity of the flora and fauna which exists in the Parish's two main areas of woodland – St Catherine's Woods and the woods of Rozel Valley.

Red squirrels are among Britain's best-loved native mammals and until recently they were found in most woods and parks, but are almost extinct in England and Wales, surviving only in a handful of areas. Although Jersey forms part of the natural range of red squirrels, none of the Channel Islands had an endemic population. In the 1890s naturalists in Jersey saw fit to introduce them from, it is thought, both Northern France and Southern England. Since then no further introductions have occurred and the Island has escaped the 'grey tide'. We have a population of about 400 squirrels in Jersey. This makes our Island important for research purposes, since it is one of the few places in the UK with a red squirrel population not at risk from grey squirrels.

Jersey's woods tend to be small and fragmented, nestling mainly on the steep valley sides where agriculture is difficult. The woods are often separated from one another by urban areas, roads or agricultural land and this means that for the squirrels to move between woods, they must rely on the integrity of the hedgerow system. Between 1974 and 1988 Jersey lost over 200,000 elm trees to Dutch elm disease and this reduced the elm-dominated hedgerows by about 98 per cent.

St Catherine's Wood and the woods in Rozel Valley are relatively large woodlands, and both have populations of red squirrels. These woods are isolated from those in the south-west of the Island and the squirrels living within them are unlikely to stray far.

219 The red squirrel (left) and grey squirrel (right) can be distinguished by their form and individual characteristics, such as the red squirrel's ear tufts, as well as by their colour.

Squirrels are mainly seed eaters and so most of their food arrives in autumn when the sweet chestnuts, acorns and beech nuts become ripe. These seeds support them through the winter months but they are nearly all gone by January. About one-third of enterprising squirrels then turn to people's gardens and receive supplemental feeding to help them through the leaner summer months. Since the Parish boundary that separates Trinity from St Martin runs through the meadows below Rozel Mill, Rozel woods span two parishes. Some squirrels exploit the generosity of Trinity folk by crossing Rozel Hill to raid bird feeders or to eat from specially-erected squirrel feeding stations. Such Viking-type cross-parish plunderings do the squirrels no harm since they continue to feed and behave naturally, just topping up their energy requirements by quick visits to feeders, sometimes commuting up to a kilometre to reach them.

Research has shown that 80 per cent of squirrels that breed in late summer are likely to need supplementary food. This is because the summer is a time of food shortages for squirrels and the female's weight must be above 325 grams for it to be able to undergo the physical rigours of pregnancy. As the summer wears on, those females not receiving extra food are less likely to be able to maintain enough weight to breed. Therefore, it is mostly supplementary-fed squirrels that breed in between July and September. Many of the houses on the edge of Rozel woods receive squirrel visitations and they run the gauntlet of Rozel Hill to reach the tasty morsels on the other side. Sadly squirrels have no road sense and about two-thirds of squirrel mortality is due to road kills or cat predation. So although supplementary feeding undoubtedly benefits squirrels, it clearly carries dangers too. Obviously squirrels also die naturally and here it is juveniles that are most at risk since they make tasty morsels for bird predators such as sparrowhawks, kestrels and occasionally barn owls.

Not only are squirrels important prey for other predators, they also fulfil an important ecological niche. When the autumn glut of food arrives, in order for it to sustain the squirrels over the winter mouths, the squirrels bury the nuts in the ground. Their incredible sense of smell (and not their memory!) helps them to retrieve the nuts when hunger strikes. As in all nature's systems there is competition, and the other woodland rodents, the less obvious but no less beautiful wood mice and bank voles attempt to steal the squirrel's booty. These smaller mammals do us no harm but are important food items for barn owls and kestrels and help to disperse seeds and keep the

220 *The barn owl, one of the squirrels' natural enemies.*

number of insects under control. Approximately five per cent of the original seed fall escapes being eaten by rodents or insect grubs, or becoming rotten, and manages to germinate. When these seeds have been expertly buried in the soil by the squirrels, the seedlings have a good start in life and may one day grow into huge trees, the seeds of which will support more squirrels, so completing the woodland cycle.

Clearly then, for successful red squirrel conservation, the planting of large-seeded broadleaf trees is important. Useful too are native pines, such as scots pine, which bear cones that squirrels eagerly exploit, particularly in late summer when the cones are still green. It is important, however, that pines are planted in sympathy with the surrounding broadleaf trees, but even small patches can provide the squirrels with a useful natural source of crucial late summer food.

Sites which have a small conifer component or where squirrels can readily receive supplemental food support nearly double the number of squirrels compared to woods where squirrels must rely on the fallen seed alone. Furthermore trees such as larch and the beautiful specimens of yew in St Catherine's Woods provide good food for the squirrels.

The conservation bodies – the Planning and Environment Committee's Environmental Services Unit, the Men of the Trees, and the Jersey Tree Advisory Council, as well as many private landowners – carry out vital work in managing the woods, so that they are a healthy habitat for all the woodland mammals, birds and insects.

Our woods retain many characteristics that are a legacy of their past management. For example, during the Occupation of Jersey in World War II, many of the Island's trees were felled when the need for fuel was great. Subsequently much of the woodlands' re-growth consisted of sycamores, which grow well but only provide food for squirrels in the spring period when they eat the growing shoots and flowers. Luckily the other dominant trees in the Parish woods are sweet chestnut and oak, both of which provide the all-important tree seeds in autumn. Therefore one desirable aspect of woodland management involves replacing over-abundant sycamore with a more diverse choice of trees.

Some trees escaped felling during the war and these mature, mostly ivy-covered trees, are

221 *The red squirrel is alive and well in the woods of St Catherine and Rozel. (Photo: Louise Magris)*

222 'Leave 'er alone – pore ole thing might be a widder. Besides, I thought you was gone on "Painted Ladies", 'Arry'. Edmund Blampied drawing. (Courtesy of The Blampied Trustees)

imperative throughout the woods where they provide nest sites and hiding places both for squirrels and the birds who eat the many insects living in the ivy. The squirrels actively choose ivy-covered trees in which to build their nests, or dreys, and many generations of squirrels remain loyal to the same tree. Therefore, ivy should never be removed from such trees. It is a plant which is often misunderstood: it is not a parasite and only uses the tree for support in its quest to reach the light. Its roots are firmly in the ground from which it gains the nutrients and water necessary for its growth.

Jersey's woods are smaller and more fragmented than would normally be considered ideal for squirrels in other places. Despite this, it is estimated that of the Island's population of about four hundred squirrels, approximately fifty are resident in the Parish. Initially there was concern about the squirrels in these north-eastern woods being isolated from those in the south-west, and so putting themselves at risk from inbreeding. However, it would appear that squirrels can occasionally move away from their homes through the network of hedges, and the results of a genetic survey suggest that St Martin's squirrels are genetically viable for the present. Future conservation plans centre around consolidating the hedgerow links so that squirrels can leave the parish and contact others elsewhere in the Island.

ST MARTIN GARDENS AND GARDENERS

The climate and conditions in Jersey are generally conducive to gardening. The soil is good, being in the main acid – there is no natural lime anywhere. The air is moist, there is sufficient rainfall, frosts are, thankfully, not often prolonged or severe – and the sun shines.

It is, therefore, mild enough to allow growth of a large range of cultivated plants from far and wide. For example, from the Himalayas, China, Japan and North America we have rhododendrons, magnolias, azaleas and wisteria – and we cannot forget the camellia. The magazine *The Jersey Gardener* said in 1883:

> If there is one thing more than another that distinguishes Jersey gardens from those on the north side of the Channel, it is the presence in the former of quantities of camellias planted in the borders, on the lawns and in all sorts of situations and all growing healthily and blooming properly.

From South Africa, Central and South America we have the agapanthus, mimosa and monkey puzzle tree (*Araucaria araucana*) – very much a Victorian phenomenon – which was introduced in the late 18th century and could often be seen in front gardens, the wild gladiolus (*G. communis*) which grows almost like a weed and is considered difficult to establish in Britain, and of course our Jersey lily or *les belles dames toutes nues* (*Amaryllis belladonna*).

However St Martin in particular is subject to bitter and savage easterly winds which sweep across from Europe in autumn and winter, and there are also examples over the years of freak weather conditions causing damage and death to the more tender of our plants. There was a serious drought in 1916 followed by a long harsh winter in 1917. The frost, as described by the then Seigneur, lasted at Rosel Manor from 22 January to 16 February. The coldest night recorded was on 4 February when the temperature dropped to -7°C (20°F). Severe frosts were recorded in 1962 and 1963 and there was a spell of cold winters in 1985, 1986 and 1987 which killed off many exotic plants. It is interesting to note that most of our cabbage-palms lost their leaves in 1985 but sprouted again in 1986. This new growth was cut down to ground level by the even harder frosts of January 1987, but many palms started to grow from the base and are still growing – a true story of triumph over adversity.

We experienced the tail-end of a hurricane in October 1964 and the great storm of October 1987 which caused such extensive damage – particularly to trees – that it is unlikely to be forgotten in a hurry. There have also been drought periods, most recently 1976 and 1983. We battle too against viruses such as Dutch elm disease, which caused almost total destruction of these trees in the 1970s, and the perpetual honey fungus.

Despite these trials and tribulations gardeners still manage to grow a wide variety of plants, shrubs and trees that are the envy of our visitors. To quote from *The Jersey Gardener* of October 1883: 'A fruitful spot is this little bit of earth called Jersey. You only have to put into the ground a root, a seed or a slip and straightway it groweth into a large tree. Flowers of all kinds grow in glorious profusion.'

And so it is in St Martin. Although a mainly agricultural Parish it boasts a variety of gardens large and small. This book cannot possibly include them all, but has concentrated on a small selection in the hope that the owners of those omitted will not be offended.

La Chaire, Rozel Valley

Before describing the gardens we should perhaps be aware of the man who originally planned and planted the gardens of La Chaire. Samuel Curtis (1779-1860) was an important botanist and

223 La Chaire, photographed in about 1880. It was the home of botanist Samuel Curtis. (Courtesy of John Brewster)

publisher, and a nurseryman of note. He was the proprietor of *Botanical Magazine*, succeeding the founder, his father-in-law and first cousin, William Curtis, author of *Flora Londinensis*. In 1846 he sold his rights in the magazine, bought two parcels of land 'in a bare and rocky valley watered by a stream' – which was La Chaire in Rozel – and there he retired. He died in January 1860 and is buried in St Martin's churchyard.

In his obituary the *Jersey Times* said he was held in great respect and an article in *Cottage Gardens* reported:

> His general disposition, and his hospitality and kindness to all visitors, his unobtrusive but unbounded beneficence towards the poor had endeared him to all who came within the circle of his acquaintance. For a long time his health had gradually failed. One of his greatest trials was the loss of his eyesight which deprived him of the pleasure of observing the growth and development of the plants and flowers to which he was so much attached. We cannot forbear saying that in Mr. Curtis the Island has lost a very worthy and universally esteemed resident. La Chaire with its valuable botanical specimens is the property of his daughter Mrs. Fothergill.

The Journal of The Royal Horticultural Society in 1933 described the garden at La Chaire as 'naturally beautiful', saying it was 'a fitting surrounding to one who all his life was so devoted to the cultivation of flowers and trees'.

Samuel Curtis built the house (now demolished and rebuilt in grander style) and terraced the rocky sides of the steep valley. He made small paths that connected these terraces, which he then planted, specialising in tender trees and plants that were carefully sheltered from storms by hedges of holm oak (*Quercus ilex*) and eucalyptus. There were two essential conditions that convinced Mr. Curtis to choose this valley, which he screened with his holm oak hedges – firstly the partiality of rhododendrons and other choice shrubs for a mild temperate climate, and secondly, this particular corner was not of granite but of purple conglomerate, which could be disintegrated by tree roots into soil eminently suited to his subtropical shrubs.

The original garden must have been quite lovely. Magnolias were trained on the walls of La Chaire with blue hydrangeas on the rocks above. Double-white and other camellias flourished off the main path facing the house. To the north-west there was a eucalyptus tree which eventually reached a height of 80 feet and was ostensibly the largest specimen in Europe. Unfortunately this was lost in the blizzard and severe weather of February 1995.

To the east, extending from the valley road up to the south face of the rocks, Curtis planted a deep belt of holm oak. Towards the west, also protected by hedging, were planted groups of Himalayan and other rhododendrons – among them a hybrid raised at La Chaire (between *R. formosum* and *R. edgeworthii*) – acacias, olive trees (*Olea sativa*, the olive of Southern Europe and *Olea fragrans*, said to be used for flavouring tea), *Eriobotrya japonica* (loquat), which fruited, and bamboos. Along paths winding up from the house over the south face of the rocks grew brilliant masses of the South African *Mesembryanthemum tricolor*.

Curtis was a friend of Sir John Le Couteur who had a beautiful garden above St Aubin's Harbour. Le Couteur had many plants from the Royal Botanic Gardens, Kew, where Curtis had been a director, and from the Royal Horticultural Society gardens in Chiswick. Like most avid gardeners, he swapped plants and cuttings. Sir John described La Chaire as 'Italy in Jersey'.

From 1852 Curtis's daughter Harriet, widow of Dr. Samuel Fothergill, lived with him at La Chaire. She too was interested in plants and preserved and mounted specimens of the many species of Jersey seaweeds. Records from *The Jersey Gardener* of 1884 of a guided tour by the then gardener. Mr. Beckford show that most of Curtis's bushes and shrubs were still flourishing. 'The Rhododendron arboretum was twenty feet high and the Falkoneri from Sikkim was growing in the open and looking as healthy as if on its own native Indian mountains.'

H.R.H. The Crown Princess Victoria Kaiulani of Hawaii frequently visited La Chaire and leased it in 1896 from Mrs. Phoebe Rooke to live there with her father the Hon. Archibald Cleghorn. In letters to her aunt she wrote that Mrs. Rooke's house was 'not very large but her garden is very beautiful'.

A Mr. Fletcher bought the property at the end of the 19th century. He pulled down the old Curtis house and built the present one in its place. He also organised a complex system for watering the gardens. Sadly, the gardens deteriorated after a while because of financial problems. When La Chaire was bought by a Mrs. Rose after the First World War, one of the few surviving reminders of the earlier gardens was the much-prized *Magnolia campbellii*.

In 1932 La Chaire was bought by Mr. V.A. Nicolle, whose wife sought expert advice from Kew on the garden. During the Occupation, the Germans dug up some of the magnolias and transported them to Germany. After a number of changes of ownership the restoration of the grounds, much of which is natural woodland, was carried out in consultation with David Ransom. As well as giving expert advice he organised the supply of trees, shrubs and flowers. There was much clearing of undergrowth, pruning and general tidying up to do before planting.

Today one walks up the path to the hotel by a wisteria-clad wall. The balustrade is covered with sweet-smelling summer jasmine (*Jasminium officinale*), honeysuckle and ivy. There are two mature sweet bay trees (*Laurus nobilis*) in the far corner. Progressing up the paths which criss-cross the old terracing, one passes a small mixed herb garden up to the woodland garden where there are interesting trees and shrubs to be seen. Among the holm oak one can find the eucryphia which in summer bears white scented flowers and which has suffered over the last 10 years, but is about to receive treatment from the tree surgeon; the huge Monterey cypress (*Cupressus macrocarpa*), again now badly damaged; a strawberry tree (*Arbutus unedo*) with its red fruits; eucalyptus, multi-stemmed pine trees and many feathery-leaved mimosas (*Acacia dealbata*).

Across the road, a stream runs along the bottom of the south side of the valley, where ferns, primulas, fuchsias, hydrangeas and semi-aquatic plants flourish. Mature trees cover the hillside – beeches, oaks (English and the evergreen holm oak), pines and holly. There are many rhododendrons and there is natural regeneration of the woodland floor with gorse, holly, oak and pine seedlings, to name but a few, as well as multitudes of foxgloves and mosses.

Magnolia Cottage

A little further up the valley, nestling at the foot of Curtis's terracing, is Magnolia Cottage. In its garden stands a *Magnolia campbellii* which is reputed to be one of the finest in Europe. The exquisite and huge rose-coloured flowers appear in March and April. At the time of writing it is about to undergo work by tree surgeons. The last time this was done was in 1972 when a specialist UK firm removed dead wood and superfluous growth and by means of steel wire braced the trunks together. The wire was fastened with screws inserted into the branches. Stumps of rotten branches were removed and all cavities sealed with a specially prepared bitumen emulsion. Concrete in the base of the tree was removed, the rotten wood beneath it gouged out and a copper pipe inserted to drain away any further accumulation of water. The cavity was then resealed with cement. This magnificent magnolia is thought to be around 140 years old and one of the very first of its type to be introduced to Europe. It could not have been planted by Samuel Curtis as *M. campbellii* was not brought from the Himalayas until some eight years after his death. It is hoped that the tree surgeons' work will prolong the flowering life of this pride of Jersey, and that it will continue to give pleasure to the large numbers of people who take the traditional drive or walk through this valley when word is passed around that the lovely flowers are blooming.

Across the road from the house, amidst the wooded area to the left of the stream and further up the valley, is a fine example of the handkerchief tree (*Davidia involucrata*) which displays its graceful cream-white pendant 'pocket handkerchief' bracts in May.

Les Vaux

A third noteworthy garden exists in this part of Rozel. This is the beautiful garden of Les Vaux, situated in its own steep-sided valley which branches out of the much larger Rozel valley. When the late Sir Giles Guthrie and Lady Guthrie bought the house in 1966 the gardens were in a very neglected state. It took two years to clear all the bracken, brambles, nettles and other weeds. The elm trees along the boundary had succumbed to Dutch elm disease and they, along with the old

224 Rhona, Lady Guthrie, who with her husband, the late Sir Giles Guthrie, established the gardens at Les Vaux. (Photo: Chris Blackstone)

half-dead fruit trees in the overgrown orchard, the 'Christmas' trees and the numerous sycamore seedlings, were felled and removed. The only trees left were a copper beech, a swamp cypress (*Taxodium distichum*), a whitebeam (*Sorbus aria* 'Lutescens') and two weeping copper beeches (*Fagus sylvatica pendula*). The main areas of lawn were then sown, the terraces grassed and pathways created which ran along and criss-crossed the steep sides of the côtils.

A water garden was constructed in 1971. A small stream runs through a series of pools at the foot of the granite wall to one side of the drive and the whole is fed by natural drainage from the farmland above. Along its length grow many moisture-loving plants, including arum lilies (*Zantedeschia aethiopica*), irises (*I. ensata, I. kaempferi, I. sibirica*), Chinese bamboo (*Nandina domestica*), primulas, hemerocallis cultivars and the striking yellow-flowered skunk cabbage. Removal of a sycamore tree exposed the huge pudding-stone rock which forms an impressive backcloth and has small and low-growing plants and shrubs springing from its fissures.

A dwarf pinetum consisting of large numbers of compact and slow-growing conifers was planted in 1972; as with most things planted in Jersey they have grown well. The côtil above is thickly covered with mature rhododendrons, camellias, magnolias and myrtles. More recently the land adjacent to the cottage at the entrance to the drive was cleared and is being planted with more of Lady Guthrie's favourite trees, shrubs and herbaceous plants as well as thousands of spring bulbs. But gardening is not always straightforward: some ten thousand *anemone blanda* bulbs were planted and every one was eaten by wood mice.

Lady Guthrie has created her garden for all-year-round colour and effect. Along the northern côtil a line of silver birches (*Betula utilis* var. *jacquemontii*) with their dazzling white trunks, underplanted with cornus and salix with their red, yellow and green stems, gives spectacular colour during the winter months. Among all the trees and shrubs, the bright yellow mahonia flowers and a scarlet-berried collection of hollies bring cheer to cold winter days. In the spring, thousands of bulbs bloom and camellias, magnolias, rhododendrons, azaleas and amelanchiers provide a blaze of colour. There is an amazing bank of low-growing rosemary (*Rosmarinus officinalis* 'Prostratus') on the north côtil. Hydrangeas (*H. mareaji* 'Perfecta'), *Buddleia lindleyana* and broom (*Genista aetnensis*) are just a few of the hundreds of plants that bloom in the summer. Then there are the brilliant autumn colours of the acers (including *A. griseum, A. davidii brilliantissimum, A. ozakazuki*), the sorrel tree (*Oxydendrum arboreum*) and the witch alder (*Fothergilla major*).

There are many fine specimen trees in this garden, including the bead tree (*Melia azederach*), ginkgo (*Ginkgo biloba*), swamp wattle (*Albizia julibrissin rosea*), kowhai (*Sophora tetraptera*), *Maackia amurensis*, winter's bark (*Drimys winteri*), the conifer, *Cunninghamia lanceolata* and the strawberry

Plate 35. 'Coral Calypso'
designed by Nancy Thelland.
1996 Prix d'Excellence, Best
Animation and Inter-Parochial.
(Photo: Jersey Evening Post)

Plate 36. 'Night on the Tiles'
designed by Nancy Thelland.
1998 Prix d'Excellence.
(Nancy Thelland Collection)

GARDENS AND GARDENERS

Plate 37. A spring showing of azaleas in the gardens of Les Vaux, Rozel. (Courtesy of Rhona, Lady Guthrie)

Plate 38. The Magnolia campbellii of unusual size and beauty at Magnolia Cottage, Rozel. (Courtesy of John Brewster)

Plate 39. Illustration by Clara Maria Pope *from* A monograph on the Genus Camellia *by Samuel Curtis F.L.S., published in 1819.*

Plate 40. The tracery of spring at Rosel Manor. (Photo: Chris Blackstone)

NATURAL HISTORY

Plate 41. *Un p'tit St Martinais pouailu (A furry little St Martinais). (Photo: Louise Magris)*

*Plate 42. A male broad-bodied chaser dragonfly (*Libellula depressa*) in the grounds of Rosel Manor. (Photo: Roger Long)*

*Plate 43. Wall lizards (*Lacerta muralis*), commonly seen at Mont Orgueil. (Photo: Sian Courts of Jersey Wildlife Preservation Trust)*

Plate 44. Common terns in courtship display. Their breeding ground at La Grand' Brecque was disturbed by the French 'invasion' of 1994. (Photo: Michael Dryden)

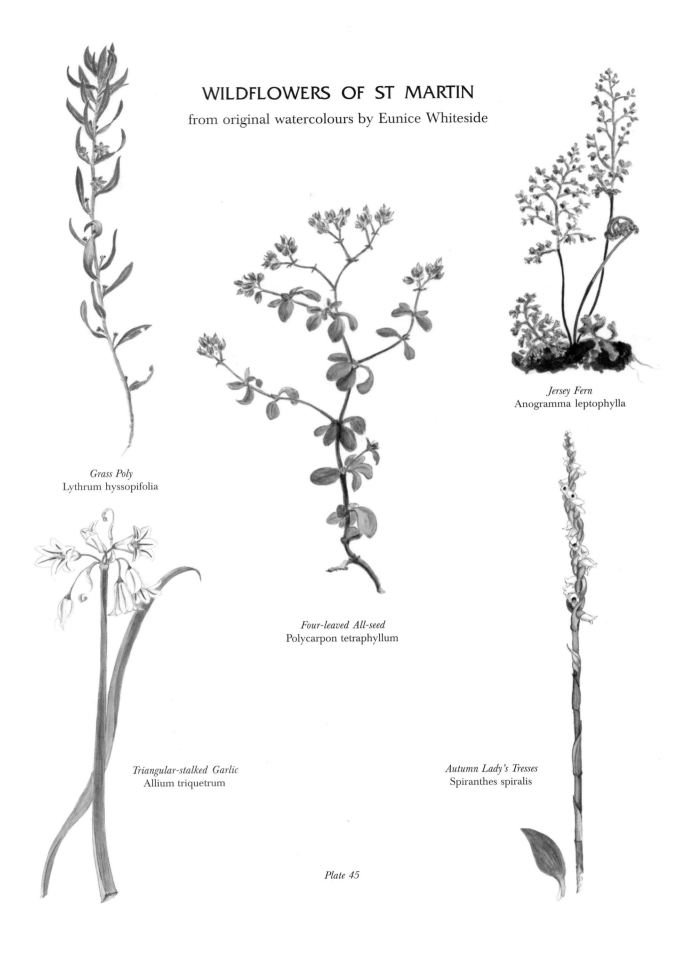

WILDFLOWERS OF ST MARTIN
from original watercolours by Eunice Whiteside

Jersey Fern
Anogramma leptophylla

Grass Poly
Lythrum hyssopifolia

Four-leaved All-seed
Polycarpon tetraphyllum

Triangular-stalked Garlic
Allium triquetrum

Autumn Lady's Tresses
Spiranthes spiralis

Plate 45

tree (*Arbutus unedo rosea*). There are a few trees native to the British Isles such as English oak, holm oak and beech but they are very much in the minority – this garden is stocked with plants from all over the world.

Finally one must not forget the dark green ivy swags which run along the dry stone wall near to the house, the life-size red-brown wire-netting sculptures of geese and chickens, and the strutting peacocks that all contribute to this lovingly-restored garden.

Rosel Manor

For centuries the home of the Lemprière family, the Manor has a mainly woodland and water garden, beautiful at all times of the year but especially so in the spring. The garden was mentioned in the 15th century, when Renaud Lemprière expected all his visitors to view and admire it. It was then rather neglected until the time of the present Seigneur's grandparents: Reginald and Clementine Lemprière lived at Rosel from 1851 to 1931. Clementine was a keen gardener and did much to reshape and plant it. This renovation work continued while Captain John Bolitho (Brigadier Lemprière-Robin's uncle) was living at the Manor (1944-1964). In the late 19th and early 20th centuries there was a vogue for plant collecting and woodland gardening in Cornwall. Captain Bolitho, a Cornishman, and his wife were keen gardeners and made many improvements – cutting paths, clearing undergrowth and planting many trees, shrubs and bushes that he had collected from many parts of England but especially from his old home county. He was responsible for planting the magnolias which are so much a feature of this garden, the *Drimys winteri* in the Palm Garden and the *Metasequoia glyptostroboides* (dawn redwood) which is below the second lake. This tree Captain Bolitho brought over from Cornwall as a small stick in his suitcase for fear that customs officers would confiscate it. He also made the lower of the two ponds which until then had been a mud pool and stream.

Brigadier Raoul Lemprière-Robin is also passionate about his garden and has made his own special improvements since returning to his ancestral home.

One enters the grounds along the drive which winds through rolling farmland where cattle graze. La Chenaie with its lovely old oaks is being enhanced with trees planted for the new millennium and for William, Brigadier Lemprière-Robin's infant grandson. In amongst the trees and shrubs, which include camellias, hydrangeas, skimmias and escallonias there is a *Sequoiadendron giganteum* – the only specimen in Jersey – planted in 1994 by the Tree Register of the British Isles to commemorate the filing of the 100,000th record.

To the rear of the Manor, whose walls are covered with virginia creeper (*Parthenocissus* sp.), is a large expanse of lawn which slopes southward to a valley that finally runs down to St Catherine. This lawn is flanked by the oak-lined 'Coronation Walk' and there is a way leading from the front of the Brigadier's study, down the '39 steps' through the Bluebell Walk to the woods.

The old Manor, the colombier and the ancient chapel of St Anne were built at the head of the steep-sided valley running south-eastward to the bay. The 12th-century granite chapel, which is clad in a wisteria planted 140 years ago, is the architectural focal point for the present garden – there is now no trace of the original garden. It contains choir stalls and pews fashioned from oak and chestnut trees felled on the estate in the 19th century.

225 A swamp cypress, officially the tallest in the British Isles, towers above Rosel Manor pond. (Photo: George Llewellyn)

The chapel garden contains the magnificent *Magnolia* × *soulangiana* 'rustica rubra' whose branches span a diameter of over fifty feet. The Palm Garden nearby has another magical magnolia, *M. mollicomata*, as well as four non-edible date palms, a *Drymis winteri* which, although badly damaged in the great storm of 1987, still survives and has new growth springing from its base, and a banana tree which did once, according to Mrs. Lemprière-Robin, bear one small banana, which was promptly picked by their daughter Emma, but has never borne fruit again!

At the lower end of the lawn which slopes down from the chapel are two small lakes, the first of which was originally a fishpond stocked with carp. Large dense swathes of arum lilies (*Zantedeschia aethiopica*) surround this upper lake which is dominated by a swamp cypress (*Taxodium distichum*), officially the tallest of its kind in the British Isles. Old-fashioned roses, azaleas and the moisture-loving primulas (*P. denticulata*) line the banks. The watercress that grows on the lake reputedly provided extra vitamins and minerals during the 1940-5 Occupation.

Between the lakes are more azaleas, primulas, forget-me-nots and cowslips (planted by Mrs. Lemprière-Robin) as well as skunk cabbage (*Lysichiton camtschatcensis*) which, despite its name, is a striking, musky-scented, white-flowering waterside perennial. In the dell between the lakes is a large fern of New Zealand origin which Captain Bolitho brought back as a seed and which itself has seeded and grown.

The lower lake, with its growing carpet of waterlilies, is surrounded by the massive-leaved gunneras, bamboos and various species of hosta (planted by the Brigadier) and the backdrop is provided by the lovely weeping willow, a coast redwood (*Sequoia sempervivens*) a black alder and *Magnolia campbellii* 'Lanarth'.

On the hillside above is what the gardeners call 'the Brigadier's Plantation', an area which he has planted fairly recently with a mixture of shrubs – mahonias, buddleias, bamboos, early-flowering azaleas and rhododendrons including a *R. fragrantissima* which has been grown from a cutting from another in the garden. Beyond the second lake by the stream is a *Corylus* 'Contorta', or corkscrew hazel, which Emma planted to mark her 21st birthday in 1986.

All the valley sides are thickly planted with a variety of trees, both native to Jersey and specimen. Tree ferns (*Dicksonia antarctica*), brilliantly-coloured rhododendrons (there are over sixty varieties in the garden), azaleas, camellias, fuchsias, genista and acacias fill the upper part of the gardens. Further down, in amongst the oaks and beeches, is another *Taxodium distichum* and *Drimys winteri*, a strawberry tree (*Arbutus unedo*), acers, giant rhododendrons and magnolias, including *M. stellata* with its fragrant, star-shaped, white flowers. Touchingly, some of these are planted to mark the grave of a beloved family pet. Underplanted throughout this beautiful garden, mostly by the Brigadier, are thousands of daffodils and cyclamen which all contribute to the blaze of colour in spring.

The great storm of 1987 caused extensive damage to trees and a great number were lost. Fortunately, however, many fine specimen trees survived, including the taxodium which lost only a few branches. Seeds were collected from fallen trees and sown (there are now some small pine trees growing very healthily as a result). Damaged trees and shrubs were pruned and tidied up, new and replacements planted, thus ensuring that the Manor garden must surely remain one of the most stunning spring gardens on the Island.

La Colline and Camellia Cottage

Mrs. Violet Lort-Phillips is synonymous with gardening in Jersey. She has a particular love for roses and camellias and was President of the International Camellia Society from 1983 to 1986. She travelled to Japan in 1999 to celebrate her 90th birthday with a talk to camellia enthusiasts at the International Camellia Congress.

In 1958 Mrs. Lort-Phillips and her husband came to live at La Colline, Gorey Hill. The garden was non-existent and of mountainous habit but there were a few good trees, so starting from scratch Vi designed, adapted and filled it with unusual plants, rare trees, shrubs and bulbs. There were a series of 'themed' gardens: the Japanese garden (for which she did research in the British Museum) contained stones arranged in traditional Japanese fashion; a rose garden and a 'John inspired' gravel garden – John Brooks was a protégé of Arthur Hellyer and gave her much advice on designing a garden for opening to the public. The Memorial Garden, built in memory of her brother Edward Fitzroy St

226 Violet Lort-Phillips, former president of the International Camellia Society and grande dame of Jersey gardening. (Photo: Astrid Haydon)

227 'Jersey Belle', a new magnolia cross, grown from seed by Mrs. Lort-Phillips. (Courtesy of Mrs. V. Lort-Phillips)

Aubyn, was planted with scarlet and gold roses and had a small waterfall leading into a pool. The stone plaque in the wall, dedicated to him, is still there. The Ruby garden was planted to commemorate the Lort-Phillips's 40th Wedding Anniversary and contained many Australian and New Zealand plants including a kowhai (*Sophora microphylla*) which was grown from seed. Naturally her great passion for camellias was reflected in the large number she planted.

Little of that garden remains except for the mimosa tree (*Acacia dealbata*) which can still be seen cascading over the wall on Gorey Hill in glorious, fragrant, yellow profusion in spring.

When Mrs. Lort-Phillips moved to her new home next door she appropriately named it Camellia Cottage. In fact she rescued one *Camellia nobilissima*, a white anemone form, and transplanted it. Her quarry garden is divided into 16 zones for ease of watering and planting. She has 82 roses from all over the world, including *R. setigera*, the prairie rose of America, *R. canina* species, wild roses from the Volga, Britain and Finland, and a red single burnet rose with red hips, grown from seed collected in China by Roy Lancaster. Her idea was to plant the roses on top of the quarry and let them cascade down over the rocky faces but the 'Man from Mattocks' told her 'Don't confuse your roses, Madam. Plant them at the bottom and let them grow up!' Other old favourite roses include *R. filipes* 'Kiftsgate', *R. banksiae* 'Lutea', Mermaid, New Dawn and Jersey Beauty, a very fragrant, creamy yellow.

As well as roses there are plenty of her beloved camellias and a magnolia, which she grew from a seed given to her by the late Contesse d'Orglandes. It proved to be the result of a natural cross between *M. sinensis* and *M. wilsonii* and has large creamy white flowers with purple stamens, an almond-like scent and pink ovoid fruits. As a new form, Mrs. Lort-Phillips registered it in 1981 and was allowed to name it *Jersey Belle*.

As a member of the Garden History Section of the Société Jersiaise, Mrs. Lort-Phillips is helping to organise a survey of Jersey's gardens for their New Millennium Project. Her own personal project is the Millennium Wall – a new three-tiered terrace wall on an area damaged by a landslip following the loss of a large holm oak tree. She set about constructing this wall herself after an estimate proved too expensive for her liking. This enterprising lady took the advice of an engineer, and, using hundreds of old *Country Life* and other glossy magazines, built a *mur de papier*. Based upon the same principles as *papier mâché*, the gloss used on the paper will help to provide a robust wall which will eventually compact into a wood-like structure. Between the terraces will be planted tree ferns and, of course, camellias.

Le Petit Coin

Off La Grande Route de Rozel, hidden behind a fuchsia hedge and dwarfed by a mimosa tree grown from a cutting of the original, lies the rose- and wisteria-covered cottage of Le Petit Coin and its lovely garden. Peter and Sonya Scott Graham moved in on the day of the Royal Wedding in 1981 and two years later set about transforming this corner of St Martin. The south-facing garden is terraced on five levels and where the old bake-house stood there is now a small raised pond. In 1982, a section of the boundary granite wall fell into the road; the stone mason who came to repair it stayed on for two years and completed all the terrace walls.

The White Garden is on the lowest tier and contains, as the name suggests, white-flowering trees and plants. It is dominated by two old fir trees which have been pruned and bolted together to stabilise them. There is a cherry tree with holly round the trunk, a hawthorn with a Rambling Rector rose climbing through it, *Viburnum carlesei*, a ribes, *Abelia grandiflora*, and camellias, including Matterhorn and *C. nobilissima* with masses of underplanted white honesty. The only concession to anything other than white is the bank of yellow and white daffodils in the spring on which there is a magnolia, 'Jersey Belle', and on top of the bank is a hedge of *Viburnum tinus*, which cuts off the upper part of the garden.

228   Mr. and Mrs. Peter Scott Graham at Le Petit Coin. (Photo: Chris Blackstone)

Behind the White Garden there are herbaceous borders along the terraces with dahlias, poppies, penstemons, tradescantias, alstroemerias and *Euphorbia wulfenii*, a favourite of Sonya. Interspersed among them are camellias and shrubs – choisyas, philadelphus, sarcococcas, ceanothus, roses and teucriums, to name but a few. Roses grow on arches along the rose walk together with clematis, especially the *macropetala* varieties. A high granite wall provides an impressive background along which are trained more roses, a *Fremontodendron californicum*, a cassia and a bright red flowered *Salvia grahamii*. In the round border there are many shrubs including *Viburnum bodnantense*, *Feijoa ellowiana*, *Hydrangea quercifolia*, photinia and a myrtle, a cutting from a bush planted by Canon Wilford, a previous owner. He used to pick a sprig to put in the bouquet of every bride in the Parish.

Camellias are Peter's passion and they abound all around the garden, with over forty varieties. His favourite is his award-winning *C. reticulata*, 'Dr Clifford Parks', a large, dark-green-leaved, glossy shrub with large double peony-pink blooms. There is a hedge of camellias, which have been grown from seeds given to the Scott Grahams by Violet Lort-Phillips, a former president of the International Camellia Society, and a camellia, the only one originally in the garden, which has been christened 'Forecast', although its real name is unknown. If it flowers before Christmas it is a good sign that the worst of winter is past, but the prospect of cold weather in January seems to hold it back.

The *Pinus wallichiana*, with its long, drooping, blue-grey needles, the slow-growing *Abies koreana* with swathes of *Clematis montana* cloaking the high walls and the large *Magnolia grandiflora* all provide foci for this garden which, not surprisingly, has been highly commended in its section of the Jersey Floral Gardening Competition.

La Chaumière Fleurie

229 Margaret Le Cornu's garden is dedicated to flower arranging. (Photo: Jersey Evening Post)

This garden is only eight years old and has been designed and planted with flower arranging in mind. According to Margaret Le Cornu very few of the plants are not used in her arrangements, for which she is well known in Jersey.

The greenery, or backbone, for her arrangements is provided by varieties of pittosporum including *P. tenuifolium* Silver Queen, Irene Patterson and Purpurea (a lovely bronze coloured leaf), hollies (e.g. Gold King and Silver Queen), cupressus, phormiums, skimmias, eleagnus, *Viburnum tinus* and copper beech amongst others. The bulrushes also provide a striking display.

Each season is planted with a different coloured theme. Spring is lime-green and yellow: *Hamamelis mollis*, narcissi and tulips. In early summer there are the cool blues and pinks of delphiniums, phlox, lupins, lilac and astilbes, leading to the 'hot' colours of July and August: tiger lilies, sunflowers and gaillardias. There are, of course, magnolias and camellias (27 at the last count) including one propagated by the air-layering method, from Cloverly in St Martin. It is singled out for special mention in the *International Camellia Journal* of October 1979 for being 'a large double white japonica which flowered from December onwards'.

Public Gardens

Mention should be made of the Public Gardens of the Parish. The States' Parks and Gardens Department provide a colourful display along the Gorey seafront and in Devon Gardens on the land side of the road. Working with a background of perennials – palm trees, phormiums, yuccas, pampas grass, viburnums and others, the Department every year plants bulbs and bedding plants for spring and summer show. One of the permanent focal points of these displays is a fascinating sculpture which commemorates the shipbuilding industry, once a vital part of St Martin life.

230   'Lady Glovetree and John the gardener'. Edmund Blampied drawing. (Courtesy of The Blampied Trustees)

Tales of Old St Martin

MEMORIES OF YOUTH ON A JERSEY FARM

The Reverend George Whitley was born in 1872 at the family home, La Haie Fleurie, St Martin. His boyhood on a Jersey farm at the end of the 19th century made a deep impression on him and he delivered this paper to the Jersey Society in London on 13 December 1949, drawing vivid and nostalgic pictures of the old Jersey way of life. He was speaking 50 years ago, and was describing a vanished age. How much more remote it seems to us now at the close of the millennium.

George Whitley was educated first at Rozel School, then in St Helier. He was ordained as a Methodist minister and lived for two years in Lausanne. He described himself as trilingual in English, French and his native Jersey Norman-French. He was a very articulate and successful preacher. He died in 1964, aged 92, and was buried in St Martin's parish cemetery.

This is the story of a vanished age, which, though not distant in time, seems so remote as to denote an almost entirely different civilisation and way of life.

In that period there were no motor cars, no tractors, no electric light, no gas in the country, wireless was unknown, cinemas did not exist, and aeroplanes were not even imagined. The tomato was a luxury, certainly not cultivated in Jersey.

I trust it will not be considered egotistic if I bring in the personal element in describing the scenes of my childhood and my youth; my tale also must of necessity be circumscribed, as it refers almost exclusively to the parish of St Martin, the home of my ancestors, and the place of my infant nurture.

The founder of our family is described as 'membre de la garrison du Mont Orgueil', and was buried in St Martin's Cemetery in 1674.

The house which has been for several centuries the home of the family is known by the picturesque name of La Haie Fleurie and adjoins the Rosel Manor estate on the way to Greencliff and Verclut. The house with its gable to the road is very old; at the further end is an annexe with the date 1805, but the main building is of a very much more ancient period.

The older house was then covered with thatch. It has a granite arch over the main entrance, and the door used to be in two parts (an upper and a lower), while at the back of the entrance hall was a stone spiral staircase. On either side were the old and best kitchens, both with their earthen floors, and enormous oak beams, with joisted floors unceiled.

231 *The Reverend George Whitley (seated) with South African cousin, Henry Whitley, at Haie Fleurie. (Courtesy of Kathleen Binet)*

The old kitchen was the centre and hub of the daily life; its wide hearth and open chimney had seats at either side, which enabled you to contemplate the firmament whilst warming yourself at the fire of wood, furze or gorse. An interesting feature in this old open fireplace, was the swinging iron bracket with adjustable hangers fixed to the wall, with a hook at the end on which you hung the kettle; when not in use it was pushed back against the wall. It was called *la cranne*, and is now in the old Farm Kitchen of the Société Jersiaise in Pier Road.

The *trépi* or iron tripod – paradoxically it sometimes had four legs – was used for supporting cooking utensils. On it was fixed the *bachîn* or wide circular pail, used on black-butter nights, and for heating water to scald the newly killed pigs.

The wide, and daily-scrubbed deal dinner table – no table-cloth but mats, with the frying pan full of eggs, and saucepans with hot potatoes boiled in their skins – those were the days of plenty and absence of coupons. Behind was the old-fashioned dresser with its antique crockery. In the corner of the room was the granite trough with the pickled pork. The trough was dated E.W. 1790. Pork was the staple food; beef or mutton only on Sundays. Bevelled boards fitted the top, on which rested the churn with its big wheel, brought down every Thursday for the butter making. Adjoining the hearth was the *jonquière*, a kind of wide bunk, which, when the curtains were drawn, provided an ideal resting place. Fixed to the joist was the *râclyi*, or bread rack, on which were placed the weekly baked loaves of gigantic proportions. Then there was the *choutchet*, or stool made out of the trunk of a tree, on which my grandmother would sit and prepare the leaven for the dough, kneaded in a tray on the wide window-sill of the enormously thick wall; in my time we had gone beyond the *crasset* lamp, and invested in candles and paraffin lamps. The other room, or best kitchen, had a sofa, grandfather's clock and a table, dresser, and food cupboard. Here visitors were entertained, and the table-cloth was used. The parlour in the annexe was only used for very special occasions.

A door of the old kitchen led into the dairy, where the milk was kept in crocks, and also the cream in readiness for the weekly churning. Another door led to the Cider House. Here was the circular granite trough (*le tou*), with a huge stone (*la meule*) which was turned by a horse for the crushing of the apples, also the *preinseu*, the press, where the pulp (*le mars*) was spread in large pieces of sacking, and placed between layers of wheat straw which squeezed the cider out of the pulp into large wooden tubs or vats beneath. On the side were the hogsheads or barrels where the sparkling cider fermented and would supply the family for the year.

Outside in the yard was the well, and over it a solid piece of granite made into a trough for the watering of the cattle, with its ancient pump. The bakehouse, with its big oven heated with faggots and gorse, was a separate building. Every Friday was baking day – huge loaves made out of our own-grown wheat, the dough being placed on wide cabbage leaves in the red-hot oven; large milk puddings; raisin and currant cakes; apple pies; *sohier*, a deep dish with layers of paste and apples; the well-known *bourdelots*, or baked dumplings, and the bread-cakes, *gâche à fouée*, eaten hot with plenty of butter. Friday was indeed a busy day. Saturday was town day, and rounded pounds of butter placed on cabbage leaves (of the 10 foot high variety), and stamped with the owner's name, would be taken to market. On Saturday evening also all papers would be locked away with the exception of the *Christian Herald* and the *Sunday at Home*, the only suitable newspapers for Sunday reading.

The Yearly Round

The big event in the early part of the year was the big plough – *la grande techéthue*, and that was a neighbourly and social event. A number of farmers would join together and plough each other's land; practically the whole of February was used for that purpose. Two ploughs were used, six or eight horses would draw the big one, and two or three the smaller one that preceded it, peeling the surface of the soil. The chief and most important function was that of the man who held the plough, and great pride was taken in the straight, deep and even furrow; others with spades would dig the corners, and truss neatly the newly turned soil. During the morning liquid refreshments and currant

233 Tom Marett working at St Martin's Forge, 1979. (Photo: Jersey Evening Post)

cake would be served in the field. The women were busy preparing the meals, and the big oven was requisitioned. Huge joints of beef, great hams, and luscious puddings all contributed to a hearty lunch. After the day's work there came a social and pleasant evening with a good supper sometimes enlivened with speech and song. It may not have been a good economic proposition judged by present-day standards, but it was certainly the communal spirit at its best.

In the vraicking [*sic*] season, the cutting of the seaweed took place on the days fixed by the Royal Court. The vraic buns baked for the purpose with a liberal supply of raisins or currants were eaten on the rocks, and at the end of the day the tired men returned with their heavy loads of fertilising manure.

Easter brings back memories of the dish of fliottes on Good Friday – a dish of flour and eggs boiled in milk – or sometimes fried codfish. Jersey wonders (*mèrvelles*) made with flour, butter and eggs and boiled in lard were a great delicacy. Easter Monday meant for a large section of the community the Grove Place Chapel tea, followed by a feast of music, song and oratory. The return of Spring was marked by the song of the cuckoo, the return of the swallows building their nests in the eaves, and fishing of mackerel and long nose in Fliquet Bay.

The busiest time was the potato-lifting season, with the arrival of Breton and Norman labourers. A curious custom was that of placing the largest potatoes – toppers – on top of the barrels, no doubt to attract the attention of the merchants on 'the bridge', that is, the Weighbridge. Horse-drawn mowing machines had only just appeared, so most of the work was done by hand, and it was good to hear the rhythm of the scythe and smell the new-mown hay.

During the summer would take place the Sunday School picnic, and as many as 35 two-horse vans, filled to capacity with children and adults, would form one great procession. Farmers would give their services, and vie with each other in the sleekness of their horses, and the shining of the harness, providing cushioned seats, and even carpets in their vehicles. On the great day remote parts of the Island would be visited, popular hymns would be sung on the way and a feast would be provided: truly a great and pleasing adventure for young and old. Then the Harvest, much of it still done by hand, was followed by the visit of the threshing machine, a great attraction for the boys, also a social and communal function, when neighbours would join in a co-operative effort.

Autumn and winter meant the flaying of the wheat in the barn, so as to have good straw for thatching of house or rick, or for the layers for cider pressing. Then followed the standing of the seed potatoes, especially on wet days. Cider-making also filled many a busy winter day: the gathering and crushing of the apples, and the cleaning and filling of the barrels with newly made cider.

An ever-popular event was the making of black butter. This is an apple preserve so named on account of its colour when cooked. For days previous, apples had been peeled and sliced, then emptied in a large circular pail or bachîn placed on a tripod in the hearth over a wood fire; cider was copiously applied, also spices and cinnamon and in some cases liquorice to darken it. The stirring had to go on for hours, in fact it was an all-night job, and neighbours would gather to join in the stirring, working in relays, by means of a long handled wooden rake; between the relays a certain amount of flirting and merry-making went on: these were called black-butter nights – *sethée de nièr beurre*. They were frequently repeated during the long winter nights and were immensely popular.

One of the great events was Guy Fawkes night and the burning of the effigy of this national hero, preceded by a great procession to the accompaniment of brass bands, sometimes mounted horsemen, facial distortions, crackers and fireworks.

Then finally came the Christmas season and the killing and salting of the pigs, the pork chops or trimmings on Christmas Eve, and the *gâche à crétons*, which was a cake made with the residue from melted pig's fat, known as cracklings, and apples mixed in dough.

As for schooling, I went first to the Dame School to which I would proceed on cold mornings with a heated pebble in each pocket to keep my hands warm. The Rozel School followed, with its most efficient master and the liberal use of the cane – an almost daily procession before our exit was in front of the master's desk where we received two sharp and stinging raps on the palm of the hands, to the envy of the girls who had to remain behind and write 25 lines while we boys boisterously roamed the countryside, often to the annoyance of the neighbours. Finally, came the Town School, and the four-mile walk each way each day – boys were tough in those days. There was no compulsory education and the Sunday School played an important role, secular as well as spiritual; infants were taught their letters and to read. Many years after, when preaching in Plymouth, I met a Jersey Captain whose only education had been derived from our Sunday School and his own efforts while at sea. On the following day I had to visit the ship of which he was Captain and part owner, as she lay off Plymouth Hoe.

234 Le Côtil, 1979. John Germain is stirring the bachîn *of Black Butter. (Photo:* Jersey Evening Post*)*

The Sunday School Anniversary, with special singing, recitations and prizegiving, was an ever-popular draw for young and old, and crowded the Chapel, despite 6d. entrance fee. Occasional Magic Lantern displays and Poole's Diorama, and the stories of missionaries at foreign mission meetings fired our youthful imaginations – while the local cattle shows, regattas and annual inter-insular rifle shooting on Gorey Common between Jersey and Guernsey were of unflagging interest.

We were exceedingly proud of our Jersey Militia, and at 16 we had to go to drill twice a week at the local arsenal. One morning the Colonel, the Adjutant, and the Sergeant of the Artillery visited us. The order was given: 'Volunteers for the Artillery, one step forward.' I stepped forward, and they tried the measuring rod on me. 'This man is rather short' said the sergeant, and my heart sank. 'What's your name' asked the Colonel. 'Whitley, sir' I replied, 'I am the grandson of Elie Whitley who was in your battery.' 'Oh, you are Elie Whitley's grandson. Take him.' And that was why I either rode on a gun, or stood by with a lanyard across my middle, and when the order was given 'Fire', I shifted my body and the gun went off – all because I had a grandfather. There were three infantry regiments, two field batteries of artillery and the town garrison artillery, the event of the year being the Queen's birthday on the 24th May and the grand review on St. Aubin's Sands, where all Jersey assembled and raised their hats and shouted 'Hurrah, for good old Queen Victoria' to the accompaniment of the booming of the guns and the rattle of the rifles.

The corvée, or road-mending, with horse and cart, was compulsory – six days a year had to be devoted to this object. The cracked stones were taken to a given spot by order of the Inspector and spread over by other worthy citizens. Needless to say the days were short, the loads were light, and everybody took the business in a leisurely fashion. The steam roller had hardly yet made its appearance, consequently the roads were fairly rough. The annual sale of the *bannelais* (road scrapings) created a certain competition among the local farmers.

My grandfather had been a man of the sea and, though retired from distant travel, yet with the farm he combined the pleasure of fishing; so from my early days I was familiar with lobsters and lobster-pots, sailing boats and visits to the Écréhous.

To every St Martinais, St Martin's is the best parish in the Island. This, of course, will be contested, but the fact remains that the Parish has Island possessions: a light house and Break-water, a Castle and a harbour. The Écréhous, half-way towards the coast of France, consist of the three main islets (and numerous rocks): Maître Île, and Marmotière with several fishing houses connected at low tide with Blanche Île, from which it is separated by a long causeway of big pebbles. Here lived for many years King Pinel of the Écréhous, fishing, basket and lobster-pot making, and drying and burning seaweed, being his main occupations. On one occasion he sent one of his baskets to his fellow sovereign, Queen Victoria, from whom he received in return a blue frock-coat with yellow buttons and a peak cap, of which he was intensely proud. In his latter days with a dwindling exchequer he sat in a tent in the cattle market – people paying 2d. to go and look at him – with cap and frock coat, as he sat in state. The throne of the islands is now vacant, but, alas, the erstwhile palace of the king was swept away by the sea a few years ago.

Gorey was a scene of great activity in those far-off days. It was the headquarters of H.M.S. *Mistletoe*, which was supposed to protect the Islands against the raids of French fishermen within British Waters, so there were always many sailors about. A daily steamer went across to Carteret, and sailing ships traded regularly with the French coast opposite, bringing butter, eggs, hay and straw, while Jersey farmers went annually to the Lessay fair to purchase their fast trotting horses. Those were the days of free trade and free travel; Colorado beetles, foot and mouth disease, prohibitive protective duties, and passports were non-existent.

Gorey was the terminus of the Jersey Eastern Railway, in existence from 1872 to 1932. Here also, though in its declining stage, was the oyster fishery in which a few boats were engaged. Oysters and scallops were fairly plentiful. Both Gorey and St Catherine's had been shipbuilding centres for many years, and I saw the last sailing ship built and launched from St. Catherine's, by

236 *'Knife and fork tea at Bill's', a watercolour by Edmund Blampied. (Courtesy of The Blampied Trustees)*

the Le Huquet firm. Picot at Gorey was apparently the last to close up. On fine moonlight nights sand-eeling was indulged in – with baskets hanging from our necks and long pointed rakes we would rake the sand with water well up to our knees; hard work it was, but gloriously compensated by a good breakfast of fried sand-eels in the morning.

This was the aftermath of the great Newfoundland cod fish industry which had caused Jersey to boom in the early and middle decades of the century. I wish someone would write the history of this great industry. Constantly you met elderly captains, sturdy sailors who had weathered many an Atlantic storm, who told thrilling tales of adventure and of the mysteries of those who go down to the sea in ships. Ex-shipwrights who had helped to build their sea-worthy craft were everywhere, while not a few erstwhile indentured clerks to the Newfoundland and Labrador coasts were frequently to be met. It has been said that wherever you travel you meet a Jerseyman. Economic conditions encouraged emigration, while the attractions of the gold-digging in Australia, and the development of Canada and other outposts of Empire, meant that there were few families who had not friends and relatives in distant lands.

Some of my relatives had been engaged in the building of the St Catherine's Breakwater and undoubtedly some of my forbears had engaged in the smuggling trade. My grandfather would tell me that in his boyhood he had seen the cider houses filled with cases of tea that had not arrived in the Island by way of St. Helier harbour. But then in the 18th century smuggling was a highly respectable and remunerative occupation. Parson Woodford, a respectable and worthy Norfolk vicar, says in his diary: 'Last night Andrews the smuggler woke me up at eleven. I came down and gave him some small beer and bought six pounds of tea from him'; and Arthur Young, the traveller, gentleman farmer, and founder of the Board of Agriculture, writes 'Lord Sheffield has asked me to send him some cabbage plants as he wants to experiment in the growing of them in Sussex,

237 *The Reverend George Whitley with George V on the occasion of the King's visit to the Channel Islands in 1921.*

but the difficulty is labour. The young men in these parts are engaged in smuggling which pays far better.' No wonder it proved attractive to enterprising Jerseymen.

As a boy I listened with avid interest and a certain awe to the folklore stories of my maternal grandmother. There were also tales of butter that would not set, dough that would not rise, physical ailment of man and beast, all put down to the nefarious activities of witches. Ghosts in white apparel, sometimes carrying a coffin, or assuming the shape of a dog (*le tchan du Bridje*) would be seen at night. Others called Springing Jacks would suddenly appear and with equal speed disappear leaving terrified pedestrians. Sometimes the ghost met his match and left his white apparel behind in his flight for safety. Weird music, singing and dancing could be heard at certain places; there were haunted houses, a typical example being Teighmore, where a succession of Barnardo Boys completely exorcised the demons. There were also tales of terror inspired by the presence of Russian soldiers in the Island during the Napoleonic wars.

Contested elections for municipal and legislative officers always created interest and excitement in our quiet way of life. There were two recognised parties in the parish, the Rose and the Laurel, red and white being the colour of the former and blue of the latter. On either side of the Parish Church was a public house, the *Royal* for the Rose party, while the *Crown* favoured the blues. For weeks before the election candidates and their friends would go from house to house soliciting support, and when the great day arrived the Parish was all agog. It was the day of open voting, and free drinks and free meals were supplied at the various hotels, and free conveyance to the polling booth. If rumour is to be relied upon, bribery was not altogether unknown; we were supposed to belong to the Laurels, but on an auspicious occasion in an election for Jurat my family were on the side of the reds, so I went to school sporting the red favours. Our candidate was the better man, and we had a good many fights in the school yard on his behalf. But, alas, to our discomfiture the other man won the day.

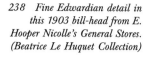

238 Fine Edwardian detail in this 1903 bill-head from E. Hooper Nicolle's General Stores. (Beatrice Le Huquet Collection)

Some old customs and superstitions still prevailed. It was considered unlucky to kill pigs at certain phases of the moon or to sow crops on certain days, or when the wind was in a certain quarter; one farmer, as he scattered his parsnip seeds, used to chant a certain slogan, 'Grosse et longue et pas frouchie' praying that his parsnips might grow big, long and not bi-forked. If you kept bees you were to put crêpe on the hives if there was a death in the family, and even the inoffensive daily visit of the Robin Red-breast was considered a bad omen – while the sight of magpies boded sinister or good news according to numbers.

Domestic events such as christenings and weddings were duly celebrated by family gatherings, and in the case of a death, undertakers would go round warning the relatives of the sad event, then on the following day invite neighbours and friends to the funeral. These would gather at the house, and, after receiving refreshments and a pair of black gloves and crêpe tied round their hats with the ends hanging behind, would follow the plumed hearse to the church or chapel for the service, then to the deceased's final resting place. Only men usually attended funerals. On the following Sunday, the family in deep mourning, would proceed to the church, and sit together in or near the pew the deceased used to occupy, remaining seated through the service, when appropriate hymns would be sung, and occasionally a funeral sermon would be preached.

Transport was slower and safer than it is today. Springcarts, vans, wagonettes, phaetons, four-wheeled pony chaises and, for the wealthy, the carriage and pair with coachmen and footman. A horse-drawn bus would go to town twice a week. A few bicycles of the bone-shaker variety were to be seen. Middle-aged gentlemen propelled a tricycle with solid tyres, while adventurous young men rode the penny-farthing (a high wheel and a small one); casualties were frequent in the way of bruises and broken bones. Well do I remember the advent of the bicycle with pneumatic tyres, the Safety as it was then called. The first women seen astride two wheels caused a sensation, people shaking their heads as a sign of disapproval, while the coming of the 'Bloomers' or shorts worn by ladies was a temporary scandal.

Itinerant musicians, German bands, one-man bands of many instruments, Italians with barrel organs and performing monkeys or a performing bear enlivened the countryside, while pedlars were ubiquitous.

The language was, of course, the Jersey patois. We were tri-lingual, for we read our Bibles, said our prayers and sang our hymns in French, wrote our letters and did our sums in English, and talked in the patois. I still remember my people saying 'Let's speak in English, the little one won't understand.'

Special events stand out in my memory:

(1) The Centenary of Robert Raikes, the founder of the Sunday Schools, in 1880. Thousands of children assembled in the People's Park, and under our respective banners we marched through the town all wearing medals with the effigy of the founder, the Anglicans repairing to the town schools, and the Methodists to Grove Place to partake of a sumptuous tea.

(2) The unveiling of the Jean de Quetteville monument in St Martin's Chapel. De Quetteville was the first native Wesleyan Minister and the apostle of Methodism in the Channel Islands. He was a native of St Martin's, and in connection with the centenary of Methodism, a fete was held at Le Câtillon, which was his home and that of his forebears. Afterwards there was a crowded meeting in the Chapel presided over by Jurat F. de Quetteville. The Reverend Mattieu Gallienne, who had known de Quetteville, came over from Guernsey to unveil the Memorial, and preached from the text 'There is a lad here with five loaves and two fishes'. Now it happened that five of us boys sat together in a pew in front, and to our momentary indignation the preacher compared us to these loaves. Years after, when I stood before an examination board of Ministers in Guernsey, the venerable old man was present, and when I reminded him of the incident, he placed his hand on my head and gave me his benediction.

(3) The failure of the Bank. One morning when I was fourteen my grandfather ordered me to put the mare in the trap, and to accompany him to town, for news had come that a prominent bank had closed its doors. When we arrived in Library Place the truth of the news was confirmed. My grand-father had what was then considered a fairly big amount on deposit. Great was the sensation caused by the arrest of the Managing Director, who after a prolonged trial was sent to the convict settlement at Portland. This grim place near Weymouth used to fill me with awe on my first visits to the mainland as I remembered that several Jerseymen had been sent there. Although since then I have been in many prisons, including Wandsworth, Wormwood Scrubs, Guernsey and Jersey gaols, even the one-cell gaol in Sark, the eventuality of my going to Portland is not very likely as it is no longer a convict prison. In those days the Police Court was under the Royal Court, and the visit of Black Maria with prisoners was an event of daily interest. While on the subject let me mention an old custom dating, no doubt, from the days when Mont Orgueil was the Island prison. Certain citizens of the Eastern parishes had to be

239 'Arrival of the English Mail, Gorey, Jersey', c.1900, at the Gorey Pier post office, opposite what is now the bus park. (Courtesy of John Jean)

present with a halberd on days of public execution, to keep the crowd back and to prevent the escape of the prisoner as he was led up to Gallows Hill for the expiation of his crime. Public executions have been long abolished, and Jersey has been free from capital crime for many years.

(4) The visit of Sequah, a quack American Doctor with a four-in-hand (a charabanc drawn by four spirited horses) and a band of players dressed as Red Indians. He extracted teeth to the rhythm of the band, made the lame to walk, and decorated his coach with the crutches of those cured by his massage and the application of his magic ointment, 'The Prairie Flower', of which he sold prodigious quantities. Great indeed was the sensation, many were the cures; then, after Sequah had gone, new crutches had to be obtained, and Sequah never came a second time.

My grandfather was a quiet, unobtrusive man of great physical strength, undaunted courage, and sterling personal character. When, at the age of seven, on the loss of my mother, I was taken to live at the farm, he became my ideal and my hero, and today I cherish his memory; but I owe much to my grandmother, a woman of deep practical piety who read me stories of the Bible and taught me to sing. She was the Priestess of her household, and every night she conducted family worship, and prayed aloud for members of her family mentioning their names. I always waited for her to mention 'little George' – sometimes after I would fall asleep, but never before my name was mentioned in prayer. My forbears were simple folk, but they left me a great legacy of deep piety and faith in God, and the example of the good life. I was brought up in the Methodist faith but I wish to pay my tribute to the worthy Rector of the Parish, a man of fine Christian principles, the friend of all, the enemy of none.

My tale is ended. Much has happened since those days. I remember with what hopes we hailed the dawn of the new century; little did we foresee the terrible days that were coming – two world wars which have shaken our Christian civilisation to its very foundations, and Jersey bears the scars of them today.

Her people have benefited by the discoveries and achievements of science – the tractor has displaced the horse-drawn plough, motor-cars, lorries and motor-cycles roam along the roads – electric light and the wireless are in nearly every home – people are much more wealthy than their fathers and enjoy many more comforts and amenities. But much of the moral shelter and isolation have gone – this is the inevitable march of time. Is it real progress? Are people happier? We, the legatees of the great Puritan tradition, often look back with nostalgic feelings to those days long past.

In the present chaotic condition of human civilisation and universal unrest, we ask, what of the future?

What of the future of this gem of the sea, so richly endowed, so highly favoured? May she continue to raise men and women of faith, integrity of character and nobility of purpose, and to that end our prayer must ever be May the God of our Fathers be with us yet, lest we forget!

A TALE OF BROKEN EGGS

This story was recorded by Vivian Richardson in 1981. It had been related to him by Charles Blampied, a carpenter whose workshop was at Rose Cottage opposite Greendale Stores, Faldouet.

Nicholas Ralph Richardson (1810-1876) was the owner of La Ferme, a large property on the Trinity border, west of Rozel. He married Esther Gaudin and, although she bore him five children, she eventually left him, returning to her family. It seems that Nicholas was over-fond of revelry and paid insufficient attention to his family and his farm.

The story relates to an era when there was no public transport, radio or TV and when country roads were largely unmetalled and indifferently maintained; when country people only infrequently moved outside the immediate area in which they lived and worked and were obliged to make their own entertainments. Rents and feudal dues were largely settled in kind.

At the top of the hill leading west from Rozel was a public house frequented by Nicholas Richardson, his cronies and other locals. Nicholas lived not far away at La Grande Maison (La Ferme) and used the pub for drinking, playing cards and dominoes as well as sociable meetings. On one particular occasion, Nicholas was in the pub with his friends. He went outside to the hill roadway for a breath of fresh air. Thomas, a local man and known to be a simpleton, happened to be passing and was greeted by Nicholas. 'Where are you going, Thomas, with that basket?' Thomas replied 'Monsieur Richardson, I am taking these eggs for my master to the seigneur at Rosel Manor.' 'Oh, are you?' said Monsieur Richardson, 'but not just yet. Come into the warmth of the pub and have a drink with us.' Thomas demurred but was dragged, protesting loudly, into the pub room.

Nicholas and his companions took a fair number of the eggs from Thomas's basket and made a large omelette which they then consumed. This caused very great distress to Thomas, who realised that he was responsible for their safe delivery. He implored the men to suggest how he could explain the reduction in the number of eggs in his basket to the seigneur. 'That's all right, Thomas, we will all go along with you to the Manor.' They, with Thomas, all set out for Rosel Manor.

Approaching the kitchen door of the Manor House, Monsieur Richardson and his friends directed Thomas to continue whilst they hid themselves in shrubbery close by, and started to make a dreadful noise. The Manor dogs rushed out barking loudly and surrounded the wretched and terrified Thomas. The seigneur rushed out to discover the cause of the frightful fracas. Seeing it was only Thomas, the seigneur called off the dogs and enquired kindly what the trouble was about. Thomas replied that he was bringing eggs from his master when the dogs attacked him. The kindly seigneur was much concerned and directed Thomas to the kitchen to have a good meal. The eggs were forgotten. Monsieur Richardson and his merry cronies slipped away un-seen.

MEMORIES

The following two brief recollections tell of a Parish and of parishioners in times past, but not long past. Monica Amy recalls the people she knew in her youth in the 1920s and '30s, and Stan Perchard recalls Gorey as he has known it. It is important that we should not forget how much has changed in a single lifetime, not just in the great strides of science, but in the day-to-day routines and places of our Parish.

Sister Monica Amy

The Parish was amazingly compact in that one was able to obtain locally most things required for our daily existence. There were also a number of recreational amenities and clubs. Trinity and St Martin shared a district nurse and at St Martin's House lived Mr. Messervy, the veterinary surgeon, who also had boarding kennels, much to the chagrin of the near neighbours who could not sleep at night for the barking of the dogs.

Mr. Robins was the blacksmith and the Forge was where it still is today. Mr. Quenault from Faldouet was the dairyman at Faldouet Dairy; Mr. Beloil was the chimney sweep, and Mr. Le Moeur kept bees and was also the local photographer. We sold his postcards of Jersey cattle and the churches in our shop. Doctor O'Connor was the village GP and had a surgery at The Briery where he and his family lived. There was a Mr. Blampied, who was a member of the Church choir, and who had a little shop just beyond Faldouet, who was a real craftsman and able to mend a variety of things from pots and pans to chairs and tables. He made 21st birthday keys both for me and for my brother Gerald. Mine was a replica of the key of Mont Orgueil Castle – but I don't know which door it might have opened.

Mr. Edward Slade ran a local bus service into St Helier and had a char-a-banc service for the many guest houses in St Martin. Another bus service attached to the Parish was run by Mr. Bob Rondel. Unfortunately there was a disastrous fire and his garage, behind Ash Cottage, was burnt down, but mercifully no lives were lost.

Recreational amenities consisted of various clubs and organisations. There was St Martin's Football Club, St Martin's Fife and Drum Band, a Brass Band attached to the Chapel Youth Club, St Martin's Girl Guide

240 A postman outside Central House, c.1929. (Gerald Amy Collection)

Company (but no Girls' or Boys' Brigade until later, and no Boy Scouts). St Martin's Fife and Drum Band used to rehearse in the shed at the back of the Public Hall. For those interested in golf (the leisured classes) there was always Grouville Golf Links not too distant.

A Mr. Reynolds, or Raynel, was the local cobbler, who had the little corner shop at the end of Crown House stores, which later became a cycle repair shop, run by Raymond Whitley after he had lost a leg in an accident. The *Royal Hotel*, the local public house, was run by the Misses Le Seelleur, who were both in the Church choir.

We were also fortunate in the Parish to have a Methodist, a Roman Catholic and a Church of England place of worship, an elementary school (which every parish had, of course), and three small private schools. Mr. Brine and his family lived at School House.

On the whole all the parishioners got on fairly well but naturally there were the inevitable storms in a teacup. Election time for Constables or Centeniers were often days of warring factions' rivalry, and some horrible tricks were played by each side against the other.

Stan Perchard

The *Beach Hotel* was previously the *Brook House Hotel* until the 1950s. Before that the property was simply Brook House. The Jersey Eastern Railway line ran through its back garden.

Margaret Terrace – a modern row of granite cottages developed by David Kirsch and named after his mother when they were completed in the 1980s – stands on the site once occupied by small single-storey cottages. These had been built by the Le Brocq family of Le Rivage Farm in the 1930s on land once used by the Eastern Railway line. There were gates at Gorey Slip.

An area now re-surfaced and used as a car park was also used by the railway line. When this was closed it was afterwards used by farmers to dump vraic and also to accommodate boats awaiting repair. Gorey Gardens have been established on the railway track to Gorey Pier Station. On the land side of the Coast Road where 'The Hut' now stands was a Morris Garage in the 1930s.

The betting shop was a grocer's shop built in around the late 1940s. *Ruellan's Village Pub* was previously *The Welcome Inn* and, earlier still, the National School. Mr. Taylor was headmaster, assisted by Mr. Coker and Miss Sybil Le Cocq. The school closed during the 1914-18 War. The Corner House was the original *Welcome Inn*. In Beach Road the doors of the beer cellar are still in place: opposite was Harry Coram's Grocery Shop.

Clos de Rivage was once Le Rivage Farm owned by the Le Brocq family. Where L'Abricotier now stands, an old stone building which was originally a house but was also used as a shipwright's workshop once stood. It was the business of Mr. J.R. Falle. La Chatelaine de Gouray was a cultivated field, part of Le Rivage Farm.

Ville Franche was Cantell & Tipping's Gorey Coaches and Taxis garage. Tennis courts stood where the Drive-in Bar-B-Q operates. Two cottages stood behind a garage, which is now used by the barbecue staff for catering purposes.

The three properties opposite the promenade shelter did not exist, these were cultivated gardens. Devon Gardens used to be a cultivated field, which was worked by, and probably belonged to, the Le Monnier family.

Of the houses that have front entrances on Gorey Hill and rear entrances on the Coast Road, Seabright was a private house, but is now a nursing home; La Cadeline, the home of Mr. and Mrs. R.A. Noël, was the home of Mr. Webley, Manager of the S.C.S. Bus Company. Next to Bronggarth, now called Louiseville, was the home of Mr. Sydney Perchard, constable's officer in St Martin. In the 1930s and 1940s the name *The Volunteer's Hotel* could faintly be seen on this building. Next door, Beachleigh was the home of Mr. A.S. Perchard, father of Sydney Perchard; together they ran the firm A.S. Perchard and Son, Builders and Decorators. The restaurant on the hill, which was Mont Orgueil Restaurant before being taken over by the Lewis family of *Longueville Manor Hotel* and becoming Suma's, was the building firm's carpenter's shop and timber store. Where Casalina now stands were two cottages. In one lived two Miss Whitleys, and in the other lived a Mrs. Baker. Homestill was a grocer's shop run by a Miss La Mare. The Jersey Diamond building was once Fairview Tea Rooms and, in the early 1900s, was a baker's shop owned and run by a Mr. Le Gresley.

Gorey Pier has also changed dramatically during the last century. There were once two hotels standing side by side: Cantell's *British Hotel* and Main's *Elfine Hotel*. They are now joined together and form part of *The Moorings Hotel*. What is now The Galley Restaurant was the Gorey Pier Sub-Post Office. Fountain Court used to be what would now be called a fancy goods shop, run by the Springate family. It was famous for their speciality: home-made ice cream. An opening exists between what is now the Old Sail Loft and the *Dolphin Hotel* which was previously *Carrel's Temperance Hotel*. Before that it was a Jersey Eastern Railway property, used by A.S. Perchard and Son to store building materials.

Between the *Dolphin* and Neptune was Ann's Little House tearooms, serving morning coffee and afternoon teas. Where the Neptune now stands was a private house named October Cottage. Fairview was a small shop owned by a Mrs. and Miss Gallichan. Where the public lavatories now stand was the Gorey Pier weighbridge.

Another feature of Gorey in the 1930s was the Gorey Castle Yacht Club, which was formed by Mr. Tom Lee, owner of Ann's Little House, and others. Moored across Gorey Harbour, approximately in line with the crane and Devon Gardens, were small sailing craft about 10 to 12 in number. These boats, all with mainsail and jib, were named after birds such as *Kingfisher*, *Curlew*, *Kestrel* and *Mallard*, and all formed part of GCYC. Also at Gorey Pier beneath the sea wall from the slip at Gorey Pier to the steps on the promenade below Devon Gardens, was a series of wooden poles, probably used as markers when the sea wall was built and reclamation took place. These poles were still in place during the German Occupation. Prior to this they were used by households living in the area as clothes poles. Housewives hung washing out to dry and, in doing so, had to fit in with the tide. When the tide was in, no washing could be dried.

Gorey Pier lighthouse is an interesting feature. The previous lighthouse stood at the very end of the pier; but this new light was erected at Gorey, having been moved from St Helier Harbour. It came down in St Helier during a storm in the 1960s. When it was erected at Gorey a new landing stage was also put in place.

On the land side of Gorey Hill, where the Pound World and Joyride now stand, was cultivated land. The angle car park was then covered in buildings used by boatowners to store boating gear; they were originally coal stores used by the Royal Navy. Opposite Seabright stood Gorey pump, operated by turning a large wheel, supplying residents in the area with drinking water. A pump house stood next to it to provide water for Gorey Pier toilets. Gorey pump was a bus stop on the S.C.S. bus route 2 from Snow Hill to St Catherine, featuring in the bus timetable.

Continuing up the hill, next to Gorey pump and close to the road, was a small building used by Mr. Bill Goode, a boot and shoe repairer. Adjacent to this was cultivated land, where Hillcrest was later built; during the 1950s and 1960s it was used as a residence and as tea rooms. On the sea side of the hill, Mount Rise was Mr. Bobby Walden's chemist's shop, later a grocery shop ran by Mrs. Baudains and her daughter. On the land side the property next to Seacliffe Guest House was another shop; in the early part of the century the proprietor was Mr. Peter Perchard; later Mr. Wherry took on the business. After the Second World War, Mr. Edwin Perchard continued for some years.

Villa Koritza was the home of Mr. Armitage, an artist. One property in the terrace opposite, which is now called Seascape, was previously 'The Studio' and used as such by Mr. Armitage. La Colline Court was known as La Colline, the home of Advocate P.N. Richardson. The rough-cast wall opposite Rockmount was erected in 1940 or 1941 for Gouray Church by Mr. William (Bill) Marett and Mr. Stanley Perchard, plasterers for A.S. Perchard and Son. Mon Plaisir at the top of Gabard, Gorey Hill, was a shop, and the proprietors were Mr. and Mrs. Le Gros.

The two cannons positioned on the pillars of The Old Cadet House were placed by Mr. C.A. Potter who lived there. These cannons were cast in cement by Bill Marett and Stanley Perchard in 1937 or 1938.

Lynton, the home of Mr. and Mrs. Maurice Lees, was Lynton Private School, run by Mrs. Stanley Blampied. Her husband was organist and choirmaster at Gouray Church for many years.

Villa Capri opposite Petit Portelet was the Café Capri owned by Mr. and Mr. Lenton.

In Petit Portelet, under the bank of Roche de Lion, stood two wooden fisherman's huts. One was used by Mr. Edwin Perchard and the other by Mr. Clarence Perchard, a professional fisherman, who operated out of Petit Portelet and owned two fishing boats named the *Pink* and the *St Martin*.

Between Roche de Lion and Jeffrey's Leap on the seaside, a wooden gate can still be seen. Before this gate was erected, a footpath led down to the small bay known as La Franine. In this small bay another fisherman's hut stood, used by the Vardon Brothers, who were also professional fishermen.

Anne Port Bay Hotel was previously *Fairbanks Hotel.*

La Crete Quarry was a working quarry during the 1930s. Four houses stand beyond La Crete Quarry; on this site was *Hotel La Reserve*, which was pulled down by German forces during the Occupation.

Port St Catherine, a Mediterranean-style house built opposite *Les Arches Hotel* was once a farm. *La Rondel Hotel* was previously *Glendale Hotel*, run by a Mr. Cotrel who also operated Gorey Coaches in the 1950s.

During the Occupation, German railway lines ran from the Grouville golf course along the sea side of the coast road to Gorey Pier. The trucks carried sand to barges which operated out of

241 Gerald Amy in St Martin's Bakery van. The headlamp shield indicates that this was taken soon after the start of World War II, but before the Occupation. (Gerald Amy Collection)

Gorey Harbour. The property next to the harbourmaster's house was turned into a small bunker, camouflaged to look like a garage door, and can still be seen. The hotels were used to provide accommodation for German troops. In about 1942, access to the pier (unless by special pass) was denied to Islanders. A large concrete bunker stood where the coach park is now. When this was being built part of the old slip, which ran seaward from where the public lavatories now stand, was revealed. The bay was fortified with poles, and some held mines. High walls were built across the slipways. Mont Orgueil was used only by German troops; the footpath to Petit Portelet was closed by barbed wire. The steps leading from opposite Gouray Church to the lower hill were closed off with barbed wire. The coastal road was designated a military zone. Some houses were occupied by the German army: these included Rockmount, La Garenne, and The Warren.

A Salvation Army hall was established in the New Road, Gorey Village, in the Parish of Grouville. During the summer months, open-air services were held on Sundays, in the mornings, afternoons and evenings. Most of these services were held either on Mont Orgueil Castle green, the top of Gorey Pier slip or Gorey Village slip.

Sixteen
The People of St Martin

INTRODUCTION

Much of the content of this book deals with places, events and organisations, all of which are important to the Parish of St Martin. However, it is people who make a community, and this book would not be complete without a glimpse, however superficial, of the parishioners themselves.

Chapter 2 describes the Seigneurs of Rosel, whose family can be traced back to the 13th century. There are also two individuals who have achieved a degree of fame beyond the bounds of the Parish itself. These are the Reverend François Le Couteur, whose interests extended beyond the church to matters military, and Edmund Blampied, an artist of international reputation whose works fetch increasingly high prices around the world.

St Martin is, and always has been, an agricultural community. In times past all the needs of everyday life were satisfied on the farm and there was no need to travel far. The concept of leisure travel is a recent development. A trip to St Helier was a major event for many farm people and their life centred on the church and those who gathered there. The transport revolution of the past 100 years has wrought a major change in lifestyle, but it has not destroyed the sense of community. Families of St Martin take an active interest in their history. Of those who can trace their origins back for a hundred years in the Parish, there can be few who do not have either a Noël, a Richardson, or a Le Seelleur among their forebears. Each of these three families is descended from ancestors who lived in the Parish before 1500; there are probably others of equal but unrecorded lineage.

Connétable John Germain indicated those who he believed had the longest family histories or closest ties with the Parish and many of these people were happy to make their records available. The following brief description of some of the families of St Martin is based on their information.

THE INCIDENCE OF FAMILY NAMES

Historical records indicate which families existed in St Martin during the last 300 years. In an attempt to collate the names which occurred most frequently in Parish data, research has been carried out in the following documents:

The 1696 Oath of Allegiance
In the light of threats from the French, who supported the deposed James II, William of Orange, King of England, asked Parliament to pass an Act of Association, requiring all 'men of importance'

242   Three fine gentlemen of St Martin: Harold Pallot, Charles Perchard (Connétable 1901-19) and Charles Billot (Connétable 1935-49), c.1910. (Courtesy of Keith Pallot)

to vow to 'combine with others for the better protection of His Majesty's Royal Person and Government'. This oath was signed, somewhat tardily, in Jersey in 1696. The record of signatories, listed by parish is held in London and was published by the Channel Islands Family History Society in 1995. The definition of 'men of importance' is questionable and in no way can the document be regarded as a reliable census.

Liste des Contributables 1861

This is the earliest parish rate list of which a complete record is maintained at St Martin's Public Hall. It lists by vingtaine the heads of households owning property in the Parish. There is a danger of duplication where one person owned properties in more than one vingtaine.

Liste du Rat 1998

This is the most recent available rate list. The same reservations apply as in 1861 and, in addition, the tendency to register properties in the name of companies could lead to further distortion.

Subject to these qualifications, the numerically most prominent families of St Martin over the years appear to have been:

	1696	1861	1998
Ahier	0	3	6
Amy	0	5	0
Aubin	1	8	1
Bellot	1	7	0
Bertram	2	2	2
Billot	0	8	5
Bisson	4	1	6
Blampied	1	3	9
Buesnel	0	6	4
Collas	3	1	0
De Gruchy	1	8	16
De Quetteville	7	7	0
Dolbel	6	0	1
Falle	1	8	2
Fauvel	1	5	4
Gallichan	7	9	6
Gaudin	7	11	1
Germain	1	1	5
Le Gresley	0	2	3
Le Huquet	1	21	1
Le Maistre	3	1	4
Le Seelleur	3	10	8
Machon	10	9	1
Mallet	7	4	1
Marrett	1	5	8
Messervy	7	3	1
Nicolle	14	11	1
Noël	10	25	3
Pallot	4	9	9
Payn	8	10	2
Perchard	3	8	17
Renouf	5	20	11
Richardson	3	10	12
Sohier	6	1	0
Vardon	1	13	0
Whitley	1	11	0

THE REVEREND FRANÇOIS LE COUTEUR

The events surrounding the Battle of Jersey – Baron de Rullecourt's invasion of the Island with a detachment of 700 Frenchmen, the battle in the Royal Square and the death of Major Francis Peirson on 6 January 1781 – are well enough known. Less well-known are the exploits of a re-markable St Martinais, the Reverend François Le Couteur.

He was, by all accounts, an exceptional man, typical of the best of the 18th-century clergy – a man of action as well as a much loved and respected priest. His great interest was in cider-making, then the major item in local trade and export. The Duke of Richmond map of 1795 highlights the hundreds of cider-apple orchards

243   The Reverend François Le Couteur's signature, taken from the parish minute book. (Courtesy of the Parish of St Martin)

which had become such a feature of the Jersey and St Martin countryside by the late 18th century. In 1790 Le Couteur founded the Jersey Agricultural Society and became its first President, devot-ing 30 years of his life to developing scientific methods designed to increase the yield and im-prove the quality of the local cider. Clearly, he was a man fully and actively involved in the life of his St Martin parishioners. However, it is his contribution to the defeat of the French invasion force for which he will be best remembered.

In the late 1700s the threat of French invasion was very real. An attack had been made in 1779 by the Prince of Nassau, who attempted to land French troops in St Ouen's Bay, and it was this event which prompted Le Couteur to purchase two cannon and keep them ready for action in St Martin's Church.

On the night of 5 January 1781, de Rullecourt, with his 700 men, landed at La Rocque and set out for what he thought would be the capture of the Island for the French. He took 500 of his best men and arrived in St Helier in the early hours. What resistance they met was ruthlessly dealt with – witness the brutal killing of Pierre Arrive who came out of his house in Colomberie and was bayoneted to death.

By mid-morning, all seemed lost. The Lieutenant-Governor, Major Corbet, had been intimi-dated into signing a capitulation document ordering the English regiments stationed in the Island to show no resistance to the occupying French troops. It was then that Major Peirson, officer commanding the 95th Regiment of Infantry, decided to ignore the Governor's order and march on the town. In the brief but bloody skirmish which followed, the French were defeated and both Peirson and de Rullecourt were killed.

However, these were not the only events of significance on that day. When de Rullecourt set off from La Rocque to march on the town, he left behind about one hundred men to guard the ships and receive reinforcements. News of the action reached the Rector of St Martin at 7 o'clock on the morning of the 7th. His response was immediate and decisive. As we can see from his later actions, vacillation was not in his nature.

We can only imagine the enthusiasm and vigour with which Le Couteur arranged for his guns to be taken from St Martin's Church and trundled down Gouray Hill towards Grouville.

The verbatim account of his evidence at the subsequent court-martial of Major Corbet rings out with the authority of a man who knew that he, at least, had acted honourably. 'We moved toward Fort Conway (now Fort Henry) in Grouville Bay to join a detachment of the East Regiment of Militia and the Glasgow Volunteers. I then being on horseback proceeded to reconnoitre the enemy shipping since it was my opinion that the fleet might be set on fire.'

The situation that met him was one of some confusion, and it was largely Le Couteur's resolution and single-mindedness which helped to resolve it. Captain Campbell, commanding officer of the 83rd Regiment, had received a message from the captured Lieutenant-Governor ordering him to take no further action. Clearly Campbell was no Peirson, and he, together with Lieutenant Robertson, made clear to Le Couteur that they intended to obey the order to the letter.

Le Couteur would have none of this; the enemy must be attacked at once and Corbet's order regarded as null and void. 'Mr Corbet is no longer to be looked upon as Governor, as he is prisoner; it is a palpable absurdity that a man deprived of his liberty should issue forth any order; it is most probable that the capitulation has been forced upon him; our engaging the enemy cannot admit a doubt of success; in short, every moment is precious; if we do not, some other corps will snatch from our hands the palm of victory.' The two officers wavered; disobeying orders would lead to a likely court-martial and dismissal; but Le Couteur had an answer for this too: 'I am a man of property, and if you should lose your commission, I will take care that you shall be fully indemnified.'

How the dispute would have ended we shall never know because at that moment a messenger arrived from Peirson informing Captain Campbell that he had taken command and that he was about to attack the enemy.

The action that followed was brief but decisive. The five companies of the 83rd, led by Captain Campbell and Lieutenant Robertson, attacked the enemy and, with the loss of seven men, succeeded in capturing the position and taking the French troops prisoner. Le Couteur, no doubt thrilled at the prospect of using his cannon, decided to fire on the French ships which were lying offshore. 'I remained with the Militia to cannonade a boat that was coming in to take off some of the French that had taken refuge among the rocks which I had the pleasure of driving back without effecting her purpose, causing 14 to be taken prisoner.'

It is clear that men of the 1st, or North (Saint Martin and Trinity) Militia Regiment took an active part in the engagement, since two are recorded as having been wounded, whilst on 5 November 1881, the three Militia Regiments were authorised to inscribe 'Jersey – 1781' upon their colours.

At the time of his death in 1808, the *Gazette of Jersey* said of François Le Couteur: 'His solid unostentatious piety, his freedom from every taint of worldliness, his scorn of frivolity, his kindness towards the poor and unfortunate, made him loved and respected by all.'

244 Edmund Blampied. Portrait by John St Helier Lander, 1932. (Courtesy of The Blampied Trustees)

EDMUND BLAMPIED

Edmund Blampied, who was without doubt one of Jersey's leading artists, is one of the Parish of St Martin's most famous sons.

He was born at Ville Brée on 30 March 1886, the youngest of four brothers. His father, John, was the son of a Trinity farmer, and his mother, Elizabeth, was the daughter of Thomas Blampied, a master mariner of St Martin. These were harsh times, and five days before Edmund Blampied was born his father caught pneumonia after a vraicing expedition and died at the age of only thirty-six.

Elizabeth then brought up four boys alone. She had help from her dead husband's sisters, in particular from Rachel Blampied, who cared for the boys while she was out working. Edmund Blampied went to school on the Rosel Manor estate, to a property now known as the Old School House close to Rozel Mill. His teacher was Mr. T.C. Stent, obviously someone the little boy admired, as, once he had become an established artist, he sent his old teacher examples of his work.

245 *'Midday meal at the farm, Jersey'. One of a set of six oil paintings of country life by Edmund Blampied presented to HMS* Jersey *on 10 July 1939. (Courtesy of The Blampied Trustees)*

Blampied, who by the beginning of the First World War had already established himself as one of Britain's leading etchers, was probably best known for his illustrations of horses. As a small boy he would watch for hours as horse-drawn carts lumbered up the hill from Rozel Bay. Even then he was fascinated by the animal's form and movement. He had an extraordinarily retentive visual memory, and there is no doubt that some of these early scenes were featured in his adult work. Indeed, Blampied wrote in 'A Few Memories of My Very Early Days', published in the *Bulletin of the Jersey Society* in London in 1959:

> These folk were all so friendly, so amusing, so hard working. Their happy chatter and laughter, the horses and the noise of cart wheels, the cackle of poultry, the bark of friendly dogs, potato planting, cider-making … the happy noise of it all. To a youngster hungering to be some day an artist, this jungle of happy life was of great educational worth. In London some years later and desperately homesick, my imagination was very pleasurably exercised in reliving these precious memories. I treasured and loved them. And it was during those very early years in Jersey that I taught myself to draw a horse in all its movements.

Blampied became a student at the Lambeth School of Art in January 1903. As he wrote for the *Jersey Society Bulletin* in London, he was very homesick. He spent some of his holidays in Jersey, visiting the places he had so much enjoyed in his younger days, including Rozel, where he loved to fish, and Ville Brée, where he visited relations.

As his career gathered pace and his reputation spread across the globe, Blampied never lost his hankering for Jersey. In the 1930s he illustrated a new edition of *Black Beauty*, designed the front cover for *The Water Babies*, and produced the illustrations for *Peter Pan and Wendy*. For this commission, his work had been chosen after he submitted a sample colour illustration, and he went on to produce 15 pages of line drawings and 12 in full colour. The book was published in London in 1939 and in New York in 1940. The publishers were pleased with the result, saying:

> There are certain qualities demanded of illustrations for this classic story. They must have the fairy atmosphere combined with humour. Mr. Blampied's pictures have this other-world feeling, yet his pirates are robust and ferocious and his picture of Mr. Darling in the dog kennel is the funniest we have seen.

In 1938, he was invited to join the Royal Society of British Artists, but less than a year later he had moved back to live in the Island, at a time when his professional life was obviously at its most happy and successful. For some it appeared a strange decision, for others who knew him better it was no surprise. One great friend wrote: 'To understand Blampied you must know something of Jersey. Were there no Jersey there would be no Blampied.' This was said of the artist who spoke to his paintings in Jersey-French. It was how he got the spirit and the inspiration.

When he returned to Jersey he did not return to St Martin. Instead he and his wife Marianne, whom he had married in 1914, made their home in St Aubin. When the Second World War began, and Jersey was occupied, the Blampieds were among those who elected to stay in the Island. They moved to Route Orange, and were familiar figures walking about St Brelade with their pet dog, a corgi called Mr. Lloyd. During the first year of the Occupation, because of the shortages and privations, Blampied lost three stone in weight.

After the war years, Blampied was as busy as ever. He had witnessed the passing of the old way of life, and through his extraordinary memory and talent, was able to portray it in authentic detail, bringing everyday scenes to life in a way which captures the imagination of those born many years too late to see them for themselves. Today, Blampied is still well-loved as one of our best-known Jerseymen. We know that it was the life he knew and loved as a small boy in St Martin which helped fire his imagination and huge talent.

THE 'FIVE HUNDRED YEAR' FAMILIES

Le Seelleur

The earliest Le Seelleur ancestors were farmers in the Rozel/St Martin area. They have been in continual ownership of farmland at Le Villot (the village) on the Rue du Villot in the Fief de Rozel since 1463. The Le Seelleur farm was originally known as Haye Hogard – Haye means hedge and Hogard a stack yard; therefore the whole would mean an enclosed area where they stacked grain. Over the years the name fell into disuse and the family became the Le Seelleurs of Le Villot until 1982 when John Alexander Le Seelleur restored the original name.

The size of the Le Seelleur landholdings has varied over the years – many of the field names on the documents of 1600 are the same today and other parcels of land came through their wives' inheritances. However the land was also divided amongst the family on each owner's death. Since John Le Seelleur inherited from his Uncle Thomas, he has regained possession of all the original fields bar one, which is presently owned and farmed by a second cousin.

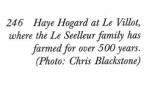

246 Haye Hogard at Le Villot, where the Le Seelleur family has farmed for over 500 years. (Photo: Chris Blackstone)

There are 46 variations in the spelling of the Le Seelleur name; the meaning is either from the English 'sellier' or 'saddler' or more probably from the French 'sceau' or 'seal', translating as 'he who seals or applies the seal'. One of the earliest variants of the name was Le Repossey, and the Extente of 1528 records that Philot Le Repossey in St Martyn had 'Herbage and Greuery due and paiable'. The most popular Christian name given to the male members of the family is Jean/John and to the females, Marie/Mary. There have been a number of family intermarriages, notably with the Renoufs of which there are 13 recorded. Over the centuries the family has expanded and moved. There are still a number in the Rozel area of St Martin area and others in Faldouet as well as in the other parishes of the Island. Members have also left Jersey for England and Canada. Their occupations have diversified too – from farming to sea captains, carpenters, shipwrights, shopkeepers, bakers, shoemakers and more.

Most of the Le Seelleurs of today are descended from Jean (son of Jean of Bas Rozel) born in 1614, who married Marie Machon, daughter of Lucas and Félice Machon of Faldouet, in 1631. They had 11 children, five of whom died in infancy. Only three of the remaining six offspring who married apparently produced children and it is these who are today's Le Seelleur forefathers.

Philippe, born in 1635, the first child of Jean and Marie, took over the farm at Le Villot and enlarged the land holding by acquiring Le Clos du Gras Vallet. He married Marguerite Le Ber in 1664 and died in 1676 leaving his widow and their three young children with the problem of running the farm. Guardians were appointed and when Jean (born January 1665) came of age he gave power of attorney to his mother. He left St Martin, probably to go to sea, but returned and married Anne Renouf in May 1689. They produced seven children but the first six died young and when Jean died in April 1723, Anne was left with their young son Thomas, born in 1717. The farm must have been run by friends and relatives until Thomas came of age. He married Elizabeth Le Feuvre and they had nine children, three of whom died in infancy. Their eldest son and heir, Thomas, was born in 1739; he married Marie Renouf in 1763 and they had eight children of whom Thomas, born in 1764, was the eldest. Haye Hogard underwent some rebuilding in 1792, for both Thomas and George (born 1766) cut their initials into a beam. They were found by the present owner, John Alexander Le Seelleur, in 1982 during restoration work and read TLSL 1792 and GLSL 1792.

The farm at Le Villot has supported a large number of dependents over the generations; in the 1841 census Thomas was 75 years old and there were 13 family members living with him. He died in 1849 leaving the farm to his eldest son Thomas, born in 1800. He married Jeanne Renouf

247 The apple crusher at Haye Hogard. The stone was pivoted on a central point and drawn around by a horse. Cider-making was a major industry in Jersey. (Photo: Chris Blackstone)

and they had six children, five girls and a boy. It is interesting to note that four of their five daughters were seamstresses, and a sampler embroidered by the eldest, Jeanne aged 10 in 1837, still survives. Thomas their only son (born 1835) married Marie Mauger and produced eight offspring of whom the eldest, Thomas, born in 1863, married Mary Ann Whitel. In the 1871 census there were 12 family members at the farm, and by 1881 the number had increased to 18, some of whom probably lived at Le Villot across the road: this farm was rented from Thomas John Le Huquet for £52 per annum, including farmhouse, outbuildings and seven vergées of land. Thomas Le Seelleur is listed in 1881 aged 18, a carpenter and living at the farm. He inherited the farm at Le Villot on the death of his father in 1911, but a month later, having just moved into Haye Hogard, he died,

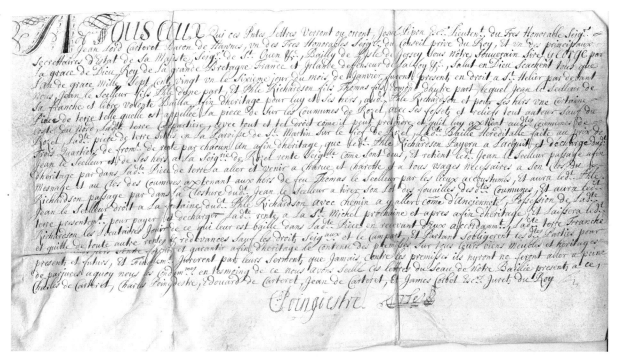

248 John Le Seelleur has retained many family documents including this deed dated 6 January 1721. It provided a right of access to the Le Seelleurs across a neighbouring property in order to reach a well, la fontaine. (John Le Seelleur Collection)

aged only 48. His eldest son Thomas was only 15, but he worked the farm with his two sisters, Lilian and Kathleen, and died, never having married, in 1979. His younger brother John Thomas Le Seelleur (the fifth child of Thomas and Mary Ann Whitel) was a farmer all his life, apart from service in World War I. He rented Manor Farm just north of Le Villot. He married Violet May Alexander in 1926 and they had two children, John Alexander and Ruby.

The family remained on the Island during the German Occupation, John Thomas being a member of the civilian police force, whilst their son John Alexander left school and began his life on the farm. Having married Margaret Perchard on 28 December 1949, he took over the renting of Manor Farm when his father retired in 1954. When John Thomas died in 1979 the farm at Le Villot was left jointly to John Alexander, 'Big John', the eldest surviving male in the family and his two children, Anne and John Robert. He undertook extensive renovation of Haye Hogard and moved into it in 1987. His son, John R., married Anne Margaret Barette on 25 September 1982 and took over the renting of Manor Farm in 1987, which he farms along with the fields of Haye Hogard since his father's retirement from active farming. He and Anne have two children, Emma Anne (born in 1984) and John Alan (born in 1986) and so the Le Seelleur dynasty continues in this corner of St Martin.

Noël and Germain

John and Gwen Germain live in the fine property, Rozel Hamlet, overlooking the grounds of Rosel Manor. The house was built in 1842, as attested by the datestone, now inside a subsequent extension. The initials on the stone, GN and AAB, are those of George Noël and Anne Aubin. George was born in 1794 and his son, George Edouard, was born in 1833, presumably in the earlier house, still in sound condition, which stands to the rear of the 'new' building.

The earlier, but not necessarily the first, house on this property bears the initials and date EN 1694, followed by a device which could be a fleur-de-lys, indicating a French origin for the family. Edouard Noël was born in 1668 and the family tree in John Germain's possession goes back a further five generations to 'Julien Noël 1480'. This tree appears to have been drawn at least 100 years ago and information on the first two generations of the family is sketchy. Nicholas Noël, who died in 1624, was the first family member of whom there is detailed information and he is described as 'Sergeant du Roi', as were his son Noé, grandson Denis and descendants for three further generations, ending with George who was born in 1738. The Sergeant was an officer of the Fief du Roi, paid variously in money or in land. His duties included the issuing of summonses, assisting the Prévôt and collecting rentes. George's younger brother, also Denis (1741-1809), bore the somewhat unnerving title of *Denonciateur et Capitaine dans la Milice*. In fact, a *denonciateur* is an official of the Royal Court whose duties included 'announcing' rather than 'denouncing'. It is interesting to note that John Germain (1939) was the last Prévôt: he succeeded his father in the office but it was abolished in recent years as being of no relevance to modern-day affairs.

Notable among the women who married into the Noël family was Rachel Syvret, granddaughter of the Reverend François Le Couteur, Rector of St Martin. This François Le Couteur is the first of four who followed in quick succession, the last of whom distinguished himself at the time of the Battle of Jersey.

Edouard Noel
né 1699, ep 1745

Rachel, fille de Thomas Sivret et de Marthe, 3ième fille du Rev Francois Le Couteur, Recteur de St Martin, et de Sara, fille de Jean Dumaresq, 3ième fils de Richard Dumaresq, et de Marie, fille et co-héritière de Nicolas Lemprière, l'un des Juges de la Cour Royale et d'Elizabeth fille de Clement Dumaresq Seigneur de Samarès et de Marguerite de Carteret.

249 An extract from the Noël family tree, detailing the ancestry of Edouard's wife, Rachel. (John D. Germain Collection)

250 George Edouard Noël (1834-1915) and his wife, Marie Anne Gaudin (1837-1925). These portraits were taken by C.P. Ouless, son of the famous marine artist. (John D. Germain Collection)

251   *The wedding of George Richardson Slade and Elsie Louisa Germain, 9 September 1915. Anne Germain (née Dorey), grandmother of Connétable John Germain, is third from left in the middle row; her husband, John, is sitting in front of her. The Slade family ran the bus service to St Martin (Chapter 5). (John D. Germain Collection)*

Many other well-known St Martin family names were joined with the Noëls: Perchard, Messervy and Renouf in the 17th century, Dumaresq, Collas, Labey, Mallet and Richardson in the 18th, and Aubin, Billot, de Gruchy and Gaudin in the 19th.

However, the family most closely connected with the Noëls is the Germains. One of the earliest recorded, Nicholas, married first Magdelene Noël and, after her death in 1645, Catherine Noël. Nicholas' son Noé also married a Noël, Susanne in 1677. After this the pattern changed and there are no further marriages recorded between the two families until the wedding of John Thomas Germain and Louisa Jane Noël in 1884. Louisa had three sisters but no brothers, so the male line in this branch of the Noël family became extinct. Louisa is the great-grandmother of Connétable John Germain.

With modern health care, infant mortality rates in Jersey are negligible and we tend to forget the distress suffered by earlier generations. John Thomas Germain (1862-91) was one of only two survivors to adulthood from six children. Even he was survived by both parents when he died at the age of 29.

In addition to the various family trees, John Germain has a massive Holy Bible. This was printed for Thomas Kelly of Paternoster Row in 1815 and originally belonged to the Cleak family of which nothing is known. As is not uncommon, the flyleaf records certain family dates, the earliest being the birth of Mary Anne Cleak in 1809. An additional point of interest is that the flyleaves contain an extensive – and decidedly un-Biblical diatribe against various 'murderers', including the Earl of Jersey! This Bible was acquired by John Thomas Germain (1862-91). Other fascinating family papers include the police diary of Centenier George Edouard Noël, which covers a period in the 1890s, and the family rentes book. The latter records the payment of *rente* to the Seigneur de Rosel starting in 1788 and ending in 1967, in which year Seigneurial rights were abolished. The *rente* was originally seven *cabots* of wheat, which was commuted to a monetary payment in later years. John Germain remembers helping to deliver the wheat to the colombier at the Manor in the years before the second world war. The *rente* book is bound in parchment and, on the inside, a religious text in Latin is still clearly visible. Obviously, this was salvaged from a much earlier document, probably a Catholic text destroyed at the time of the Reformation.

Richardson

Ralph Richardson, a mercenary soldier, is said to have been the captain of King Richard III's bodyguard at the Battle of Bosworth in 1485. After the battle he fled from England and came to Jersey. In 1507, he leased from the Seigneur of Rosel the property known as La Grande Maison de Rozel, later called La Ferme, which the family held until 1957.

252   Clement Richardson (1792-1878) and his wife Susan Le Huquet (1795-1883). They built the present house at Bas Rozel. Susan was a member of the shipbuilding family and Clement was also involved briefly in this business. (Courtesy of Maurice and Nancy Vautier)

*253   Captain Thomas
Richardson of the Royal Jersey
Militia, c.1800. (Courtesy of the
Richardson family)*

The two branches of the family which remain in St Martin separated at an early date. John (born 1599) is recorded as being of Bas Rozel and this property remained in the ownership of his descendants for many generations. The present house has a datestone 18 CRCS SLHQ 29, having been built in 1829 by Clement Richardson and Susan Le Huquet. The Le Huquet family were one of the leading shipbuilders at St Catherine and Clement Richardson also entered this business for a while. However, the family's main occupation continued to be farming and Clement (b.1851) is said to have accumulated a considerable fortune. He married Mary Ann Amy (1851-86) and, after her death, Bella Le Brun. He had one daughter, Amy Mary (1880-1954), and no male heir. Bas Rozel passed out of the family. The farming tradition was maintained by Clement's younger brother, John Dorey, whose grandson Gerald Arthur and his family, wife Doreen and sons Colin, Mervyn and Lester, continue farming in St Martin, now at North Lynn, near St Martin's Arsenal. They have bred a long line of champion cattle, winning numerous trophies, including the McLean Cup of the Comice Agricole de St Martin, won outright in 1986.

The junior branch of the family is descended from John's younger brother, Nicholas (b.1602). They came to prominence in the 17th century: Philip Richardson was an advocate and Jurat of the Royal Court; Nicholas was a signatory of the Proclamation of Charles II in 1648; his son, also Nicholas (b.1633) was captain of the Island of Sark and Philippe was Connétable of St Martin (1674-91). Also at that time a branch of the family was established in Jamaica, where they acquired large estates. Abraham, returning from Jamaica in 1709, was killed by pirates and his wife, Elizabeth (née de Carteret), was later lost at sea off Les Casquets. The family of Abraham's younger brother Clement and Jacqueline Reserson continued the line with some distinction. Clement himself was Connétable from 1731 until his death in 1752, having succeeded his nephew, Abraham, in that office (1723-32). Their eldest son, Clement (d.1795), served in the Royal Navy and was

254 The Richardson family at Bas Rozel, c.1883. Clement (1822-99) and his wife, Nancy Dorey, are in the centre. In the doorway are John Dorey and his wife, Jane Anley, grandparents of Gerald Richardson of North Lynn. (Courtesy of Maurice and Nancy Vautier)

255 Philip Mourant Richardson (1847-1925) and his wife, Susannah Norman. (Courtesy of the Richardson family)

appointed British Consul in Sardinia; second son, Nicholas, was Connétable (1761-70) as was his son, also Nicholas (1790-93).

Nicholas was the ancestor of the branch of the family which continued at La Ferme. However, his brothers also had notable careers. Clement and Philip were both in the Royal Navy, the latter winning the Nile Gold Medal: he served on H.M.S. *Bellerephon* in the Battle of the Nile and his early death in 1806 was attributed to the wounds he suffered. He is buried in St Martin's churchyard. Brother Thomas served as a captain in the Royal Jersey Militia.

This branch descends through a further Nicholas to Nicholas Ralph (1810-76); one of these two is said to have shot the last fox in Jersey and had a top hat made from its fur. Nicholas Ralph was notorious for his heavy drinking and gambling, much of which took place at a public house at Rozel. A curator was finally appointed to look after his affairs and the ancestral home was let. Nicholas Ralph, who built the present house at La Ferme, was the last of his line to farm; his wife, Esther Gaudin, returned to her family at Stonewall, where she brought up her children, including Philip Mourant Richardson who became an écrivain and also Deputy for St Saviour. His son, Philip Norman (1875-1957), was an advocate and St Helier Deputy and later a Senator. After his death La Ferme and most of his other properties were sold. His son Denys carried on his father's legal practice, Ogier & Le Cornu, and he also continued the family tradition of service to St Martin, as procureur du bien public. His three sons have moved out of the Parish, but his daughter, a successful artist, lives at Gorey.

ST MARTIN FAMILIES

256   Headstrong Edwardian Ladies. A Copp family wedding at Oakhurst, c.1910. (Courtesy of Maurice and Nancy Vautier)

Ahier

Donald Ahier of Seymour Farm can trace his family in Jersey to the middle of the 15th century, including such noteworthy ancestors as Sire Thomas (b.1442), a priest, and Jean (d.1784), who was imprisoned for refusing to drill on Sundays; his son Aaron was one of the last survivors of the Battle of Jersey and his grandson Philippe served on a Jersey privateer and lost a leg fighting the French.

However, the first to come to St Martin was Philip John (1856-1941), who leased La Ferme from Nicholas Richardson's Curator and later bought Seymour Farm from Philip Le Masurier; his prowess as a farmer is related in chapter 11. One of his four sons, Philip, served as Deputy for St Martin (1936-45) and another, Henry, despite suffering from tuberculosis as a child, was Connétable (1950-63). The other two boys spent much of their lives overseas: Walter emigrated to Canada and lost a leg at the Battle of the Somme fighting in the Canadian Scottish Regiment, and Francis served as Commodore on the P. & O. Line, returning to Jersey to become a Jurat. Henry's son, Donald, ran Seymour Farm until his retirement in 1992. As neither he nor brother Philip nor sister Christine has children, Seymour Farm has been sold.

Amy

The Amys are primarily a Grouville family, where they can trace their ancestry back to Raulin Amy in 1460.

The St Martin branch originated with Charles, born in 1801 and married in St Martin in 1822. His son, also Charles, was born in 1824 and married Ann Elizabeth Richardson. They owned the house next to the tower at St Catherine, known as 'Amy's House'. Their son, Frederick Charles, born in 1856, was a fisherman, operating from St Catherine. In 1886 he was awarded the Jersey Humane Society's certificate for saving the life of John Billot at Les Écréhous. When Billot's fishing boat, *Fear Not*, got into difficulties, Amy and his friend Elias Whitley went to the rescue and managed to save Billot, though his son was drowned.

John Thomas, son of Frederick, was born in 1889 and served in the Hampshire Regiment. He was captured at the Battle of Mons in 1914 and spent the remainder of the war in a prison camp. As a recruit in the British Expeditionary Force, he became a member of the much honoured and decorated body of men known as 'The Old Contemptibles'. After the war, he served as a vingtenier and started the business of J.T. Amy, St Martin's Bakery: the business later became Central Stores and was continued by his son, Gerald, until his retirement in 1987.

257 John T. Amy of the Hampshire Regiment, 1914, with his parents (seated) and Stan Rondel. John Amy was captured at the Battle of Mons. (Gerald Amy Collection)

Billot

The name Billot is first recorded in the Island in 1309. It is believed that the family came from the district of Billot, near Lisière in Normandy. The family became established in Trinity, where La Billoterie is situated, close to Les Croix, but there was also another La Billoterie in St Peter,

258 *Four generations of the Billot family at La Chasse, 1932. Lydie Billot née Tourgis (91), Charles Billot, Connétable 1935-49 (56), Thomas Billot, Connétable 1963-72 (24), Anne Billot (10 months). (Courtesy of Anne Perchard)*

mentioned in a document of 1677. Billots are also to be found in St Saviour, where several fields are named Le Clos de Billot. A Billot in Trinity signed the Oath of Allegiance in 1696, but the name is not found amongst the St Martin signatories.

The Godfray map of 1849 shows a number of properties in the Parish owned by Billots. They acquired what is still the family property in St Martin, namely Holmdale in La Rue de la Ville Brée, in the second half of the 18th century. The original name of the property was La Gaupette, and meadows to the west of Holmdale include Gaupette in their names. The date stone over the front door is engraved '18 PBL DDF 22'. The date 1822 is not the date of the marriage of Phillipe Billot to Douce du Fresne (whose initials they are) but the date on which Holmdale was built onto an older house, part of which remains as the kitchen. Philippe was the son of another Philippe who married Elizabeth Godfray in 1793 and who was either lost at sea or died in a French prison shortly after his son's birth. Thereafter, Elizabeth never used her married name and was even buried as Elizabeth Godfray. She financed the construction of the new house and a family anecdote is that the granite was carted to the present site of the house, then to the top of La Ville Brée and, when Elizabeth changed her mind again, back to the bottom of the road. Her initials, EGF, also appear on the front of Holmdale.

During the 20th century the family has been prominent in municipal affairs. Charles Philip Billot served the Parish for almost forty years, including service as Deputy and then as Connétable from 1935 to 1949, a period which included the difficult years of the Occupation. His younger brother George became a Jurat, after his return to Jersey from a banking career in London and was subsequently appointed a Lieutenant-Bailiff and awarded the OBE. George's son, Commander Godfray Billot, captain of HMS *Hartland*, won a DSO for his bravery at Oran. Charles's two sons, Charles and Thomas, both farmed in La Ville Brée and bred some celebrated strains of Jersey cows. Holmdale Oxford Pride, bred by Charles, Reserve Champion in 1921, was sold to an American breeder for the enormous sum of £1,000 and was Grand Champion in America the following year. Thomas bred Visiting Design whose three sons were sold for £1,000 each during the 1950s.

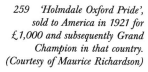

259 'Holmdale Oxford Pride', sold to America in 1921 for £1,000 and subsequently Grand Champion in that country. (Courtesy of Maurice Richardson)

Charles was Deputy of St Martin from 1963 to 1969. He was a fervent advocate for *la consèrvâtion et de la pèrpétuâtion d'l'usage dé la vielle langue nouormande du pays*, the objective of L'Assembliée d'Jèrriais of which he was president for several years. Thomas served as centenier from 1953 to 1963 and then as Connétable until 1973; he was a founder member and first president of the Rozel Rovers Football Club from 1943 to 1959.

Charles Perchard Billot, the son of Charles, after being a successful jockey at local races, became a racehorse trainer and was champion trainer for several years. Thomas's daughter Anne (Mrs. Perchard of La Ferme) has since 1989 been chairman, and later president, of the World Jersey Cattle Bureau which brings together associations of Jersey cattle breeders around the world.

De Gruchy

Although the De Gruchys have been in Jersey since the latter part of the 13th century, the earliest recorded baptism of the Surville branch in St Martin, of Esther Mary, daughter of Jean De Gruchy and Esther de Quetteville, was recorded on 18 November 1828. Jean De Gruchy was known to be farming in La Vingtaine de Faldouet in 1851, and his son Thomas farmed 42 vergées at Surville, Vingtaine de La Quéruée in 1868. The family has continued to farm Surville to the present day.

François, a twin brother of Thomas, emigrated to South Africa. His son Charles lived for a period of time with his uncle at Surville, before emigrating to Perth, Western Australia. A third brother William was a master mariner living with his family at Faldouet.

260 Thomas Renouf De Gruchy (1868-1936), Connétable 1926-35. (Courtesy of Harold De Gruchy)

Thomas's son, Thomas Renouf De Gruchy, was Connétable of St Martin (1926-35) and was also founder secretary of the Comice Agricole de St Martin in 1894 and president of that body in 1920. His son, Thomas Raymond, followed in his father's footsteps by being elected Connétable in 1949 serving until his untimely death the following year. His three sons Raymond, Harold and Vernon continued working the family farms in La Vingtaine de La Quéruée until their retirement in 1995.

De La Haye

The first record of the De La Haye family in the Parish was of Gedeon De La Haye c.1600. However, the family moved to Trinity and onward to St Helier and did not re-establish a presence

261   Stanley John De La Haye. (Photo: Stuart McAlister)

in St Martin until 1913, when Stanley De La Haye married Lydia Lucas and purchased Beuvelande.

This Stanley (1888-1939) served as a Constable's Officer in the Parish. His son, also Stanley, gave extended service to the Parish. Stanley John De La Haye was born in 1918 and was one of the first pupils at Hilda Ahier's School at Springside. The certificate given to him by a grateful Parish when he retired as Connétable listed his service as:

Vingtenier La Quéruée	1939-40
Aumonier	1946-52
Surveillant	1952-88
Constable's Officer, La Quéruée	1958-72
Expert (Rate Assessor)	1968-72
Centenier	1972-87
Connétable	1987-94

This certificate ends with the delightful salutation:

J'vos souhaitons à la Normande, bouan yi, bouanne dent, bouan pid, et le Paradis à la fin d'vos jours.

We wish you in the Norman fashion, good sight, good teeth, good feet and Paradise at the end of your days.

Stanley De La Haye and his sons, Richard, Colin and Stephen, all live in St Martin and Beuvelande remains the family property.

Dorey

Laurence Dorey's grandfather, George Dorey, was born in Trinity and spent time at sea as ship's captain. After his marriage to Anne Le Gros of St Lawrence, the couple set up Les Buttes Stores in St Martin, which remained in the family until granddaughter Hilda Ching retired in 1986.

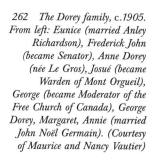

262 The Dorey family, c.1905. From left: Eunice (married Anley Richardson), Frederick John (became Senator), Anne Dorey (née Le Gros), Josué (became Warden of Mont Orgueil), George (became Moderator of the Free Church of Canada), George Dorey, Margaret, Annie (married John Noël Germain). (Courtesy of Maurice and Nancy Vautier)

George and Anne had six children, of whom George became Moderator of the Free Church of Canada, Josué (Joe) was Guardien of Mont Orgueil from 1939-59, Frederick farmed at Grasfort and Annie married John Noël Germain, grandfather of the Connétable. Frederick's son, Frederick George, also served at Mont Orgueil. His second son, Laurence, now retired, lives at La Rue de la Mare des Reines.

Falle

Although the name of Falle is recorded in St Saviour as early as the *Extente* of 1274 the first known family in St Martin dates back to Simon, who died in 1606.

In the 19th century there was a line of three successors each called George James, the eldest of the three being the son of Jean Falle, who was baptised in St Martin in 1764.

George James, born in 1821, served as a sergeant in the Jersey Militia and worked as a blacksmith. He married Betsy Mollet in 1846. His brother, Thomas, was a fisherman at Anne Port: he and his wife, Fanny Le Huquet, had 13 children.

Fanny lived to the age of 93 and is reputed to have been a matriarch of forceful character. Her daughters ran the tearooms at Anne Port, which she enjoyed visiting. However, she considered the sea breezes to be injurious to health and her son and son-in-law, Philip Le Gresley, had to walk alongside, holding up sheets to shield her from the wind. Philip, who was married to Fanny's daughter, Ada Mary, was the organist at Les Landes Methodist Chapel and they ran a Sunday school at their home, St Agatha, then held on a Crown lease.

George James (born 1850) was at sea for some years and subsequently became a photographer's assistant in St Helier. He also served in the militia, including service in France in the First World War. He married Susan Pallot of St Saviour and their daughter, Alice, married George De Gruchy Noël, a descendant of the St Martin family of that name.

263 *Betsy Mollett, who married Sergeant George Falle. (Courtesy of Janet Ferbrache)*

Fauvel

The Jersey Chantry Certificate of 1550 mentions a Johan Favel who was due one *cabot* of *rente* in the Parish.

Francis Fauvel had a shipyard at Gorey in the 19th century and is recorded as having built the 24-ton cutter *Love* in 1853. The property, now occupied by the Drive-In Bar-B-Q, remained in family ownership for some years after the demise of the shipbuilding industry.

The family also owned a farm at Faldouet, which included the site of the dolmen. Mr. Fauvel carried out a series of excavations from 1839 to 1863, and in 1933 the artefacts which he recovered were presented to the Société Jersiaise by his heirs.

Gaudin

The first record of the family in St Martin is of Philippe Gaudin in 1540. The Gaudins were established in Vingtaine de la Quéruée from 1659 and at Green Farm there is a date stone for Philippe Gaudin, who married Elizabeth Aubin in 1781. The family spread widely and at various times owned a number of properties in the Parish, including Haut de Rué, Le Fleurion (from 1832), Green Farm, Lowland (now Ambleside) and Glenvale. There is a datestone at Haut de Rué of Philippe Gaudin, 1638, and the property remained in the family certainly till the later years of the 19th century, when it was acquired by Philip Mourant Richardson, who had been brought up at Stonewall by his mother, Esther Gaudin.

The family has been prominent in service to the Parish: George Gaudin was chef de police *c.*1845, when his portrait was painted by P.J. Ouless (fig.123); Philippe George Gaudin of Green Farm was elected Deputy in 1875, as was Thomas Gaudin in 1890.

Over the years, many of the family travelled extensively and there are now several branches in Canada and at the settlement of St Martin's Bay in South Island, New Zealand.

264 *Wash day at the Gaudin property of Green Farm, late 19th century. The traditional Jersey bonnets are a particularly delightful feature. (Courtesy of the Richardson family)*

Philip Gaudin (1863-1938) married Margaret Noël and after farming at La Davisonnerie Farm in St Saviour they moved to Le Fleurion. Philip's grandson, Cyril, still lives in the Parish, with his son Paul, daughter-in-law, Megan, and grandchildren Celia and Philip.

Le Huquet

The Le Huquet family of Elmore were prominent in the shipbuilding industry at St Catherine, where they had several yards at various times.

Captain Philippe Le Huquet was also a leading light in the Wesleyan Chapel and managed the St Martin Fife and Drum Band.

Beatrice Le Huquet taught at St Martin's School from 1920 to 1966 and, after her retirement, worked as a St John Ambulance nurse. At the age of 93, she still takes a keen interest in parish life.

Pallot

The Pallot family can be traced back to Jean Pallot du Port Querière who was baptised *c.*1588.

265 *Philip Gaudin (1863-1938) and his wife, Margaret Noël, at La Davisonnerie. (Courtesy of Paul Gaudin)*

266   Captain Charles Pallot, photographed by Constant Peigné of St Nazaire. (Courtesy of David Pallot)

He was Regent (Headmaster) for 60 years at St Mannelier School, which had been established in Jersey in 1477. Jean married Jeanne Faultrart, the daughter of the Reverend Helier Faultrart, Rector of St Martin in 1613, since when the family has had a continuous presence in the Parish. Their son, Josué, became Rector of St Clement and later Rector of Grouville and signed the Proclamation of Charles II on 17 February 1648. Another Pallot ancestor, referred to as Dr. Pallot in Payn's *Armorial*, was Physician to Louis XIV of France. It is recorded in the *Lancet* of 2 January 1864 that, for curing the King's bout of malaria with a secret remedy, Dr. Pallot was rewarded with 48,000 *livres*, 2,000 *livres* for life and the grade of *chevalier*. Louis also ordered that the medicine, which was quinine, should be introduced into the pharmacopoeia.

During the late 18th and the 19th centuries many of the Pallot men were mariners and ship owners.

Nicholas Pallot (1793-1870) was variously, between 1825 and 1847, Master of *John, Charles, John and Mary* and *Queen*. He married Jeanne Le Sueur, lived at Les Landes, and their five sons John (b.1821), Clement (b.1827), Elias George (b.1829), Philip (b.1831) and Charles (b.1833) all went to sea. At times the brothers served on the same ships, which were family-owned, including *Ocean, Lavinia, Adelina, John and Mary, Eliza and Maria* and *C. T. Sutton*.

Clement and his brother Elias George married the Cantell sisters, Mary Elizabeth and Maria, and lived together at Weldon House, Faldouet and later at nearby Melbourne House. Clement owned a number of ships including *Bonny Mary* (149-ton schooner), *Ocean Queen* (149-ton brigantine), *Alexandra* (306-ton barque), *Britain's Pride* (178-ton brig), *Gemini* (426-ton barque) and *Morning Star* (178-ton brig). Elias was the master of the *Bonny Mary* and is recorded as having arrived at Bristol from Rio carrying 7,985 wet hides. His son, Captain Elias Nicholas, gained his master's

267 *The ship's bell of the* Iris *served as the farm bell at La Tourelle for many years.* Iris *was built in St Helier in 1820 and rated about 250 tons. Captain John Pallot commanded her on her last voyage as a Jersey registered ship to Bristol in 1869. (Courtesy of David Pallot)*

certificate at Plymouth and was on the *Eliza and Maria* trading to South America, until she was lost in a collision in September 1872. He then took command of the *Bonny Mary* until 1880 when he transferred to Cardiff steamships and was master of several vessels. The offspring of Elias and Clement also joined the Royal Navy and Mercantile Marine and variously settled in Cardiff, Canada and New Zealand.

Charles, the youngest brother, was also a master of *Bonny Mary* and then of the barque *Gemini*. In March 1866 he arrived at Bristol from Mauritius with 9,000 bags of sugar. He also voyaged to the west coast of South America, the West Indies and New York in 1868/9 with a crew of 14, 12 of whom were Jerseymen. He retired to live at Elm Bank on Gorey Pier as Autorisé (Harbourmaster) for Gorey Harbour from 1886 to 1901.

Nicholas' brother Jean (1797-1870) was also a mariner, Master of *Laurel* and *Traveller*. He and his wife Marie Le Seelleur had three sons: John(b.1821) who was Master and owner of *Queen* and of the schooner *Why Not?* (105 tons), built by Le Huquet at St Catherine, which in 1862 won the Round-the-Island race; Nicholas (b.1823) and Philip (b.1825) were both Masters as well. They served on, amongst others, *Morning Star, C. T. Sutton, Antelope, Souvenir, Regalia* and *Queen of the Isles*. Philip was owner of a number of vessels including the last named, an 80-ton ketch. The family also owned *St Catherine*, another race winner.

John Pallot, the eldest son of Nicholas and Jeanne left the sea and moved to La Tourelle in Faldouet to farm. His elder surviving son, John, became Connétable of St Martin in 1919. He was elected following the sudden death of the former Connétable, Charles Perchard, and served until 1926. The two families – the Perchards and the Pallots – intermarried. Horace, the eldest Perchard son, married Mabel, John Pallot's daughter, and Harold, the second and only surviving

268 *The wedding of Harold Pallot and Janet Maud Perchard at La Chasse, 19 April 1911*
Back row: Rodney Perchard, Garnet Perchard, Charles Billot
Middle row: John Pallot, Julia Le Huquet (née Pallot), Aunt Kate, Jack Le Huquet, Annie Le Huquet, Rev. Balleine, Louisa Billot, Horace Perchard, Philip Le Huquet, Josephine, Capt. Philippe Le Huquet.
Front row: Miss Valpy, Mary Anne Pallot (née Laffoley), Gertrude Billot (née Perchard), Harold Pallot, Janet Pallot (née Perchard), Charles Perchard, Jane Pallot (née Le Gros), Aunt Mary Ann, Mabel Perchard (née Pallot), Elise Pallot (née Perchard)
Children: Thomas Billot, Charles Billot

(Courtesy of Mary Lacey)

son of John, married Janet, the younger of Charles Perchard's two daughters, and they had five sons, all of whom served their country as officers in the army and navy throughout the Second World War. Two of them returned to St Martin to live; Colonel John to La Tourelle, which he and his wife Beatrice lovingly restored, and Colonel Norman to nearby La Chouquetterie.

Perchard

Jersey Place Names gives the derivation as 'a man from Perche in southern Normandy'. Associated place names in St Martin include Les Courtils de Perchard ès Mares (1615), La Pièce de Perchard (1663, 1675) and Le Clos Perchard (1701).

Philip Perchard is recorded as being a juryman in Trinity in 1331, and in 1527 Michael Perchard was Rector of St Saviour. The family tree of the St Martin branch, as far as it has been traced, starts with Jean c.1520, whose son, Gautier Perchard, married Thomasse Le Repossey from a branch of the Le Seelleur family. Their son Hugh (also spelt 'Hiou') was baptised at St Martin in 1565.

The family spread widely in the Parish and has been associated in marriage with many of the other long-established families: Noël (five instances), de Quetteville, Le Seelleur, Richardson, Marett and others. Jean Edouard (1819-1902) married three times and produced a large family. He held a pilot's licence for Jersey's east coast and many of his descendants also made their living at sea. His sons, Edouard and Francis, also held pilot's licences and the latter was lighthouse keeper and harbour pilot at Gorey. Another brother, Winter, was stationmaster there. Grandson John Edward (1875-1950) served for an extended period on Lord Brassey's world-girdling yacht, *Sunbeam*, thus becoming widely known as 'Sunbeam Jack'. Today, this branch of the family lives mostly in Gorey Village (Grouville) and is without male heirs.

269   A party of Perchards on Harold Robin's Try Again. *Colonel Dresser, 'Sunbeam' Jack and three of his Perchard uncles, Harold Robin. (Courtesy of Irene Morley)*

The late Sidney Perchard of Lower Gorey Hill was captain of the yacht *Teazer* and used to do much work taking parties to Les Écréhous. His family originated in Guernsey.

Charles Perchard was Connétable of St Martin 1901-19. He was the building contractor responsible for building the sea wall, slipway and roadway in the Bay of St Catherine in 1882 for £3,010 and the sea wall in the Bay of Fliquet in 1883 for £425. He was the father of Gertrude, who was married to Charles Phillipe Billot, later Connétable, and Janet, who was married to Harold Pallot of La Tourelle. Rodney George, his youngest son, went to sea and ended his career as assistant harbourmaster of Montreal, Canada during the Second World War.

The Perchards now living at La Chasse, Rue des Cabarettes, and La Ferme, Rozel, originate in St Saviour.

William George of La Chasse (1909-1999), was a Deputy and Senator of the States for a period of 12 years and subsequently president of the Royal Jersey Agricultural and Horticultural Society for six years. His famous 'Keeper' strain of cattle won many Island championships in the years following the Second World War. Colin Perchard OBE, CVO, his elder son, is with the British Council and has held senior posts in many countries.

Renouf

The first Renouf identified as being from St Martin is Renauld, who was buried there in January 1640. By the 18th century, the family was well represented in the parish. Nicholas Renouf (1788-1867) served as a constable's officer.

There were a number of marriages between different branches of the family. In 1861 William Charles Renouf married Amelia Renouf. In due course, they had a daughter, Medora Amelia, who married Thomas George Renouf. William Charles (1840-1918) was a general merchant at

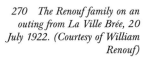

270   The Renouf family on an outing from La Ville Brée, 20 July 1922. (Courtesy of William Renouf)

Highlands, near Rozel Mill. It is apparent that he prospered as he bought a property at Ville Brée from George Noël. His descendants still farm in the same locality today.

271 *19th-century butter stamp of Elie Whitley, St Martin. (Courtesy of Cynthia Binet)*

Whitley

The first of the Whitleys came to Jersey in 1651 in Admiral Blake's fleet. He joined the Mont Orgueil garrison and died in 1674 and was buried in St Martin's cemetery. The family acquired land at Haie Fleurie: there is also a Chasse Fleurie and a Côtil Whitley near St Catherine's Breakwater.

A stone salting trough has the inscription EW 1790 and there is a datestone on the west end of the house, 18 EW ELH 05, which records Elie Whitley and his wife Elizabeth Le Huquet. The last of the Whitleys to live at Haie Fleurie was another Elie (this name is common in all branches of the family), who died in 1930. The property then passed to his sister Ann, from her to her nephew, John Whitley Starck, and thence to his niece, Kathleen Binet (née Nicolle), who has now lived there for nearly 80 years. Mrs.

Binet was aged five and living at Diélament when her mother died. She remembers well her journey to Haie Fleurie in the bread van of the Vardon sisters of Rozel Mill.

Elie Whitley was awarded the Royal National Lifeboat Institution Silver Medal for rescuing the crew and passengers of the Danish vessel *Isabella Northcote*, which was wrecked on Les Écréhous in November 1872. Elie, Charles Blampied and another made two trips in an open rowing boat, 'in a strong westerly gale and a heavy sea'. The certificate cites his 'extraordinary perseverance and gallant conduct in putting off a distance of several miles in a small boat'.

One of the family treasures is a sampler made by 'Anne Susan Whitly [*sic*] aged 8 1839'. This is a work of high quality for one so young and features Adam and Eve.

272 *Sampler stitched by Ann Susan Whitley in 1839. (Courtesy of Kathleen Binet)*

The Reverend George Whitley (1872-1964) was brought up at Haie Fleurie and his memories of youth are detailed in Chapter 15. He was a Methodist preacher of some prominence and travelled extensively.

Appendix 1
GEOLOGICAL TABLES

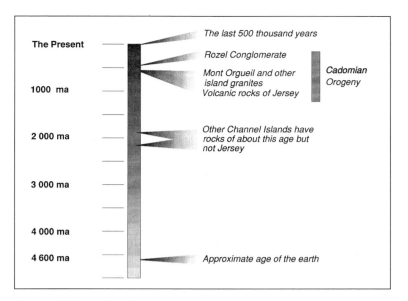

The Present — The last 500 thousand years

Rozel Conglomerate

Mont Orgueil and other
island granites
Volcanic rocks of Jersey

Cadomian
Orogeny

1000 ma

2 000 ma — Other Channel Islands have
rocks of about this age but
not Jersey

3 000 ma

4 000 ma

4 600 ma — Approximate age of the earth

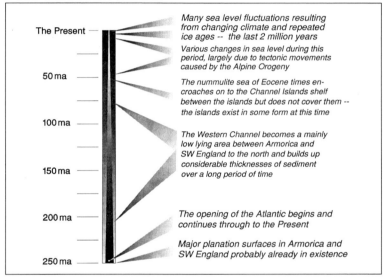

The Present — Many sea level fluctuations resulting
from changing climate and repeated
ice ages -- the last 2 million years

Various changes in sea level during this
period, largely due to tectonic movements
caused by the Alpine Orogeny

50 ma

The nummulite sea of Eocene times en-
croaches on to the Channel Islands shelf
between the islands but does not cover them --
the islands exist in some form at this time

100 ma

The Western Channel becomes a mainly
low lying area between Armorica and
SW England to the north and builds up
considerable thicknesses of sediment
over a long period of time

150 ma

200 ma — The opening of the Atlantic begins and
continues through to the Present

Major planation surfaces in Armorica and
SW England probably already in existence

250 ma

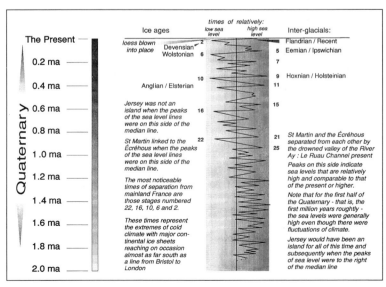

341

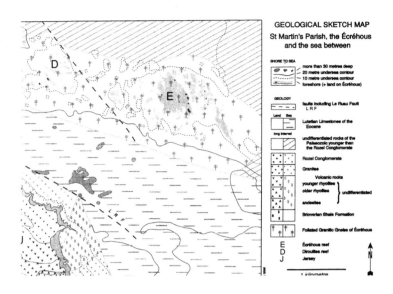

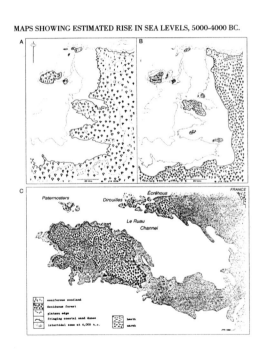

MAPS SHOWING ESTIMATED RISE IN SEA LEVELS, 5000–4000 BC.

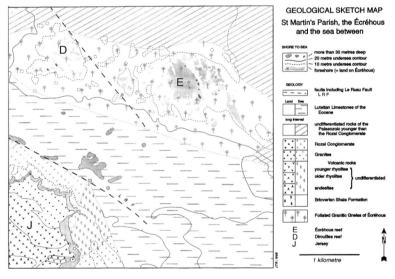

Appendix 2

THE CONNÉTABLES OF ST MARTIN

1490-96	Jean Nicolle	1752-56	Thomas Syvret
1528	Philippe Payn	1756-61	Elie de Quetteville
1531-36	Edmond Perrin	1761-70	Nicolas Richardson
1539	Philippe Payn	1770-73	Elie de Quetteville
1541-47	John Messervy	1773-79	Philippe Collas
1547-51	Thomas Le Hardy	1779-82	Nicolas Richardson
1551-53	Henry Mallet	1784-90	Philippe Collas
1553	Edouard Crafford	1790-93	Nicolas Richardson
1553-60	Servais Nicolle	1793-99	Philippe Nicolle
1560-80	Clement Dumaresq	1799-08	George Bertram
1584-86	John Gray	1808-11	Jean Mallett
1586-87	François Le Maistre	1811-14	Philippe Godfray
1587-97	Edmond de Quetteville	1815-21	George Bertram
1597-16	Edouard Payn	1821-25	Jean Nicolle
1616-29	Abraham Payn	1825-34	Philippe Godfray
1629-32	Philippe Dumaresq	1835-41	Francis Godfray
1632-41	Thomas Le Maistre	1841-44	Thomas Messervy
1641-47	Abraham Payn	1844-62	Chefs de Police*: George Gaudin, George Sohier,
1647-51	Abraham Le Maistre		Edouard Elie Le Sauteur, George Asplet
1652-55	Thomas Bandinel	1862-65	Edouard Le Huquet
1655-56	Clement Dumaresq	1865-77	Thomas William Messervy
1657-60	Jean Nicolle	1877-80	Philippe Amy jnr.
1660-66	Abraham Le Maistre	1880-83	Reginald Raoul Lemprière
1666-74	David Bandinel	1883-86	Frédéric Nicolle de Quetteville
1674-91	Philippe Richardson	1886-01	Frédéric Richardson Le Brun
1691-94	George Bandinel	1901-19	Charles Perchard
1694-97	Thomas Lemprière	1919-26	John Pallot
1697-04	George de la Garde	1926-35	Thomas Renouf de Gruchy
1704-07	Thomas Lemprière	1935-49	Charles Philip Billot
1707-08	David Bandinel	1949-50	Thomas Raymond de Gruchy
1708-14	Thomas Lemprière	1950-63	Henry Ahier
1714-17	George de la Gard	1963-72	Thomas George Billot
1717-20	Thomas Lemprière	1972-81	George Rive Le Masurier
1720-21	James Corbet jnr	1981-87	Winter Chevalier de Gruchy
1721-23	George Bandinel	1987-94	Stanley John de la Haye
1723-31	Abraham Richardson	1994-	John Baudains Germain
1731-52	Clement Richardson		

* On 10 December 1844, an election for the office of Connétable was held between Thomas Messervy and Thomas Laffoley. Messervy polled 177 votes to Laffoley's 140, but the latter protested that there had been irregularities. He claimed that a 'considerable number' of voters should not have been included in the rate list as electors, others were not old enough to vote, and that Messervy had employed bribery and threats to induce electors to vote for him and to keep Laffoley's supporters away from the election. The Royal Court's Inferior Number heard the case in January 1845, but after much legal argument on formalities-some of it bordering on the absurd-the Court refused to hear Laffoley's witnesses. He then appealed to the Court's Superior Number, but they upheld the lower Court's judgment. Laffoley was determined not to let the matter rest there, and he gave notice of appeal to the young Queen Victoria's Privy Council. While this was going on, Messervy was unable to take his oath as Connétable, and so the parish was effectively run by the various Chefs de Police for nearly 18 years. In March 1862 Laffoley was granted leave to abandon his appeal and his claim and this left Messervy free to take the oath of office, but by this time Messervy was an old man and the Royal Court excused him from taking the oath and ordered a fresh election.

ST MARTIN HONORARY POLICE

Officers, 1887-1999 – from the Parish Records

CENTENIERS

Philip Cabot	1887	Thomas George Billot	1953-63
Josué Francis snr	1887	Walter Herbert de la Mare	1958-72
Charles Ahier	1887-99	John Dorey Germain	1971-81
Charles Perchard	1887-92	George Rive Le Masurier	1962-72
John Pallot	1893-98	Winter Chevalier de Gruchy	1971-81
George Journeaux jnr	1893-1904	Stanley John de la Haye	1972-87
Winter John Philip Proper	1900-04	Francis John Lucas	1976-85
John Sidney Le Gresley	1905-20	John Baudains Germain	1981-94
John George Pallot	1905-20	Maurice Lees	1985-98
Philip Ahier	1920-29	Silvanus Arthur Yates	1987-91
Charles Philip Billot	1920-29	David Alexander Thelland	1991-94
Charles P. Journeaux	1929-46	Nelson George Le Cornu	1994-
Clifford George Pallot	1929-46	John Gerard Poole	1997-
Henry Ahier	1946-50	Sarah Julie Frank	1998-
John Noel Germain	1946-55	Maurice Gotel	1998-
John William Messervy	1950-58		

VINGTENIERS AND CONSTABLE'S OFFICERS 1949-1999

VINGTAINE DE ROZEL

VINGTENIERS

Thomas G. Billot	1945-53	Nelson G. Renouf	1953-58
John D. Germain	1958-63	Gerald A. Richardson	1963-82
Alan L. Barette	1982-	William C. Renouf	1982-91
Clifford G. Pallot	1991-		

CONSTABLE'S OFFICERS

John T. Le Seelleur	1938-58	John N. Germain	1943-46
Kenneth G. Richardson	1943-55	George R. Slade	1946-55
Nelson G. Renouf	1931-55	Clifford W. Renouf	1953-76
John G. Germain	1955-58	Gerald A. Richardson	1955-63
Winter C. de Gruchy	1958-71	Richard O. Norman	1958-64
Denys P. Renouf	1963-76	Garnet J. Perchard	1964-80
John B. Germain	1971-83	Alan L. Barette	1976-82
William C. Renouf	1976-82	Sydney J. Payn	1980-83
Clifford G. Pallot	1982-91	Graham M. de Gruchy	1982-91
Peter F. Blampied	1982-94	David A. Thelland	1990-91
Thomas R. Channing	1991-94	Colin S. de la Haye	1991-
John B. Dingle	1995-96	Desmond A. Dunne	1995-97
James J. Young	1997-	Alan Phillips	1997-

VINGTAINE DE FALDOUET

VINGTENIERS

John W. Messervy	1946-50	George Le Masurier	1950-69
Francis J. Lucas	1969-77	Gerald G. Richardson	1977-83
Francis W. Tadier	1983-92	Richard J. Farrow	1992-95
Maurice F. Gotel	1995-		

CONSTABLE'S OFFICERS

Sydney R. Perchard	1933-58	Wilfred P. Le Seelleur	1931-64
George Le Masurier	1943-52	Walter H. de la Mare	1946-58
Raymond J. le Gresley	1952-66	Arthur J. Le Boutillier	1958-64
Francis J. Lucas	1961-69	Laurence R. J. Labey	1964-68
Neill A. Ohlssen	1964-68	Harold G. Perchard	1966-73
Charles P. Richomme	1968-74	Gerald G. Richardson	1968-77
Herbert A. de la Mare	1969-85	John W. Le Seelleur	1970-86
John A. Crosby	1973-81	Robert J. Messervy	1980-92
Francis W. Tadier	1982-83	Michael A. Richecoeur	1983-89
Roy N. Smith	1985-	Peter E. Sangan	1986-92
Barry F. Maindonald	1989-92	Maurice F. Gotel	1993-95
Malcolm S. Noel	1993-	Stuart D. McAlister	1993-
Julie Frank	1995-97		

VINGTAINE DE LA QUÉRUÉE

VINGTENIERS

William G. Perchard	1942-55	George R. le Masurier	1955-62
Thomas R. de Gruchy	1962-81	Harold J. de Gruchy	1981-90
Michael O. Stevens	1990-		

CONSTABLE'S OFFICERS

George R. Le Masurier	1943-55	Charles W. Gilbert	1943-52
Frederick G. Dorey	1952-58	Thomas R. de Gruchy	1955-62
Stanley J. de la Haye	1958-72	Harold J. de Gruchy	1962-81
Harold C. Noel	1972-85	John A. Burns	1981-90
Michael O. Stevens	1985-91	John G. Poole	1990-95
Stanley J. M. Perchard	1991-94	Michael D. Blampied	1994-
Judith M. Gindill	1995-		

VINGTAINE DE L'ÉGLISE

VINGTENIERS

John T. Amy	1945-61	John N. Richard	1961-64
Leslie T. Le Seelleur	1964-73	Percy G. Baudains	1973-79
John R. Renouf	1979-85	Laurence Barette	1985-88
Nelson G. Le Cornu	1988-94	Stanley J. Perchard	1994-97
Desmond A. Dunne	1997-		

CONSTABLE'S OFFICERS

John N. Richard	1946-61	Leslie T. Le Seelleur	1961-64
Percy G. Baudains	1964-73	John R. Renouf	1973-79
Laurence Barette	1979-85	Nelson G. Le Cornu	1985-88
Jason P. Laffoley	1988-91	George K. Borg	1991-

VINGTAINE DE LA FIEF DE LA REINE

VINGTENIERS

Percy G. Robins	1936-67	Ulric V. Noel	1967-79
John J. Marett	1979-83	Douglas E. Huelin	1983-89
John N. Brée	1989-95	Michael B. Le Couteur	1995-

CONSTABLE'S OFFICERS

Ulric V. Noel	1946-67	Michael J. Kempster	1967-70
Raymond L. Le Cornu	1970-73	John J. Marett	1973-80
Douglas E. Huelin	1980-83	John N. Brée	1983-89
Richard J. Farrow	1989-92	Michael B. Le Couteur	1992-95
Charles S. Hornby	1995-		

DEPUTIES OF ST MARTIN

	Elected
James Godfray	1857
François Charles Gruchy	1872
Philippe George Gaudin	1875
Thomas William Messervy	1878
Thomas Gaudin	1890
Josué François Noel	1895
Charles William Binet	1898
George Journeaux	1905
John Pallot	1914
Edward Slade	1920
Charles Philip Billot	1929
Philip Ahier	1936
Edward Slade	1946
John Noel Germain	1953
David Charles Le Seelleur	1957
Charles Philip Billot	1963
Brigadier Raoul Charles Lemprière-Robin, O.B.E.	1969
Helen Baker	1978
Henri Leon Dubras	1984
Terence Ahier Jehan	1990
Frederick John Hill, B.E.M.	1993

On 6 November 1856 the States passed an Act adding 14 elected Deputies to the Assembly, one for each parish and three for St Helier.

The first sitting of the States with the new Deputies was held on 29 January 1857.

The Slade and Billot families have the distinction of having had both a father and son serving as Deputy.

John Pallot and Charles Philippe Billot both served as Deputy before becoming Connétable.

Thomas William Messervy served as Connétable for 12 years before becoming Deputy, in which office he served a further 12 years.

THE RECTORS OF ST MARTIN

1195	Robert Le Hougue
1196-1208	Robert Florie
1208-1242	Thomas de Vauville
1242	Thomas de la Hougue
1295	Geoffroy de Carteret (became Dean in 1315)
1299	Thomas de Ausses (was still Rector in 1309)
1346	Johan de Hamelton
1348	Richard Corbyn
1349	Pierre Malecovenant
1371-1374	William de Gerlethorpe
1374	Thomas de Riby
1414	Peter Amnener
1432-1463	Thomas Le Hardy
1494	Jean du Val (Dean)
1495-1500	Pierre Le Penec
1500-1505	Guillaume Nicolson
1505-1508	Thomas Coubray
1509	Nicolas l'Evesque (Dean)
1514-1543	Richard Mabon (Dean)
1550	Clement Gosselin
1550-1553	Charles Mabson
1553-1565	John Poulet (Dean)
1566	Thomas Johanne
1574-1583	Pierre Henry dit Dangy
1587-1628	Helier Faultrart
1629-1645	David Bandinel (Dean)
1645-1660	Pierre d'Assigny
1661-1671	Philippe Le Couteur (Dean)
1672-1706	François Le Couteur (brother of the Dean)
1708-1717	François Le Couteur (son of his predecessor)
1717-1765	François Le Couteur (Vice-Dean; son of his predecessor)
1765-1775	François Payn (Dean)
1776-1789	François Le Couteur (nephew of François Le Couteur 1717/65)
1789-1798	Philippe de La Garde
1799-1818	Charles Le Touzel
1818-1829	George Bertram (Vice-Dean)
1829-1856	George Balleine
1856-1875	Philippe Guille
1875-1901	Thomas Le Neveu
1901-1917	George Philip Balleine
1917-1941	Reginald Le Sueur
1941-1947	(During the German Occupation, Canon John Russell Wilford was Ministre Desservant)
1947-1959	Edward Cecil Lemprière
1960	William Kilshaw (Ministre Desservant)
1960-1961	Ernest William Rendell Guymer
1962-1981	Franklin Osmond Brackley (Vice-Dean)
1981-1982	Arthur Charles Granger (Ministre Desservant)
1982-	Lawrence John Turner

N.B.   When only one date is given, the man mentioned is known to have been Rector in that year, but the dates of his appointment and retirement are unknown.

THE INCUMBENTS OF ST MARTIN'S CHURCH, GOURAY

CHAPLAINS

1834	J. Gallichan	1837	W. Hamond
1839	C.D. Robinson	1848	G. Poingdestre
1850	J. Le Maistre	1857	A. Bibby
1874	F.W. Foster	1875	E. Luce
1877	J. Hammond	1877	L.W. Strong
1879	A.G. Hogg Harding	1880	F. Cardon
1881	C.M. Godfray	1885	C.W. Sillifant
1886	H.R. Holme	1887	J.F. Harris
1887	R.W. Hamilton	1893	R.D. Grindley
1895	W. Cotes	1895	A.J. Abbey
1896	O.T. Bulkeley	1898	C.W.H. Connelly

VICARS

1900	C.W.H. Connolly	1908	R.D.D. Love
1929	E.S. Collins	1930	C.M. Turnell
1939	S.R. Knapp	1966	C.L. Penn
1972	P.G. Newby		

PRIESTS IN CHARGE

1978	J.D. Dodd	1994	L.W. Matthews

THE SHIPBUILDERS OF GOREY AND ST CATHERINE

ST CATHERINE

Edward Le Huquet

Vessel Name	Tonnage	Rig	Date	Owner
Ann & Eliza	10	Cutter	1836	Whitley & Co.
Ann & Eliza			1842	Le Huquet & Whitley
Bellona	100	Schooner	1837	P.Vardon & Co.
Ebenezer	13	Cutter	1875	Le Gros & Co.
Freedom	50	Cutter	1852	Bisson & Le Couteur
Hebe			1874	Du Fresne & Bellot
Jane	8	Cutter	1875	P. Renault
Joseph & William	18	Cutter	1842	T. de la Mare
Larch	12	Cutter	1828	T. de la Mare
Laurel	16	Cutter	1824	J. Le Huquet & Co.
Napier	12	Cutter	1841	C. Aubin
Nelson			1841	E. Le Huquet & Co.
Rolla	164	Brig	1839	Giraudot & Miller
Swan			1840	Baudains & De Garis
Thetis	22	Cutter	1840	F. Du Fresne
Tom & Mary	60	Schooner	1846	Le Huquet & Filleul

J. & T. Le Huquet

Vessel Name	Tonnage	Rig	Date	Owner
Alzina			1876	Perchard & Co.
Arcana	29	Cutter	1848	T. Stevens
Atlas	29	Cutter	1851	Godfray & Le Gros
Blanche	33	Cutter	1854	Philip Messervy
Britain's Pride	182	Brig	1858	C. Pallot & Co.
Caroline K. Ferrer	4	Cutter	1851	G. Asplet
Ceres			1841	J. Le Huquet
Chance			1872	F. Mollet
Comet	80	Cutter	1853	H. Noel & Co.
Crown	42	Cutter	1863	J. Messervy
Czarina	55	Schooner	1874	J. Pascoe
Daring	60	Cutter	1868	G. Asplet & C. Le Quesne
Eclair	69	Cutter	1856	J. Barbier
Enchantress	45	Schooner	1875	F. Mollet
Escape	183	Brig	1861	G.N. Le Quesne
Fawn	26	Cutter	1858	Jury & Williamson
Fearless	14	Cutter	1844	F. Du Fresne & Co.
First	51	Cutter	1853	Blampied & Arthur
Fleetwing	38	Cutter	1859	F.J. Mollet
Flying Foam	160	Schooner	1879	P. Noël
Friend of the Isle	47	Ketch	1852	T. Cabot
Graphic	60	Schooner	1874	Le Huquet & Co.
Hydra	52	Cutter	1852	George Noël
Louisa	60	Cutter	1859	G. Asplet
Mistletoe	60	Schooner	1876	J. Le Gros
Orient			1859	C. Le Sueur & Co.
Progress	69	Schooner	1877	F. Mollet
Resolute	76	Schooner	1877	G. Noël
Rifle	41	Ketch	1860	C. Pirouet

Royal	35	Cutter	1856	Pascoe & Le Huquet
Secret			1850	C. But
Snowdrop	149	Brig	1873	J. Le Masurier & Co.
St Catherine	107	Schooner	1877	C. Pallot
St Martin	46	Cutter	1854	R.R. Lemprière
St Saviour	36	Cutter	1864	Joshue & Le Jeune
Surprise	49	Ketch	1858	Newman & Williams
Swallow			1859	C. Le Sueur & Co.
Traveller	60	Schooner	1846	T. Renouf & Co.
Unity	23	Cutter	1870	Day & Le Seelleur
Waverley	80	Schooner	1873	F. Mollet
Why Not	105	Schooner	1862	L. Pallot

Clement Richardson

Brisk	105	Cutter	1845	Richardson & Renouf
Iris			1844	Dorey & de la Mare
Jason	21	Cutter	1845	J. Le Huquet
Lively			1842	C. Richardson
Susan				C. Richardson

Vardon & Le Huquet

Bellona	100	Schooner	1837	J. Perrée
John & Mary	50	Cutter	1851	Pallot & Co.
Mars	288	Barque	1839	J. Pellier
Penelope	134	Brig	1840	Huelin & Le Feuvre
Rolla	165	Brig	1839	Giraudot & Miller
Swan	54	Schooner	1841	Baudains & de Garis
Welcome	120	Brig	1840	J. Godfray

GOREY

George Asplet

Onward	199	Schooner	1850	Henry Hoskins
Freedom	78	Schooner	1850	Gallichan & Noel
Annie	260	Barque	1860	Austin & Co.
Jeffrey	70	Schooner	1860	Thomas Lavan
Montrose	265	Barque	1861	Scrutton & Co.
Vivid	102	Schooner		George Asplet

Charles W. Aubin

Alvina	57	Schooner	1874	Philip Payn
Belladonna	69	Schooner	1877	P. Le Gresley
C.E.C.B.	47	Cutter	1859	C. Cotgrove
Columbine	35	Cutter	1877	Cole & Colman
Design	66	Ketch	1874	Philip Payn
Emma Jane	55	Dandy	1872	J. Le Gros
Excelsior	92	Cutter	1875	R. Foster
Gorey Lass	49	Dandy	1868	J.M. Kent
Lady of the Isles	44	Dandy	1865	Philip Payn
Lizzie	50	Cutter	1875	
London	59	Dandy	1867	Aubin & Le Seelleur
Lydia	40	Cutter	1870	W. Wright

Matje	50	Schooner	1876	
Mermaid	53	Ketch	1869	J.G. Pascoe
Nellie	80	Ketch	1873	E. Seager
Prairie Flower	56	Schooner	1877	Arms & Aubin
Prince	44	Dandy	1867	Aubin, Richmond & Le Seelleur
Rapid	52	Cutter	1856	Philip Payn
Red Gauntlet	74	Schooner	1876	J. Adams
Saucy Lass	38	Cutter	1870	Harvey & Stacey
Sea Nymph	56	Schooner	1877	Arms & Aubin
Seabird	70	Schooner	1873	F.G. Renouf

Philip Bellot

Advance	229	Brig	1858	George Asplet
Agricola	50	Ketch	1871	Cantell & Co.
Albatross	70	Schooner	1872	J. Wright
Bonny Mary	149	Brigantine	1854	Clement Pallot
Camelia	68	Schooner	1876	
Castella	77	Schooner	1876	P. Le Masurier
Chagamau	83	Cutter	1878	Charles Robin & Co.
Challenger	55	Ketch	1878	Charles Robin & Co.
Charlotte	108	Schooner	1874	Cantell & Co.
Excellent	70	Ketch	1868	E. Seager
Fanny	43	Ketch	1855	J.C. Cartwright
Gazelle	59	Ketch	1873	J. Moses
Gauntlet	52	Ketch	1875	J.C. Renouf
Hernhutt	34	Cutter	1871	P. Wheeler
Laurite	69	Schooner	1866	W. Downing
Lucinda	59	Schooner	1869	Downing & Morrisey
Milton	140	Brigantine	1853	Gallichan & Noël
Orient Star	102	Schooner	1872	P. Cabot
Racer	59	Ketch	1859	Charles Whitley
Rambler	83	Schooner	1875	Charles Whitley
Willing	100	Schooner	1858	B.J. Cantell
Zephyr	148	Schooner	1855	J.B. Falle

John Messervy

Engineer	65	Schooner	1864	F. Le Feuvre
Express	56	Dandy	1862	Le Gros & Gallichan
Flying Cloud	70	Schooner	1863	John Buhts
Honour	36	Cutter	1861	Hamon & Le Gros
Isabel	42	Cutter	1858	Cantell & Co.
Jane & Mary	54	Ketch	1865	Gavey & McKeown
John & Eliza	140	Brigantine	1857	J. Messervy
Lily of the Valley	54	Dandy	1864	Cantell & Co.
London	68	Cutter	1854	Renouf & Co.
Morning Star	51	Dandy	1859	Messervy & Pallot
Morning Star	47	Cutter	1861	Cantell & Co.

Francis Picot

Active	30	Ketch	1854	Charles Whitley
Agile	88	Schooner	1874	G. de Ste Croix
Angela	7	Yacht	1883	

Aura	94	Schooner	1872	John Fauvel
Bride	24	Yawl	1877	J.A. Laws
Bud	47	Cutter	1852	F. Hamon & Co.
Conqueror	69	Schooner	1875	J. Blampied
Dolphin	54	Schooner	1862	T. Renouf
Donna Maria	84	Schooner	1875	W. Pickford
Eclipse	59	Schooner	1879	Picot
Emily	40	Cutter	1859	J. Swain
Fairwater	64	Ketch	1877	Kent & Baker
Forest Girl	66	Cutter	1863	J. Young
Forest Lad	63	Ketch	1865	George Wheeler
Flying Fish	74	Schooner	1878	Picot & Cole
Gazelle	224	Brig	1864	Le Gallais & Le Gros
Gypsy King	33	Cutter	1857	J. Bennewith
Hero	67	Ketch	1872	C. Whitley
Island Queen	48	Dandy	1868	L. Godfray
Laura	30	Cutter	1879	J. Swain
Lily	23	Cutter	1871	Delapine & Lafolley
Louisa Jane	49	Dandy	1861	Le Couteur, Gallichan & Woods
Main	33	Cutter	1860	W. Wright
Ocean Branch	59	Cutter	1858	George Wheeler
Ocean Bride	47	Cutter	1858	Philip Wheeler
Ocean Pet	74	Schooner	1876	W. Pickford
Pallas	62	Ketch	1871	Cantell & Co.
Queen	60	Cutter	1876	P.E. Guille
Queen of the Isles	81	Ketch	1873	Philip Pallot
Regalia	46	Ketch	1872	Picot, Pallot & Frith
Regina	59	Schooner	1866	H.P. Frith
Reward	30	Cutter	1879	J. Swain
Royal Arch	46	Ketch	1866	F. Picot
Silver Cloud	82	Schooner	1873	Cantell & Kent
Standard	67	Ketch	1867	S.P. Wright
Stormbird	113	Schooner	1852	J. Le Boeuf
Susan	65	Ketch	1875	W. Swain
Swan	59	Schooner	1875	G. Balleine
Sultan	65	Ketch	1867	Pallot & Gavey
Triumph	81	Ketch	1874	P.J. Le Huquet
Union	193	Brig	1865	Charles Robin & Co.
Volant	52	Dandy	1867	A. Anderson
Welsh Girl	65	Schooner	1868	Larman & Paskins
Winifred	44	Cutter	1883	P. Bailhache & Co.

Jean Vardon

Antagonist	50	Cutter	1855	Esnouf & Mauger
Bliss	32	Cutter	1845	Philip Jeune
Commander	120	Schooner	1845	J. Dorey
Elizabeth Taylor	180	Schooner	1845	J. Taylor
Emerald	52	Schooner	1846	J. Renouf
Emperor	58	Cutter	1847	Le Couteur & Bisson
Freedom	47	Cutter	1847	G. Asplet
General Don	40	Cutter	1844	J. Fauvel
Governor	59	Cutter	1847	Bertram & Noël
Handy	59	Cutter	1846	Drélaud & Anley

Appendix 8
ST MARTIN MARINERS

Compiled by John Jean

Name	Baptised	Dates as Master	Notes
AHIER, Thomas Amice	1815	1851-1870	Master of *Ant*.
AHIER, Thomas	1794	1836-	
AMY, George			Lived at 2 Union Place, Gorey 1898-1909.
AMY, John	Grouville		Lived at La Vallette, Gorey 1861-70. Master of *Zephyr* 1864, *Circassian* 1869-73.
ASPLET, Charles	1823		Master in Massachussets c.1840.
ASPLET, Thomas	1819		Lived at La Vallette, Gorey 1855-68.
AUBIN Francois	1823		Lived at Clare Vale 1849-65.
AUBIN, John	1773		Master of lugger *Plymouth* 1798.
BANDINEL, F.			Master of *Mary Ann* 1764.
BANDINEL, Thomas			Master of *Peggy* 1790.
BAUDINS, Philip			Master of small vessel at Chausey.
BELLOT		1791-1794	
BELLOT, Elie			Mate on *Minerva* 1832.
BELLOT, Francis	1797	1823-1836	Master of *Experiment* 1831, *Young Peggy* 1823.
BILLOT, Elias	1787	1808-1851	Murdered, found in St Helier Harbour.
BILLOT, Frederick George	1860		Lost when S.S. *Euterpe* was mined.
BILLOT, Francis	1817	1852-1868	
BILLOT, Philip			Master of *Jenny* 1790 on voyage to Newfoundland
BONNEL, John	1836		Master of *Diamant* 1859.
BRAND, William John	1822 (Essex)	1859-1874	Lived St Martin 1851. Master of *Isabella & Jane* 1859.
BUTT, Edward	1820 (Isle of Wight)		Uncle of Dame Clara Butt, opera singer. Master of *Victory* 1852.
BUTT, Henry Albert	1848	1844-1884	Master of *Osprey* 1848, *Crystal* 1874.
CABOT, Noé	1765		Master of conger fishing boat.
CANTELL, Alfred George	1842	1863-1874	Lived St Martin c.1851.
CANTELL, Francis John	1832 (Southampton)	1856-1868	Lived *British Hotel*, Gorey c.1866.
CANTELL, George John	1840	1861-1899	Lived St Martin c.1851. Master of *Willing* 1868, *Owney Belles* and *Telegraph* 1899. Died 1911.
CANTELL, John	1806 (England)	1861-1870	Lived in St Martin c.1851.
CARDY, Derek James	1851		Lived Gorey Harbour 1899-1910. Died in Fife, Scotland.
CARTWRIGHT, Joseph	1845		Master of *Fanny* 1870. Widow kept Cartwright's Tavern on Gorey Pier.
CHEVALIER, Charles	1804		Lived in St Martin 1851. Master of *Enterprise*.
CHEVALIER, Louis John	1844	1868-1869	
CLARKE, Frederick	1852		Died 1896, buried in St Martin.
CLARKE, Thomas Barry	1815 (Cowes)	1856-1871	Master of *Lalla Rookh* 1860. Lived in St Martin c.1851.
DAVEY, James	1818 (Essex)	1861-1868	Lived in St Martin.
DAVEY, Mark	1839		Lost without trace *en voyage* Newfoundland to Jersey.
DAVEY, Robert	1802		Master of *Mary Ellen* 1836, *Virginia* 1842-48. Lived in St Martin 1836-48.
DAVEY, William	1848	1892-1916	
DE GRUCHY, John Walter	1838	1869-	Lived in St Martin.
DE GRUCHY, Philip	1834	1860-1878	Lost with ship 1878.
DE GRUCHY, Philip George	1877	1909	Lived in Le Catel, Rozel.
DE LA MARE, Jean			Lived in St Martin. Master of a conger boat at Chausey.
DE LA MARE, Thomas	1800	1827-1854	

DICKENSON, John	1816	1836-1856	Lived in St Martin c.1851. Drowned with vessel 1856.
DOREY, George	1842	1864-1868	Born in Trinity. Lived Les Bottes, St Martin.
DOWNER, Alfred Philip	1845		Lived Archirondel Farm. Died 1927, buried in St Martin cemetery.
DOWNER, John F.	1842	1861-1870	Lived at Archirondel Farm.
DU FRESNE, Francis	1816	1853-1861	Died 1861.
ERITH, Henry Philip	1832	1859-1874	Died 1904, buried Les Croix cemetery Grouville. Master of *Regina* 1866, *Regalia* 1872.
FALLE, George Nelson	1838	1868-	Lived St Martin.
FEREY, Philip	1813	1847-1868	
GALLICHAN, Frederick		1867-	Lived St Martin.
GALLICHAN, Thomas			Drowned Rozel Bay 1887.
GAUDIN, James	1839	1864-1870	Lived at Le Câtillon. Died 1884 in USA.
GAUTIER, William	1914		Lived at Les Landes, St Martin. Master of SS *Achibster*, c.1914.
GERMAIN, Noé	1639		Master and owner of a vessel at Rozel.
GODFRAY, Hugh	1794	1826-1835	Son of Hugh.
GODFRAY, John Charles	1794	1835-1836	Son of Philip. Master of *Cerus*.
HOUGET, François	1823		Lived St Martin. Mate 1881-82.
JEUNE, Herbert P.			Son of G.M. Jeune of La Croix, St Martin. Chief Officer of *Colombo Maro* 1904.
JEUNE, Jean	1814	1830-	
JEUNE, John	1857	1877-1882	Lived Hilgrove Terrace, Gorey.
JEUNE, Philip	1802	1838-1869	
JOURNEAUX, Thomas	1831	Mate 1866-68.	
KENT, Edward Thomas	1829 (Portsmouth)	1855-1861	Lived in Gorey 1851-85. Married Charlotte Rachel Cantell.
KENT, George	1815 (Portsmouth)	1857-1864	Lived in St Martin 1851-91.
KENT, John	1815 (Portsmouth)	1859-1868	Lived in St Martin. Twin of above?
KENT, Matthew John	1810 (Portsea)	1846-1865	Lived in St Martin.
KENT, Matthew John (Junior)	1833 (Portsmouth)	1857-1865	Lived in St Martin.
LAFFOLEY, John Joseph Clement	1831	1859-1861	Lived at Dudley House, Faldouet 1850-98. Master of *Take Care* and *Voyageur*.
LE BASTARD, Jean			Master of *Ebenezer* 1826.
LE BOUTILLIER, Charles			Lived in St Martin 1836-51, Master of *John* 1836, *Nameless* 1840, *Ipswich* 1849, *Voyageur* 1851.
LE BRETON, Francis André	1794	1826-71	Lived at Railway Lodge 1871.
LE COCQ, Charles	1876		Mate 1890-1903. In 1956 still fishing from Rozel aged 80.
LE COCQ, Thomas	1834	1861	
LE COCQ, Thomas	1874	1892-1931	Lived at Les Butieres, Faldouet
LE FOUR, George	1846	1870-1875	Lived Gorey until 1885. Married Mary Louisa Tardiff.
LE FOUR, Samuel	1809	1847-1868	Lived St Martin. Master of *Samuel and Mary* 1848.
LE FOUR, Samuel	1829	1862-1868	Lived St Martin.
LE GROS, Daniel	1802	1836-1874	Son of Jean. Master of *Laurel* 1836, *Mary Jane* 1847-55.
LE GROS, John	1823	1861-1883	Lived at Spring Villa, Faldouet.
LE GROS, Jean	1799	1836-1850	Drowned 1850.
LE HUQUET, Abraham John	1838	1868-1874	Master *Cornucopia* and *Orient Star*.
LE HUQUET, Edward	1810	1847-1863	Died at Sussex Lodge, Faldouet, 1896.
LE HUQUET, Jean	1764	1793-1826	Married Susanne Godfray. Died 1831, buried St Martin cemetery.
LE HUQUET, John	1850		Died 1907, buried St Martin cemetery.

Name	Born	Years	Notes
LE HUQUET, Philippe	1873		Lived at Elmore.
LE HUQUET, Philip	1795	1826-1846	
LE HUQUET, Philip	1820		Brother of Thomas and John. Lived at Les Champs.
LE HUQUET, Thomas	1805	1831-1869	Married Anne Starck. Died 1898, buried St Martin cemetery.
LE SAUTEUR, Alfred	1863	1879-1888	Lived at Le Chalet, La Corbière.
LE SEELLEUR, A.J.	1846		Lived at Battery House, Gorey.
LE SEELLEUR, George	1848		Lived at Battery House, Gorey.
LE SEELLEUR, John	1839	1865-1868	Lived in St Martin.
LE SEELLEUR, Philip	1845	1874-	Lived in St Martin.
LE SEELLEUR, Thomas Edmund	1837	1867-1868	Married Anna Touret. Died of yellow fever in Rio de Janeiro, 1868.
MAUGER, Philip Edward	1842	c.1860	Lived in St Martin.
MESSERVY, Philip	1796	1861-1864	Lived in St Martin.
MOLLET, Edward J.	1871-1878		Lived in St Martin. Master of *Welcome*.
MOLLET, Francis John	1864-1889		Lived in Union Place, Gorey. Master of *Galatea* and *Waverley*.
MOLLET, Frederic	1846	1874-1882	Lived in Gorey. Master of *Energy* and *Progress*. Lost at sea 1882.
MOSES, Alfred J.	1861-1874		Lived at 4 Wesley Place, Gorey 1885. Master of *Gazelle*.
NICOLLE, Edward Godfray	1840		Lived at Carteret View, Faldouet. Married Ann Jane Noël. Buried in St Martin cemetery.
NICOLLE, F.G.	1864	1898-1916	Lived at Tivoli, St Martin. Master of various English vessels.
NOËL, David	1866	1914-	Lived Sussex Lodge, Faldouet. Master of S.S. *Philotis*, torpedoed but saved. Still at sea in the 1930s.
NOËL, George	1909-		Lived Clifton House, Faldouet and Bank Dale, Gorey, (1908).
NOËL, George	1829 (Grouville)	1861-1880s	Lived at Ville Brée 1891.
NOËL, Hugh	1861-1880s		Master of small vessel at Chausey 1765.
NOËL, Matthew J.	1827	1848-1866	
NOËL, Philip	1834	1866-1879	Lived Sussex Lodge, Faldouet. Married Eliza Susan Le Huquet. Buried in St Martin cemetery.
NOËL, Philip	1801	1836-1861	Lived in St Martin.
NOËL, Philip Elie	1859		Lived at Faldouet House, 1898.
PALLOT, Charles	1833	1858-1870	Lived in St Martin c.1851. Died at Elm Bank.
PALLOT, Clement	1820	1853-1870	Lived in St Martin.
PALLOT, Elias George	1829		Son of Nicholas. Lived at Welton House. Master of schooner *St Catherine* 1857.
PALLOT, Elias Nicholas	1849		Lived in St Martin. Master of Morel vessels in Cardiff. Died 1896.
PALLOT, John	1821	1855-1868	Lived at La Tourelle in St Martin.
PALLOT, Nicholas	1823	c.1871	Lived in St Martin.
PALLOT, Nicholas	1793	1825-1847	Son of Philip. Lived in St Martin. Master of *Charles, John, John and Mary* and *Queen*.
PARK, Samuel Henry	1849	1870-1879	Lived in St Martin.
PAYNE, Helier	1821	1887	Lived in St Martin. Master of S.S. *Brentford*.
PERCHARD, John Edward	1819	1867-1869	Lived at Elfine Cottage, Gorey. Master of *Heather Belle* and *Elfine*.
PERCHARD, Rodney George	1886	1914-1918	Lived in St Martin. Master of S.S. *Denbighshire*.
RENOUF, Alfred Joshua	1840	1867-1868	Lived in St Martin.
RENOUF, Francis George	1826	1854-1873	Lived in St Helier.
RENOUF, Thomas	1781	1828-1839	Son of Philip. Master of *Traveller*. Lived in St Helier.

RICHARDSON, John	1819	1864-	Lived in St Martin.
RICHARDSON, Leighton T.	1895	1914-	Lived in St Martin. Master of H.M.H.S. *St David* 1914, and G.W.R.'s *St Julien*.
RICHARDSON, Thomas	1828	1856-1865	Lived in St Martin.
RICHMOND, William	1909-1915		Lived in Union Place, Gorey.
STARCK, Charles	1866		White Star Line vessel Master. Buried in St Martin cemetery, 1919.
SWAIN, Charles	*c.*1900		Lived at Vine House, Gorey.
SWAIN, John	1817 (Essex)	1856-1874	Lived in St Martin, 1851.
TURNIDGE, Edmund	1826 (Essex)	*c.*1906	Lived Gorey Pier, 1891-1909.
WHEELER, George	1828 (Sussex)	1859-1865	Lived in St Martin *c.*1851. Master of *Olive Branch* and *Forest Lad*.
WHEELER, Philip	1828 (Essex)	1859-1878	Lived in Gorey.
WHITLEY, Charles Elias	1849	1870-1896	Married Fanny Hocquard. Master of *Alabama*.
WHITLEY, Charles Elias	1874		Lived at La Maison des Fiefs, Rozel. Retired from sea 1896. Son of above.
WHITLEY, Elias	1811	1830-1859	Drowned at sea 1859.
WOODS, Alfred Porter	1842 (Portsmouth)	1865-1873	Lived in Gorey *c.*1851.
WRIGHT, John	1859-1874		Lived at Beulah House, Gorey. Master of *King*.
YOUNG, James Henry	1832 (Portsmouth)	1857-1868	Lived in St Martin, 1851.

FAMILY TREES

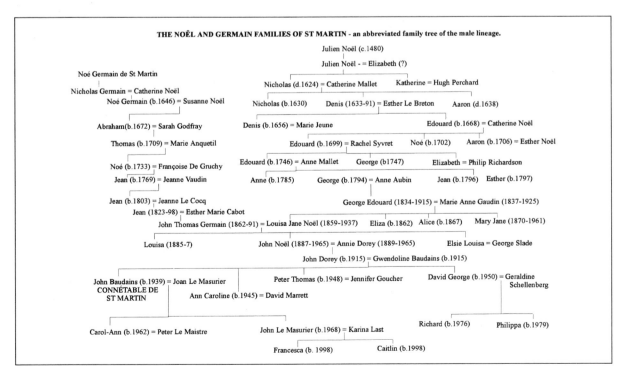

RICHARDSON OF ST MARTIN - an abbreviated family tree of the male lineage.

Ralph Richardson, reputedly Captain of Richard III's body guard at the Battle of Bosworth, 1485. Leased La Ferme from Seigneur of Rosel 1507.

Edmund = Colette Soulas of 'Lower Rozel'

Thomas

John Reserson of Guernsey

Hugh (d.1598) = Philippene de Quetteville

Nicholas = Jeanette Le Quesne

Jean of Bas Rozel (b. 1599) = Marie Anquetil

Nicholas (b.1602) = Abigail Dumaresq

Thomas (b.1638) = Marguerite Dorey

Philippe (b. 1631) (Jurat, Connétable)

Nicholas (b. 1633) Capt of Isle of Sark

Abraham (b. 1637) to Jamaica

Philippe (b.1676) = Marie Arthur

Clement = Jacqueline Reserson of Guernsey (Connétable)

Clement (1715-92) = Catherine Estur

Clement, Lieut. RN

Nicholas (Connétable)

Clement (1743-1826) = Elizabeth Cabot

Nicholas (b. 1764) (Connétable)

Clement, Lieut. RN

Philip, Lieut. RN (d.1807)

Clement (1770-1837) = Jeanne Le Huquet

Nicholas (b. 1795)

Clement (b. 1792) = Susan Le Huquet (of Bas Rozel)

Nicholas Ralph (1819-76) = Esther Gaudin

Clement (b. 1822) = Nancy Dorey

Philip Mourant (1847-1925) = Susannah Norman

John Dorey (b. 1854) = Jane Anley

Philip Norman (1875-1957) = Florence Aubin

Anley John (b. 1886) = Eunice Dorey

Vivian (b. 1902)   Hugh (b. 1903)   Denys (b.1906)   Edward (b.1910)

Andrew

John Dorey   Kenneth George   Douglas Anley   Gerald Arthur

Martin   David   Peter

Leighton

Kenneth   Wynford

Douglas   Gerald   Mervyn   Lester

Tobias   Piers   Miles   Laurence

Paul Leighton

Marcus

Danny   Joshua

CHAPTER NOTES AND AUTHORS

1. ANCIENT TIMES

The geology and topography of St Martin – Dr. John Renouf

St Martin in pre-history: the first farmers of the Neolithic – Dr. John Renouf and Mary Gibb

The Dolmens of St Martin – Mary Gibb

2. MEDIEVAL HISTORY

Mont Orgueil Castle – Christopher Aubin

Rosel and the Lemprière-Robins – Katie Le Quesne

Le Saut Geoffroi – Bob Hill and Katie Le Quesne

Les Chefs Tenants du Fief de la Reine – Anthony Paines

> *Page 27.* Strictly, chefs tenants were tenants of the fief, but with the decline of the feudal system their rights over, and duties in respect of, the commune – the common land – became the important aspect. The title used here is embossed on the leather bound covers of the 19th- and 20th-century minute books.

> *Page 34.* A translation of the 19th-century minutes has been provided by Mrs. E.M. Bois.

3. 17TH TO 19TH CENTURIES

The Don roads – Graham Crosby

> *Page 36.* For an account of the Reverend Le Couteur's contribution to the Battle of Jersey see the section in Chapter 16.

> *Page 37.* Copies of both the Duke of Richmond map and the Godfray map are displayed in St Martin's Public Hall and can be examined in the Société Jersiaise Library.

> *Page 38.* A full plan of Jersey's Don roads is printed on the front endpaper of Joan Stevens' *Old Jersey Houses, Vol.2*.

The Jersey Eastern Railway – Chris Blackstone

The mills of Rozel – Anne Perchard

The defensive towers of St Martin – Mary Gibb

> Machicoulis. A parapet furnished with openings between supporting corbels for dropping stones etc. on assailants.

Rozel, or Le Couperon, Barracks – Mary Gibb

St Martin's Arsenal – Mary Gibb

Haut de la Garenne – Helen Baker and Katie Le Quesne

Sash windows, round arches and shutters – Christopher Scholefield

Date stones – Gerald Le Cocq

4. THE GREAT WAR 1914-1918 – Nigel Le Gresley

5. MICROCOSM NO MORE – THE FORCES FOR CHANGE

St Martin and the motor car – Peter Tabb

The bus family Slade – Graham Crosby

Page 76. El Hassa is situated 100 yards north of St Martin's Garage with the bus garages, now overgrown, still visible on the left-hand side of the road.

Page 76. The photograph shows El Hassa in its original state as a single-storey cottage. The second storey was added by Edward Slade around the turn of the century.

Page 77. The forge was already there in the 1881 census when Charles Garnier was listed as a blacksmith, the house then being called Orkney Cottages.

Page 79. A Slade Dennis 'Lancet' appeared on the 31p stamp in 'Jersey Transport – Buses' series in April 1998. It is pictured at Archirondel with St Catherine in the background.

Page 79. Edward's sister-in-law, Iris Falle, lived at Waverley Farm.

Tourism and St Martin – Graham Crosby

6. THE GERMAN OCCUPATION 1940-1945

The Island's story – Anthony Paines

My memories of the Occupation – Beatrice Le Huquet

Occupation childhood memories – Anne Perchard

The Occupation of the Parish – Monica Amy

German fortifications in the Parish of St Martin – Michael Ginns

A Jersey widow's thoughts . . . – poem – Jackie De Gruchy

The Roll of Honour – 1939-1945

7. LES ÉCRÉHOUS – Chris Blackstone

Prehistoric and monastic periods

Quarrying

Fishing and the disputes between Jersey and France
Long-term residents and recreational visitors

8. THE CHURCHES

The Parish Church – Lawrence Turner and Katie Le Quesne

St Martin's Church, Gouray – Lawrence Turner

St Martin of Tours – Lawrence Turner

The Roman Catholic Church – Katie Le Quesne

The Methodist Church – Betty Brooke

The St Martin perquage – Katie Le Quesne

The Housewife's corner

9. THE JERSEY MILITIA – Maurice Lees

10. THE MUNICIPALITY

The Parish administration – Helen Blampied

St Martin's Public Hall – Helen Blampied

Parish finances – Chris Blackstone

The Honorary Police – Maurice Lees

Page 166. The 'Clothier Report' was named after its Chairman, Sir Cecil Clothier, KCB, QC. The other members of the Committee were Mr. Bernard Binnington, OBE, Mrs. (now Jurat) Sally Le Brocq, Mr. Ronald Mitchell and Jurat Michael Rumfitt; Secretary, Mr. Anthony Paines.

Planning & development – Maurice Lees

Party politics – Anne Perchard

11. FARMING: THE STAPLE INDUSTRY – Anne Perchard

Farming

Comice Agricole de St Martin

12. MARITIME ST MARTIN

Ship-building at Gorey and St Catherine – Anthony Paines

Page 196. Information about vessels built in St Martin has been derived from John Jean's works and data provided by Alex Podger. There are some inconsistencies in the various lists. Two of the vessels whose names are inscribed on the Shipbuilders' Fountain at Gorey are not in Appendix 7 – *Supply* and *St Peter.*

St Catherine – the harbour that never was – Hamish Marett-Crosby

The Royal Naval Training School – Katie Le Quesne

The oyster fisheries – Katie Le Quesne

The Newfoundland trade – Anthony Paines

Vraic – Anthony Paines

St Catherine's Lifeboat – Paul Richardson and Sarah Johnson

Gorey Regatta – Chris Blackstone

The design of the banner at the head of this section is based on medieval seals such as those of the English Cinque Ports and Flemish sea ports. It was designed by Major N.V.L. Rybot, D.S.O. The banner depicts, in medieval heraldic style, a cog (ship) of the 14th century in full sail. A stylised representation of Gorey Castle (Mont Orgueil) is shown in the sail. The ensign at the stern carries the cross of St George, the patron saint of England as well as of Gorey Castle. The flag at the ship's jackstaff on the fo'castle head bears arms emblematic of Saint Nicolas, Bishop of Myra. He is patron saint of children as well as of sailors. The three golden 'besants' represent the purses he threw secretly into the house of three sisters to save them from destitution or shame. The wavy bands symbolise the sea. The high hill facing the Castle at Gorey is named Mont St Nicolas.

St Catherine's Sailing Club – Chris Blackstone

Gorey Castle Yacht Club – Chris Blackstone

Gorey Boat-Owners Association – Hugh Fauvel

13. THE COMMUNITY

Ma Pâraisse – **poem** – Amelia Perchard

St Martin's Battle of Flowers Association – Peter Germain, Percy Gicquel and Pauline Perchard

The schools of St Martin – Gerald Le Cocq and Chris Blackstone

Jèrriais in St Martin – the language shift – Professor Nicol Spence

The St Martin Bands – Katie Le Quesne

St Martin's Olde Tyme Music Hall – Trevor Green

The St Martin tapestry – Nancy Thelland

Gorey Fête – Katie Le Quesne

Jumellage – Bob Hill

St Martin's Football Club – Katie Le Quesne

Rozel Rovers – Gerald Le Cocq

La Préférence, St Martin – Katie Le Quesne

St John Ambulance – Jenny Pallot

St Martin's Women's Institute – Kath Richardson

The Girls' Brigade – Jenny Pallot

The Boys' Brigade – Jenny Pallot

St Martin's Diamond Club – Jenny Pallot

St Martin's Flower Club – Jenny Pallot

14. NATURAL HISTORY

Bird life – Mike Stentiford

Wild flowers – Eunice Whiteside

The squirrels of the woods of St Martin – Dr. Louise Magris

St Martin gardens and gardeners – Jenny Pallot

15. TALES OF OLD ST MARTIN

Memories of youth on a Jersey farm – The late Reverend George Whitley

A tale of broken eggs – The late Vivian Richardson

Memories – Monica Amy and Stan Perchard

16. THE PEOPLE OF ST MARTIN

Introduction – Katie Le Quesne and Chris Blackstone

The incidence of family names – Anthony Paines

The Reverend François Le Couteur – Katie Le Quesne

Edmund Blampied – Katie Le Quesne

The 'five hundred year' families – Chris Blackstone and Jenny Pallot

    Page 317. Le Seelleur – From interviews with John Le Seelleur.

    Page 320. Noël and Germain – From interviews with John D. Germain and family documents.

    Page 323. Richardson – From family records maintained by the late Advocate Denys Richardson and from interviews with Gerald Richardson and Nancy Vautier.

St Martin families – Chris Blackstone

GLOSSARY

abreuvoir	A roadside watering place for animals.
advocate	The Jersey equivalent of an English barrister, with sole right of audience in all courts except the Petty Debts Court, where an Advocate shares such right with the solicitors.
aumones	Alms.
bachin	A large, open cooking pan, usually made of metal, which can be put directly on the fire.
bailiff	Chief magistrate and head of the States of Jersey. Appointed by the Crown, the Bailiff is also President of the Royal Court.
bannelais	Road sweepings, usually auctioned to farmers as fertilizer.
banon	The right to graze one's cattle on the stubble lands of the fief between harvest and ploughing
botte	A sheaf.
branchage	Branches of trees, which must not overhang neighbouring property.
branchage, visite du	A twice-yearly perambulation of the parish roads by the Connétable and Parish police to order the removal of any overhangs, or encroachments. Defaulters are fined.
centenier	The second rank in the Parish Honorary Police. Originally so called because he was charged with the well-being of a hundred families. A Centenier is elected for a period of three years by the electorate of the Parish to keep order within its boundaries. The senior Centenier is known as the 'Chef de Police' and may deputise for the Constable in his absence.
chaume	Thatch.
colombier	Dovecot or Pigeon House. The right to have a colombier was strictly controlled. It was the prerogative of 'Francs Tenants' only, i.e. Seigneurs or owners of some private fiefs.
comice agricole	An agricultural show.
constable (connetable)	The civil head of the Parish, who presides over Parish Assemblies and is a member of the States of Jersey. He is elected by the electorate of the Parish for a term of three years.
côtil	Field or land on hillside or slope.
dénonciateur	An executive officer of the Royal Court, subordinate to the vicomte and appointed by the Bailiff.
deputy (député)	A member of the States of Jersey elected by the Parish to represent them for a period of three years.
droit	Right (in Law).
États	The States of Jersey, the island's legislative assembly, which governs in the name of the Crown.
expert	Expert (witness). Experts form the panel which sets the parish rate.
extente	A listing of Crown property.
fief	The basic feudal holding.
fief du roi (de la reine)	The Crown Fief, out of which various private fiefs were granted.
foncier (-ière)	Concerning or pertaining to land.
fontaine	A spring.
garenne	Rabbit warren.
germain	A relation of the whole blood. In the law of inheritance there is a difference in entitlement between those of the whole- and those of the half-blood.
greffe	A registry or office of a clerk.
greffier	Registrar or keeper of records. Since 1930, there has been a States Greffier and a Judicial Greffier. Some Seigneurial courts had their own Greffier.
halberdier	A duty attaching to certain properties in St Martin, St Saviour and Grouville. They were to provide a man armed with a halberd to act as a guard of honour on certain occasions for the Governors, and to act as a guard during the transfer of prisoners to and from Mont Orgueil Castle to the Royal Court for trial. Some sources say there were 12 in Grouville, 18 in St Saviour and between 100 and 120 in St Martin.
héritage (cour d')	One of the divisions of the Royal Court, which deals with disputes concerning land.
hougue	An artificially constructed hillock, usually covering prehistoric remains.

inspecteurs des chemins	Roads inspectors, two of whom are elected in each vingtaine to supervise the repair of roads.
jardin à potage	Vegetable garden.
Jèrriais	The native Jersey language of Jersey, or Norman French.
Jersey Royal Fluke	The proper name of the variety of potato introduced in about 1880 which has been the basis of the new potato industry ever since.
Jurat (Juré-Justicier)	One of 12 honorary judges who, with the Bailiff, constitute the Royal Court, where the Bailiff is the judge of law and the Jurats are the judges of fact.
lavoir (douet à laver)	A communal washing place for laundry.
livre tournois	The basic currency of Jersey from the 12th century until 1834, when it was replaced by sterling.
officier du connétable	(Constable's Officer) The fourth rank in the Parish Honorary Police.
ormer	A local shellfish. A contraction of the name 'oreille de mer', the shell being the shape of an ear. The interior of the shell is covered with mother-of-pearl.
parish (Paroisse)	From early medieval times Jersey has been divided into 12 parishes which serve as both ecclesiastical and civil administrative units. Each has a Rector, appointed by the Crown, a Constable and other elected officials; also an ancient Parish Church, a rectory and Parish buildings.
perquage	A path which was a public right of way.
perque	A measure of length and area, equalling 22 feet (Imperial), or 484 square feet (Imperial).
pied	A measure of length and area. One pied in length equals 11 (not 12!)Imperial inches. This can cause confusion when taking measurements from Jersey legal contracts.
prévôt	Fief officer originally elected by the principal *tenants* of the fief from among their number. His duties included collecting *rente* and issuing summonses.
procureur du bien public	One of two trustees elected in the parish to pass deeds and contracts, conduct Parish law-suits and oversee the use of parish funds.
pouquelaye	Prehistoric burial ground marked by stones.
rât	Rates, levied by the Parish on all property.
rente	An annual payment charged on land, a form of mortgage. There are several kinds of *rente* which, though usually in wheat can also be found due in many other products or services, e.g. flour, barley, oats, rye, beans, peas, butter, eggs, hens, capons, wax, cider, apples, pepper (pound, ounces or corns), oranges, money, day's labour, sheep, geese, chicks, wine, congers, vraic or ash, in fact just about anything! It could also be apportioned so that half a hen or even the tenth part of an egg was owed!
seigneur *or* dame	The lord or holder of a fief.
sergent	A fief officer, sometimes paid in money or land. Duties could include the issuing of summonses, assisting the Prévôt and collecting *poulage rentes.*
States of Jersey	The island's legislative assembly or chamber. It is composed of 12 Senators (voted in by an all-island electorate); 12 Constables, each representing a parish; 29 deputies, each representing a parish or an electoral district within a parish. The President of the States is the Bailiff, who is appointed by the Crown.
surveillants	Churchwardens. Two are appointed for each parish by the Ecclesiastical Assembly. Their job is to keep the church in repair and to see that everything necessary for the church's ministry is supplied.
tenant	Holder of land on a fief, or of the fief, in relation to his overlord.
town	As St Helier is Jersey's only real conurbation, it is universally known as 'Town' in the island.
trésor	A communal institution relating to the maintenance of the parish church fabric.
vergée	A measure of land area. One vergée equals 40 perches or 19,360 square feet (Imperial). Approximately two and a quarter vergées are equivalent to one English acre.
vicomte *or* viscount	The chief executive officer of the Royal Court.
vingtaine	All Jersey parishes, with the exception of St Ouen, are divided into vingtaines. St Martin has five vingtaines, each of which has a vingtenier who is responsible for collecting the rates. In general the fiefs respect the vingtaine boundaries. Their names in St Martin are: Vingtaine de

	Rozel; Vingtaine de Faldouet; Vingtaine de la Quéruée; Vingtaine de l'Eglise; Vingtaine du Fief de la Reine.
vingtenier	The third rank in the Parish Honorary Police, after the Constable and the Centeniers.
visite royale	A perambulation around a parish by the Royal Court to inspect the roads.
vivier	A fish pond.
voyeur	A sworn witness who participates in the Visite Royale. Twelve voyeurs are sworn in for each Parish.
vraic	Seaweed washed up by the tide. Vraic is collected from the beaches to be used as fertilizer on Jersey's fields.
Wonders	Jersey Wonders or 'Des Mèrvelles' are a variety of doughnut with a twist in their shape. It is said that Wonders should only be cooked when the tide is falling as a rising tide will cause the fat to boil over.

Many of the above definitions were taken from *A Glossary for the Historian of Jersey* by C.N. Aubin.

BIBLIOGRAPHY

Ahier, Philip, *Stories of Jersey's Seas, Jersey's Coasts and Jersey's Seamen* (published privately, Huddersfield, 1955-7)

Ahier, Philip, 'The History of Primary School Education in Jersey from Early Times till 1872' (unpublished MS, Société Jersiaise, 1966)

Anon., *Caesarea: The Island of Jersey* (Simpkin Marshall, London, 1840)

Anon., *Code of Laws for the Island of Jersey* (1771)

Anon., *Comice Agricole de St Martin, Centenary Show Programme* (1994)

Anon., *Minute books of Gorey Regatta Association*

Anon., *Trees in Jersey* (The Jersey Association of The Men of the Trees, Jersey, 1997)

Arnold, J. and Appleby, J., *Catalogue Raisonné of Etchings, Drypoints and Lithographs of Edmund Blampied* (John Appleby Publishing, Jersey, 1996)

Aubin, C.N., *A Glossary for the Historian of Jersey* (Jersey Archives Service, 1997)

Aubin, C.N., 'Bordage, Bedelage and Sergenté Tenure in Jersey' (*Annual Bulletin*, Société Jersiaise,1997, 26(2), 246-62)

Aubin, C.N., 'The Perquages of Jersey, the Sanctuary Paths of Legend' (*Annual Bulletin*, Société Jersiaise, 1997, 27(1), 103-60)

Balleine, G.R. , *A Biographical Dictionary of Jersey* (Staples Press, 1948)

Barton, K.J., 'Excavation of the Middle Ward, Mont Orgueil, Jersey' (*Archaeological Journal*, 141, 1984, 216-42)

Barton, K.J., 'Preliminary Report on Excavations at Mont Orgueil Castle, Jersey, July 1972' (unpublished manuscript, Société Jersiaise)

Bender, B., *The Archaeology of Brittany, Normandy and the Channel Islands* (Faber & Faber, 1986)

Birt, P., *Lé Jèrriaise Pour Tous* (Don Balleine Trust, Jersey, 1985)

Bisson, M., *Islands in Bloom, Gardens and Gardening in the Channel Islands* (Michael Stephen, Jersey, 1988)

Bois, F. de L., *A Constitutional History of Jersey* (States Greffe, Jersey, 1972)

Bonsor, N.R.P., *The Jersey Eastern Railway and the German Occupation Lines* (The Oakwood Press, Lingfield, 1965)

Brett, C.E.B., *Buildings in the town and parish of St Helier* (National Trust for Jersey, 1977)

Campbell, P., 'La Côte de la Pallière' (*Jersey Life*, 3(22), January 1968)

Corbet, F.L., *A Biographical Dictionary of Jersey, Vol.2* (Société Jersiaise, 1998)

Cruickshank, C., *The German Occupation of the Channel Islands* (Imperial War Museum, 1975)

Cunliffe, B., *Jersey in Prehistory* (Société Jersiaise, 1994)

Davies, B., *Gaspé, Land of History and Romance* (Ambassador Books, Toronto, 1949)

Davies, W., *The Coastal Towers of Jersey* (Société Jersiaise, 1991)

Davies, W., *Fort Regent – A History* (published privately, 1971)

Davies, W., *The Harbour that Failed* (Ampersand Press, Alderney, 1983)

De Gruchy, F.A.L., 'Royal Jersey Militia and the Military Rôle of Jersey in History' (*Annual Bulletin,* Société Jersiaise, 1956, 16(4), 365-72)

De Gruchy, G.F.B., *Medieval Land Tenures in Jersey* (Bigwood, Jersey, 1857)

De Gruchy, J., *The Way to the Bay* (La Haule, Jersey, 1996)

Dixon, P. *et al., Mont Orgueil Castle: A Report on the Archives* (University of Nottingham, 1998)

Falle, Ph., *An Account of the Island of Jersey* (1st edition, 1694; 2nd edition, 1734; edition with notes by E. Durell, 1837)

Ford, D., 'The Jersey Oyster Fisheries' (unpublished MS)

Gallishet, J., *Les Fermes de L'Île de Jersey* (Bureau de la Science Sociale, Paris, 1912)

Gibb, B., 'St Martin Treasures Survey' (unpublished manuscript, 1982)

Ginns, M., *Transport in Jersey – 1788-1961* (Transport World, 1961)

Glendenning, A., *Société Jersiaise Web site*

Hawkes, J., *The Archaeology of the Channel Islands, Vol.II: The Bailiwick of Jersey* (Société Jersiaise, 1938)

Hillsdon, S., *Jersey Witches, Ghosts and Traditions* (Jarrold, Norwich, 1984)

Inglis, H.D., *The Channel Islands* (Whittaker & Co., 1835)

Jamieson, A.G., *A People of the Sea* (Methuen, 1986)

Jean, J., *Jersey Sailing Ships* (Phillimore, Chichester, 1982)

Jean, J., *Stories of Jersey's Ships* (La Haule Books, Jersey, 1987)

Jean, J., *Jersey Ships and Railways* (La Haule Books, Jersey, 1989)

Jean, J., *Tales of Jersey's Tall Ships* (La Haule Books, Jersey, 1994)

Jee, N., *Landscape of the Channel Islands* (Phillimore, Chichester, 1982)

Johnston, D.E., *The Channel Islands: An Archaeological Guide* (Phillimore, Chichester, 1981)

Johnston, Peter (ed.), *The Archaeology of the Channel Islands. A Symposium* (Phillimore, Chichester, 1986)

Jones, R. *et al., Past Landscapes of Jersey* (Société Jersiaise, 1990)

Kelleher, J.H., *The Triumph of the Country* (John Appleby Publishing, Jersey, 1984)

Kinnes, I. and Hibbs, J., *The Dolmens of Jersey: A guide* (La Haule Books, Jersey, 1988)

Layzell, A (ed.), *Who's Who in The Channel Islands* (Jersey, 1987)

Le Dain, J., *Jersey Alphabet* (Seaflower Books, Bradford-on-Avon, 1997)

Le Maistre, F., *Dictionnaire Jersiais-Français* (Don Balleine Trust, Jersey, 1966)

Le Quesne, C., *A Constitutional History of Jersey* (Longman, 1856)

Le Sueur, F., *A Natural History of Jersey* (Phillimore, Chichester, 1976)

Likeman, J., 'École Élémentaire or Elementary School' (*Annual Bulletin,* Société Jersiaise, 1991, 25(3), 501-12)

McCormack, J., *Channel Island Churches* (Phillimore, Chichester, 1986)

Matthews, M., 'Le Câtel de Rozel – A Survey' (*Annual Bulletin,* Société Jersiaise, 1986, 24(3), 183-98)

Mavins, J. and Y., *Le Seeleur, A Jersey Heritage* (Canada, 1963)

Mayne, R., *The Battle of Jersey* (Phillimore, Chichester, 1981)

Mayne, R. and Stevens, J., *Jersey Through the Lens* (Phillimore, Chichester, 1975)

Nicolle, E.T., *Mont Orgueil Castle* (The Beresford Library, Jersey, 1921)

Ouless, P.J., *The Death of Major Frs. Peirson* (Le Lievre Bros, Jersey, 1881)

Ouless, P.J., *Les Écréhous* (Chronique, Jersey, 1884)

Patton, M., *Jersey in Prehistory* (La Haule Books, Jersey, 1987)

Plees, W., *An Account of the Island of Jersey* (T. Baker, Southampton, 1817)

Quayle, T., *Survey of the Norman Isles* (Sherwood, Neely & Jones, 1815)

Ragg, A.E., *A Popular History of Jersey* (W.E. Guiton, Jersey, 1895)

Renouf, J. and Urry, J., *The First Farmers in the Channel Islands* (Education Department, Jersey, 1976)

Rodwell, W., *Les Écréhous, Jersey* (Société Jersiaise, 1995)

Rooke, O., *The Channel Islands: Pictorial, Legendary and Descriptive* (L. Booth, 1856)

Rybot, N.V.L., *Gorey Castle, Jersey* (States of Jersey, 1933)

Rybot, N.V.L., *The History of Gorey Regatta* (Gorey Regatta Programme, 1954)

Shepard, H.G., *One Hundred Years of the Royal Jersey Agricultural and Horticultural Society* (Jersey, 1933)

Sinel, L., 'The German Occupation of Jersey: A Diary' (*Evening Post*, Jersey, 1946)

Sinel, L., *The Geology of Jersey* (J.T. Bigwood, Jersey, 1912)

Société Jersiaise, *Annual Bulletins* from 1875 to 1998

Société Jersiaise, *Glossaire du Patois Jersiaise* (Société Jersiaise, 1924)

States of Jersey, *Report for the Census of 1989*

Stevens, C., 'Windmills, watermills and streams of Jersey' (unpublished MS, Société Jersiaise)

Stevens, C.G., Arthur, J.F. and Stevens, J.C., *Jersey Place Names* (Vols.1 and 2, Société Jersiaise, 1985)

Stevens, Joan, *Old Jersey Houses, Vol.I* (Commercial Art, Jersey, 1965)

Stevens, Joan, *Old Jersey Houses, Vol.II* (Phillimore, Chichester, 1980)

Stevens, J., *Victorian Voices* (Société Jersiaise, 1962)

Syvret, M., *Edmund Blampied* (Robin Garton Ltd., 1986)

Syvret, M., 'Jersey Settlements in Gaspé' (*Annual Bulletin*, Société Jersiaise, 1963, 18(3), 281-95)

Syvret, M. and Stevens, J., *Balleine's History of Jersey* (Phillimore, Chichester, 1998)

Wyatt, H., *Jersey in Jail* (Ernest Huelin, Jersey, 1945)

INDEX

1709

Ce 3e. jour d'Aoust 1709. en Assemblée de psse. en St. Mari
á été ordoné que la place du Banc situé en l'Eg. de lad. m.
paroisse. Entre le Banc me. Phtte. Fauvel & Celuy de me.
phtte. Richardson f. Jean, ey devant appartenant á me. Augustin
Clemt. le Feuvre & á la famille de feu Augustin
Nicolle moitié par moitié demeure vá l'avenir audit
me. Clemt. le Feuvre & sa famille sans jnquietude ny
trouble desd. heritiers sinon que Marie Nicolle veue de Gideon
le sueur fille dud. Augustin Nicolle ce poura assoir au Banc quy
sera fait su vie durante et s'oblige led. le Feuvre de faire
transporter led. ancien Banc po. la famille de lad. Marie
Nicolle á ses propres fraix dans la chappelle du Nord
de lad. Eglise au Costé de Celuy de James Mallet et en
outre payer le travail qui á été fait aud. Banc ey
devant & aussy donne led. le Feuvre dix livres pour
les pouvres de lad. paroisse po. la Place du Banc,
ce fait en pressence des Principaux, Ministres, Con ble.
Centrs. surveillants & Proer. de lad. psse. & autres offen.
& du Consentement de lad. Marie Nicolle & en sa
presence //   signé en l'original

G. Bandinel: Fr. le Couteur R.r   Tho. Lempriere Con ble

Clemt. Machon: Centr. Tho. de Queteville Proer.

Fr. le Maistre   sur veillants   Tho. Aubin
                                       Tho. Gallichan

David de Quetteville

Jean du Fresne

Ce 12e. jour d'avril 1710. en Assemblée de Paroisse il á été acordé
unne place dans l'Eglise de St. Martin en la Chapelle du Nord
derriere le Banc mt. Tho. Gallichan, a Isaac Renouf fs. Jean, &a
Jean Renouf fs. Isaac po. y placer un Banc moitié par moitié
pour assoir leur familles sans aucune preuciance, suivant
ce qui en avoit été arresté en assemblée de lad. Paroisse
il y a viron deux ans   signé en l'original

Fr. le Couteur R.r

D. la Garde   Fr. le Maistre: surveillt.   Tho. Lempriere. Conest ble.
                                            Jean Nicolle surv ll.

Tho. Aubin   Tho. de Queteville Proer.

                  Tho. Gallichan